Developing Solutions for Microsoft Azure AZ-204 Exam Guide

Discover the essentials for success when developing and maintaining cloud-based solutions on Azure

Paul Ivey

Alex Ivanov

<packt>

BIRMINGHAM—MUMBAI

Developing Solutions for Microsoft Azure AZ-204 Exam Guide

Copyright © 2022 Packt Publishing

Group Product Manager: Rahul Nair
Publishing Product Manager: Niranjan Naikwadi
Senior Editor: Shazeen Iqbal
Content Development Editor: Romy Dias
Technical Editor: Rajat Sharma
Copy Editor: Safis Editing
Project Coordinator: Ashwin Dinesh Kharwa
Proofreader: Safis Editing
Indexer: Pratik Shirodkar
Production Designer: Shankar Kalbhor
Marketing Coordinator: Nimisha Dua

First published: September 2022

Production reference: 1230922

Published by Packt Publishing Ltd.
Livery Place
35 Livery Street
Birmingham
B3 2PB, UK.

ISBN 978-1-80323-706-0

www.packt.com

Contributors

About the authors

Paul Ivey is an experienced engineer and architect specializing in Microsoft technologies, both on-premises and in the Azure cloud.

In his four years at Microsoft, Paul has been a secure infrastructure engineer and an app innovation engineer, where he helped hundreds of enterprise customers adopt DevOps practices and develop solutions for Azure.

Paul is now a Microsoft Technical Trainer, providing training for Microsoft customers to help them with preparing to pass Azure exams.

In his spare time, Paul is a keen PC gamer and enjoys traveling abroad to experience foreign sights, cultures, and food (mostly food).

Originally from Devon in the UK, Paul currently lives in Cheltenham in the beautiful Cotswolds area of England.

I want to thank my amazing fiancée, Krishelle, for being my motivation and biggest supporter in all things. I'd also like to thank my friends and colleagues that supported me and provided learning opportunities over the years, with a special shoutout to Gary, Ira, Liam, and Suren. The whole Packt team has helped make my first authoring experience a pleasant and successful one, particularly Ashwin Kharwa and Romy Dias.

Alex Ivanov is an experienced cloud engineer with a primary focus on supporting companies in their journeys to adopt Azure services. Alex has worked for Microsoft for eight years as a cloud support engineer and four years as an Azure Technical Trainer.

Alex is an expert in software engineering and digital transformation who has helped many customers to migrate their solutions to Azure. His experience has helped him gain multiple certifications in software development, AI, and data platforms. As a professional trainer, Alex has already educated thousands of clients and helped them to prepare for and pass the Azure certification exams.

In his free time, while not being jumped on by his three kids, he enjoys camping, boating, running, and building RC models.

I want to thank my beautiful wife, Olga, and my kids, Sofia, Daniel, and Peter, who give me space and inspired me to write this book. I'd also like to thank the whole Packt editing team for helping me with my first authoring experience. Special thanks to Romy Dias, who edited most of my work.

About the reviewer

Massimo Bonanni specializes in cloud application development and, in particular, Azure compute technologies. He is a Microsoft Technical Trainer at Microsoft, and his goal is to help customers utilize their Azure skills to achieve more and leverage the power of Azure in their solutions. He is also a writer (he has written a couple of books about serverless in the past two years), a technical speaker at national and international conferences, and a Microsoft Certified Trainer. He was a Microsoft MVP (for six years in Visual Studio, development technologies, and Windows development), an Intel Software innovator, and an Intel Black Belt.

I would like to thank my wife and family for their patience and the support they give me in my work. Without their contribution and support, everything would be much more difficult.

Table of Contents

Part 2: Developing for Azure Storage

5

6

Part 3: Implementing Azure Security

7

Implementing User Authentication and Authorization   157

8

Implementing Secure Cloud Solutions   181

Part 4: Implementing Monitoring, Troubleshooting, and Optimization Solutions in Azure

9

Integrating Caching and Content Delivery within Solutions   205

10

Troubleshooting Solutions by Using Metrics and Log Data   227

Part 5: Connecting to and Consuming Azure and Third-Party Services

11

Implementing API Management 257

12

Developing Event-Based Solutions 279

13

Developing Message-Based Solutions   301

Part 6: Exam Preparation

14

Mock Exam Questions   327

Preface

Cloud developers are in high demand right now, and as this demand continues to grow, so too does the requirement for up-to-date knowledge of the ever-evolving plethora of cloud technologies and features. One of the most popular ways in which to provide evidence of possessing the knowledge required to be a successful cloud developer is by obtaining relevant certifications.

The chapters of this book are structured in a way that aligns with the skills measured in the AZ-204 exam, so you can see which area of the exam is being addressed in each chapter. You'll explore all the services and features covered by the exam in a clear, succinct way, including practical exercises to follow along to get a firm understanding of concepts, with access to downloadable code examples if required.

Who this book is for

This book is intended to help professional developers with experience in Microsoft Azure in preparing to take and pass the AZ-204: Developing Solutions for Microsoft Azure exam, as well as developers looking to increase their existing knowledge of how to develop solutions for Azure.

What this book covers

Chapter 1, Azure and Cloud Fundamentals, recaps some of the fundamentals of cloud computing and some important concepts of Azure, providing a sound foundation for the rest of the book.

Chapter 2, Implementing IaaS Solutions, builds on the topics discussed in the previous chapter by exploring Infrastructure as a Service solutions, including virtual machines and ARM templates, finishing with containers and their associated Azure solutions.

Chapter 3, Creating Azure App Service Web Apps, covers one of the most used services in Azure development, Azure App Service. This chapter introduces App Service and goes into detail about authentication and authorization within App Service, networking features, and app settings and logging within App Service.

Chapter 4, Implementing Azure Functions, starts with an introduction to Azure Functions, including hosting, scaling, and binding options. We explore developing, testing, and deploying functions, along with stateful durable functions.

Chapter 5, Developing Solutions That Use Cosmos DB Storage, explores NoSQL solutions hosted in Azure, including coverage of Azure Table storage and its features and leveraging service from the code. This chapter also provides a deep dive into Cosmos DB, explaining Cosmos DB scaling, high availability, consistency, and recovery features. It demonstrates querying from the Azure portal and the SDK.

Chapter 6, Developing Solutions That Use Azure Blob Storage, covers Azure Blob Storage and its role in supporting deployed applications and services in Azure. You will learn about the features of the Azure Blob Storage service and study cases where Azure Blob Storage can help to host web applications.

Chapter 7, Implementing User Authentication and Authorization, is where, after a detailed introduction to the Microsoft identity platform, we implement authentication with the Microsoft Authentication Library. Building on this, we explore Microsoft Graph and demonstrate making calls to it within code. We then finish with a detailed look at shared access signatures for authorizing access to storage resources in Azure.

Chapter 8, Implementing Secure Cloud Solutions, is where we explore using Azure Key Vault to secure application secrets, including authorization and authentication with Key Vault. This leads us on to the topic of managed identities, including options and best practices. The final topic of this chapter is Azure App Configuration, for centrally and securely managing your application configuration settings and feature flags.

Chapter 9, Integrating Caching and Content Delivery within Solutions, starts with an introduction to dynamic content caching with Azure Cache for Redis and continues to explore static content caching with Azure CDN, including different caching patterns, high availability, pricing models, and integration with Azure platform services such as Azure App Service and Azure Blob Storage.

Chapter 10, Troubleshooting Solutions by Using Metrics and Log Data, explores a variety of telemetry and monitoring topics, including troubleshooting crashes with Application Insights, monitoring web logs with Azure Monitor, and creating live dashboards and workbooks using Kusto queries.

Chapter 11, Implementing API Management, is all about web APIs, Swagger, and the API Management service, with a deep dive into advanced configuration using policies.

Chapter 12, Developing Event-Based Solutions, explores a variety of the event-based services available in Azure, including Event Hubs for ingesting big data, Event Grid for reactive programming, IoT Hub for telemetry monitoring, and Azure Relay for hyper-cloud communication.

Chapter 13, Developing Message-Based Solutions, is all about the implementation of messaging patterns. We will introduce messaging services in Azure, starting with Azure Storage and then moving on to Azure Service Bus. We provide guidelines for reliable content delivery with message-based services. We finish with an introduction into the concept of DevOps and some examples of DevOps practices.

Chapter 14, Mock Exam Questions, is a mock exam to build your familiarity with the types of questions you might be presented with in the exam. We introduce the different types of exam questions and timings and then get straight into the mock exam questions.

To get the most out of this book

You will need the latest version of Visual Studio Code, .NET, PowerShell Core, the Azure CLI, Git, and Docker Desktop. All code examples have been tested using .NET 6.0, PowerShell Core 7, and version 2.37.0 of the Azure CLI on Windows 10 and Windows 11. However, they should also work with future releases as well.

Software/hardware covered in the book	Operating system requirements
Visual Studio Code	Windows, macOS, or Linux
Docker Desktop	Windows, macOS, or Linux
PowerShell Core	Windows, macOS, or Linux
Azure CLI	Windows, macOS, or Linux
.NET 6.0	Windows, macOS, or Linux
Git	Windows, macOS, or Linux
Azure Functions Core Tools	Windows, macOS, or Linux

Check the license requirements for Docker Desktop if you want to follow along with the exercises in *Chapter 2, Implementing IaaS Solutions*. A Docker Personal plan is free for personal, individual use. Each chapter details which (if any) Visual Studio Code extensions are required.

If you are using the digital version of this book, we advise you to type the code yourself or access the code from the book's GitHub repository (a link is available in the next section). Doing so will help you avoid any potential errors related to the copying and pasting of code.

As every chapter in this book relates to Microsoft Azure, you will also need a non-production Azure tenant and subscription that can be used to follow the exercises and enable your own learning and experimentation.

Download the example code files

You can download the example code files for this book from GitHub at `https://github.com/PacktPublishing/Developing-Solutions-for-Microsoft-Azure-AZ-204-Exam-Guide`. If there's an update to the code, it will be updated in the GitHub repository.

We also have other code bundles from our rich catalog of books and videos available at `https://github.com/PacktPublishing/`. Check them out!

Code in Action

The Code in Action videos for this book can be viewed at `https://bit.ly/3LtUSAp`.

Download the color images

We also provide a PDF file that has color images of the screenshots and diagrams used in this book. You can download it here: `https://packt.link/1TGWe`.

Conventions used

There are a number of text conventions used throughout this book.

`Code in text`: Indicates code words in text, database table names, folder names, filenames, file extensions, pathnames, dummy URLs, user input, and Twitter handles. Here is an example: "The URL includes the `scope` parameter, `scope=openid+profile+email`, which consists of the standard OIDC permissions that the `User.Read` permission uses."

A block of code is set as follows:

```
using Microsoft.Identity.Client;
const string _clientId = "<app/client ID>";
const string _tenantId = "<tenant ID>";
var app = PublicClientApplicationBuilder
```

When we wish to draw your attention to a particular part of a code block, the relevant lines or items are set in bold:

```
var app = PublicClientApplicationBuilder
    .Create(_clientId)
    .WithAuthority(AzureCloudInstance.AzurePublic, _tenantId)
    .WithRedirectUri("http://localhost")
    .Build();
```

Any command-line input or output is written as follows:

```
$ dotnet new console -n "<app name>"
```

Bold: Indicates a new term, an important word, or words that you see onscreen. For instance, words in menus or dialog boxes appear in **bold**. Here is an example: "Select **Microsoft** for **Identity provider**, leave everything as default, and click **Add**."

> **Tips or important notes**
> Appear like this.

Get in touch

Feedback from our readers is always welcome.

General feedback: If you have questions about any aspect of this book, email us at customercare@packtpub.com and mention the book title in the subject of your message.

Errata: Although we have taken every care to ensure the accuracy of our content, mistakes do happen. If you have found a mistake in this book, we would be grateful if you would report this to us. Please visit www.packtpub.com/support/errata and fill in the form.

Piracy: If you come across any illegal copies of our works in any form on the internet, we would be grateful if you would provide us with the location address or website name. Please contact us at copyright@packt.com with a link to the material.

If you are interested in becoming an author: If there is a topic that you have expertise in and you are interested in either writing or contributing to a book, please visit authors.packtpub.com.

Share your thoughts

Once you've read *Developing Solutions for Microsoft Azure AZ-204 Exam Guide*, we'd love to hear your thoughts! Scan the QR code below to go straight to the Amazon review page for this book and share your feedback.

https://packt.link/r/1803237066

Your review is important to us and the tech community and will help us make sure we're delivering excellent quality content.

Part 1: Developing Compute Solutions in Azure

We'll begin with a recap of some cloud computing fundamentals before we start exploring Microsoft Azure, covering the key need-to-know concepts of Azure. We'll then introduce the relevant compute solutions available within Azure. You will learn how to create and use ARM templates and provision Azure virtual machines, as well as some important considerations when doing so. We'll cover an introduction to containers and the relevant services for managing containers and container images. We'll introduce Azure App Service, covering creating and deploying code to an App Service web app, along with scaling and configuration options. The final topic of this part is Azure Functions, where we'll cover creating, developing, and deploying Azure Functions, along with durable functions for the stateful orchestration of serverless functions

This part covers 25-30% of the AZ-204 exam questions.

The following chapters will be covered under this section:

- *Chapter 1, Azure and Cloud Fundamentals*
- *Chapter 2, Implementing IaaS Solutions*
- *Chapter 3, Creating Azure App Service Web Apps*
- *Chapter 4, Implementing Azure Functions*

1
Azure and Cloud Fundamentals

With the prevalence of cloud technologies and DevOps ways of working, the industry demands developers that can develop and deploy cloud solutions and monitor them throughout the application life cycle. Becoming a Microsoft-certified *Azure developer* can differentiate developers from the competition, but with such a plethora of information out there, it can be difficult to structure learning in an effective way to obtain the certification. This book aims to make the process of gaining the required knowledge to pass the **AZ-204: Developing Solutions for Microsoft Azure** exam less of a challenge.

If you didn't already know, then I'm sorry to break it to you, but there is no mystical cloud floating around providing IT resources to organizations; there are some incredibly powerful machines in your cloud provider's data centers from which you can use resources, configurable through a web portal (often, other options are available as well).

With cloud computing, you can quickly create servers, web applications, storage, and virtual machines – to name just a few – within seconds. When you need more resources, you can get them; when you no longer need them, you can scale back and save money – you pay only for what you use. The cloud provider looks after the hardware, maintenance, and underlying infrastructure.

During this chapter, we will take a moment to recap the different cloud deployment and service models, benefits, and considerations, before going into some Azure specifics. By the end of this chapter, we will have discussed the most fundamental concepts that will be referenced throughout this book, ensuring that we start with the same fundamental understanding before going deeper into our topics.

In this chapter, we will cover the following main topics:

- Understanding the benefits of cloud computing
- Reviewing cloud deployment models
- Examining cloud service models
- Exploring the core concepts of Azure

Technical requirements

If you would like to follow along with the examples in this chapter, you will require the following (later chapters will have these requirements as well):

- A Microsoft Azure subscription: If you don't already have a subscription to use, you can set up an account for free here: `https://azure.microsoft.com/free/`

- The Az PowerShell module: Instructions can be found here: `https://docs.microsoft.com/powershell/azure/install-az-ps`

- The Azure CLI: Instructions can be found here: `https://docs.microsoft.com/cli/azure/install-azure-cli`

- A Windows, macOS, or Linux device with the latest version of PowerShell installed: Installation information can be found here: `https://docs.microsoft.com/powershell/scripting/install/installing-powershell`

- A supported web browser: Supported browsers can be found here: `https://docs.microsoft.com/azure/azure-portal/azure-portal-supported-browsers-devices`

Code in Action videos for this chapter: `https://bit.ly/3qOiMgC`

> **Important Note**
>
> Whether you intend to use an Azure account with free Azure credit or not, you are responsible for monitoring and managing your account. If you are going to follow along with the hands-on exercises throughout this book, you need to understand potential costs and monitor your usage and budget responsibly. Consumption models are great, but if you create resources and leave them running 24/7, for example, the costs will soon start adding up – make sure you keep on top of any costs you may incur from following the exercises in this book.

Understanding the benefits of cloud computing

Before cloud computing became an option, companies would have physical network components and server hardware to host roles that would allow them to manage identity, storage, databases, and web applications, among others. Each of these would need skills and cost to install, configure, maintain, patch, and eventually upgrade.

If there was a sudden rise in web requests to one of your web servers, for example, you may have had a drop in service availability because your hardware lacks the resources required. If you predicted the sudden rise, perhaps due to seasonal patterns, you may have gone through a **capital expenditure (CapEx)** process. Once (if) approvals are obtained and everything gets set up, if the actual traffic isn't what was forecast, or once the traffic drops again, you might be stuck with expensive hardware that isn't being fully utilized, while still having ongoing running and maintenance costs (as well as potentially grumpy financial controllers!). This alone presented a problem, and we're not even touching on disaster recovery or high availability requirements.

Enter cloud computing…

Perhaps the most noticeable change when a company moves to a cloud-based infrastructure is that the requirement to have many physical components is greatly reduced. Identity management can be achieved without a single physical server for you to manage – just log in to a web portal and do everything from there. Users no longer need to be connected directly to your internal network for secure connectivity.

Depending on the **service-level agreement (SLA)** you have with your cloud provider, even when something goes wrong, the cloud infrastructure can help keep your applications highly available with no noticeable downtime. With the previous scenario of a sudden rise in web requests, you may have decided to scale your application vertically (also known as scaling up/down), providing it with more resources, but that often results in some downtime while the application is upgraded.

You could have configured automatic horizontal scaling (also known as scaling in/out) – if your application hits a certain metric, more instances of your application could be automatically created to handle the spike, and the number of instances could be scaled back down automatically once demand reduces again – preventing any downtime while being cost-effective.

To demonstrate this, I created a web app in **Microsoft Azure** that only took 30 seconds to create and be up and running, and then configured auto-scaling. When monitoring the instances of my web app, there was a spike in the number of requests (the lower line) over a period, the instances (the upper line) increased to 2, and once that spike subsided, the instances were reduced to 1:

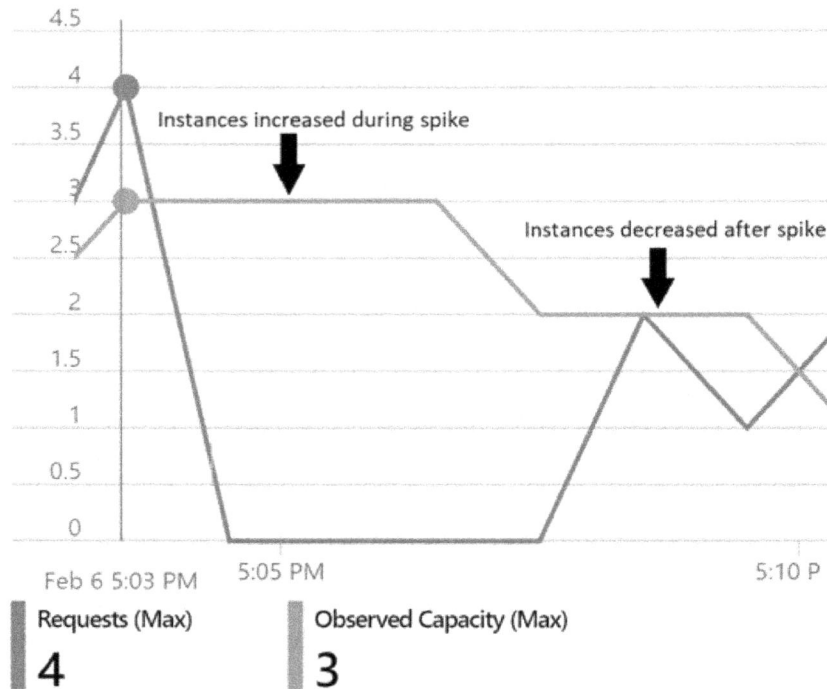

Figure 1.1 – Auto scaled instances during a requests spike

Due to the elasticity that cloud computing brings, my application had the resources it needed without any downtime and scaled the resources back down when they were no longer needed. I mentioned that I was able to provision my web app and have it accessible to the internet in just 30 seconds – no CapEx, no hardware, no delays, and no complications. I had the option to deploy the app to one of many locations around the world, thanks to the global distribution of my cloud provider's data centers.

With cloud computing, you not only have all the benefits mentioned here and more, but because cloud services are typically consumption-based, you only pay for the resources you use. No upfront costs, just **operational expenditure (OpEx)** costs, depending on what you use. To some, one of the biggest benefits of cloud computing is that you no longer need to deal with quite as much of an *Ethernet jungle* as before. As this chapter is intended to recap these fundamentals, we won't delve any deeper at this time.

With the benefits just covered and many others, it's no surprise that the number of workloads being migrated to the cloud is increasing exponentially. When thinking about moving workloads to the cloud, it's important to understand the hosting options available to you, the most common of which we will cover in the next section.

Reviewing cloud deployment models

There are three main types of cloud deployment models available from cloud providers: **public cloud**, **private cloud**, and **hybrid cloud** (other cloud models exist, such as *Community Cloud*, but we won't discuss those other models here). Here is a summary of these models:

- **Public cloud**:

  - This is the most common model and where services and resources are offered over the public internet to anybody that wishes to *purchase* them. All cloud resources are owned and maintained by a cloud provider, so it's more like renting resources than purchasing them.

  - Pay only for what you use with a consumption-based model.

  - The cloud provider handles maintaining and updating the hardware.

- **Private cloud**:

  - Unlike the public model, services and resources are available exclusively for one organization. Often, this model is chosen when strict security controls and isolation are required.

  - Hardware, software, configuration, maintenance, updates, and security are all managed by the organization exclusively using the available resources.

  - Hardware needs to be purchased and all running costs fall to the organization if the hardware is running, even if resources aren't being used.

- **Hybrid cloud**:

  - You can compose public and private cloud models, taking advantage of the benefits of each.

  - Flexibility to store sensitive information on private resources, while allowing interconnection to an application on the public cloud, for example.

  - Ability to decide where to host workloads, depending on the requirements.

It's important to note that although a private cloud may be required to meet certain regulatory standards, public clouds are often more than secure enough for most scenarios. The physical data centers hosting cloud hardware follow strict security controls that comply with many external regulations, as well as bring the benefits of availability and redundancy.

The security features available from cloud providers are comprehensive, industry-leading, and often offer better protection, monitoring, alerting, and remediation than most organizations achieve when they manage their resources. Unless otherwise stated, this book will be assuming that the public cloud is the chosen model (which is the most common by far).

Now that we understand the main cloud deployment models, of which the public cloud is the most common, we should discuss the service models available. You will encounter the models we are about to cover numerous times if you haven't already, and every service you deploy in Azure will come under one of these models.

Examining cloud service models

No cloud computing discussion would be complete without mentioning **Infrastructure as a Service (IaaS)**, **Platform as a Service (PaaS)**, and **Software as a Service (SaaS)**. Although other cloud service models exist, these are the most common cloud models offered by cloud providers and are the standard models per the **National Institute of Standards and Technology (NIST)**. Let's briefly recap these models before we get into Azure specifics:

- **Infrastructure as a Service (IaaS)**:

  - As the name suggests, with this model, the cloud provider manages the underlying infrastructure. One of the most common examples of this implementation is cloud-based virtual machines – you can request virtual machines with certain specifications and the cloud provider has automation take care of provisioning them for you. You don't need to worry about the underlying host or infrastructure. You will manage the virtual machine, including installing software, updates, and more.

  - This is the closest model to managing physical machines, without needing to manage any hardware. Provisioning virtual machines is much faster than having to procure and set up physical machines – as is scaling and removing them. You get the most flexibility and control with this model.

  - With the consumption-based model, you only pay for the resources you use (OpEx). For example, if you have a virtual machine and enable daily auto-shutdown, automation will take care of shutting the machine down each day at the desired time, allowing the machine to be stopped and *deallocated*, at which point the virtual machine itself no longer incurs any costs until it's started again (other resources attached to the virtual machine may still incur separate costs).

- **Platform as a Service (PaaS)**:

  - From a developer's perspective, this is becoming the most popular model. With this model, developers can deploy their applications to a managed hosting environment.

  - The cloud provider manages all the underlying hardware and infrastructure as with IaaS, but with PaaS, they also manage any virtual machines, the operating systems, patching, and more. You, as a developer, just manage the application, along with the data and access to it.

- The consumption-based model makes this a cost-effective model. Being able to provision an environment where you can host your application quickly, deploy and test your application, then potentially remove the environment (an Azure App Service, for example) without needing to worry about any of the details of the machines on which this environment is hosted greatly improves developer agility.

- **Software as a Service (SaaS):**

    - With this model, the cloud provider provides you with the software. You just manage who can use the software and which features.

    - One of the most common Microsoft-hosted examples of SaaS is Microsoft 365, which includes applications from what was previously called Office 365 – you are provided with the software; you just need to define who can access what features. The cloud provider handles everything else.

    - Typically, this is a pay-as-you-go model – monthly or annually, regardless of how much the software is used. The software is provided *as-is*. Because you don't manage the software, if features of the software have limitations, you don't have control over these features, unlike if you were managing the software itself.

The following diagram shows the service models compared to on-premises, showing which aspects you manage in each. There are many similar illustrations of this all over the internet, so you will have likely come across something similar at some point:

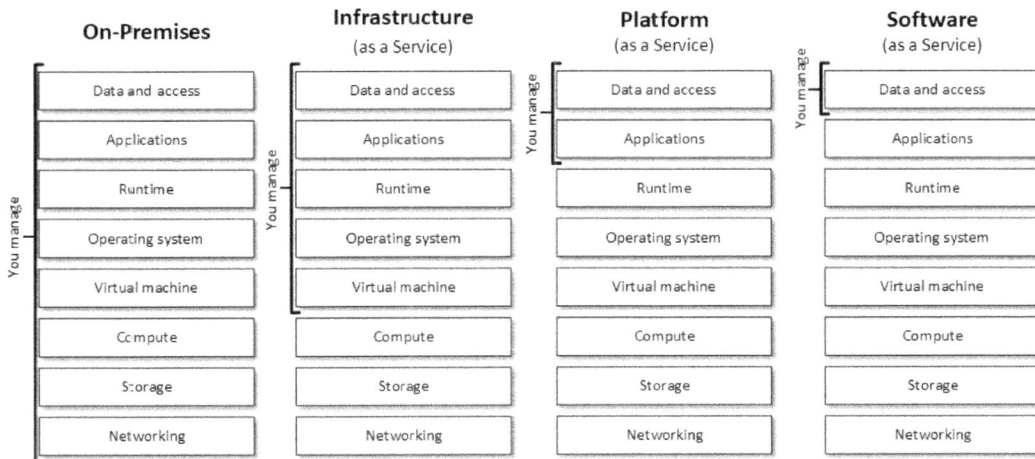

Figure 1.2 – Illustration of the different cloud service models and management responsibility

Increasing numbers of applications are being redesigned for hosting on PaaS services, allowing developers to focus on developing and have the infrastructure details not be a concern, greatly improving **developer velocity**. Whether that is the design decision or not, it's important to understand the different options available. Now that we've had a recap of some cloud fundamentals, it's time to start delving into Azure specifics.

Exploring the core concepts of Azure

Microsoft Azure is Microsoft's globally distributed cloud platform and provides over 200 products and services, covering all the service models previously discussed – from virtual machines to cognitive services. Managing all your services and subscriptions can be done through the **Azure portal**, which can be accessed via `https://portal.azure.com`. The portal isn't the only option – Azure also offers a comprehensive API and CLI, both of which will be explored throughout this book. There is also a marketplace where Microsoft partners, **independent software vendors** (**ISVs**), and startups can offer their solutions and services that have been optimized to run on Azure.

Azure's giant of an identity platform is known as **Azure Active Directory** (**AAD**), which will be referred to throughout this book many times. At no point will we be covering all aspects of AAD in depth – only the areas that are relevant to this exam. Subscriptions provide you with access to Azure products and services. Companies can have multiple subscriptions, allowing for a separation of billing and access control, as well as management groups that group together multiple subscriptions. Within those subscriptions, you can create your resources, grouped into **resource groups** (discussed shortly).

Regions and availability zones

When you create a resource in Azure, you often need to specify the **region** in which to create the resource. As potentially heartbreaking as *"there is no cloud, it's just someone else's computer"* might be, this phrase and others similar have become popular in recent years, and we covered the meaning behind it previously. With Azure consisting of a global network of data centers around the world, you have the flexibility to select the region in which the data center hardware that will host your service is located.

So, what is an Azure region? A region is a geographical area within which one or more (usually more) Azure data centers reside, connected through a dedicated regional low-latency network. With data centers being grouped within a latency-defined perimeter (of less than 2 milliseconds), Azure ensures that workloads are balanced between them appropriately. Note that some services are only available in certain Azure regions. Regions allow you to create your resources as close as possible to you or your users, as well as cater to data residency requirements you might have. There are special Azure regions that have been created for certain government bodies, keeping them isolated from the public infrastructure.

Availability zones consist of one or more physically separate data centers within the same Azure region, connected through high-speed fiber-optic networks, with independent power, cooling, and networking. If one availability zone goes down, the other continues to operate. There are a minimum of three zones within a single region. Depending on the region and service, you may be able to select whether your data is replicated across the same zone, other zones within the same region, or another region entirely. There is plenty of documentation available out there, should you wish to read more on this topic. For this recap, we have gone into enough detail for now.

When it comes to the deployment and management of Azure resources, a topic you must understand is Azure Resource Manager.

Azure Resource Manager

Before **Azure Resource Manager (ARM)** was introduced in 2014, resources were deployed and managed using **Azure Service Manager (ASM)**. With ASM, all resources were deployed and managed individually – if you wanted to manage resources together according to your application life cycle, for example, you would need to create scripts to do so

In 2014, Microsoft introduced ARM, adding the concept of a resource group. Resource groups are units of management for your logically related resources. With ARM, all resources **must** be a member of a resource group, and only one, although supported resources can be moved between resource groups.

Resource groups provide a logical grouping of resources, so you can organize resources that share the same life cycle into a resource group. When the time comes to remove said resources, you can remove the resource group, which will remove all those related resources. Resource groups can also be used as a scope for applying **role-based access control (RBAC)** – so accounts that need access to resources within a resource group can be provided with access at the resource group level, without needing permissions to all other resources/resource groups, or at a higher level, such as the subscription level.

One organizational concept I'll mention here is **tags**. While resource groups are great for organizing and grouping resources, their organizational usefulness has limits, especially when a resource can only be a member of one resource group at a time. Tags can be added to resources for additional organization and categorization.

Tags work as name-value pairs and can be used however you see fit – perhaps for a cost center, an environment, department, classification, or any other purpose (see the *Recommended content* section of the *Cloud Adoption Framework* guide, which contains guides on tagging decisions). At the time of writing, supported resources can have as many as 50 tags, with tag names limited to 512 characters (storage account tag names are an exception, where the limit is 128 characters) and tag values limited to 256 characters.

Any request – be it from the Azure portal, Azure PowerShell, the Azure CLI, SDKs, or REST clients – is received by ARM, which will then authenticate and authorize the request before sending the request to the Azure service. All methods, including via the portal, make use of the same ARM REST APIs – you just can't interact with the APIs directly. Some example services can be seen in the following diagram:

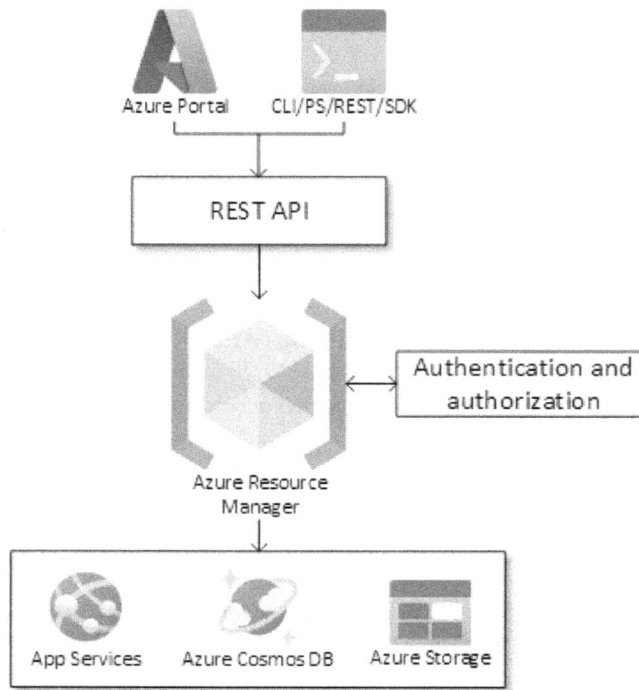

Figure 1.3 – Illustration of the role ARM plays in handling Azure requests

In addition to being able to manage, secure, and monitor resources as a group with resource groups, ARM also introduced **Azure Resource Manager templates** (**ARM templates**) – a JSON file that defines one or more resources as a declarative template. You define what resources you want to deploy and any dependencies, and ARM will handle the orchestration. ARM templates allow you to repeatedly and consistently deploy resources, defined in code – Azure's native **Infrastructure-as-Code** (**IaC**) solution.

IaC will be explored in more depth later in this book; for now, just know that if your infrastructure is defined in code, you can programmatically deploy your infrastructure consistently and rapidly, reducing the risk of human error, as well as being able to remove resources from a resource group that haven't been defined in an ARM template, should you wish. You can even take an existing resource or resource group and export them to an ARM template for future automation.

Another benefit of ARM is **idempotence** – by default, redeploying an ARM template to a resource group that already contains resources that match those in the ARM template won't affect those resources. This means that you can deploy the ARM template to reduce environment drift, without risking impacting those resources that match the specification in the template. If resources are missing from the resource group that are present in the ARM template, those resources will be deployed, bringing the environment aligned with the desired setup.

ARM templates

We just touched on ARM templates being a great way of deploying resources in a consistent, repeatable way, using a declarative template. Here's a very simple example of an ARM template, which I will use to deploy a storage account to my resource group:

```
{
    "$schema": "https://schema.management.azure.com/
schemas/2019-04-01/deploymentTemplate.json#",
    "contentVersion": "1.0.0.0',
    "parameters": {
        "storageAccountName": {
        "type": "string",
        "defaultValue": 'stdemoaz204"
        },
        "purpose": {
        "type": "string"
        }
    },
    "resources": [{
        "name": "[parameters('storageAccountName')]",
        "type": "Microsoft.Storage/storageAccounts",
        "apiVersion": "2021-04-01",
        "tags": {
            "purpose": "[parameters('purpose')]"
        },
        "location": "[resourceGroup().location]",
        "kind": "StorageV2",
        "sku": {
            "name": "Premium_LRS",
            "tier": "Premium"
        }
    }]
}
```

This template was created with relative ease using the *Azure Resource Manager (ARM) Tools for Visual Studio Code* extension for Visual Studio Code.

As you can see, the template specifies the schema and content version, followed by the `storageAccountName` and `purpose` parameters, the former having a default value set. The last part of the template specifies the resource I would like to deploy via this template. The name pulls the value from the `storageAccountName` parameter. Skip down a few lines, and you can see I'm setting a tag on the resource called `purpose` and that a value is getting pulled from the `purpose` parameter. On the next line, we specify that the location (region) this resource will be created in is going to be the same one as the resource group where I will deploy this template. The last few lines are specific to storage accounts and specify the kind of storage account, tier, and replication settings (yes, I know we skipped `type` and `apiVersion`; bear with me).

With this file saved as `deploy.json` (the name doesn't matter, although the extension needs to be `.json`), let's look at the commands for creating the resource group and deploying the resource using the Az PowerShell module (more on that shortly). The Azure CLI or portal could have also been used:

- `New-AzResourceGroup -Name "<group name>" -Location "<desired location>"`, substituting `<group name>` with the desired name of the resource group, and `<desired location>` with the relevant Azure region (which will also be used as the region for the storage account).

  To avoid any confusion, my example verbatim is `New-AzResourceGroup -Name "rg-az-204" -Location "uksouth"`.

- After receiving confirmation that the resource group was created, the `New-AzResourceGroupDeployment -Name "<deploymentName>" -ResourceGroupName "<group name>" -TemplateFile "<ARM template path>" -storageAccountName "<storage account name>" -purpose "<purpose tag value>"` command creates the deployment and specifies the parameters. Substitute `<deploymentName>` with a deployment name without whitespaces (it's a good idea to make this unique per resource group for accurate deployment monitoring), `<group name>` with your resource group name, `<ARM template path>` with the relevant path to your ARM template, `<storage account name>` with the desired storage account name (numbers and lowercase letters only), and `<purpose tag value>` with whatever purpose value you want for the tag. Strictly speaking, not all these need to be surrounded by quotes – it's more of a habit. I'd rather use them and not need them than need them and not use them!

  To avoid any confusion, my example verbatim is `New-AzResourceGroupDeployment -Name "StorageDeployment_1" -ResourceGroupName "rg-az-204" -TemplateFile ".\ARM templates\deploy.json" -storageAccountName "strfirstarm" -purpose 'AZ-204 book'`.

Once completed, I could run the last command again the same as I did previously, but because the resource declared in the template already exists with the same configuration as in the template, the resource wouldn't be touched. I could also just change the resource name and ARM would deploy another resource with a different name but with the same configuration – the beauty of IaC.

Although we're discussing ARM templates as Microsoft's first-party IaC solution, there are plenty of third-party solutions available that can also deploy and configure Azure resources. Microsoft also has another tool called Bicep that provides a more developer-friendly experience and greater functionality. At the time of writing, Bicep is not part of the exam, so we won't go into further detail here. However, you can find a link to its documentation in the *Further reading* section.

Back to the template and the two properties we didn't talk about – *type* and *apiVersion* – they both relate to resource providers and types. We'll cover these in the next section.

Resource providers and resource types

Now that we have introduced ARM, it's worthwhile going one level deeper and discussing Azure **resource providers**. ARM relies on a variety of resource providers to manage distinct types of resources. For example, when deploying a resource, the request will come to ARM, which will then use the appropriate resource provider for that resource type. Resource providers are identified by a resource provider namespace – some common examples of resource providers are `Microsoft.Compute`, `Microsoft.Storage`, and `Microsoft.Web`. Each resource provider has one or more **resource types**. If we take the example of a virtual machine – ignoring all the additional resources that can be deployed alongside it for the moment (network resources, for example) – ARM will use the `Microsoft.Compute/virtualMachines` resource type, which – as you can see – falls under the `Microsoft.Compute` resource provider.

Why am I telling you this? For a couple of reasons:

- If you try to deploy a resource and the relevant resource provider hasn't been registered within your subscription, you may not be able to deploy that resource, depending on the permissions for registering resource providers in the subscription.

- When you start looking at deployments via ARM templates or even within the Azure portal, you will see a reference to resource providers and resource types, so it makes sense to introduce them beforehand (look back at the previous ARM template and you will see).

Here's an example deployment from the Azure portal. I deployed a virtual machine and the required additional resources. You can see the resource type (comprised of the resource provider namespace and resource type) in the **Type** column:

Resource	Type
✓	Microsoft.Compute/virtualMachines
✓	Microsoft.Network/networkInterfaces
✓	Microsoft.Network/virtualNetworks
✓	Microsoft.Network/publicIpAddresses

Figure 1.4 – Resource providers and resource types in the Azure portal

Resource providers provide extensibility, allowing new resource providers to be added in a consistent way when new services are added to Azure. You can also write a resource provider for managing custom resource types. The availability of resource providers and resource types (and specific API versions) vary, depending on the Azure region. There is also a tool within the Azure portal called **Resource Explorer** that allows you to explore the various resource providers and types that are available. Every resource type will have one or more API versions available. More on that later.

Resource definitions

One last topic before we move on is resource definitions. Although certain properties will be present in some resources and not others, all resources managed by ARM have the following properties in their definition:

- Name
- ResourceGroupName
- ResourceType
- Location
- ResourceId
- Tags (optional)

It's useful to become familiar with what a typical resource definition looks like as you will likely encounter them often, in various forms. Most of these have been discussed already (location is the same as a region in this context), except for ResourceId. Resource IDs are globally unique identifiers for a specific resource, in the /subscription/<subscription ID>/resourceGroups/<resource group name>/providers/<resource provider>/<resource type>/<resource name> format. Here is an example of a virtual machine with a single tag name and value:

```
Name              : my-vm
ResourceGroupName :
ResourceType      : Microsoft.Compute/virtualMachines
Location          : uksouth
ResourceId        : /subscriptions/                                    /resourceGroups/
                                 /providers/Microsoft.Compute/virtualMachines/my-vm
Tags              :
                    Name       Value
                    =====      =====
                    purpose    AZ-204 book
```

Figure 1.5 – Example resource definition including a tag

How did I get that information? Using Azure PowerShell. In the next section, we'll look at how to use the Azure CLI and Azure PowerShell.

Azure CLI and Azure PowerShell

As this chapter is intended to be a recap, we won't be going into too much depth here. If you have installed the Az PowerShell module and haven't already signed in with it, you can use the Connect-AzAccount cmdlet. If you have installed the Azure CLI and haven't already signed in with it, you can use the az login command. For this chapter, I will be using Azure Cloud Shell from within my browser. If you would like to do the same, you can find instructions here: https://docs.microsoft.com/azure/cloud-shell/overview. Let's explore a few basic commands that touch on some of the topics we've discussed so far. We will go through examples for both PowerShell and the Azure CLI.

Az PowerShell module

Here are a few basic commands you can run within your PowerShell session (whether locally or via the PowerShell Azure Cloud Shell):

- List all Azure locations available to your current subscription with Get-AzLocation. Notice that Location is slightly different from DisplayName.

- List the resource providers available to your current subscription with Get-AzLocation | Select -ExpandProperty Providers | sort.

- List some of the locations in which the Microsoft.Compute/virtualMachines resource type is available and which API versions are available with (Get-AzResourceProvider -ProviderNamespace Microsoft.Compute).ResourceTypes | where ResourceTypeName -eq "virtualMachines".

- If you already have a resource deployed, you can list the resource details as in my previous PowerShell screenshot with Get-AzResource | Where Name -eq "<resource name>", substituting <resource name> with the name of your resource.

Azure CLI

Here are a few basic commands you can run within your CLI session (whether locally or via the Bash Azure Cloud Shell):

- List all Azure locations available to your current subscription with `az account list-locations`. Notice that although you can immediately see additional information, `displayName` and `name` are reflective of what we saw with PowerShell. To filter out the noise and just list the names, use `az account list-locations --query [].name -o tsv`.

- List the resource providers available to your current subscription with `az provider list --query [].namespace -o tsv`.

- List the locations in which the `Microsoft.Compute/virtualMachines` resource type are available and which API versions are available with `az provider show --namespace Microsoft.Compute --query "resourceTypes[?resourceType == 'virtualMachines'].{Locations:locations[], apiVersions:apiVersions[]}"`.

- If you already have a resource deployed, you can list the resource details with `az resource list --name "<resource name>"`, substituting `<resource name>` with the name of your resource.

These were just a few basic examples of using the Az PowerShell module and the Azure CLI to get information from Azure. There will be many examples throughout this book, so having an introduction to them early on – if you weren't already familiar with them – can be beneficial.

Summary

In this chapter, we had a recap of some generic facts and benefits of cloud computing while discussing the most common deployment and service models. Then, we went into some Azure specifics – starting with high-level information about Azure, subscriptions, Azure Active Directory, and resources. From there, we touched on regions and availability groups before looking at ARM – what it is, how it works at a high level, and resource groups and tags, and then looked at how to use ARM templates to deploy in a programmatic, consistent way while making use of ARM's idempotence.

We continued looking at ARM by covering resource providers, resource types, and resource definitions. We then brought some of these topics together using the Az PowerShell module and the Azure CLI to get information from Azure. If you are taking the AZ-204 exam, it's likely you already knew a lot – if not all – of the topics we have covered. If not, then this fundamental starting point should serve you well throughout the rest of this book.

In *Chapter 2, Implementing IaaS Solutions*, we will build on some of the topics discussed in this chapter, specifically around IaaS and ARM. We will look at provisioning virtual machines in more detail, including programmatic deployment, before looking at containers and their associated Azure services.

Questions

Answer the following questions to test your knowledge of this chapter:

1. What is the difference between scaling vertically (that is, scaling up/down) and scaling horizontally (that is, scaling in/out)?

2. What is the resource provider for virtual machines?

3. With SaaS, you, as the consumer, manage data, access, and the operating system running the software. True or false?

4. Azure virtual machines are an example of which cloud service model?

5. What is the maximum number of resource groups an Azure resource can be a member of?

Further reading

To learn more about the topics that were covered in this chapter, take a look at the following resources:

*   You can read more about Azure regions and availability zones here: `https://docs.microsoft.com/azure/availability-zones/az-overview`

*   You can read more about Azure Resource Manager here: `https://docs.microsoft.com/azure/azure-resource-manager/management/overview`

*   You can read more about ARM templates here: `https://docs.microsoft.com/azure/azure-resource-manager/templates`

*   Documentation on Bicep can be found here: `https://docs.microsoft.com/azure/azure-resource-manager/bicep/`

*   You can read more about **role-based access control (RBAC)** here: `https://docs.microsoft.com/azure/role-based-access-control/overview`

*   You can find several design decision guides from the Cloud Adoption Framework here: `https://docs.microsoft.com/azure/cloud-adoption-framework/decision-guides`

*   You can read more about queries with the Azure CLI here: `https://docs.microsoft.com/cli/azure/query-azure-cli`

- To learn more about the Azure CLI and PowerShell, check out the Microsoft learning path here: `https://docs.microsoft.com/en-us/learn/modules/automate-azure-tasks-with-powershell/`

- For further information on the fundamentals of Azure, check out the Azure Fundamentals learning path from Microsoft here: `https://docs.microsoft.com/learn/paths/az-900-describe-cloud-concepts/`

2
Implementing IaaS Solutions

We'll now build on some of the fundamentals we covered in the previous chapter, focusing on **Infrastructure as a Service (IaaS)** solutions. We will explore Azure **virtual machines (VMs)** in depth, covering topics of design decisions, additional resources related to VM creation, and availability options.

We'll take what we've already covered about **Azure Resource Manager (ARM)** and build on this knowledge further, focusing on ARM templates in more depth and discussing some of the more complex outcomes that ARM templates can enable, such as multi-tiered templates, conditional resource deployments, and the different deployment modes available.

One of the most exciting and game-changing recent innovations in the developer world is containers. We'll start off with an introduction to what **containers** and **container images** are and why the interest in containers is rapidly growing among developers. We'll discuss the components of a **Dockerfile** and use it to build and run a container image. With a grasp of containers, we'll then move into Azure specifics with **Azure Container Registry** and **Azure Container Instances**, having our container image running and managed within Azure.

By the end of this chapter, you'll understand the important considerations and design decisions when provisioning Azure VMs, as well as how to perform more complex deployments with ARM templates. You'll also understand what containers and container images are, their value, and the solutions Azure provides to manage them. This chapter will be our entry into more hands-on practical exercises.

In this chapter, we will cover the following main topics:

- Provisioning VMs in Azure
- Exploring ARM templates
- Understanding containers
- Managing container images in Azure Container Registry
- Running container images in Azure Container Instances

Technical requirements

In addition to the technical requirements outlined in *Chapter 1*, *Azure and Cloud Fundamentals*, you will require the following to follow along with the exercises:

- Visual Studio Code – downloadable from here: `https://code.visualstudio.com/Download`.

- The ARM Tools Visual Studio Code extension installed – found here: `https://marketplace.visualstudio.com/items?itemName=msazurermtools.azurerm-vscode-tools`.

- Git, which can be downloaded from here: `https://git-scm.com/downloads`.

- For container exercises, if using a Windows machine, enable the **Windows Subsystem for Linux** (**WSL**): `https://docs.docker.com/desktop/windows/wsl`.

- To build and run Docker images locally, the recommended tool to use is Docker Desktop. A Docker Personal plan is free for personal, individual use and can be found here: `https://www.docker.com/products/personal`.

- The code files for this chapter can be downloaded from here: `https://github.com/PacktPublishing/Developing-Solutions-for-Microsoft-Azure-AZ-204-Exam-Guide/tree/main/Chapter02`

Code in Action videos for this chapter: `https://bit.ly/3RVP1GA`

> **A Note on Docker Desktop**
>
> Although Docker Desktop is listed here as a technical requirement, and there will be exercises that make use of it, if you don't want to sign up for a Docker Personal plan, skipping the exercises that use Docker Desktop and following along in theory is completely fine. There are alternatives as well, so feel free to do your own research into those should you wish.

Provisioning VMs in Azure

Although – as mentioned in the previous chapter – **Platform as a Service** (**PaaS**) services are becoming more popular, there are certainly times when you need more flexibility and control over your environment than PaaS can offer. Azure VMs provide the flexibility that virtualization offers, without the need to manage your own underlying infrastructure. As you will know by now, the management activities of VMs – such as installing software, patching, and configuration – are for you to perform.

Because of the flexibility that VMs offer, they can often be the logical choice for various scenarios, such as rapidly building and destroying development and test environments, providing quick and convenient means to scale environments should they be needed. Other scenarios might include **high-performance computing** (**HPC**) for complex computational workloads, as well as extending your existing infrastructure by connecting your corporate network to the Azure cloud network seamlessly, without the need to purchase additional hardware.

A mistake that often gets made when building out an application infrastructure in the cloud is not taking the many important design decisions into consideration before doing so. The following aspects should be considered before provisioning VMs:

- Availability
- Disks
- Limits
- Location
- Naming
- Operating system image
- Post-provision configuration
- Size
- Pricing model

Before we tackle the preceding list, the very first consideration should be the network. Without considering how all resources – both on-premises and cloud – should communicate, as well as how they are intended to be secured, provisioning VMs can quickly become more of a distraction than a means to empower and deliver productivity.

Availability

There are several **Availability options** that Azure offers for VMs, depending on your availability needs. You should avoid running a production workload on a single VM, as it wouldn't be resilient in the face of planned or unplanned maintenance. When creating a new VM within the Azure portal, you are prompted to select your desired availability choice – **Availability zone**, **Virtual machine scale set**, or **Availability set**:

Availability options ⓘ	No infrastructure redundancy required ⌄
Security type ⓘ	**No infrastructure redundancy required**
Image * ⓘ	Availability zone
	Physically separate your resources within an Azure region.
	Virtual machine scale set
Azure Spot instance ⓘ	Distribute VMs across zones and fault domains at scale
Size * ⓘ	Availability set
	Automatically distribute your VMs across multiple fault domains.

Figure 2.1 – VM availability options during creation

We should cover some terminology here first:

- **Fault domains**: Fault domains are logical groups of hardware within a data center that share the same power and network hardware. Distributing your resources across fault domains limits the impact of physical hardware failures and power interruptions.

- **Update domains**: Update domains are logical groups of hardware within a data center that might undergo maintenance or be rebooted at the same time. Only one update domain is rebooted at any one time and given 30 minutes to recover before maintenance is initiated on another update domain. As you might imagine, availability options that distribute resources across multiple update domains increase availability.

Now that we've got an understanding of what fault domains and update domains are, we can make more informed decisions about our infrastructure redundancy selection. Here are the options available to us:

- **Availability zones** were discussed in the previous chapter, so there's no need to discuss those in more depth. You can choose which availability zone within your selected region to deploy the VM to, which will also apply to all resources created as part of the VM provisioning.

- **Virtual machine scale sets** allow you to create and manage a group of load-balanced VMs. High availability is achieved by distributing VMs across multiple availability zones and fault domains, also allowing your application to automatically scale based on demand or a pre-defined schedule.

- **Availability sets** are logical groups of VMs within a data center, where VMs are distributed across fault domains and update domains. Availability sets themselves don't carry any costs; you only pay for the VM instances that you create. Each VM in the availability set should be able to handle the same requests, so you can benefit from the redundancy offered.

You could also combine an availability set or availability zone with an **Azure Load Balancer** for better application resiliency. You can read more about the Azure Load Balancer service in the *Further reading* section.

Another option you have when provisioning a VM is to assign it to a **proximity placement group**, which is a logical grouping used to ensure resources are physically located close to each other when low latency between resources is essential. You can read more information about proximity placement groups via the link in the *Further reading* section.

Disks

When it comes to disks, there are two main considerations – **disk type** and **disk storage**. The two types of disks available are **standard** and **premium**. For development and testing, standard disks can be cost-effective while still being performant. For production workloads, it's recommended to use premium disks, which offer higher performance and lower latency, at a higher cost than standard.

The two options for disk storage are **managed disks** and **unmanaged disks**. With unmanaged disks, the storage account that holds the virtual disks is your responsibility. I/O operation limits per storage account and the requirement to add additional storage accounts when scaling is required are factors you need to consider and manage yourself.

The current recommendation and default option is to use managed disks, where the storage is managed by Azure – you define the disk size (which could be up to 4 TB), and Azure will create and manage both the disk and the storage behind it. There's no need to concern yourself with storage account limits and thresholds, making scaling much easier with managed disks.

Limits

At the time of writing, there is a default limit of 25,000 VMs that a subscription can have per region and 20 **virtual Central Processing Units (vCPUs)**. Yes, a limit of 20 vCPUs effectively means a limit of 20 VMs, but a support request can be raised to have a limit (such as vCPUs) increased. This is an important design decision because it may be more appropriate to choose another service on which to host your application when you consider this limit.

Location

Location – or region – was discussed in the previous chapter, so we won't go over old ground explaining what it is. In the context of a VM, the location is also where the virtual disks will be created.

Naming

A decision that's often overlooked is the naming convention to use for your VMs. The name is more than just an identifier within Azure – the name of a VM is used as the hostname as well. For Windows, the limit is 15 characters, whereas Linux has a limit of 64 characters. Changing the names of VMs after provisioning isn't a trivial task, so the name should be considered carefully before you create the VM. A recommended practice in naming convention is to include some of these things: environment (is this for development or production?), location, the product or service the resource supports, the role of the resource, and – if applicable – the instance, when there's more than one named instance. For example, the first production web server in the West Europe region might be called `prodweu-webvm01`.

Operating system image

Azure offers a variety of different operating system images that you can select to have installed on the VM during provisioning, both from the Windows and Linux families. Note that Azure only supports 64-bit operating system images. In addition to the base images, you can find images on **Azure Marketplace** that include additional software to support a specific scenario, saving you from having to install all the software components individually. You can also create your own disk image, upload it to Azure Storage, and use it to create a VM.

Within the Azure portal, you can view many available images from different publishers, including those that are custom-built for a specific type of workload. However, when we're talking about programmatic deployment, it's important to understand how to find the image details so that you can specify that in your script, command line, or ARM template. Azure Marketplace images are defined within a categorization hierarchy – a **publisher** contains one or more **offers**, and an offer can contain one or more **stock keeping units (SKUs)**, which can have one or more **versions** (the *latest* can usually also be selected for the version). The following tables are example values for Windows and Linux images:

Linux		Windows	
Publisher	Canonical	Publisher	MicrosoftWindowsServer
Offer	UbuntuServer	Offer	WindowsServer
SKU	16.04-LTS	SKU	2016-Datacenter
Version	Latest	Version	Latest
Exact version	16.04.202109280	Exact version	14393.4908.220116

Figure 2.2 – Image category breakdown examples for Linux and Windows

Here, I will show you how to get the details of images available per region using the Az PowerShell module, as well as the Azure CLI (assuming you're already authenticated in your session):

1. To list all publishers available in the Central US region using PowerShell, use the following:

    ```
    Get-AzVMImagePublisher -Location 'centralus' | select
    PublisherName
    ```

    Using the CLI, use the following:

    ```
    az vm image list-publishers --location 'centralus'
    --query [].name -o tsv
    ```

    If we scroll, we can see both publishers from *Figure 2.2* in the list.

2. With the name of the publisher identified, we can find all offers from that publisher (we will use MicrosoftWindowsServer in this example) using PowerShell:

    ```
    Get-AzVMImageOffer -Location 'centralus' -PublisherName
    'MicrosoftWindowsServer' | select Offer
    ```

    Using the CLI, use the following:

    ```
    az vm image list-offers --location 'centralus'
    --publisher 'MicrosoftWindowsServer' --query [].name -o
    tsv
    ```

    We will make a note of the WindowsServer offer for the next step.

3. With the publisher and offer names obtained, we will list all the SKUs available under the WindowsServer offer using PowerShell:

```
Get-AzVMImageSku -Location 'centralus' -PublisherName
'MicrosoftWindowsServer' -Offer 'WindowsServer' | select
Skus
```

Using the CLI, use the following:

```
az vm image list-skus --location 'centralus' --publisher
'MicrosoftWindowsServer' --offer 'WindowsServer' --query
[].name -o tsv
```

We can see that the SKU from *Figure 2.2* is listed, so we will make a note of that for the next step.

4. Now that we have found the SKU, we can find all available image versions for that SKU using PowerShell:

```
Get-AzVMImage -Location 'centralus' -PublisherName
'MicrosoftWindowsServer' -Offer 'WindowsServer' -Skus
'2016-Datacenter'
```

Using the CLI, use the following:

```
az vm image list --all --location 'centralus' --publisher
'MicrosoftWindowsServer' --offer 'WindowsServer' --sku
'2016-Datacenter'
```

At the time of writing, the version shown in *Figure 2.2* is listed among others. I purposely didn't filter these results, so you can see the output showing all the properties we've just discussed. Also, note that if you used the CLI command, you also see the urn property. **URN** stands for **Uniform Resource Name**, and you can see that it combines all those properties, separated by a colon (:). Some tools accept an image URN, so I wanted to make sure it was pointed out. In fact, we will be using URNs shortly.

Post-provision configuration

If the VM you are provisioning is a Windows machine, you can take advantage of the VM extensions that Azure offers. These extensions enable additional configuration for things such as running custom scripts, collecting diagnostics data for monitoring the health of your application, and setting up **Desired State Configuration (DSC)** to manage the configuration of the environment after the machine is created, so any common tasks can be automated.

While ARM templates can provide **desired state deployment**, the configuration state of the deployed VM is not managed by ARM and can be managed through DSC. See the *Further reading* section for further information on DSC. Azure also supports **cloud-init** (https://cloud-init.io/) for most Linux distributions that support it.

Size

With Azure VMs, you don't define the specifications for individual components such as processor, storage, or memory separately. Instead, Azure has the concept of **VM sizes**. The size determines the different specifications for the VM, and there's a wide range available – you can also use **Azure Policy** to limit which sizes can be selected should you need to. A recommended way to determine which size you should select is to consider the type of workload the VM will be running.

The current workload types range from general-purpose for less demanding workloads, such as development and testing scenarios, to workloads with additional optimizations in either compute, memory, storage, or graphics, as well as high-performance compute, which was mentioned earlier in this chapter. Within each of these families, there is a variety of different sizes for you to choose from to best suit your needs. To help you select an appropriate VM size, Microsoft provides a useful *VMs selector* tool (which can be found here: `https://azure.microsoft.com/pricing/vm-selector`), allowing you to answer some questions about your requirements before providing recommendations on size. The very first selection in this tool is to indicate the type of workloads your VM will be responsible for, as you can see here:

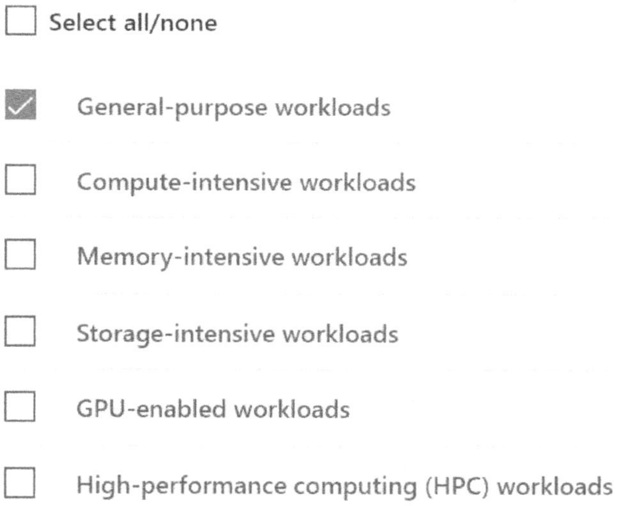

☐ Select all/none

☑ General-purpose workloads

☐ Compute-intensive workloads

☐ Memory-intensive workloads

☐ Storage-intensive workloads

☐ GPU-enabled workloads

☐ High-performance computing (HPC) workloads

Figure 2.3 – Workload selection within the VMs selector tool

From within the Azure portal, you can also apply a filter to the visible sizes based on workload type, so you are only presented with those sizes appropriate to that type of workload. If you need to change the size of your VM after provisioning, you can upgrade or downgrade if the current hardware configuration is supported in the new size. When you do resize a VM, be aware that it will be rebooted, which can potentially cause a temporary outage and change some configuration settings, such as the IP address.

If you would like to see which VM sizes are available within a specific region, you can use the Az PowerShell module that was introduced in the previous chapter, as well as the Azure CLI. To list all sizes and the respective specifications available in the West US region, for example, you could use the following PowerShell command:

```
Get-AzVMSize -Location 'westus'
```

For the same information using the Azure CLI, you could use the following command:

```
az vm list-sizes -l 'westus' --output table
```

Pricing model

Another important point that should be considered before creating a VM is cost. There are two main costs for each VM: storage and compute. You are charged separately for storing data in virtual hard disks that VMs use. Even if the VM is stopped/deallocated, the storage is still being used and therefore still incurs a charge, which was alluded to in the previous chapter.

Compute prices are shown per hour, but you get billed per minute that the VM is running. When the VM is stopped and deallocated, Azure releases (or deallocates) the hardware, so you will not incur compute costs during that time. As the Windows operating system has a license charge but Linux doesn't, the compute charges for a Linux VM will be lower than that of a Windows machine of the same size (you may be able to save money by reusing an existing Windows license with the **Azure Hybrid Benefit**).

There are two different payment options available for compute costs: **pay-as-you-go** and **Reserved VM Instances**. With the pay-as-you-go option, you pay for compute capacity by the second, without any long-term commitment or upfront payments, with the ability to scale capacity up or down at any time. Reserved VM Instances allow you to purchase a VM in advance, with a commitment of 1 or 3 years. This option can provide up to 72% cost savings compared to pay-as-you-go. This option is more common when the VM needs to be running continuously or you need budget predictability and can commit to having the VM for at least a year.

The list we have just gone through isn't exhaustive, but they represent the main design decisions that need careful consideration before any deployment occurs. Once those are decided, we can start thinking about creating our VM.

Creating a VM

As with other services in Azure, the availability of options can vary depending on the region you select. As we touched on previously, most resources in Azure can be created in the Azure portal, via PowerShell, the CLI, the REST APIs, the SDKs, and using ARM templates. We're not going to go over how to open the VM creation wizard within the portal, as that's something you are likely already familiar with; you should see all the options discussed up to this point when you start the wizard.

One thing I would like to point out is that you can make your life a little easier with URLs – if you want to head straight to the VM creation wizard, you can use this URL: `https://portal.azure.com/#create/Microsoft.VirtualMachine-ARM`. To head straight to the same wizard, but with the Windows Server 2016 Datacenter image selected, you can use this URL: `https://portal.azure.com/#create/Microsoft.WindowsServer2016Datacenter-ARM`. If you would like to find the URLs for other resources, head to Azure Marketplace, select your resource, and note the URL.

The quicker and more efficient way to create VMs is programmatically, also providing you with the flexibility to create multiples at once should you need to. We're going to use PowerShell and the CLI to provision VMs next (we won't give examples for both throughout the entire book; this is just demonstrating how the same things can be achieved with both).

We're not going to look at the REST APIs right now because that would require a conversation around authentication and bearer tokens, which is a topic for later in this book. The exam just requires you to be aware that the REST APIs are an option for deploying and managing resources. You can see the REST API documentation for creating or updating VMs here should you wish: `https://docs.microsoft.com/rest/api/compute/virtual-machines/create-or-update`.

At the time of writing, the default image that gets used when you don't specify an image for a new VM is Windows Server 2016 Datacenter. In the following exercises, we will create a Windows Server 2019 Datacenter VM and an Ubuntu Server 19.04 VM.

Image URNs

Using the same process that we followed earlier to get the image names, we can easily find the Windows Server 2019 Datacenter SKU using the following PowerShell command (or use the CLI if you prefer and substitute my location value with your own):

```
Get-AzVMImageSku -Location 'westeurope' -PublisherName
'MicrosoftWindowsServer' -Offer 'WindowsServer'
```

We can see that *2019-Datacenter* is listed there.

For the Ubuntu version, we can use the following:

```
Get-AzVMImageSku -Location "westeurope" -PublisherName
"Canonical" -Offer "UbuntuServer"
```

This lists the SKU of *19.04*.

For our Windows VM, the URN for the latest version of that SKU would be `MicrosoftWindowsServer:WindowsServer:2019-Datacenter:latest`.

For our Ubuntu VM, the URN for the latest version of that SKU would be `Canonical:UbuntuServer:19.04:latest`.

Armed with our URNs, let's create some VMs! The syntax we will be using is very simple compared to what you can do, but you won't be expected to know all the complexities available for the exam. I want to use a cheap VM, so I'm going to use `Standard_B1s`, which is available in my subscription and desired region.

Within your already established and authenticated PowerShell session (make sure the context is set to your correct subscription as well by using `Get-AzContext`, and use `Set-AzContext`, passing in the *subscription* and *tenant* if needs be, should you need to change it):

1. Open **Visual Studio Code** (**VS Code**), navigate to a sensible location (create a new folder if it makes sense to do so), and create a new file with the `.ps1` file extension. Your file explorer might look something like this now:

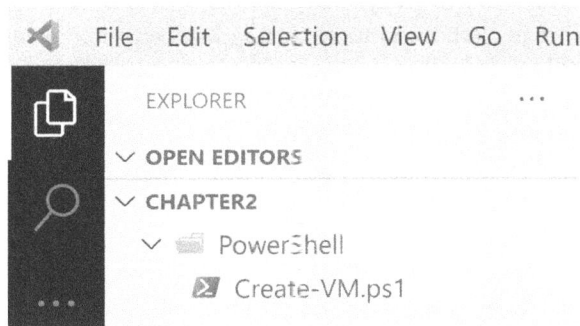

Figure 2.4 – New directories and PowerShell scripts in VS Code's file explorer

2. Set up the variables we're going to use:

```
$rgName       = "RG-AZ-204"
$location     = "westeurope"
$vmSize       = "Standard_B1s"
$winVmName    = "VM-WIN-WEU-C2-1"
$ubuVmName    = "VM-UBU-WEU-C2-1"
$winURN       = "MicrosoftWindowsServer:WindowsSer
ver:2019-Datacenter:latest"
$ubuURN       = "Canonical:UbuntuServer:19.04:latest"
$creds        = (Get-Credential -Message "Admin
credentials for the VMs:")
$text         = "Hello, World!"
```

```
$userData    = [System.Convert]::ToBase64String([System.
Text.Encoding]::Unicode.GetBytes($text))
$tag         = @{"chapter" = 2}
```

Most of these should already make sense to you by now, and you should be able to comfortably switch any names and the location to suit you (remember Windows' 15-character limit for hostnames). The `$creds` variable will use `Get-Credential` to prompt for a username and password, which will be used for both VMs (otherwise, we would be prompted for each one individually). You can customize the `$text` variable to be whatever string you like. `$userData` converts the value of `$text` into a Base64 string, as that's what the user data property requires – you'll see what this looks like shortly. We're also adding a variable containing the key-value pair for a tag we're going to add to the resource group, with the name of `"chapter"` and the value of 2 (it's lowercase for a reason – bear with me), just for some additional basic customization.

3. Add code to create the resource group, the Windows VM, and the Ubuntu VM, making use of all the variables we just set up. Without adding any exception handling or anything else that you would usually add (for the sake of simplicity and readability), your script should look something like this:

```
# Variables
$rgName      = "RG-AZ-204"
$location    = "westeurope"
$vmSize      = "Standard_B1s"
$winVmName   = "VM-WIN-WEU-C2-1"
$ubuVmName   = "VM-UBU-WEU-C2-1"
$winURN      = "MicrosoftWindowsServer:WindowsSer
ver:2019-Datacenter:latest"
$ubuURN      = "Canonical:UbuntuServer:19.04:latest"
$creds       = (Get-Credential -Message "Admin
credentials for the VMs:")
$text        = "Hello, World!"
$userData    = [System.Convert]::ToBase64String([System.
Text.Encoding]::Unicode.GetBytes($text))
$tag         = @{"Chapter" = 2}

# Create resource group
New-AzResourceGroup -Name $rgName -Location $location
-Tag $tag -Force

# Create Windows VM
```

```
New-AzVM -Name $winVmName -ResourceGroupName $rgName
-Location $location -ImageName $winURN -Credential $creds
-Size $vmSize -UserData $userData

# Create Ubuntu VM
New-AzVM -Name $ubuVmName -ResourceGroupName $rgName
-Location $location -ImageName $ubuURN -Credential $creds
-Size $vmSize -UserData $userData
```

4. Open a new terminal window:

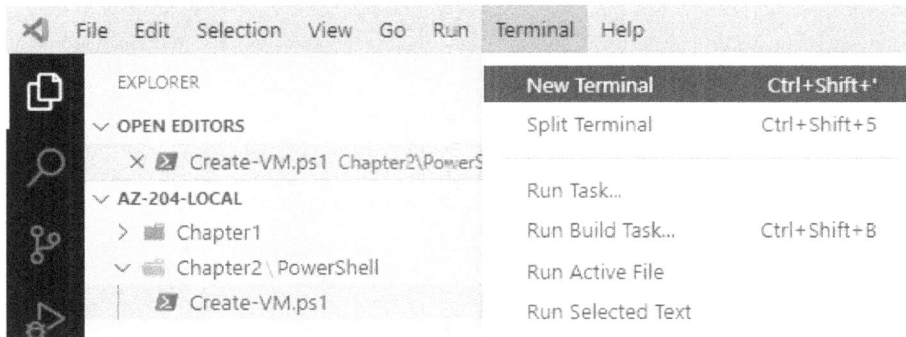

Figure 2.5 – Opening a new terminal session within VS Code

5. If PowerShell isn't your default terminal, switch to a PowerShell terminal, using the dropdown next to the plus sign next to the terminal window:

Figure 2.6 – Selecting a PowerShell terminal from a VS Code terminal window

6. When you're ready, run your script (make sure you have the correct path)!

7. When prompted, due to our $creds variable using Get-Credential, input the desired admin username and password for the VMs.

8. Once the script has finished, check in the Azure portal, and you should see your new resource group with the `chapter 2` tag and the new VMs, along with their related resources.

9. Click on one of the newly created VMs, and under **Settings**, go into the **Configuration** blade.

10. Scroll down, and you can see our text in the **User data** field:

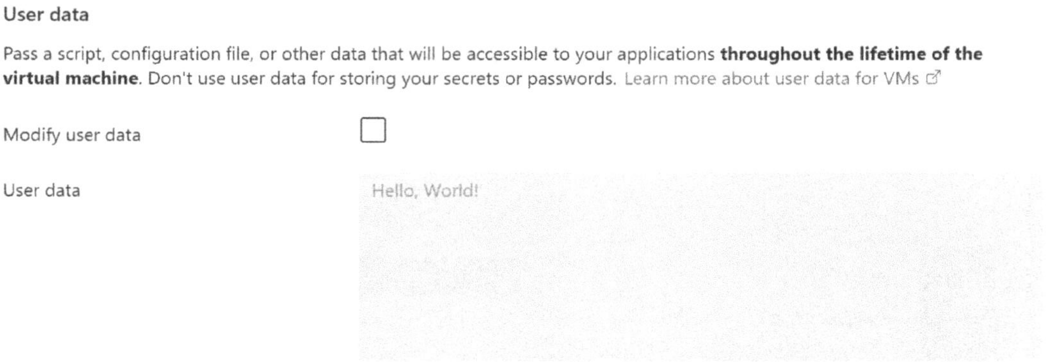

User data

Pass a script, configuration file, or other data that will be accessible to your applications **throughout the lifetime of the virtual machine**. Don't use user data for storing your secrets or passwords. Learn more about user data for VMs ☐

Modify user data   ☐

User data   Hello, World!

Figure 2.7 – The User data field showing our custom data

11. Make a change to the `$tag` hashtable (we can capitalize the `C` in `chapter`), and then save and rerun your script again.

    The script should complete much faster because ARM can see the resources already exist and the changes don't require redeployment, so the changes are pushed rather than the resources being redeployed.

12. Refresh your browser page and go back into the resource group to see the change in the tag.

13. You can also verify the image that was used by using the following:

    ```
    (Get-AzVM -ResourceGroupName "RG-AZ-204" -Name "VM-UBU-
    WEU-C2-1").StorageProfile.ImageReference
    ```

    You can do the same using the Windows VM name and see that they have indeed used the image we specified with the URN.

14. Delete the resource group and all the resources we just deployed with the following:

    ```
    Remove-AzResourceGroup -Name "RG-AZ-204"
    ```

    You will be prompted before it carries out the deletion, as we didn't use `-Force`. This will take a few moments.

I used PowerShell for this example, but you can find the Bash equivalent within the GitHub repository at `https://github.com/PacktPublishing/Developing-Solutions-for-Microsoft-Azure-AZ-204-Exam-Guide/tree/main/Chapter02/02-bash-script` should you want to check that out.

Although understanding basic commands such as the ones we've used so far is useful for the exam, be aware that we could have also done the same thing with the REST APIs and the **Azure client SDK**. For the exam, you don't need to go into the details of exactly how that could be done; just know that it's an option. Being aware of how to provision resources using PowerShell and the CLI is important, but for more complex orchestration, ARM templates are the more pragmatic way to deploy repeatable infrastructure as code, which we will explore next.

Exploring ARM templates

In the previous chapter, we introduced **Azure Resource Manager** (often referred to as **ARM**), resource providers, and types, along with ARM templates. We went through a very basic example of an ARM template, highlighting a couple of the most basic elements. Let's start off with an overview of all the elements you can use within an ARM template.

ARM template structure

Here is an empty template, showing all the main sections available:

```
{
    "$schema": "https://schema.management.azure.com/
schemas/2019-04-01/deploymentTemplate.json#",
    "contentVersion": "1.0.0.0",
    "parameters": {},
    "functions": [],
    "variables": {},
    "resources": [],
    "outputs": {}
}
```

We will briefly cover each of these.

$schema (required)

This element defines the location of the schema that describes the version of the template language to be used. Some editors are only able to process older versions of the schema, whereas VS Code can use the latest version. Note the filename of deploymentTemplate – this shows that the schema being used is for resource group deployments. If we were intended to perform a subscription deployment, we would use a schema with the filename subscriptionDeploymentTemplate. For management group deployments, it would be managementGroupDeploymentTemplate, and for tenant deployments, it would be tenantDeploymentTemplate. When using VS Code, the **ARM Tools** VS Code extension listed in *Technical requirements* will populate the empty template, including pre-populating the $schema and contentVersion elements.

contentVersion (required)

This element helps to version your templates. Using versioning can help ensure the right template is being used for your deployments.

parameters (optional)

You'll know from our first ARM template example in the previous chapter that this element allows you to specify input parameters for the template to use. Each parameter needs to have a name and type (the allowed types are `array`, `bool`, `int`, `object`, `secureObject`, `secureString`, and `string`). Other optional elements within a parameter are `defaultValue`, `allowedValues`, `minValue`, `maxValue`, `minLength`, `maxLength`, and `description`.

functions (optional)

This element allows you to create your own functions for your template to use, which will typically have complex expressions that you'd rather avoid having to type multiple times throughout a template. For example, you might define a function that takes a certain prefix for a resource name as its input parameter (functions can't access template parameters, only the parameters defined by the function) and uses that to create a unique name to avoid naming conflicts. Each resource can then just call the function within its name declaration, passing in whatever prefix, and the function will make sure the name it outputs is unique and has that prefix. Each function needs to have a namespace defined (which can be whatever you want, helping you avoid naming conflicts), a name, along with an output type and output value. You can also have parameter types and values if you wish.

variables (optional)

This element allows you to create variables that your template can use. Unlike parameters, variables don't need their type defined, as it will be inferred from the value of the variable. Another difference from parameters is that variables don't have their value defined by input at deployment time. Variables are often used to simplify values in much the same way as functions, although variables don't get called to provide an output as functions do – they resolve a value, and that value is immutable once resolved and can be referred to throughout the template.

resources (required)

This element – unsurprisingly – allows you to define the resources you want to deploy or update as part of the template deployment. The required resource elements are `type`, `apiVersion`, `name`, and often (but not always) `location`. From what we covered in the previous chapter, this shouldn't come as a surprise. There are several other resource elements, depending on the resource type. You can also add conditions, explicit dependencies, tags, and more. One thing to note about the `type` and `name` elements is if the resource is a child of another resource, the type and name of the parent resource are included in those of the child resource. For example, a SQL database needs to be parented to a SQL server. You have two options for setting the name of the child resource:

- If the child resource is defined separately from the parent, you will need to add the parent's type with a forward slash (/), followed by the child's type. The same applies to name. For example, if the parent's type is `Microsoft.Sql/servers`, then the type of the child database will be `Microsoft.Sql/servers/databases`. If the name of the parent resource is `parentsqlsvr` and you want the child's name to be `childsqldb`, the name of the child resource will be `parentsqlsvr/childsqldb`.

  Here is an example snippet:

```
{
    "type": "Microsoft.Sql/servers",
    "apiVersion": "2021-02-01-preview",
    "name": "parentsqlsvr",
    "location": "North Europe",
    "properties": {}
},
{
    "type": "Microsoft.Sql/servers/databases",
    "apiVersion": "2021-02-01-preview",
    "name": "parentsqlsvr/childsqldb",
    "location": "North Europe",
    "properties": {}
}
```

- If the child resource is deployed within the same template as the parent, you can also define the child resource within the parent resource definition, and just define the type and name of the child resource without adding the type or name of the parent, as they will be assumed from that of the parent. We will show this in the upcoming exercise.

outputs (optional)

This element allows you to return values from deployed resources. In our previous example, you may need to return `resourceId` for the SQL server. Outputs need to have a name and type, with other optional output elements. Here's a basic snippet of JSON from our ARM template that will output `resourceId` for our SQL server:

```
"outputs": {
    "resourceidsvr": {
        "type": "string",
```

```
   "value": "[resourceId('Microsoft.Sql/servers',
'parentsqlsvr')]"
  }
}
```

You can see here that I'm using the `resourceId()` function. This is an example of an **ARM template function**. A link to further information on the functions available can be found in the *Further reading* section at the end of this chapter.

An element I haven't mentioned is the `apiProfile` element, which allows you to define `apiVersion` for resource types in your template, so you don't have to define `apiVersion` for each resource – just define that all `Microsoft.Compute/virtualMachines` resources should use a specific `apiVersion`, for example. This doesn't come up in the exam, and it's not something often used, but I thought I'd mention it because it could make your life a little easier.

Note that when you deploy an ARM template, ARM converts your template into REST API operations, which then get sent to the relevant resource provider. At the start of this section, I mentioned that ARM templates allow for more complex deployments of multiple resources. Armed (pun intended) with a better understanding of the structure of an ARM template, we can start exploring how to deploy multiple resources using ARM templates.

Deploying multiple resources

There are two approaches to deploying multiple resources – **multi-tiered templates** and **nested templates**. A multi-tiered template will deploy multiple resources – some potentially depending on others within the same template – within a single template. This is a common approach for less complex solutions because you can have a single file – ideally stored in a source control repository – that can deploy your entire solution to a resource group.

You could also have a subset of the resources in your solution stored in their own templates, with a parent template linking them all together. This allows for granular reuse of templates across multiple solutions, which is useful when certain resources need to have certain properties defined or they need to have additional resources linked to them, regardless of what solution is being deployed. Hard-coding full names of resources isn't very scalable or repeatable for different deployments, so we're going to look at both defining parameters at the command line and making use of parameter files.

With that out of the way, let's go through a few key points to be aware of when deploying multiple resources via ARM templates.

Multi-tiered templates

As we already inadvertently discussed multi-tiered templates when we talked about parent-child resource relationships while going through the structure of an ARM template, we'll look at those first. This example will deploy an App Service plan along with a web app, which will conditionally deploy a staging **deployment slot** if a *production* Boolean parameter is true. This way, we can also cover conditional resource deployments at the same time.

As this exam assumes some previous experience in this area, I'm not going to walk you through a step-by-step guide on how to create an ARM template. I will, however, give you a ready-made ARM template and point out some key elements. The ARM Tools extension allows you to create a .json file and type arm! to have it create the ARM template structure for you to use. You can also make use of *Ctrl* + spacebar to get helpful suggestions for resource types, API versions, and most of the other important properties you might need.

Let's look at an ARM template and cover the important elements:

1. Download the ARM template or copy and paste the file contents from the following repository location and save it as a .json file on your local machine: https://github.com/PacktPublishing/Developing-Solutions-for-Microsoft-Azure-AZ-204-Exam-Guide/tree/main/Chapter02/01-arm-template.

    For the appName value, I made use of the uniquestring() template function. This generates a deterministic string based on whatever string values we provide it. I provided the *subscription ID* and *resource group ID* as parameters to the function, ensuring that the 12-character string returned is unique for our subscription and resource group. If we did the exact same thing for another resource within the same subscription and resource group, using the same appPrefix, the name wouldn't be unique, so we might want to include the deployment name or some other parameters to ensure that it's truly unique. For this example, we're fine without that. I added this string to the end of our appPrefix value.

    Look through the rest of the template, where there shouldn't be any real surprises. The creation of the dependsOn sections that implement the resourceId() function was simplified by the ARM Tools extension, which provides suggestions of applicable resources within the template. These suggestions were triggered with the keyboard shortcut *Ctrl* + spacebar. Based on my selection from the suggestions, the extension populated the function parameters for me. Note that we're using the production parameter value for the condition controlling the deployment of the staging slot resource, which is a child of the app.

2. Create a resource group using the CLI:

    ```
    az group create --name "RG-AZ-204" --location
    "westeurope"
    ```

    Alternatively, use PowerShell:

    ```
    New-AzResourceGroup -Name "RG-AZ-204" -Location
    "westeurope".
    ```

3. Deploy the template by navigating to the same directory as the ARM template and using the CLI:

```
az deployment group create --resource-group "RG-AZ-204"
--name "MyDeployment_1" --template-file .\web-app.json
--parameters appPrefix="myprefix"
```

Alternatively, use PowerShell:

```
New-AzResourceGroupDeployment -Name "MyDeployment_1"
-ResourceGroupName "RG-AZ-204" -TemplateFile .\web-app.
json -appPrefix "myprefix"
```

Note that you can see the *resource ID* of the web app as an output once deployment completes.

4. Navigate to the Azure portal and find the resources within your resource group; check the app settings are there under the **Configuration** blade for your web app and that no deployment slots other than the default production one have been created as well. You can also view your deployment history from the **Deployments** blade of the resource group should you wish.

5. Run the same deployment command – only this time, set the value of the production parameter to true ($true in PowerShell). This will deploy the staging slot to the web app.

6. Create any kind of resource you like in the resource group.

7. Run the same deployment command again, but this time, set the deployment mode to complete by adding -Mode complete in PowerShell or --mode complete in the CLI.

    Note that the newly created resource was deleted. When you use complete mode, any resources that are present in the deployment scope that aren't defined in the template are removed. The idea is that the ARM template defines what the environment should look like, and complete mode enforces that by ensuring only those resources in the template are present. The default deployment mode is incremental, which won't affect resources in the template that don't need changing, and any resources not in the template won't be touched either.

8. Clean up resources by deleting the resource group with the CLI:

```
az group delete --name "RG-AZ-204"
```

Alternatively, use PowerShell:

```
Remove-AzResourceGroup -Name "RG-AZ-204"
```

Nested and linked templates

When solutions become larger and more complex, it can often be more pragmatic to split parts of a solution into separate templates and then use another template that connects them all together. **Nesting** a template is when you have the contents of another template defined as a Microsoft. Resources/deployments type of resource within the main template, which then contains all the template contents of that child template. Here's an example of a template being defined as a resource within another template:

```
"resources": [
    {
        "type": "Microsoft.Resources/deployments",
        "apiVersion": "2021-04-01",
        "name": "nestedTemplate1",
        "properties": {
          "mode": "Incremental",
          "template": {
            "$schema": "https://schema.management.azure.com/
schemas/2019-04-01/deploymentTemplate.json#",
            "contentVersion": "1.0.0.0",
            "resources": [
              {
                "type": "Microsoft.Storage/storageAccounts",
                "apiVersion": "2021-04-01",
                "name": "[parameters('storageAccountName')]",
                "location": "West Europe",
                "sku": {
                  "name": "Standard_LRS"
                },
                "kind": "StorageV2"
              }
            ]
          }
        }
      }
    }
]
```

Linking a template is when you do the same thing, but instead of the template contents being in the main template, you provide the **uniform resource identifier** (**URI**) to a template file, whether that's local or over the network. Here's an example of a template being linked as a resource within another template:

```
"resources": [
    {
```

```
      "type": "Microsoft.Resources/deployments",
      "apiVersion": "2021-04-01",
      "name": "linkedTemplate",
      "properties": {
        "mode": "Incremental",
        "templateLink": {
          "uri":"https://mystorageaccount.blob.core.windows.
net/AzureTemplates/newStorageAccount.json",
          "contentVersion":"1.0.0.0"
        }
      }
    }
  ]
```

So far, we've just been specifying parameters in the deployment command. When there are only a couple of possible parameters, this is usually fine. When the number of parameters increases, this approach becomes less practical. This is where **parameter files** can come in useful.

Parameter files

Parameter files can be used to define values for parameters in ARM templates, so you can have a set of parameters in one file that relates to a specific environment (development, for example) and another file with the parameters relevant to the production environment. You can then just reference the relevant file during deployment. The parameter file is another JSON file, and here's an example for our ARM template, which I have called web-app.parameters.json:

```
{
    "$schema": "https://schema.management.azure.com/
schemas/2019-04-01/deploymentParameters.json#",
    "contentVersion": "1.0.0.0",
    "parameters": {
        "production": {
            "value": false
        },
        "appPrefix": {
            "value": "myprefix"
        },
        "location": {
            "value": "westeurope"
```

```
            }
        }
    }
```

If I wanted to use this file, I would remove my parameter arguments in the command lines and instead add `--TemplateParameterFile <path to parameter file>` in PowerShell or `--parameters @{path to parameter file}` in the CLI. I could conceptually have another file that has the production parameter set to `true`, along with changes to any of the other parameters, and just reference that file when I'm deploying to production.

Now that we're able to deploy our infrastructure in a consistent way using ARM templates (as mentioned in the previous chapter, Bicep is another Microsoft tool you can use, but we won't cover that, as it's not yet part of the exam), let's explore another topic. Having to manage and maintain full VMs, when your applications only use a subset of the services and resources from those VMs, can quickly become heavy in terms of maintenance, and potentially impact agility. Let's look at how containers are changing the world in this space.

Understanding containers

When VM technology was introduced, you were able to run multiple VMs on the same physical hardware with resource isolation. This allowed for **hardware virtualization** – any communication with the host was through a hypervisor. VMs could offer immutability with VM images, so when you needed a new VM, you could use an existing VM image, and the environment would be consistent without all the previously required manual or scripted steps – great! With all the benefits that VMs bring, for certain workloads, they became somewhat *heavy*. Each VM has a full operating system kernel, all the relevant binaries, libraries, and applications, and anything else needed specifically for the application to run.

> **A Quick Stop for Some Terminology**
>
> Modern operating systems separate virtual memory into **kernel space** (which is used by the operating system kernel, drivers, and a few other things) and **user space** (which is where applications run). So, when I want to think about my application, I'm only concerned with the user space; when I want to think about the underlying operating system, I can be concerned with kernel space.

Containers came along (look up **LXC** – short for **Linux Containers** – for more information about Linux containers) providing **operating system virtualization**, which allowed us to run multiple isolated user space instances on the same host kernel. Each container has its own isolated set of processes and resources, without needing a full operating system kernel. The container runtime brokers the communication between each container and the shared host kernel. This allows us to create more lightweight, standardized, immutable environments, all able to share the same host kernel. As long as the host has a kernel that's compatible with the container, I can take a container image and run it on any host machine and get the environment up and running, much faster than even a high-performance VM most of the time.

Building on this technology, **application containers** were introduced. While operating system containers would usually run multiple services, application containers were designed to only run what your application needs and only intended for a single service per container. Each component in your solution can have its own container, deployed independently, with its own configuration.

Docker

Docker is a popular containerization platform used for developing and running containers. Docker images are created using a Dockerfile, where you define what the container should do when it gets built, working in **layers**. You start with a base image, which might use another base image and make some changes. Once you have the base image, you might want to copy files to a location within the container, maybe build your application, and then run the application from the container, so it becomes a fully functional web server, with all the application dependencies but without the overhead of a full VM. A change made to a base image is considered a layer, and Docker combines the layers and runs the container. Containers are intended to be **ephemeral** – that is, they should be able to start up and run for as long as needed, then they can be stopped and destroyed until needed again, at which point a fresh new container with the exact same setup gets created. Container states are not persistent – any changes to the state of the container while it's running won't persist beyond the life cycle of the container by default (we'll talk more about this later in this chapter).

There is much more to containers and even Docker architecture should you be interested. For the exam though, you only need a somewhat high-level awareness of what containers are and how to use Docker. Essentially, containers (Docker isn't the only container runtime or platform out there, but it's the platform referenced in the exam, hence its discussion here) become the packaged application distribution unit – if I want to build and run an application in an ephemeral, immutable, lightweight, and consistent way, I will package my code and any dependencies into a container image, knowing that it can run on any host with a compatible operating system kernel – no more cries of "*It works on my machine!*" For simplicity, the terms *Docker images* and *Docker containers* will be used throughout this section interchangeably with *container images* and *containers*.

Phew! That was a lot of theory! Let's start creating and using containers. These steps will assume you have Docker Desktop installed, as per the *Technical requirements* section at the start of this chapter. You should have it running now:

1. Open a new terminal session.

2. Before building our own container image, pull down the official ubuntu image with the following:

```
docker pull ubuntu
```

Note that the first thing it says is `Using default tag: latest`. Every Docker image has a version tag associated with it. In this case, if we wanted to explicitly pull the latest `ubuntu` image, we could've used `docker pull ubuntu:latest`.

A Note on the Latest Tag

It's important to understand that `latest` is simply the name of a tag. It doesn't guarantee you will pull down the latest version of any specified image. A common practice when building an image is to create a versioned tag and a `latest` tag at the same time, but that may not always be the case.

---

3. To list all your local Docker images, run the following command:

    ```
    docker images
    ```

4. Note that we now have the `ubuntu:latest` Docker image listed.

    `IMAGE ID` shows the first few characters of the **Secure Hash Algorithm 256-bit (SHA256)** hash ID. Note the tiny size of the image as well.

5. Let's run the container interactively (using the `-it` switch) with the following:

    ```
    docker run -it ubuntu:latest
    ```

    Note that the prompt has changed to be in the context of the container.

Pulling Images

Although we pulled the image beforehand, you don't have to. If you run a container from an image that you don't have locally, Docker will look to pull the relevant image from – by default – Docker Hub. The Ubuntu image, for example, can be found here: `https://hub.docker.com/_/ubuntu`.

---

6. If you are familiar with Linux, feel free to look around, and maybe create some files (they won't exist once the container stops anyway, which we'll demonstrate later in this chapter). If not, just print out the version of Ubuntu the container is running with:

    ```
    cat etc/issue
    ```

    This shows that you're running a very lightweight Ubuntu container on your machine.

7. Without exiting out of the interactive session or closing your existing terminal, open a new terminal session and run the following:

    ```
    docker container ls
    ```

    We can see that we are indeed running a container from the `ubuntu:latest` image.

8. Close this extra terminal session when ready.

9. Exit out of the interactive session with the following:

    ```
    exit
    ```

10. If we were to run the `docker container ls` command again, we would see no containers running. If the container is still running, stop it with the following command, using the first few characters from `container id`:

    ```
    docker container stop <container id>
    ```

    We could have also used `docker ps` as a shorter command to list our containers. The `docker container ls` and `docker ps` commands show running containers but not stopped containers. Whenever you see `docker container ls` commands such as the one in the next step, they could be swapped with `docker ps`.

11. List all containers with the following:

    ```
    docker container ls -a
    ```

12. Note `CONTAINER ID` and remove the container with the following:

    ```
    docker container rm <container id>
    ```

    We could have also used `docker rm <container id>` as a shorter command.

> **Fun Fact**
>
> If you don't give your container a name – which we didn't – one will be created for you, randomly combining an adjective with the name of a scientist.

13. Open VS Code if not already open and create a new folder for containers, with a subdirectory called `hello-world`.

14. Within the `hello-world` directory, create a new text file called `hello-world.txt`, add a short sentence (I just used `"Hello, World!"` in mine), and then save the file.

15. Within the same directory, create a new file called `Dockerfile`. There's no file extension, just `Dockerfile` as the complete name of the file:

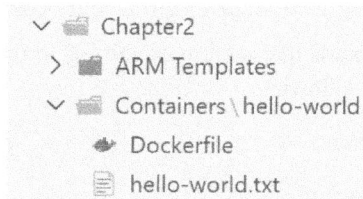

Figure 2.8 – The Dockerfile and the text file in the same new directory

16. Open `Dockerfile` and specify that our container should use the `ubuntu:latest` base image that we just used by adding `FROM ubuntu:latest`. Save the file.

17. From the terminal session already opened within the `hello-world` directory, build the container image from our Dockerfile and tag it as `demo:v1` using the following:

    `docker build -t demo:v1 .`

    The full stop at the end is important, as it tells Docker to use the current directory as its context. Any COPY actions will use the current directory as the root directory.

18. Check that our container image was built with the following:

    `docker images`

    This is now exactly the same as the `ubuntu:latest` container we looked at previously.

19. When the container builds, have it copy the `hello-world.txt` file to its local root directory by adding `COPY hello-world.txt /` (the forward slash indicates that the root directory is the desired destination).

20. With that file copied, let's have it print out the contents of our text file by adding `CMD ["cat", "hello-world.txt"]`. Save the file.

21. Your Dockerfile should look like this:

    ```
    FROM ubuntu:latest
    COPY hello-world.txt /
    CMD ["cat", "hello-world.txt"]
    ```

    To recap, this Dockerfile contains the definition for our Docker/container image. When we build from this Dockerfile, the latest version of the `ubuntu` base image is pulled (if not already cached), and then the text file is copied to the root directory within the container, which adds a second layer to the container. When we run a container using that image, the `cat hello-world.txt` command will run, which will output the contents of the text file. This is a very simple example, but I hope it helps those of you unfamiliar with containers.

22. Build a container image just as before but this time with the `demo:v2` tag by running the following:

    `docker build -t demo:v2 .`

    Note that this time we have `[2/2] COPY hello-world.txt /` in the output. This 2/2 indicates this is the second of two layers in that image. The CMD line doesn't count as a layer because it's an execution that only happens when the container is running; it's not part of the image-building process.

23. List the images as before with the following:

    `docker images`

24. Confirm that our latest image is listed. Run a container from it using the following:

```
docker run --rm demo:v2
```

We're using --rm to automatically remove the container once it exits to keep things clean, but you don't have to. You should see the contents of the text file output to the terminal window by the container.

In a very short time, we've created a new container from an ubuntu image and read the contents of a text file. If we had to power up a VM and have it run the same command, it's not likely to have happened so fast, and certainly wouldn't have been such a small image.

For a slightly more real-world example, we're going to build and run an ASP.NET application with .NET 6.0, without needing any .NET SDK installed on our local machine. For this example, we're going to use an existing GitHub repository, which has multiple samples and explanations that can be helpful for you. The purpose of this exercise isn't to test your coding ability but rather to provide a good foundational knowledge of containers, so reusing an existing solution makes sense:

1. Navigate your VS Code terminal to the containers folder you created during the last exercise and clone the repository with the following:

```
git clone https://github.com/dotnet/dotnet-docker.git
demo-v3
```

2. Once cloned, navigate to the demo-v3\samples\aspnetapp\ directory within your terminal and the VS Code explorer.

3. Examine the Dockerfile found within this directory.

   Most of this file should make sense by now. To summarize, it will pull the .NET 6.0 SDK image from the Microsoft container registry rather than Docker Hub, giving it the build alias. It will set the working directory, creating the directory if it doesn't exist, copy the solution and C# project files, and then run the dotnet restore command. Once that completes, it will copy the remaining files and runs the dotnet publish command. Finally, it will pull the ASP.NET 6.0 image from the Microsoft container registry, set the working directory and create it if needed, copying all the files from the publish location that build used, and ending with an instruction for the container to run the compiled binary, starting the web server.

4. Build the Docker image with the following:

```
docker build -t demo:v3 .
```

At this point, we have a container image that could essentially be our packaged unit of software. Any machine with a compatible kernel (Linux or Windows with WSL) can now run a container from this image and the experience will be the same. This container contains all the binaries and anything else it needs for the application to run.

5. Run a container from this image that will be removed when it stops, running it interactively and mapping port 81 on our local machine to port 80 in the container with the following:

```
docker run -it --rm -p 81:80 demo:v3
```

Note how quickly this container spun up from a container image and is now running as a web server – try achieving that same speed with a VM and VM image!

6. From your chosen web browser, navigate to `http://localhost:81/`. Our container is running as a functional web server.

7. Close the browser window and stop the container within the terminal using *Ctrl + C*.

The container (and therefore the web server) has now stopped and been removed. If we wanted to run it again, we would just use the `docker run` command, and it would run and be in the same initial state as last time. I say initial state because (as I've already mentioned) if you happen to make some changes to a container while it's running interactively, once you stop that container and run again, the changes you make don't persist – Docker images are immutable.

Having Docker container images locally is only useful for so long. At some point, you will likely need to share the images within your organization. Azure offers a managed, private Docker container registry service, where you can store and manage your Docker images in the cloud, ready to be used by other services, such as App Service, Batch, Service Fabric, and Kubernetes.

Managing container images in Azure Container Registry

I hope that by now you're comfortable with the concept of container images and containers. A common development workflow includes making changes to source code and building a Docker image from your Dockerfile that copies files, and runs tests on and compiles your code, ready for a container to run from it. That built image gets pushed to a repository within a container registry, which can then be pulled from another machine or service and have a container instance created from it. Microsoft's managed service for storing your images is called **Azure Container Registry** (**ACR**), which is available in three SKUs:

- **Basic**: Most appropriate for lower usage scenarios, such as learning and testing environments, due to the lower storage capacity and image throughput available with this SKU

- **Standard**: Suitable for most production scenarios, due to the increased storage and image throughput

- **Premium**: Increased storage and image throughput than the other SKUs but also adds other features, such as geo-replication

ACRs can store Docker container images, Helm charts, and images built to the **Open Container Initiative** (**OCI**) image specification. All SKUs offer **encryption at rest** for container images, regional storage (so that data is stored within the location the ACR was created), zone redundancy, and the ability to create as many repositories, images, layers, or tags as you want, up to the registry storage limit (although having too many can affect the performance of your registry).

In summary, an Azure container registry can contain one or more repositories, which can contain one or more image versions. A repository in this context is similar to a source control repository, storing versioned container images. Repositories relate to the name of your image and the version relates to the image tags. For example, in our last example, we created a demo:v3 tag; if that was pushed to ACR, the repository would be demo, and within that repository, there would be a v3 version, which is a snapshot of that image. You can also use repository namespaces to group images together. In the upcoming exercise, we will group our images in the demos repository namespace.

Let's create our container registry in Azure. With more emphasis on the Azure CLI in the exam than PowerShell when it comes to containers, we're going to start using the Azure CLI for the rest of this chapter. We started by showing you both to demonstrate that they can both be used to perform the same tasks. Personally, I prefer using PowerShell when more complex scripting is required but the Azure CLI for everything else. Also, for arguments that we've already covered, such as --name and --location, we will start using the short-form versions, -n and -l respectively:

1. Create a resource group if you don't already have one with the following:

   ```
   az group create -n "<resource group name>" -l "<your
   region>"
   ```

2. Create a new container registry, which will need to have a globally unique name, using the following:

   ```
   az acr create --resource-group "<resource group name>" -n
   <registry name> --sku Basic
   ```

   Instead of --resource-group, we could have also used -g. So, don't be surprised to see that throughout the book instead.

3. Once completed, open the newly created registry within the Azure portal.

4. From the **Overview** blade, note the **Login server** value listed (<acr name>.acurecr.io). This is important because this is what we will use to log in and push images to.

5. Go through the **Networking, Replications, Content trust**, and **Retention** blades, and you'll see that these are some of the features offered only in the Premium SKU.

We've created container images and run them locally, and now we've created a cloud-based registry in which to store our container images. Let's look at how we can use the Docker tools to push our container images to our new container registry.

Docker build and push

Let's send our latest `demo:v3` image to the container registry:

1. First, log in to the registry with the following:

   ```
   az acr login -n "<acr login server>"
   ```

   When using the Azure CLI, you only need the name and not the full login server name. If you were using `docker login`, you would need the entire login server name.

2. Create an alias for the `demo:v3` image that has the fully qualified path to your registry, including the desired `demos` repository namespace, and give it the `v1.0` tag with the following:

   ```
   docker tag demo:v3 <registry name>.azurecr.io/demos/
   demo:v1.0
   ```

3. List the local container images using the following:

   ```
   docker images
   ```

   Note that you have the newly created alias, which has the same `IMAGE ID` as the `demo:v3` image. This is because it's the same image, just with an alias containing the fully qualified name of your registry, plus the repository namespace.

4. Push the image to your repository using the following:

   ```
   docker push <registry name>.azurecr.io/demos/demo:v1.0
   ```

5. Go back to your registry in the Azure portal and the **Repositories** blade. Note that we now have a `demos/demo` repository, and within that repository, we have a `v1.0` tag.

6. Click on the `v1.0` tag, and note that it lists **Docker pull command** as well as the manifest, listing all the layers that the image uses and their hashes.

7. Back in your terminal session, remove the fully qualified tag we just pushed with the following:

   ```
   docker image rm <registry name>.azurecr.io/demos/
   demo:v1.0
   ```

   We could have also used `docker rmi <registry name>.azurecr.io/demos/demo:v1.0`.

8. Confirm that it has been removed with the following:

   ```
   docker images
   ```

9. List the repositories within your ACR with the following:

   ```
   az acr repository list --name <registry name> -o tsv
   ```

10. List the tags within your repository with the following:

```
az acr repository show-tags --name <registry name>
--repository demos/demo -o tsv
```

11. Pull and run a container locally from the image in your registry with the following:

```
docker run -it --rm -p 81:80 <registry name>.azurecr.io/
demos/demo:v1.0
```

Note that it says the image can't be found locally, so it downloads the image from your registry before running the container.

12. Navigate to `http://localhost:81` in your chosen browser to confirm that the container is running. We have now pulled our image from ACR and run a container locally using it.

13. Stop the container with *Ctrl* + *C*.

So far, we have used the Docker CLI to build an image using our Dockerfile locally, then run another command to tag the image for a fully qualified alias, followed by another command to push the image to our ACR. While it's important to understand the process, ACR provides a suite of features that can perform these tasks for you on a cloud-based agent in fewer steps. These are known as **ACR tasks**.

ACR tasks

Using a single ACR task command, the relevant files can get uploaded to the cloud, and an agent will build our image and, upon successful build completion, push that image to your registry. You don't even need to have the Docker Engine installed locally.

There are several scenarios supported by ACR tasks:

- **Quick tasks:**

  - This is what was just described – have your image built, tagged, and pushed from within the cloud.

  - You can also run your image in a temporary container within ACR itself.

- **Automatically triggered tasks – trigger tasks on one or more of these events:**

  - **Source code update**: When a commit is made to a specified Git repository, an ACR-created Webhook triggers a quick or multi-step task.

  - **Base image update**: When a base image that's stored in a public Docker or ACR repository, or one of your ACRs, is updated, a task can rebuild your image, ensuring that your image has the latest patches.

- **Schedule**: Set up one or more timer triggers to run container workflows on a defined schedule. The schedule is defined using the *cron* syntax.

- **Multi-step tasks**: Perform multiple `build` and `push` tasks in series or parallel.

Using the previously downloaded Dockerfile for the `aspnetapp` sample, let's have ACR take our code, build and push an image, and then run a container, all without any of it happening on our local machine.

Build, push, and run quick tasks

Make sure you have your terminal session open in the directory we used before that contains the `aspnetapp` Dockerfile:

1. Run the ACR build quick task using the following:

   ```
   az acr build --image demos/demo:v2.0 --registry
   "<registry name>" --file Dockerfile .
   ```

   Note that the output shows everything we saw locally and additional information, including runtime and build time dependencies.

2. Confirm the new `v2.0` tag is in your repository with the following:

   ```
   az acr repository show-tags --name "<registry name>"
   --repository demos/demo -c tsv
   ```

3. Run our latest image in a container from a cloud-based agent with the following:

   ```
   az acr run --registry "<registry name>" --cmd '$Registry/
   demos/demo:v2.0' /dev/null
   ```

   Using `$Registry` just states that the command should run from the registry. A context is required for this command, but using `/dev/null` allows us to set a `null` context, as it's not required in this case.

4. Stop the container with *Ctrl + C*, and then confirm locally that the image doesn't exist and there are no containers running with the `docker images` and `docker container ls -a` (or `docker ps -a`) commands, which should be familiar by now.

5. Go to the Azure portal and into the **Tasks** blade of your registry. From there, go to the **Runs** tab and look through the stream log outputs for each task (note that each is listed as **Quick Task**). Don't worry about the latest showing as failed – that's because we terminated it manually.

   We could have also used the `az acr task list-runs --registry "<registry name>" -o table` command.

A link to further information on ACR tasks can be found in the *Further reading* section of this chapter. Now that we've seen how to build and store container images in our registry under our chosen repository, we should talk about running containers in Azure outside of the temporary container that `az acr run` provides.

The simplest and fastest way to run containers within Azure without needing to provision VMs or adopt a higher-level service is by using **Azure Container Instances** (**ACI**).

Running container images in ACI

ACI is a great solution for scenarios that can operate in isolated containers. If you want to use images from your ACR, you will need to enable the *admin user* on your ACR, which we'll go through in the upcoming exercise.

ACI also has the concept of **container groups**, within which multiple containers share a life cycle, resources, network, and so on because they'll be running on the same host. If you're familiar with a **Pod** in Kubernetes, this is a similar concept. Multi-container groups currently only support Linux containers. One use case for this can be having a container for the frontend of an application, with another container for the backend within the same container group. The frontend will serve the web application, while the backend will be retrieving data, for example. Any containers within a container group share the same public IP address and port namespace on that IP address. Because of this, port mapping isn't supported.

A single container instance is technically its own container group, isolated from all other container instances, so when you deploy a container instance, you'll still see a reference to the `containerGroups` resource type. A link to further information on container groups within ACI can be found in the *Further reading* section of this chapter.

Creating a simple container instance

Let's get started with a simple container that just runs our `demo:v2.0` image:

1. First, update the ACR to enable the admin user with the following:

    ```
    az acr update -n "<acr name>" --admin-enabled true
    ```

    Note that we're using `-n` instead of `--name`. The short versions of arguments are available across most resource types.

2. Go to the ACR within the Azure portal, and under the **Access keys** blade, note that the admin user is enabled with some credentials listed. Note also that the username is the same as the registry.

3. Although we saw the credentials in the portal, get the password programmatically using the following command:

    ```
    az acr credential show -n "<acr name>" --query
    "passwords[0].value"
    ```

4. Copy the value to use shortly (depending on which type of terminal you're using, feel free to assign the output of the command as a variable instead).

5. Create a container instance using our demo:v2.0 image, with a public IP and DNS label that's unique within the region to which we are deploying, with the following:

```
az container create -g "<resource group name>" -n
"<desired container name>" --image "<registry name>.
azurecr.io/demos/demo:v2.0" --cpu 1 --memory 1
--registry-login-server "<registry name>.azurecr.io"
--registry-username "<registry name>" --registry-password
"<password obtained in the previous step>" --ports 80
--dns-name-label "<unique DNS label>"
```

Being able to specify custom specifications of CPU and RAM granularly rather than by sizes like VMs makes container instances all the more compelling. We could have also set a restart policy with the --restart-policy argument, but the default of Always is fine for us. Also, note that we're listing port 80 and not using 81:80, as we did previously – this is because within container groups, port mapping isn't supported (and even a single container instance is in its own container group).

6. Once completed, verify the provisioning state is Succeeded with the following:

```
az container show -g "<resource group name>" -n
"<container instance name>" --query "provisioningState"
```

Feel free to check out our new container instance in the Azure portal.

7. Obtain the **fully qualified domain name (FQDN)** for your container with the following:

```
az container show -g "<resource group name>" -n
"<container instance name>" --query "ipAddress.fqdn"
```

8. Navigate to the FQDN in your chosen browser, and you should see the same page we saw when running the container locally.

As we discussed previously, containers are immutable and stateless – if you make a change to a running container, when it restarts, those changes will not persist. If you want to persist the state of a container beyond its life cycle, you need to mount an external volume.

Mounting volumes to containers

We're going to use an Azure file share for this, which only works for Linux containers:

1. Create a new storage account in our resource group with the following:

```
az storage account create -n "<storage account name>" -g
"<resource group name>" -l "<location>" --sku "Standard_
LRS" --kind "StorageV2"
```

2. Create a file share within that storage account with the following:

```
az storage share create -n "acishare" --account-name
"<storage account name>"
```

If you get an authentication error during this command, you can get an access key for the storage account and provide that with the --account-key argument. The next step shows how to get the access key, so feel free to follow that and go back if needs be.

3. Obtain an access key for the storage account with the following:

```
az storage account keys list -g "<resource group name>"
-n "<storage account name>" --query "[0].value"
```

4. Create a container with our newly created file share mounted as a volume using the following command:

```
az container create -g "<resource group name>" -n
"demowithshare" --image "<registry name>.azurecr.io/
demos/demo:v2.0" --dns-name-label "<unique DNS label>"
--ports 80 --azure-file-volume-account-name "<storage
account name>" --azure-file-volume-account-key "<storage
account access key obtained in the last step>" --azure-
file-volume-share-name "acishare" --azure-file-volume-
mount-path "/acishare" --registry-login-server "<registry
name>.azurecr.io" --registry-username "<registry name>"
--registry-password "<registry password obtained
previously>"
```

Note that the output mentions that the volume was successfully mounted.

5. When completed, open the newly created container instance in the Azure portal, go to the **Containers** blade, then the **Connect** tab, and click **Connect**:

Figure 2.9 – Connecting to the container instance

6. Create a new text file in the current directory with the following:

    ```
    touch wontpersist.txt
    ```

7. Confirm that it's been created with the following:

    ```
    ls
    ```

8. Go into the newly created mount location from the container's terminal session with the following:

    ```
    cd ../acishare
    ```

9. Confirm that there are no files in this location with the same `ls` command we just used.

10. Create a new text file in this directory with the following:

    ```
    touch persistent.txt
    ```

11. Confirm that the file has been created with the `ls` command again.

12. Stop the container from the **Overview** blade (you can use the CLI if you really want to).

13. Navigate to our file share within the storage account, and note that `persistent.txt` is there.

14. Start the container back up. Once it's up and running, connect to it the same as before.

15. Check that the `wontpersist.txt` file is no longer where we created it with the familiar `ls` command.

16. Navigate to our mounted volume with the following:

    ```
    cd ../acishare
    ```

17. Confirm that the `persistent.txt` file we created last time did indeed persist beyond the container's life cycle with the `ls` command.

18. Clean up the resources created during this chapter by removing the resource group via the portal or using the CLI command:

    ```
    az group delete -n "<resource group name>"
    ```

Having the ability to run containers within ACI can be extremely helpful when you have a workload that can run in an isolated container, allowing you to focus on designing and building your applications instead of managing the infrastructure that runs them. Hopefully, you can now see how ACI can greatly increase developer agility.

Summary

In this chapter, we built up our knowledge of some of the IaaS services that Azure has to offer. We went into detail about the design considerations when provisioning VMs, including programmatically obtaining image information. We then proceeded to provision a couple of VMs with both the Azure CLI and PowerShell. We covered one of the most fundamental and powerful deployment orchestration tools at your disposal with ARM templates, including the structure and more complex orchestration with multi-tiered templates, as well as nested and linked templates.

The last section of this chapter was all about containers – building container images and running containers from those images. With the fundamentals of containers out of the way, we looked at how ACR can help with the storage and maintenance of container images, followed by running containers within ACI, including the more advanced topic of mounting Azure file shares as volumes for persistent storage of containers.

In the next chapter, we will dive into Azure App Service web apps. We will go through an overview of the service, authentication and authorization, networking features, configuration options, monitoring, scaling, and deployment slots (which were briefly referenced earlier in this chapter).

Questions

1. What does the `Docker rmi my-image:latest` Docker CLI command do?
2. If your solution needs two containers within the same container group, which host operating system should you use?

    -   Linux

    -   macOS

    -   Windows

3. Which element can you add to an ARM template to define `apiVersion` for all resources of a specific type, so that you don't have to specify `apiVersion` for each resource?
4. We know we can run Linux containers on a Windows machine; can we also run Windows containers on a Linux machine?
5. What is the minimum number of containers you can have within a container group?

Further reading

- Read more about VM availability options here: `https://docs.microsoft.com/azure/virtual-machines/availability`.

- Read more about proximity placement groups here: `https://docs.microsoft.com/azure/virtual-machines/co-location`.

- Read about availability best practices for VMs here: `https://docs.microsoft.com/azure/architecture/checklist/resiliency-per-service#virtual-machines`.

- For information about Azure Load Balancer visit this site: `https://docs.microsoft.com/azure/load-balancer/load-balancer-overview`.

- Further information on managed disks can be found here: `https://docs.microsoft.com/azure/virtual-machines/managed-disks-overview`.

- Read more about Azure DSC here: `https://docs.microsoft.com/azure/virtual-machines/extensions/dsc-overview`.

- Details of Azure VM sizes can be found here: `https://docs.microsoft.com/azure/virtual-machines/sizes`.

- Useful Azure documentation for developers can be found here: `https://docs.microsoft.com/azure/developer/`.

- Information on the VM serial console can be found here: `https://docs.microsoft.com/troubleshoot/azure/virtual-machines/serial-console-windows`.

- Information on ARM template functions can be found here: `https://docs.microsoft.com/azure/azure-resource-manager/templates/template-functions`.

- Learn more about Docker containers here: `https://docs.microsoft.com/learn/modules/intro-to-docker-containers/`.

- Further information on ACR tasks can be found here: `https://docs.microsoft.com/azure/container-registry/container-registry-tasks-overview`.

- Useful information on container groups within ACI can be found here: `https://docs.microsoft.com/azure/container-instances/container-instances-container-groups`.

3
Creating Azure App Service Web Apps

We've covered some good ground so far with hosting applications on **Infrastructure as a Service (IaaS)**. We're now going to step into **Platform as a Service (PaaS)** with **Azure App Service**. Developers that traditionally had web apps hosted on an **Internet Information Services (IIS)** server – even if it was a cloud-based VM with IaaS – are moving their applications so that they're hosted on App Service, which brings even more benefits to this scenario than IaaS.

It's important to understand that Azure App Service is more than just for hosting web apps, so we'll start with an overview of App Service as a whole before turning our focus to web apps. We'll also take what we learned about containers in the previous chapter and show how containers and App Service can work together to bring you even more value.

By the end of this chapter, you'll have a solid understanding of Azure App Service. You'll also understand how you can manage your web applications throughout their life cycle in the cloud, including configuring, scaling, and deploying changes in a controlled and non-disruptive way.

In this chapter, we will cover the following main topics:

- Exploring Azure App Service
- Configuring app settings and logging
- Scaling App Service apps
- Leveraging deployment slots

Technical requirements

The code files for this chapter can be downloaded from `https://github.com/PacktPublishing/Developing-Solutions-for-Microsoft-Azure-AZ-204-Exam-Guide/tree/main/Chapter03`

Code in Action videos for this chapter: `https://bit.ly/3qPjR7R`

Exploring Azure App Service

Azure App Service is an HTTP-based PaaS service on which you can host web applications, RESTful APIs, and mobile backends, as well as automate business processes with **WebJobs**. With App Service, you can develop in some of the most common languages, including .NET, Java, Node.js, and Python. With WebJobs, you can run background automation tasks using PowerShell scripts, Bash scripts, and more. With App Service being a PaaS service, you get a fully managed service, with infrastructure maintenance and patching managed by Azure, so you can focus on development activities.

If your app runs in a Docker container, you can host the container on App Service as well – you can even run multi-container applications with **Docker Compose**. As early as *Chapter 1, Azure and Cloud Fundamentals*, we alluded to App Service allowing you to scale – automatically or manually – with your application being able to be hosted anywhere within the global Azure infrastructure while providing high availability options.

In addition to the features covered in this chapter, App Service also provides the option for **App Service Environments** (**ASEs**), which provide a fully isolated environment for securely running apps when you need very high-scale, secure, isolated network access and high compute utilization.

From a compliance perspective, App Service is **International Organization for Standardization (ISO)**, **Payment Card Industry** (**PCI**), and **System and Organization Control** (**SOC**)-compliant. A good resource on compliance and privacy is Microsoft Trust Center (`https://www.microsoft.com/trust-center`).

Azure Marketplace was mentioned in both previous chapters as a source for resource images. Application templates can also be found within the marketplace for things such as WordPress, among others. With the rich Azure ecosystem, there are many other integrations for convenience and security (including Visual Studio and Visual Studio Code integrations), the list of which is increasing all the time.

App Service also provides **continuous integration and continuous deployment (CI/CD)** capabilities by allowing you to connect your app to Azure DevOps, GitHub, Bitbucket, FTP, or a local Git repository. App Service can then automatically sync with code changes you make, based on the source control repository and branch you specify.

App Service is charged based on the compute resources you use. Those resources are determined by the **App Service plan** on which you run your applications. App Service apps always run in an App Service plan, so this seems like the logical point at which to introduce App Service plans.

App Service plans

If you're familiar with the concept of a **server farm** or **cluster**, where a collection of powerful servers provide functionality beyond that of a single machine, App Service plans should make sense (in fact, the resource type for App Service plans is `Microsoft.Web/serverfarms`). As we just mentioned briefly, an App Service plan defines the compute resources web apps use. I use the plural context because – just like in a server farm – you can have multiple apps using the same pool of compute resources, which is defined by the App Service plan. App Service plans define which operating system to use, the region in which the resources are created, the number of VM instances (under the hood, VM instances are running, but this is PaaS, so they're maintained for you), the size of those VMs, and the pricing tier.

As you might be used to by now, some pricing tiers will provide access to features that aren't available in others. For example, the *Free* and *Shared* tiers run on the same VM as other App Service apps, including other customers' apps, and are intended for testing and development scenarios. These tiers also allocate resource quotas for the VM, meaning you can't scale out. All remaining tiers other than *Isolated* and *IsolatedV2* have dedicated VMs on which your apps can run unless you specifically place the apps within the same App Service plan. The *Isolated* and *IsolatedV2* tiers run on dedicated VMs, but they also run on dedicated Azure **Virtual Networks** (**VNets**), providing network and compute isolation, as well as the maximum scaling out capabilities. Azure **Function apps** also have the option to run in an App Service plan.

A common misunderstanding is that you need to have one App Service plan per App Service application. This is not always necessary (you can't mix Windows and Linux apps within the same App Service plan, so you'd need multiple plans if you have that). Remember – an App Service plan defines a set of resources that can be used by one or more applications. If you have multiple applications that aren't resource-intensive and you have compute to spare within an App Service plan, by all means, consider adding those applications to the same App Service plan. One way to think of an App Service plan is as the unit of scale for App Service applications. If your App Service plan has five VM instances, your application or applications will run across all five of those instances. If you configured your App Service plan with autoscaling, all the applications within that App Service plan will scale together based on those autoscale settings. Within the Azure portal, App Service plans are described as representing the collection of physical resources that are used to host your apps:

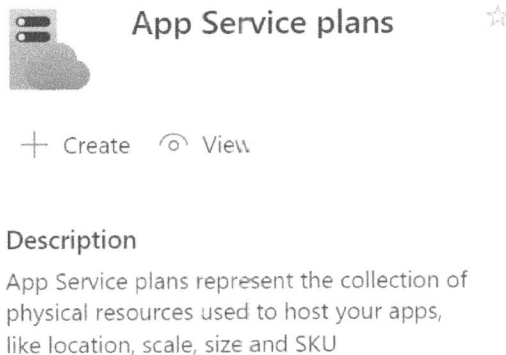

App Service plans ☆

＋ Create   ◎ View

Description

App Service plans represent the collection of
physical resources used to host your apps,
like location, scale, size and SKU

Figure 3.1 – The Azure portal description of App Service plans

We'll explore the Azure portal experience of creating an App Service plan here since this will make it easier to illustrate the configuration options:

1. Either navigate from `https://portal.azure.com` to **Create a resource** and select **App Service plan** or use the following URL to jump straight to it: `https://portal.azure.com/#create/Microsoft.AppServicePlanCreate`.

2. Select your subscription from the **Subscription** dropdown and select an existing resource group from the **Resource Group** dropdown, if you have one that you'd like to use. Alternatively, select the option to create a new one.

3. Enter the desired name for your App Service plan, select **Windows** for the **Operating System** option, and select your **Region**, as shown in the following screenshot:

Figure 3.2 – App Service plan details within the Azure portal

4. Click on the **Change size** link to be taken to a different kind of specification picker than you might be used to from other resource types. Look through the different tabs (**Dev / Test**, **Production**, and **Isolated**) while selecting different tiers and noticing the changes in hardware and features available for the different tiers. Also, notice that there is a **See additional options** link, which reveals further tiers that are available.

    We're going to be making use of staging slots and auto scale later in this chapter, so select the least expensive **Production** tier that provides these features. For me, that's **S1**:

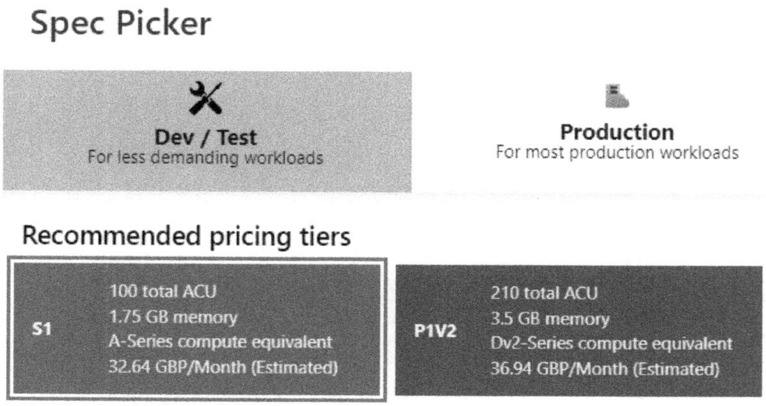

Figure 3.3 – App Service Spec Picker within the Azure portal

5.   Select **Apply**.

Notice that, depending on which tier you selected, the option to enable **Zone redundancy** is disabled, because that's only available in higher tiers. Make a note of the SKU code, not the name. In this example, the SKU code is **S1**, not just **Standard**:

Sku and size *

Standard S1
100 total ACU, 1.75 GB memory
Change size

Figure 3.4 – SKU code showing in the Azure portal

6.   Click on **Review + Create**, but don't select **Create**; instead, click on **Download a template for automation** to the right of the **Create** button. Look through the generated JSON ARM template, which should make sense now if it didn't before you started this book. You could, in theory, take this ARM template and deploy it in the same ways we covered in the previous chapter. If you click on the **Parameters** tab, you'll see that skuCode is listed, which is what we need.

7.   Close the template with the cross (**X**) toward the top-right of the current screen (*not the one that closes the entire browser window!*) Alternatively, you could scroll to the left to navigate to a previous screen.

8.   Click on **Create** to provision the new App Service plan. Once completed, go into your new App Service plan and look through the available settings. You will be able to see any apps running within the plan, storage use, networking settings, as well as horizontal and vertical scaling options.

9.   Open a terminal session, make sure you're logged in, and set it to the right subscription.

10.   Create a Linux App Service plan using the following CLI command:

```
az appservice plan create -n "<plan name>" -g "<resource
group>" -sku "<SKU code>" --is-linux
```

Alternatively, use the following PowerShell command:

```
New-AzAppServicePlan -Name "<plan name>"
-ResourceGroupName "<resource group>" -Tier "<SKU code>"
-Location "<region>" -Linux
```

While the CLI accepts but doesn't require a location because it will inherit from the resource group, PowerShell requires the location to be specified.

Now that we've explored the App Service plans that provide the underlying compute resources for your apps, we can move on to App Service web apps and put these App Service plans to good use.

App Service web apps

Originally, App Service was only able to host web apps on Windows, but since 2017, App Service has been able to natively host web apps on Linux for supported application stacks. You can get a list of the available runtimes for Linux by using the following CLI command:

```
az webapp list-runtimes --linux -o tsv
```

The versions you see relate to the built-in container images that App Service uses behind the scenes. If your application requires a runtime that isn't supported, you can deploy the web app with a custom container image. If you want to use your own custom containers, you can specify the image source from an ACR (which we'll do shortly), Docker Hub, or another private registry.

Now, let's create a basic web app using the Azure portal since – as with App Service plans – it's easier to illustrate certain elements:

1. Navigate to **Create a resource** in the portal and select **Web App** or go straight to the URL: `https://portal.azure.com/#create/Microsoft.WebSite`.

2. Make sure you've got the correct subscription and resource group selected (or create a new one). Enter a globally unique web app name and select **Code** next to **Publish**.

   Select the .NET runtime stack that matches the version we used in the containers demo in the previous chapter (it was **.NET 6.0** at the time of writing), then select **Linux** for the **Operating System** option, along with your appropriate region. Notice that the Linux App Service plan has already been selected for you in the **Linux Plan** field and that you can't select the Windows one, despite it being in the same subscription and region (the resource group doesn't matter).

   Although we're using pre-created App Service plans, notice that you can create a new one at this point. If you were to use the `az webapp up` (don't do it right now) CLI command, it would automatically create a new resource group, app service plan, and web app.

3. Progress to the **Deployment** screen and set the **Continuous deployment** radio button to **Enable**. Just notice the options available to you and then toggle the radio button back to **Disable**. At the time of writing, the only option available is **GitHub Actions**, but you do get more options within the **Deployment Center** area of the app once created.

4. Continue through the wizard and create the web app. Once completed, go to the resource.

5. From the **Overview** blade, notice that **App Service Plan** is listed.

6. Navigate to the **Deployment Center** area and view the **Continuous Deployment (CI/CD)** options that are available in addition to GitHub under the **Source** dropdown.

7. Back to the **Overview** blade, select **Browse** to open the web app in your browser. You will be presented with the generic starter page:

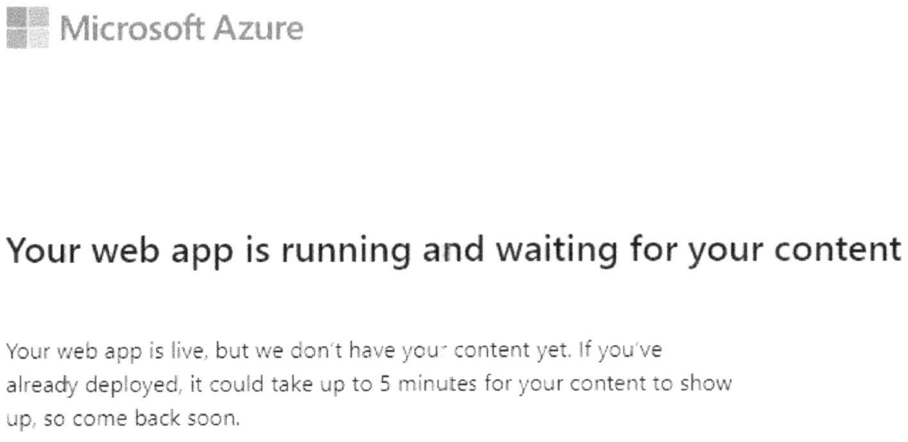

::: Microsoft Azure

Your web app is running and waiting for your content

Your web app is live, but we don't have your content yet. If you've
already deployed, it could take up to 5 minutes for your content to show
up, so come back soon.

Figure 3.5 – Web app starter page content

8. Create a Windows web app with the following CLI command:

```
az webapp create -n "<globally unique name>" -g
"<resource group>" --plan "<name of the Windows App
Service plan previously created>"
```

Alternatively, use the following PowerShell command:

```
New-AzWebApp -Name "<globally unique app name>"
-ResourceGroupName "<resource group>" -AppServicePlan
"<name of the Windows App Service plan previously
created>"
```

A location isn't required here since it will inherit from the App Service plan (App Service plans will only be available within the same subscription and region).

9. Once created, open the resource and the **Extensions** blade, then browse the available extensions, which we referred to in the previous chapter.

With that, we've created some App Service plans and web apps. Now, let's deploy some very basic code to one of our web apps:

1. If you haven't already cloned our code repository, do so now from an appropriate directory by using the following command from a terminal session:

```
git clone https://github.com/PacktPublishing/Developing-
Solutions-for-Microsoft-Azure-AZ-204-Exam-Guide
```

Feel free to either work from the Chapter03\01-hello-world directory or create a new folder and copy the contents to it.

2. Change the terminal directory to the correct directory.

3. Deploy this basic static HTML application to the *Windows* web app and launch it in the default browser using the following CLI command:

```
az webapp up -n "<name of the Windows web app>" --html -b
```

Here, we added the `-b` (the short version of `--launch-browser`) argument to open the app in the default browser after launching, but you don't need to. It just saves time because you should browse to it now anyway. Using the `--html` argument ignores any app detection and just deploys the code as a static HTML app.

4. Make an arbitrary change to some of the contents of the `index.html` file and run the same CLI command to update and browse to your updated application.

5. Optionally, to save on costs and keep things simple, go to the Azure portal and delete the *Windows* App Service and the Windows App Service plan with it.

    We will only be using the Linux App Service for the rest of this chapter, so the Windows one is no longer required unless you want to compare the experience with Linux/containers as we go along.

That was about as simple as it can get. We're not going to run through every different type of deployment (deploying using a Git repository, for example), but feel free to check out the Microsoft documentation on that, should you wish. We'll talk about CI/CD toward the end of this book as well. For now, the last deployment method we will look at before moving on is custom containers.

We're going to reuse the `aspnetapp` sample we downloaded in the previous chapter, create an ACR, store our container image there, and then use that to deploy the containerized application to our App Service. Let's get started:

1. Create a new folder for this exercise. I've called mine `app-service-container`.

2. Copy the `aspnetapp` folder from the `demo-v3` folder we cloned the sample container repository to:

Figure 3.6 – Copying the aspnetapp folder within VS Code

3. Paste it into the newly created folder. This will result in a structure similar to this:

Figure 3.7 – New folder structure with the copied aspnetapp folder in VS Code

4. From a terminal session open at the `app-service-container\aspnetapp` directory, create a new ACR with the following CLI command:

    ```
    az acr create -g "<resource group>" -n "<ACR name>" --sku
    "Basic"
    ```

5. Enable the admin user with the following CLI command:

    ```
    az acr update -n "<ACR name>" --admin-enabled true
    ```

6. Copy the admin password or assign the value to a variable by using the following CLI command:

    ```
    az acr credential show -n "<ACR name>" --query
    "passwords[0].value"
    ```

7. Create a new container image from the Dockerfile using the *ACR build* task, giving it both a `1.0.0` tag and a `latest` tag using the following CLI command:

    ```
    az acr build --image "chapter3:1.0.0" --image
    "chapter3:latest" --registry "<ACR name>" --file
    "Dockerfile" .
    ```

    We used two tags to illustrate how you can version your images with **semantic versioning** while also making sure that the most recent version is tagged with the `latest` tag as well. A link to information on semantic versioning can be found in the *Further reading* section of this chapter.

8. Update the Linux App Service so that it uses the container image with the following CLI command:

    ```
    az webapp config container set -g "<resource group>" -n
    "<app-service>" -r "https://<ACR name>.azurecr.io" -i
    "<ACR name>.azurecr.io/chapter3:latest" -u "<ACR name>"
    -p "<password obtained from step 6>"
    ```

9. Navigate to the Linux App Service within the Azure portal and view the **Deployment Center** area, which now shows the container configuration.

10. Open the **Configuration** blade. You will see that a few DOCKER_ application settings have been added, which your App Service will use.

11. Browse to your App Service URL in your browser. You will see that the same web app we ran within a container instance in the previous chapter is now running on App Service within a container.

At the moment, anybody with a browser and an internet connection could access your web app if they had the URL. Now, let's learn how authentication and authorization work with App Service so that we can require users to authenticate before being able to view our shiny new containerized web app.

Authentication and authorization

Many web frameworks have authentication (signing users in) and authorization (providing access to those that should have access) features bundled with them, which could be used to handle our application's authentication and authorization. You could even write tools to handle them if you'd like the most control. As you may imagine, the more you handle yourself, the more management you need to do. You should keep your security solution up-to-date with the latest updates, for example.

With App Service, you can make use of its built-in authentication and authorization capabilities so that users can sign in and use your app by writing minimal code (or none at all if the out-of-the-box features give you what you need). App Service uses federated identity, which means that a third-party identity provider – Google, for example – manages the user accounts and **authentication flow**, and App Service gets the resulting token for authorization.

Authentication and authorization module

Once you enable the authentication and authorization module (which we will shortly), all incoming HTTP requests will pass through it before being handled by your application. The module does several things for you:

- Authenticates users with the identity provider
- Validates, stores, and refreshes the tokens
- Manages the authenticated sessions
- Injects identity information into the request headers (which we'll also look at shortly)

On Windows App Service apps, the module runs as a native IIS module in the same sandbox as your application code. On Linux and container apps, the module runs in a separate container, isolated from your code. Because the module doesn't run in-process, there's no direct integration with specific language frameworks, although the relevant information your app may need is passed through using request headers, making this a good time for the authentication flow to be explained.

Authentication flow

It's important to understand, at least to some extent, what the authentication flow looks like with App Service, which is the same regardless of the identity provider, although different depending on whether or not you sign in with the provider's SDK. With the provider's SDK, the code handles the sign-in process and is often referred to as **client flow**; without the provider's SDK, App Service handles the sign-in process and is often referred to as **server flow**. We'll discuss some of the theory first, before checking it out in practice.

The first thing to know is that the different identity providers will have different sign-in endpoints. Here are the currently **generally available (GA)** identity providers and their respective sign-in endpoints:

- **Microsoft Identity Platform**: `/.auth/login/aad`
- **Facebook**: `/.auth/login/facebook`
- **Google**: `/.auth/login/google`
- **Twitter**: `/.auth/login/twitter`
- **Any OpenID Connect provider**: `/.auth/login/<provider name>`

The following diagram illustrates the different steps of the authentication flow, both using and not using the provider SDK:

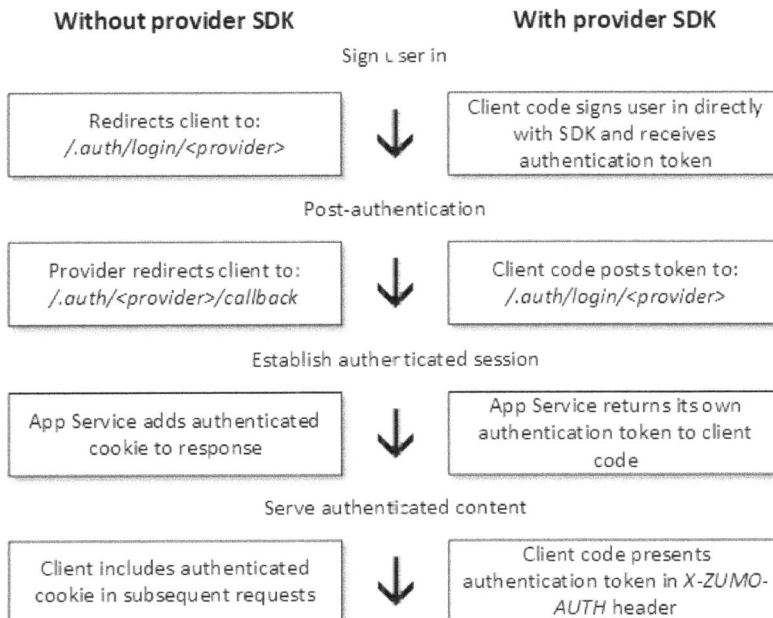

Without provider SDK		With provider SDK
Sign user in		
Redirects client to: /.auth/login/<provider>	↓	Client code signs user in directly with SDK and receives authentication token
Post-authentication		
Provider redirects client to: /.auth/<provider>/callback	↓	Client code posts token to: /.auth/login/<provider>
Establish authenticated session		
App Service adds authenticated cookie to response	↓	App Service returns its own authentication token to client code
Serve authenticated content		
Client includes authenticated cookie in subsequent requests	↓	Client code presents authentication token in *X-ZUMO-AUTH* header

Figure 3.8 – Authentication flow steps

You can configure the behavior of App Service when incoming requests aren't authenticated. If you allow unauthenticated requests, unauthenticated traffic gets deferred to your application, and authenticated traffic gets passed along by App Service with the authentication information in the HTTP headers. If you set App Service to require authentication, any unauthenticated traffic gets rejected without getting passed to your application. The rejection can be a redirect to `/.auth/login/<provider>` for whichever provider you choose. You can also configure the rejection to be a `401` or a `403` response for all requests.

Seeing the authentication flow and authorization behavior in action will help cement your understanding of the topic, so let's configure our App Service to make use of the authentication and authorization module. We're going to use the Azure portal for this exercise, as that will be easier to illustrate and understand. The exam doesn't require you to know all the commands to set this up programmatically; you just need to have some understanding of the setup and behavior. We'll also go into more detail in *Chapter 7, Implementing User Authentication and Authorization*:

1. Open your App Service within the Azure portal and navigate to the **Authentication** blade.

2. Select **Add identity provider** and notice the providers available (some are in preview at the time of writing, so they won't be in the exam for a while, hence not being listed as providers in this book).

3. From the provider list, select **Microsoft**. Take note of the available settings and how they relate to what we've just been discussing. Leave everything as default and progress to **Permissions**.

    For simplicity, we're going to create a new app registration because a detailed conversation about app registrations and service principles will come in *Chapter 7, Implementing User Authentication and Authorization*.

4. Leave the permissions as default, but just know that this is where you can specify the permissions your app should request from users when they go through the authentication process. In this case, we just want to get information on the user's claim so that we can identify them with rudimentary information. We'll see this in action in a few steps.

5. Select **Add**. You will see that your App Service has a new identity provider configured and that authentication is required to be able to access the app. Notice **App (client) ID**? We'll see that referenced again shortly.

6. Within the **Configuration** blade, notice there's a new application setting for the provider authentication secret of the app registration we just created.

7. Go over to **Azure Active Directory** and open **App registrations**. Find and open the app registration that we created (if you left the name as the default, it will be the same name as your App Service).

8. Notice that **Application (client) ID** here is the same as we saw in the **Authentication** blade of the App Service. Then, navigate to the **Branding & properties** blade, noticing that **Home page URL** matches the URL of our App Service.

9. Within the **Authentication** blade, notice that the **redirect URI** property for the application includes the **/.auth/login/<provider>/callback** pattern we just discussed, with **Azure Active Directory (AAD)** being the provider.

10. Take a look at the **API permissions** and **Expose an API** blades. You'll see the **Microsoft Graph** permission we were presented with when configuring authentication, as well as the `user_impersonation` API scope, which allows the application to access the app on behalf of the signed-in user.

11. Open a new *InPrivate/Incognito* browser session, open the built-in developer tool (often, you can open it with *F12* for most browsers by default), and navigate to the **Network** tab. I'm using Microsoft Edge (not the old Edge; Chromium Edge), so my references will relate to the Edge:

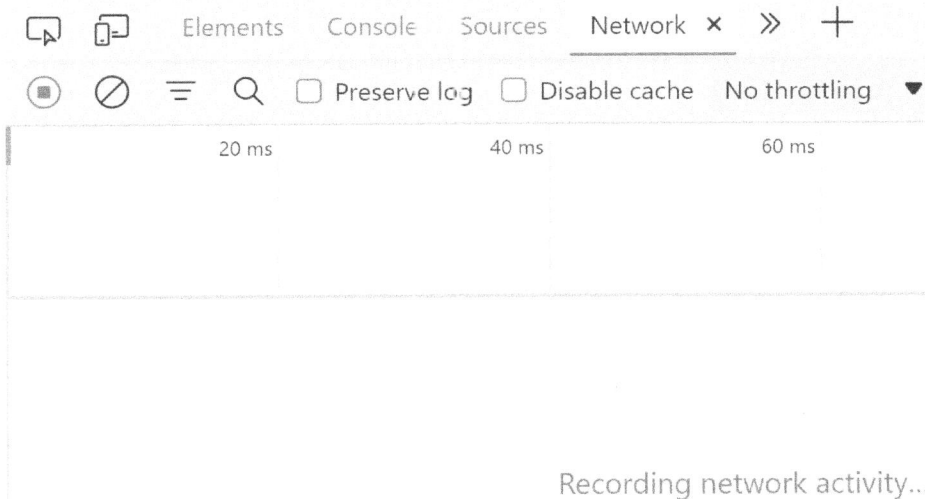

Figure 3.9 – In-browser developer tool's Network tab

Although I'm referring to the in-browser developer tool, you're more than welcome to use other tools if you wish.

12. In this new browser session, browse to the URL of your web app (copy it from the Azure portal if you need to). You will be faced with the familiar Microsoft sign-in screen. Within the developer tools, select the entry that just lists the URL of your app, and you'll see a **302 Found** status code:

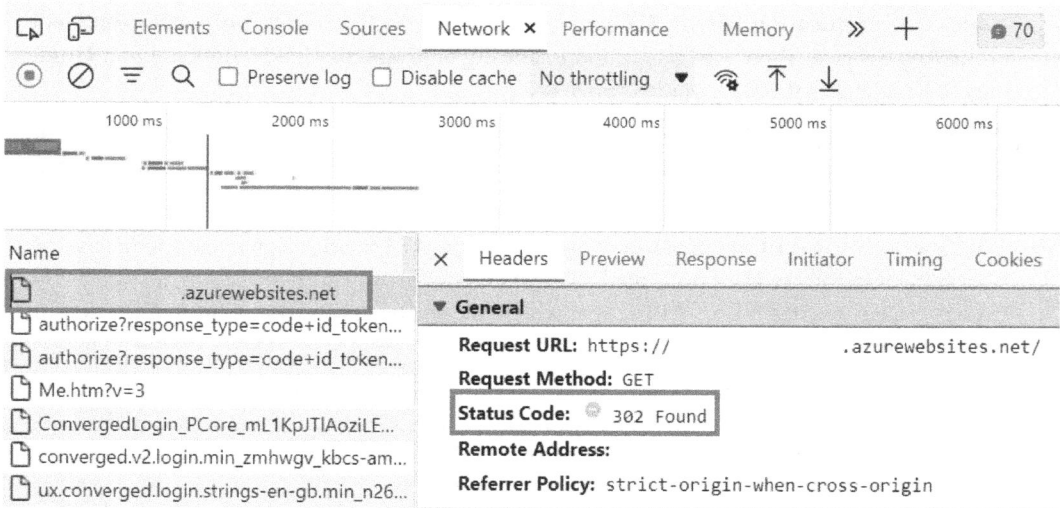

Figure 3.10 – In-browser developer tools showing a 302 status code

If you haven't connected the dots yet, we can review the authentication settings for our app and see that we configured unauthenticated requests to receive an HTTP **302 Found** response and redirect to the identity provider (Microsoft, in our example):

Authentication settings   Edit

App Service authentication	Enabled
Restrict access	Require authentication
Unauthenticated requests	Return HTTP 302 Found (Redirect to identity provider)
Redirect to	Microsoft
Token store	Enabled

Figure 3.11 – Authentication settings summary showing the 302 status configuration

13. Select one of entries with `authorize?` at the start. Notice that, on the **Payload** tab, `redirect_uri` and `client_id` are what we just saw in the app registration, telling the provider where to redirect once authentication is completed. Also, notice that the response it expects is an **ID token**:

Name								
pauliveylinuxa...	×	Headers	Payload	Preview	Response	Initiator	Timing	Cookies
authorize?res...	▼ Query String Parameters view source view URL-encoded							
authorize?res...	response type: code id token							
Me.htm?v=3	redirect_uri: https:// .azurewebsites.net/.auth/login/aad/callback							
ConvergedLo...	client_id: 1091571f-2d1b-4ef4-83ae-5eeb62076d6e							

Figure 3.12 – In-browser developer tool showing the redirect URI and client ID

At this point, you may want to clear the network log when you're about to finish the sign-in process to start from a clean log when we sign in. You don't have to, but it may make it easier to select entries when there are fewer.

14. Sign in with your account. Notice that you have to consent to the permissions the app registration has configured, so accept them to proceed:

Permissions requested

This application is not published by Microsoft.

This app would like to:

∨ View your basic profile

∨ Maintain access to data you have given it access to

☐ Consent on behalf of your organisation

Accepting these permissions means that you allow this app to use your data as specified in their Terms of Service and Privacy Statement. You can change these permissions at https://myapps.microsoft.com. Show details

Does this app look suspicious? Report it here

Cancel   Accept

Figure 3.13 – Permissions requested by the app registration

15. Select the `callback` entry and, from the **Payload** tab, copy the value of `id_token` (only copy the value, not the `id_token` wording or any other properties – which is easier to view parsed rather than source). The value should begin with `ey`. The format of this token is **JSON Web Token (JWT)**.

16. With the `id_token` value copied, open a new tab and browse to `https://jwt.ms`, then paste the `id_token` value you just copied.

    On both the **Decoded token** and **Claims** tabs, any app-specific roles your account has assigned would look as follows:

    ```
    "roles": [
      "Demo.Value"
    ],

    roles                    Demo.Value
    ```

Figure 3.14 – Decoded token and claims entries showing assigned roles

17. Go to the **Cookies** tab to see the **AppServiceAuthSession** cookie that was provided in the server's *response*. Going to the **Cookies** tab for all subsequent network log entries will show that same authenticated cookie as a *request* cookie, which is in line with the authentication flow previously illustrated.

I hope that going into that extra bit of detail and showing the authentication flow in action helped your understanding more than simply telling you the steps. We'll now move on to the final topic of our App Service exploration by briefly looking at some of the available networking features.

Networking features

Unless you're using an ASE, which is the network-isolated SKU we mentioned earlier in this chapter, App Service deployments exist in a multitenant network. Because of this, we can't connect our App Service directly to our network. Instead, there are networking features available to control inbound and outbound traffic and allow our App Service to connect to our network.

Outbound flows

First, let's talk about outbound communication. App Service roles that host our workload are called **workers**; the roles that handle incoming requests are called **frontends**. The Free and Shared App Service plans' SKUs use multitenant workers (that is, the same worker VMs will be running multiple customer workloads). Other SKUs will run on workers that are dedicated to a single App Service plan.

This leads us to a quick mention of worker VM types – the *Free*, *Shared*, *Basic*, *Standard*, and *Premium* SKUs all use the same type of worker VM. *PremiumV2* uses a different VM type, while *PremiumV3* uses another VM type again.

Why is this important? Because if you scale your App Service to an SKU that uses a different worker VM type, the outbound IP addresses of your App Service will change. Several IP addresses get used for outbound calls from your app, which you can see in the Azure portal by going to the **Properties** blade under the **Outbound IP addresses** heading. Alternatively, you can use the following CLI command to list them for your app:

```
az webapp show -g "<resource group>" -n "<app-service>" --query
outboundIpAddresses -o tsv
```

If you wanted to get a list of all possible outbound IP addresses that your app could use, including whether you were to scale your app up to another SKU, check the **Additional Outbound IP Addresses** heading in the same portal location, or use the following CLI command:

```
az webapp show -g "<resource group>" -n "<app-service>" --query
possibleOutboundIpAddresses -o tsv
```

To allow your app to make outbound calls to a specific TCP endpoint, you can use the **Hybrid Connection** feature. At a very high level, you would install a relay agent called **Hybrid Connection Manager** (**HCM**) on a Windows Server 2012 or newer machine within the network that you want to connect to, which could also be on-premises, so long as outbound traffic to Azure over port 443 is allowed. If you're already aware of the **Azure Relay** feature, this is built on the Hybrid Connections capability of that feature, but this is specialized for App Service specifically, only supporting making outbound calls to a specific TCP host and port. Both the App Service and HCM make outbound calls to the Relay, providing your app with a TCP tunnel to a fixed host and port on the other side of the HCM. When a DNS request from your app matches that of a configured Hybrid Connection endpoint, the outbound TCP traffic gets redirected through the Hybrid Connection.

The other networking feature for outbound traffic is **VNet integration**. VNet integration allows your app to securely make outbound calls to resources in or through your Azure **virtual network** (**VNet**), but it doesn't grant inbound access. If you connect VNets within the same regions, you need to have a dedicated subnet in the VNet that you're integrating with. If you connect to VNets in other regions (or a classic VNet within the same region), you need a **VNet gateway** to be created in the target VNet.

Inbound flows

Unlike outbound IP addresses, each App Service will just have a single inbound IP address, as you may imagine. There are several features for handling inbound traffic, just as there are for outbound. If you configure your app with SSL, you can make use of the **app-assigned address** feature, which allows you to support any IP-based SSL needs you may have, as well as set up a dedicated IP address for your app that isn't shared (if you delete the SSL binding, a new inbound IP address is assigned). **Access restrictions** allow you to filter inbound requests using a list of allow and deny rules, similar to how you would with a **network security group** (**NSG**). Finally, we have the **private endpoint** feature, which allows private and secure inbound connections to your app via Azure **private link**. This feature uses a private IP address from your VNet, which effectively brings the app into your VNet. This is popular when you only want inbound traffic to come from within your VNet.

There's much more to Azure networking, but these are the headlines specific to Azure App Service. As you may imagine, there's a lot more to learn about the features we've just discussed here. A link to App Service networking can be found in the *Further reading* section of this chapter, should you wish to dig deeper.

This ends our exploration of Azure App Service. Armed with this understanding, the remainder of this chapter should be a breeze in comparison. Now that we've gone into some depth regarding web apps, let's look at some additional configuration options, as well as how to configure logging for our web app.

Configuring app settings and logging

It's important to understand how to configure application settings and how your app makes of use them, which we will build on in the last section of this chapter. There are also various types of logging available with App Service, some of which are only available to Windows and can be stored and generated in different ways. So, let's take a look.

Application settings

In the previous exercise, we navigated to the **Configuration** blade of our App Service to view an application configuration setting. We did the same thing in the previous chapter, without explaining the relevance of those settings in any detail. We'll fill this gap now.

In App Service, application settings are passed as environment variables to your application at runtime. If you're familiar with ASP.NET or ASP.NET Core and the `appsettings.json` or `web.config` files, these work in a similar way, but the App Service variables override the `appsettings.json` and `web.config` variables. You could have development settings in these files for connecting to local resources such as a local MySQL database, for example, but have production settings stored safely in App Service – they are always encrypted at rest and transmitted over an encrypted channel.

For Linux apps and custom containers (like ours), App Service uses the `--env` flag to pass the application settings to the container, which sets the environment variables on that container. Let's check these settings out:

1. Within the Azure portal, find and open your App Service app and navigate to the **Configuration** blade once more. Here, you will see some already existing application settings, most of which we've mentioned.

2. Click on the **Advanced edit** button above the settings. This will bring up a JSON representation of the current application settings. This is where you can make additions or amendments in bulk, rather than making changes one by one.

3. Add a new setting (don't forget to add a comma after the last one, but before the closing square bracket). In my case, I'm calling it MY_CUSTOM_GREETING and giving it a value of Hello, World! (I've outdone myself this time, I know):

```
{
    "name": "MY_CUSTOM_GREETING",
    "value": "Hello, World!",
    "slotSetting": false
}
```

Don't worry, we'll cover what slotSetting means later in this chapter. For now, don't worry about it.

4. Click **OK** and then **Save** at the top of the page.

5. Check out the **General settings** tab and then the **Path mappings** tab to see what configuration settings we have available. The terminology within the **Path mappings** tab should be somewhat familiar from the previous chapter.

   If we were in this same area with a Windows App Service app, we would also have a **Default documents** tab, which would allow us to define a prioritized list of documents to display when navigating to the root URL for the website. The first file in the list that matches is used.

6. Browse to the URL of the web app to confirm nothing has changed. The container now has a new environment variable, but we're not doing anything with it yet.

7. From our previous aspnetapp example, open the aspnetapp\Pages\Index.cshtml file:

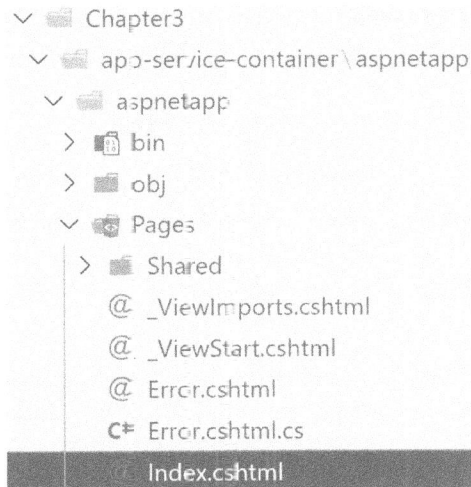

Figure 3.15 – The Index.cshtml file within VS Code

8. Add some basic code to display the value of our newly created environment variable somewhere obvious, like how I've put the `<h3>@(Environment.GetEnvironmentVariable("MY_CUSTOM_GREETING"))</h3>` line beneath the main heading:

```
28
29    <div class="text-center">
30        <h1>Welcome to .NET</h1>
31        <h3>@(Environment.GetEnvironmentVariable("MY_CUSTOM_GREETING"))</h3>
32    </div>
```

Figure 3.16 – h3 heading showing the new environment variable value

9. Save the file and open a terminal session from the directory containing the Dockerfiles.

10. Have the ACR build task update your ACR with a new version `1.1.0` container image for your app to use with the following command:

```
az acr build --image "chapter3:1.1.0" --image
"chapter3:latest" --registry "<ACR name>" --file
"Dockerfile" .
```

11. As we configured the web app to use the `latest` tag from the ACR repository, we just need to restart the app for it to pick up our latest image. Either use the **Restart** button within the portal or use the following CLI command:

```
az webapp restart -g "<resource group>" -n
"<app-service>"
```

12. Browse to the URL for the web app (or refresh if it's already open). You should now see that the application setting has indeed been passed to the container, which has been used by our code:

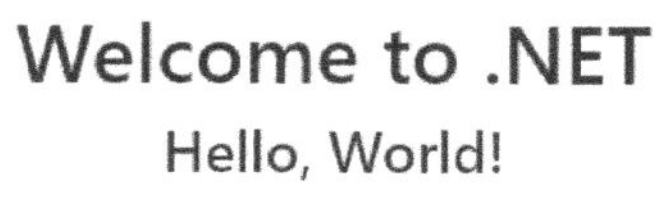

Welcome to .NET

Hello, World!

Figure 3.17 – Application setting value showing through application code

13. Update your custom application setting with whatever value you want with the following CLI command:

```
az webapp config appsettings set -g "<resource group>" -n
"<app-service>" --settings "MY_CUSTOM_GREETING=Oh, hello
again!"
```

Give the App Service a few moments to restart, then refresh the website for the app and see that your new value has been implemented.

One final configuration you should be aware of is **cross-origin resource sharing** (**CORS**), which comes supported with RESTful APIs for App Service. At a high level, CORS-supported browsers prevent web pages from making requests for restricted resources to a different domain to that which served the web page. By default, cross-domain requests (Ajax requests, for example) are forbidden by something called the **same-origin policy**, which prevents malicious code from accessing sensitive data on another site. There may be times when you want sites from other domains to access your app (if your App Service hosts an API, for example). In this case, you can configure CORS to allow requests from one or more (or all) domains.

In terms of the flow, the browser will make what's known as a **pre-flight** request to the app URL using an OPTIONS verb to determine whether they have permission to perform the action. This request will include headers detailing the origin and the request method (GET, PUT, and so on). The response will show what actions (if any) the app is willing to accept. Although our app isn't an API, we can still use it to prove the most basic functionality:

1. From the Azure portal, open your App Service and, within the **Authentication** blade, **Edit** the **Authentication settings** option, then set it to **Disabled** and **Save**. This will make the following steps easier to follow.

2. Enable CORS on the App Service and ensure it only accepts cross-origin requests from a specific URL (it doesn't need to exist; just pick any, even localhost) by going to the **CORS** blade and adding a domain to the **Allowed Origins** field (don't check the box to request credentials). The same can be achieved with the following CLI command:

   ```
   az webapp cors add -g "<resource group>" -n
   "<app-service>" --allowed-origins "http://somedomain.
   notreal"
   ```

3. From a terminal session, execute the following **cURL** command, passing in the OPTIONS verb and checking whether a GET request from a domain other than what we allowed is permitted:

   ```
   curl -v -X OPTIONS "https://<app-service>.azurewebsites.
   net" -H "Access-Control-Request-Method: GET" -H "Origin:
   http://someotherdomain.notreal"
   ```

   Notice the lack of helpful information in the response other than the line that contains something similar to { "code":400,"message":"The origin 'http:\/\/ someotherdomain.notreal' is not allowed."}.

4. Check that GET requests from http://somedomain.notreal (or whatever domain you configured CORS with) are permitted with the following command:

   ```
   curl -v -X OPTIONS "https://<app-service>.azurewebsites.
   net" -H "Access-Control-Request-Method: GET" -H "Origin:
   http://somedomain.notreal"
   ```

Notice that this time, the response includes the `Access-Control-Allow-Origin: http://somedomain.notreal` response header. This is enough to tell us that CORS is working without actually creating an API. API management will be covered in *Chapter 11, Implementing API Management*, so there's no need to go through this at this point. In a real-world situation, the JavaScript client would send the pre-flight request using the `OPTIONS` verb (like we did with cURL) and the server would respond, telling the client what the server is willing to accept (if anything). If it is, the actual request would then be made.

If you're wondering why we haven't touched on the **App Configuration** feature, that's because we will look at it in more detail in *Chapter 8, Implementing Secure Cloud Solutions*. For now, we can move on to the topic of logging.

Logging

There are various types of logging available within App Service – some are Windows-specific while others are available for both Windows and Linux:

- Windows only:

  - **Detailed error logging**: When an application HTTP error code of `400` or greater occurs, App Service can store the `.htm` error pages that would get sent to the client browser within the App Service filesystem.

  - **Failed request tracing**: Detailed tracing information on failed requests, including a trace of the IIS components used to process the request, is stored within the App Service filesystem.

  - **Web server logging**: Raw HTTP request data is stored in the W3C extended log file format within the App Service filesystem or Azure Storage blobs.

- Windows and Linux:

  - **Application logging**: Log messages that are generated by either the web framework being used or your application code directly (we will demonstrate this shortly) are stored within either the App Service filesystem (this is the only option available with Linux apps) or Azure Storage blobs.

  - **Deployment logging**: Upon publishing content to an app, deployment logging occurs automatically with no configurable settings, which helps determine reasons for a deployment failing, stored within the App Service filesystem.

For logs stored within the App Service filesystem, you can access them via their direct URLs. For Windows apps, the URL for the diagnostic dump is `https://<app-service>.scm.azurewebsites.net/api/dump`. For Linux/container apps, the URL is `https://<app-service>.scm.azurewebsites.net/api/logs/docker/zip`. Within the portal, you can use **Advanced Tools** to access further information and the links just mentioned.

Let's enable application logging in our app and have our code generate a log message to see this in action. We'll start in the portal because that's easier to show the options that are different between Linux and Windows apps:

1. Within the Azure portal, open the App Service and click on the **App Service logs** blade.

2. Turn **Application logging** on by setting the toggle to **File System** and clicking **Save**.

   To illustrate the differences between Linux and Windows apps, this is what you'd see if you went to the same location from a Windows app:

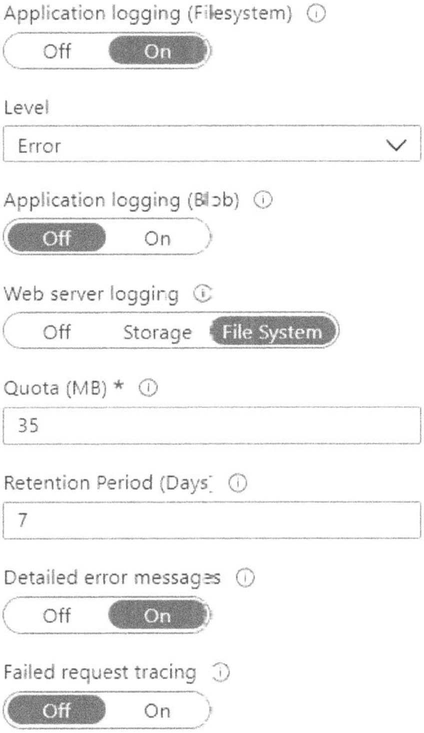

Application logging (Filesystem) ⓘ

    Off   On

Level

    Error   ⌄

Application logging (Blob) ⓘ

    Off   On

Web server logging ⓘ

    Off   Storage   File System

Quota (MB) * ⓘ

    35

Retention Period (Days) ⓘ

    7

Detailed error messages ⓘ

    Off   On

Failed request tracing ⓘ

    Off   On

Figure 3.18 – App Service logging options for a Windows App Service

3. Open the same `aspnetapp` folder we've been working with in this chapter within VS Code.

4. For the sake of simplicity, open the `aspnetapp\aspnetapp\Pages\Index.cshtml.cs` file and add the following line with whatever log text you want, within the `OnGet()` method:

```
_logger.LogInformation("This is my custom information
level log message.");
```

Then, save the file.

5. Use the ACR build task to push the update to your ACR with the following CLI command:

```
az acr build --image "chapter3:1.2.0" --image
"chapter3:latest" --registry "<ACR name>" --file
"Dockerfile" .
```

Then, restart the App Service however you wish (remember, we configured it to use the `latest` tag, so a restart is enough).

6. Within the Azure portal, open the **Log stream** blade for the App Service. Then, on another browser tab, navigate to the URL of the App Service. You should see the new application log showing something similar to the following:

```
{"EventId":0,"LogLevel":"Information","Category":
"aspnetapp.Pages.IndexModel","Message":"This
is my custom information level log
message.","State":{"Message":"This
is my custom information level log
message.","{OriginalFormat}":"This is my custom
information level log message."}}
```

Now that we've got a good understanding of some key concepts of App Service and have run through some detailed topics and enabled logging, we'll look at a topic that was very briefly touched on in *Chapter 1, Azure and Cloud Fundamentals*: scaling.

Scaling App Service apps

In *Chapter 1, Azure and Cloud Fundamentals*, we mentioned that the cloud offers elasticity so that it can scale and use as much capacity as you need when you need it. We specifically touched on scaling up (that is, vertical scaling) and scaling out (that is, horizontal scaling). Let's jump into the portal once more and take a look:

1. From within the Azure portal, open either your App Service or the App Service plan and open the **Scale up** blade. If you're in the App Service, notice that it has (**App Service plan**) to point out that it's the App Service plan controlling resources, as we discussed earlier in this chapter. Don't change anything here; just notice that these options increase the total resources available – they don't increase instances. A restart of the app would be required to scale up.

2. Open the **Scale out** blade and notice that this is currently set to a manually set instance count. While this can be useful, what we want to demonstrate here is autoscale, so select the **Custom autoscale** option.

3. Set the instance limits to a minimum of 1 and a maximum of 2 (it's up to you, but this is the lowest cost while still being able to demonstrate this – you're welcome to change the values but be aware of the cost).

4. Leave **Scale mode** set to **Scale based on a metric** and click on the **Add a rule** link. Here, you can define the metric rules that control when the instance count should be increased or decreased, which is extremely valuable when the workload may vary unpredictably.

5. Check out the options available but leave the settings as default for now. The graph on this screen helps identify when the rule would have been met based on the options you select. For example, if I change my metric threshold to be greater than 15% for CPU percentage, the graph will show that this rule would have been matched twice over the latest 10-minute timeframe (when the lines rise above the dashed line):

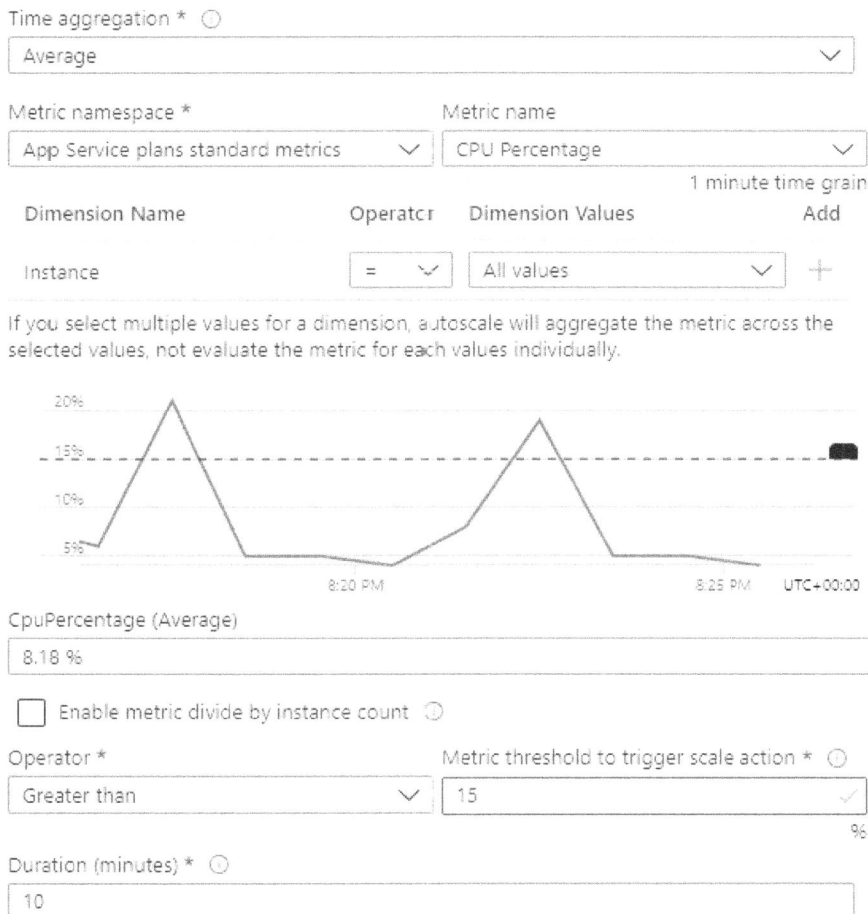

Figure 3.19 – Custom metric condition visual

6. Click on **Add**. With this rule added, it's usually desirable to add a rule to scale back down, so click on **Add a rule** and repeat this process, but this time, use a **Less than or equal to** operator, change the threshold figure to put some margin between the rules, and select **Decrease count by**. You should now have a scale-out rule increasing the instance count and a scale-in rule decreasing the instance count.

7. Scroll to the bottom of the page and click on **Add a scale condition**. Notice that this time, you can set up date and time periods for the rule to apply, either scaling to a specific count during that period or based on a metric, as we did previously. The first condition we configured acts as a default, only executing if none of the other conditions are matched.

8. Feel free to add and customize conditions and rules until you're comfortable. Either save or discard. We won't be forcing autoscale to kick in, but you're welcome to by changing thresholds and sending a lot of traffic to the app, for example.

You can view any autoscale actions through the **Run history** tab, as well as via the App Service **Activity Log**. The following are a few quick points on scaling out when using autoscale outside of self-learning as we are:

- Consider the default instance count, as that will be used when metrics aren't available for any reason.

- Make sure the maximum and minimum instance values are different and have a margin between them to ensure autoscaling can happen when you need it.

- Don't forget to set scale-in rules as well as scale-out. Most of the time, you probably won't want to scale out without being able to scale back in.

- Before scaling in, autoscale will estimate what the final state would be after it has scaled in. If the thresholds are too close to each other, autoscale may estimate that it would have to scale back out immediately after scaling in, and that would likely get stuck in a loop (known as "flapping"), so it will decide not to scale in at all to avoid this. Make sure there's a margin between metrics to avoid this.

- A scale-out rule runs if *any* of the rules are met, whereas a scale-in rule runs only if *all* rules are met.

- When multiple *scale-out* rules are being evaluated, autoscale will evaluate the new capacity of each rule that gets triggered and choose the scale action that results in the greatest capacity of them, to ensure service availability.

- When there are no scale-out rules and only *scale-in* rules – providing all the rules have been triggered – autoscale chooses the scale action resulting in the greatest capacity of them, to ensure service availability.

One important point to remind you of is that since scaling rules are created on the App Service plan rather than the App Service (because, as we know, the App Service plan is responsible for the resources), if the App Service plan increases the instances, all of your App Services in that plan will run across that many instances, not just the App Service that caused the scaling.

So far, any impactful changes we've pushed to the App Service would cause the service to restart, which would lead to downtime. This is not desirable in most production environments. App Service has a powerful feature called **deployment slots** to allow you to test changes before they hit production, control how much traffic gets routed to each deployment slot, and then promote those changes to production with no downtime. Let's wrap up this chapter by learning about deployment slots.

Leveraging deployment slots

The first thing to know about deployment slots is that they are live apps with hostnames, content, and configuration settings. In a common modern development workflow, you'd deploy code through whatever means to a non-production deployment slot (often called **staging**, although this could be any name and there may be multiple slots between that and production) to test and validate. From there, you may start increasing the percentage of traffic that gets routed to the staging slot or you may just swap the slots – whatever was in production goes to staging and whatever was in staging goes to production, with no downtime.

Because it is *just* a swap, if something unexpected does happen as a result, you can swap the slots back and everything would return to before the swap occurred. Several actions take place during a swap, including the routing rules changing once all the slots have warmed up. There's a documentation link in the *Further reading* section of this chapter, should you wish to explore this further.

We spoke about application configuration settings earlier in this chapter, but we purposely didn't address what the slotSetting meant. With each deployment slot being its own app, they can have their own application configuration as well. If a setting isn't configured as a deployment slot setting, that setting will follow the app when it gets swapped. If the setting is configured as a deployment slot setting, the setting will always be applied to whichever app is in that specific slot. This is helpful when there are environment-specific settings; you can have the same code in staging and production, but the settings will change, depending on which deployment slot that code is running from.

Different App Service plan tiers have a different number of deployment slots available, so that could be a consideration when deciding on which tier to select or scale to. As with some other settings we've discussed, Windows apps have an additional setting that's not available with Linux/container apps: *auto-swap*.

Under the **Configuration** blade of a Windows App Service, under the **General settings** tab, you'll see the option to enable auto-swap when code is pushed to that slot. For example, if you enable this setting (again, only available on Windows App Service apps) on the staging slot, each time you deploy code to that slot, once everything is ready, App Service will automatically swap that slot with the slot you specify in the settings. Don't be disheartened if you want something like that but you're using Linux/container apps – CI/CD pipelines can do so much more than that, and we'll go into some detail at the end of this book on this kind of automation.

For now, let's see deployment slots in action:

1. From the Azure portal, open the **Configuration** blade within your App Service and change the value of the custom application setting that was created previously, with some text referencing the `production` slot – I simply changed mine to `Hello from the production app`. Click **Save**.

2. Go to the **Deployment slots** blade and click **Add Slot**. Enter the name of the `staging` deployment slot and choose to clone the settings from the default/production slot (indicated by having just the App Service name), which will copy all of the application settings to the staging slot.

    You can also use the following CLI command:

    ```
    az webapp deployment slot create -g "<resource group>"
    -n "<app-service>" -s "staging" --configuration-source
    "<app-service>"
    ```

    Alternatively, you can use the following PowerShell command:

    ```
    New-AzWebAppSlot -ResourceGroupName "<resource group>"
    -Name "<app-service>" -Slot "staging"
    ```

3. Select the `staging` deployment slot and from within the **Configuration** blade, change the value of your custom application setting to mention `staging` rather than `production`. Conceptually, we have some different configurations between the staging and production slots, which we could have also replicated with different code.

4. In another browser tab/window, browse to the production slot URL for the App Service – that is, `https://<app-service>.azurewebsites.net` – and confirm that the production text is there. Now, do the same with the staging URL – that is, `https://<app-service>-staging.azurewebsites.net` – and confirm that the staging text is there. Once confirmed, navigate back to the main/production URL so that you're ready for the next step.

    This shows how you could test changes in the staging slot/app before pushing it to production. The documentation also explains how you can use a query string in a link to the App Service, which users could use to opt into the staging/beta/preview app experience.

5. From the main App Service (not the staging app), open the **Deployment slots** blade and notice that you can change the percentage of traffic that flows to each slot. This allows you to control the exposure of the staging slot before making the switch. Rather than using that right now, just click on **Swap**. Notice that you get to preview the changes that will be made, which will be the text changing in the custom application setting. Confirm this by clicking on **Swap**.

6. Go back to the tab/window with the production site showing and periodically refresh the page. You should notice no downtime. At some point, the text will change from `production` to `staging`, showing that the staging slot was swapped with production and that your changes are now live in the production app.

7. When you're done with this exercise, feel free to clean up your resources by deleting the resource group containing all of the resources we created in this chapter.

If you wanted to, you could revert the changes by swapping the slots again. If our application setting was configured as a slot setting, we wouldn't have noticed any changes because rather than following the app, the setting would have been stuck to the specific slot.

One final point to note is that although the default behavior is for all the slots of an App Service to share the same App Service plan, this can be changed by changing the App Service plan in each slot individually.

With that final point, we have come to the end of our exploration of App Service – congratulations! A lot of the concepts we've discovered here will help with the topics that will be covered throughout this book, as a lot of them will dive deeper or reference concepts we've already covered in some detail.

Summary

In this chapter, we dived into Azure App Service by looking at some fundamental features, such as App Service plans, as well as some basics of App Service web apps. We then delved into authentication and authorization, stepped through the authentication flow, and provided a summary of some networking features. Once our app was up and running, we went into some detail about configuration options and how application settings can be used by the application and are exposed as environment variables. We learned about the different types of built-in logging available with App Service and went through an exercise to have our application code log messages that App Service could process. Then, we learned how to automatically scale our App Service based on conditions and rules to make use of the elasticity that the cloud offers. Finally, we walked through how to make use of deployment slots to avoid downtime, control how changes are rolled out, and how to roll back changes, should this be required.

I hope that the topics and exercises we went through in this chapter have helped you understand the concepts that will be discussed later in this book. If you understand the fundamental concepts, you are much better prepared for the exam, which may contain some abstract questions that require this kind of understanding, rather than just example questions.

In the next chapter, we will introduce Azure Functions and what they do, while comparing with other services. We'll also cover scaling. Then, we'll start looking at developing Azure functions, triggers, and bindings, before moving on to developing stateful durable functions.

Questions

Answer the following questions to test your knowledge of this chapter:

1. Can you have separate auto scale settings for each App Service within an App Service plan?

2. With authentication enabled and not using the provider SDK, once a user has authenticated with the identity provider, which URL does the provider redirect the client to?

3. Application logging can be enabled for both Windows and Linux App Service apps. True or false?

4. The private endpoint feature of App Service can be used to prevent access to your application from outside of your specified VNet. True or false?

5. Which networking feature can be configured to allow your application to make outbound calls to resources within your on-premises network?

Further reading

To learn more about the topics that were covered in this chapter, take a look at the following resources:

*   Details on the networking features of App Service can be found here: `https://docs.microsoft.com/azure/app-service/networking-features`

*   For more information on configuring deployment credentials, check out this page: `https://docs.microsoft.com/azure/app-service/deploy-configure-credentials?tabs=cli`

*   Details on semantic versioning can be found here: `https://semver.org/`

*   Further information on the networking features available to App Service can be found here: `https://docs.microsoft.com/azure/app-service/networking-features`

*   You can find additional information on App Service deployment slots here: `https://docs.microsoft.com/azure/app-service/deploy-staging-slots`

4

Implementing Azure Functions

So far, we've covered some of the in-depth topics around **Infrastructure as a Service** (**IaaS**) and **Platform as a Service** (**PaaS**). Another popular service model that we haven't discussed yet is **Function as a Service** (**FaaS**). **Azure Functions** is Microsoft's FaaS solution, which takes the benefits of PaaS further by completely abstracting the underlying infrastructure, with pay-per-execution billing and automatic scaling available.

During this chapter, we will introduce and explore the Azure Functions service and use cases. We will introduce some of the fundamental concepts of Azure Functions and run through a development workflow for a **function app**, including development, testing, and deployment. After creating several functions, we will expand on this further by introducing stateful durable functions.

By the end of this chapter, you will understand the benefits and use cases, and have some familiarity with the development workflow of Azure Functions.

In this chapter, we will cover the following main topics:

- Exploring Azure Functions
- Developing, testing, and deploying Azure Functions
- Discovering stateful durable functions

Technical requirements

To follow through the examples in this chapter, the following are required in addition to VS Code:

- The latest version of Azure Functions Core Tools: https://docs.microsoft.com/azure/azure-functions/functions-run-local.
- The Azure Functions VS Code extension: https://marketplace.visualstudio.com/items?itemName=ms-azuretools.vscode-azurefunctions.
- To follow along with the VS Code development of a function in C#, install the .NET 6.0 SDK: https://dotnet.microsoft.com/en-us/download/dotnet/6.0.

- To follow along with the VS Code development of a function in C#, install the C# VS Code extension: `https://marketplace.visualstudio.com/items?itemName=ms-dotnettools.csharp`.

- To follow along with the VS Code development of a function, install the Azurite VS Code extension, which provides a local storage emulator: `https://marketplace.visualstudio.com/items?itemName=Azurite.azurite`.

Code in Action videos for this chapter: `https://bit.ly/3xC0ao5`

> **Note on Programming Language Examples**
>
> Remember, this book is an exam preparation guide, so we may not be covering examples using your preferred programming language. If you can understand the concepts with the language (C#) we use in this chapter, you should be able to answer exam questions on other languages as well. For documentation on supported languages, check out the *Further reading* section of this chapter.

Exploring Azure Functions

The Azure Functions service allows you to create code that can be triggered by events coming from Azure, third-party services, and on-premises systems, with the ability to access relevant data from these services and systems. Essentially, Azure Functions provides you with a serverless platform on which to run blocks of code (or **functions**) that respond to events. The unit of deployment in Azure Functions is a **function app**.

Within Azure, you create a function app, within which you can create one or more functions that share some common configuration such as app settings. The functions within a function app will all scale together, which is a similar concept to what we discussed in the last chapter with App Service plans. With this in mind, it often makes sense to group functions that are logically related together within a function app.

At the time of writing, the latest Azure Functions versions (4.x) support the following languages: C#, F#, Java, JavaScript, PowerShell, Python, and TypeScript. C# and JavaScript have been supported for longer than any of the other languages, so code samples in the exam are more likely to be in either of these two languages. The examples in this chapter use C#.

A topic that used to form part of the exam but no longer does is **custom handlers**. Custom handlers let you implement function apps in languages that aren't currently offered out of the box, such as Go and Rust, for example. You can also create a custom handler to implement a function app in a runtime that's not currently featured by default. As this topic is no longer in the exam, we won't explore the topic further here, but a link to customer handler documentation can be found in the *Further reading* section of this chapter.

Azure Functions is often the service of choice for tasks such as data, image, and order processing, maintenance of files, simple APIs and microservices, and other tasks you might want to run on a schedule. While there are similarities between Azure Functions and services such as **Logic Apps** and App Service **WebJobs**, there are some key differences to be aware of:

- Logic Apps development is more **declarative**, with a designer-first focus, whereas Azure Functions is more **imperative**, with a code-first focus. You can monitor Azure Functions using **Application Insights** (a topic for *Chapter 10, Troubleshooting Solutions by Using Metrics and Log Data*), while Logic Apps can be monitored using the Azure portal and **Azure Monitor** logs.

- App Service WebJobs and Azure Functions are built with the WebJobs SDK, both built on App Service, with support for extensibility, as well as features such as source control integration, authentication, and Application Insights monitoring. Azure Functions has several features that can offer developers more productivity than WebJobs:

  - A serverless application model with automatic scaling without additional configuration

  - The ability to develop and test within the browser

  - Trigger on HTTP/webhook and Azure Event Grid events

  - More options for languages, development environments, pricing, and integrations with Azure services

  - Pay-per-use pricing

For details on some common scenarios and the suggested implementations of Azure Functions for each, check out the *Further reading* section of this chapter. The last point in the list of differences between WebJobs and Azure Functions can help dramatically reduce your compute cost, depending on the hosting plan selected. This leads us to the topic of hosting options, as there are different options with different use cases.

Hosting options

There are three main hosting plans available for Azure Functions, all of which are available on both Windows and Linux VMs. Here's a brief summary of these plans:

- **Consumption** (also referred to as **Serverless**): This is the default hosting plan for function apps, providing automatic scaling of function instances based on the number of incoming events, as well as providing potential compute cost savings by billing only for the number of executions, execution time, and memory used by your functions. This is measured in what's known as **GB-seconds**.

  For example, if a function uses 0.5 GB of memory when it runs and runs for a total of 5 seconds, the execution cost is 2.5 GB-seconds (0.5 GB * 5 seconds). If the function isn't executed at all during that period, the execution cost is nothing. You also get a free grant of 1,000,000 executions and 400,000 GB-seconds each month.

After a period of being idle, the instances will be scaled to zero. For the first requests after scaling, there may be some latency during a cold startup while the instances are scaled up from zero.

- **Premium**: Unlike the Consumption plan, this plan automatically scales using pre-warmed workers, meaning there's no latency after being idle. As you might imagine, this plan also runs on more powerful instances and has some additional features, such as being able to connect to virtual networks. This plan is intended for function apps that need to run continuously (or nearly continuously), run for longer than the execution time limit of the Consumption plan, or run on a custom Linux image. This plan uses **Elastic Premium** (**EP**) App Service plans, so you'll need to create or select an existing App Service plan using one of the EP SKUs. Unlike the autoscale settings we saw with App Service plans from the last chapter, you can configure **Elastic Scale out** with the number of always-ready instances.

  The billing for this plan is based on the number of core seconds and memory allocation across all instances. There's no execution charge – unlike with the Consumption plan – but there is a minimum charge each month, regardless of whether or not your functions have been running, as a result of the requirement to have at least one instance allocated at all times.

- **App Service plan** (also referred to as **Dedicated**): This plan uses the same App Service plans we became familiar with in the last chapter, including all the same scaling options. The billing of this plan is exactly the same as any other App Service plan, which differs from the Consumption and Premium plans. This plan can be useful when you have underutilized App Service plan resources running other apps or when you want to provide a custom image for your functions to run on.

  If you're going to use the App Service plan, you should go into the **Configuration** blade of your function app and, under the **General settings** tab, ensure that **Always on** is toggled to **On**, so that the function app works correctly (it should be on by default). This can also be configured using the CLI, as you might imagine.

You also have the option of hosting your function apps on **App Service Environments** (**ASEs**) for a fully isolated environment, which was mentioned in the last chapter, as well as on **Kubernetes**, neither of which are in the scope of this book. Regardless of which plan you choose, every function app requires a general Azure storage account of a type that supports queues and tables for storing the function code files, as well as operations such as managing triggers and logging executions (we will see this in the *Discovering stateful durable functions* section of this chapter). HTTP and webhook triggers are the only trigger types that don't require storage.

Storage accounts are billed separately from functions, so bear that in mind for billing. A link to the Azure Functions pricing page can be found in the *Further reading* section of this chapter if you'd like to see further information on the price details.

While we're already familiar with the scaling options available with App Service plans, we should briefly discuss scaling when using the Consumption or Premium plans.

Scaling Azure Functions

The number of instances that Azure Functions scales to is determined by the number of events that trigger a function.

> **Remember**
>
> Function apps are the unit of deployment for Azure Functions, but they are also the unit of scale for Azure Functions – if a function app scales, all functions within the app scale at the same time.

The **scale controller** – which monitors the rate of events to decide whether to scale in or out – will use different logic for the scale decision based on the type of trigger being used. For example, it will take the queue length and age of the oldest queue message into consideration when you're using an Azure Queue Storage trigger. For functions using HTTP triggers, new instances can be allocated at a maximum rate of once per second. For functions using other trigger types, that rate is a maximum of once every 30 seconds (although it is faster on the Premium plan).

A single instance of a function app might be able to process multiple requests at once, so there isn't a limit on concurrent executions; however, a function app can only scale out to up to a maximum of 200 instances on the Consumption plan and 100 on the Premium plan. You can reduce this limit if you wish.

We've mentioned triggers a few times and with Azure Functions being event-driven, it's worth going into some detail about triggers, as well as getting and sending data from connected services and systems with input and output bindings.

Triggers and bindings

In a nutshell, triggers cause your functions to run, and bindings are how you connect your function to other services or systems to obtain data from and send data to these services or systems. If you don't need to send or receive data as part of your function, don't use additional bindings – they're optional. The exam mentions triggers using **data operations**, **timers**, and **webhooks**, so we'll touch on each of those in the next section of this chapter.

Input bindings (the data your function receives) are received by the function as parameters and **output bindings** (the data your function sends) use the return value of the function. The trigger creates an input binding by default, so it doesn't need an additional binding to be made in order to provide data to the function. Triggers and bindings are defined differently based on the language being used:

- **C# class library**: You can configure triggers and bindings by decorating methods and parameters with C# attributes.
- **Java**: You can configure triggers and bindings by decorating methods and parameters with Java annotations.
- **C# script/JavaScript/PowerShell/Python/TypeScript**: You can configure triggers and bindings by updating the `function.json` file.

To declare whether a binding is an input or output, you specify the direction as either `in` or `out` for the `direction` property of the binding. Some bindings also support a special `inout` direction. Each binding needs to have a `type`, `direction`, and `name` value defined.

Consider this basic scenario: each time a new message arrives in **Azure Queue Storage**, you want to create a new row in **Azure Table Storage** to store some data from the queue message. You would use an Azure Queue Storage trigger (`queueTrigger`), which creates an input binding, and you would create an Azure Table Storage output binding (`table`).

With an awareness of the basic concepts of Azure Functions, including triggers and bindings, we are now ready to start creating functions.

Developing, testing, and deploying Azure Functions

Each function is made up of two main parts: your code and some configuration. The configuration file is created automatically for compiled languages based on annotations in the code; for scripting languages, the configuration file needs to be created – this is the `function.json` file we previously mentioned.

The files required and created depend on the language being used. The folder structure may change depending on the language as well. Our first examples will be using quite minimal C# script projects with no additional extensions for the most part, which will have a folder structure as follows:

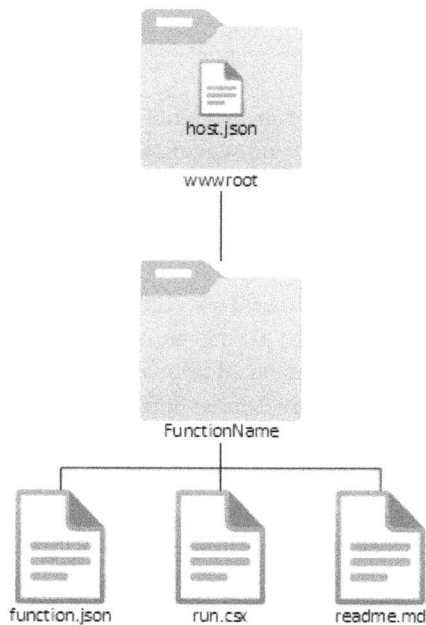

Figure 4.1 – An example folder structure of a function app

Within the wwwroot folder, you will see a host.json file, which contains configuration options for all the functions within the function app. A link to further information about the host.json file can be found in the *Further reading* section of this chapter. There would be more files and folders if we were to use extensions, and the structure would also differ if we used a different language. As you might imagine, if we had multiple functions within this example function app, we would have an additional folder with a different name containing those files underneath the wwwroot folder.

Depending on the language being used and your preference, you can develop and test your functions within the portal, or you can work on them locally using VS Code, for example. You should decide how you wish to develop early on because you shouldn't mix developing functions locally with developing them within the portal in the same function app. If you create and publish a function from a local project, don't try to maintain or modify the code from within the portal. In fact, once you deploy a project that was developed locally, you no longer have the option to create new functions within the same function app using the portal for development.

With all that being said, let's head to the Azure portal and create a function app that will contain some basic functions using all three required trigger types, to see all the concepts we've explored so far in action:

1. Within the Azure portal, create a new **function app**. The direct URL is https://portal.azure.com/#create/Microsoft.FunctionApp.

2. Select the correct subscription from the **Subscription** dropdown, and either select an existing resource group or create a new one in the **Resource Group** field.

3. Provide a globally unique name in the **Function App name** field.

4. Make sure that **Code** is selected under the **Publish** setting.

5. Select **.NET** for the **Runtime stack** setting and set the **Version** setting to the latest available one (which is **6** at the time of writing).

6. Select your desired **Region** setting and progress to the next screen of the wizard.

7. Set the **Hosting** options to their defaults, which should be to create your new **Storage account** name, set **Operating System** to **Windows**, and select the **Consumption (Serverless)** plan.

8. Next, move past **Networking** on to **Monitoring**, where you should set **Enable Application Insights** to **No**.

    You're welcome to leave the setting enabled, but we won't be covering Application Insights until *Chapter 10, Troubleshooting Solutions by Using Metrics and Log Data*.

9. Complete the wizard and click **Create** to create the resource.

10. Once created, go to the newly created function app, and open the **Configuration** blade.

There are several application settings already present, including the following:

- **WEBSITE_CONTENTSHARE**: This is used by a Premium plan or Windows Consumption plan and contains the path to the function app code and configuration files, with a default name starting with the function app name.

- **AzureWebJobsStorage**: This contains the storage account connection string for the Azure Functions runtime to use in normal operations, as mentioned previously.

A reference for the Azure Functions application settings can be found in the *Further reading* section of this chapter.

With the function app resource deployed, we can start creating our functions within it. In this case, we're going to do everything within the Azure portal for simplicity. When developing C# functions in the portal, C# script is used rather than compiled C#.

The data operation trigger

We'll start by creating a function that uses a data operation trigger in the following scenario – each time a new message arrives in Azure Queue Storage, we want to create a new row in Azure Table Storage with some data from the queue message:

1. Open the **Functions** blade and select **Create** to start creating our first function.

2. For the **Development environment** setting, make sure it's set to **Develop in portal**.

3. Select **Azure Queue Storage trigger**, enter the name `QueueTrigger1` in the **New Function** field, set **Queue name** to `myqueue-items`, leave the **Storage account connection** setting as **AzureWebJobsStorage** (for simplicity, we'll just use the same storage account for everything in this function), then click **Create**.

4. Once created, open the newly created function, if it doesn't automatically open.

5. Open the **Integration** blade, where you will see a visual representation of the trigger, as well as input and output bindings (as mentioned previously, the trigger will have an input binding already, so we won't need to create another input binding in our scenario):

Figure 4.2 – A visual representation of function integrations

Notice the trigger has **myQueueItem** in parentheses. This is the parameter name to identify our trigger within our code so that we can obtain data from it.

6. Open the **Code + Test** blade and from the file dropdown, select the `function.json` file, which you will see contains the schema for the bindings we previously discussed, with the expected details from the trigger.

7. Head back to the **Integration** blade and click on **Add output** under **Outputs**. We could have created the output binding directly in the `function.json` code, but we will use this for now.

8. Change **Binding Type** to **Azure Table Storage** (because we want to create a new row for each message received), and change **Table parameter name** to `$return`, which is how we tell it to use the return value of the function. Set **Table name** to `outTable` and click **OK**. The diagram will now show the output binding.

9. Head back to the **Code + Test** blade and open the `function.json` file again. This time, you will see our output binding configuration added to the file.

At this point, your `function.json` file should resemble the following:

```
{
    'bindings": [
      {
        "name": "myQueueItem",
        "type": "queueTrigger",
        "direction": "in",
        "queueName": "myqueue-items",
        "connection": "AzureWebJobsStorage"
      },
      {
        "name": "$return",
        "direction": "out",
        "type": "table",
        "connection": "AzureWebJobsStorage",
        "tableName": "outTable"
      }
    ]
}
```

Notice that the `connection` value is `AzureWebJobsStorage`, which relates to the application setting pointed out earlier. When connecting to other Azure services, the bindings refer to the environment variables created by the application settings, rather than using hardcoded connection string values directly. Some connections will use an identity rather than a secret, in which case you can configure a managed identity and provide relevant permissions to it. We will discuss managed identities further in *Chapter 8, Implementing Secure Cloud Solutions*, so we won't go into detail at this stage.

10. At the bottom of the screen, expand the **Logs** section to view the filesystem log streaming console. Here, you can see any logs from the function, as well as compilation logs.

11. Switch the file to the run.csx file and delete the existing code.

12. Enter the following code into the run.csx file:

```
using Microsoft.Extensions.Logging;

public static DemoMessage Run(string myQueueItem, ILogger
log)
{
    return new DemoMessage() {
        PartitionKey = "Messages",
        RowKey = Guid.NewGuid().ToString(),
        Message = myQueueItem.ToString() };
}

public class DemoMessage
{
    public string PartitionKey { get; set; }
    public string RowKey { get; set; }
    public string Message{ get; set; }
}
```

Notice that we're accessing myQueueItem, which is the trigger parameter name (also acting as an input binding). The return value of the method is passed to the output binding, which will create a new row with a PartitionKey value of Messages, a new GUID for the RowKey value, and the Message column will contain the value from myQueueItem.

13. Save the file and confirm that the log shows that the compilation was successful.

14. Click **Test/Run** and type a message into the **Body** field of the **Input** tab, then click **Run**.

15. Upon completion, the log should show that the function was called and succeeded, with the **Output** tab showing a **202 Accepted** response code.

16. Open the storage account, and within the **Storage browser** blade, navigate to **Tables** and open the newly created **outTable** table. You should see a new row containing the message:

PartitionKey	RowKey	Timestamp	Message
Messages	601402b3-54aa-4d9c-8...	2022-04-12T20:40:42.55...	Hello, World!

Figure 4.3 – A new row created in Azure Table Storage using the function test run

Congratulations! You've successfully created and tested a new function. The code and bindings work.

Let's set up the queue and confirm that everything works as intended outside of the test functionality:

1. While still in the **Storage browser** blade, navigate to **Queues**, select **Add queue**, and name it myqueue-items, which was the value of queueName in our input binding.

2. Click on the newly created queue and click **Add message**. Type a message and click **OK** to add the message to the queue.

    For simplicity, we're just using text, but we could have passed in JSON and had our function interpret the JSON elements to create an entry with multiple pieces of data.

3. Periodically refresh the queue until the message is removed from the queue.

4. Navigate to **Tables** and open **outTable** again. All being well, you should now see that a new row has been created with the message text you input as the queue message.

5. While we're here, open **File shares** and open the file share (notice that the name is the value from the **WEBSITE_CONTENTSHARE** application setting of the function app).

6. Navigate to site\wwwroot and you'll see the file and folder structure previously discussed.

That's the data operation trigger taken care of – next, we'll tackle timers. We won't list every single step for the remaining trigger types, only the relevant differences.

Timers

Here are the alternative steps required for creating a function that implements a timer trigger:

1. Create a new function within the same function app we just used, this time selecting the **Timer trigger** option modifying the schedule however you want.

    You'll see this uses the **NCrontab** syntax. A link with more information on NCrontab can be found in the *Further reading* section of this chapter. If the schedule was set to 0 */5 * * * *, then the function would trigger every 5 minutes of every day. Feel free to modify the timing for this exercise.

2. Open the function and review the files and code as before to see how this is implemented. Notice that the type here is timerTrigger. Open the logs as before to confirm the timer successfully triggers and the function runs on the configured schedule.

The final trigger type we're going to look at in this section is webhooks, or HTTP triggers.

Webhooks

Here are the alternative steps required for creating a function that implements an HTTP trigger:

1. Create another function within the same function app we've been using, selecting the **HTTP trigger** option and accepting the rest of the settings as their defaults.

2. Open the newly created function and once again view the `function.json` file to see the `httpTrigger` type being used, as well as an array of accepted methods that can trigger the function.

    Notice the output binding uses the return value from the code. Notice also the `authLevel` value is set to `function` by default. This means that the function won't be triggered by just any GET or POST request, but only if that request contains an API key from the function.

3. Open the `run.csx` file and review the code. You can see that it has a default response if there's no query string or request body, and a personalized response if a name is passed in the query string or request body.

4. Click **Get function URL**, leaving the dropdown as the **default** function key, and copy the URL.

5. In a new browser tab or window, navigate to the URL just copied and your function should display a generic message.

6. Remove ? and everything after it from the URL, and try again. The function doesn't run because it's configured to require a function key, so you get a **401** HTTP error instead.

7. Re-add the full URL, including the code string, adding &name=Azure to the end of the URL, and try again. Notice the personalized greeting, which reflects the code we saw.

Feel free to explore further, but for now, we've looked at the three trigger types mentioned in the exam.

Serverless functions are typically intended to be single purpose, short-lived, and stateless, which is great for scaling. Certain kinds of applications are difficult to implement without persistent state and being unable to incorporate a state can be somewhat of a constraint. Durable functions allow you create stateful functions using Azure Functions, which is the final topic for this chapter.

Discovering stateful durable functions

Durable Functions is an extension of Azure Functions that allows you to write stateful, serverless workflows (or **orchestrations**). You define the stateful workflows with **orchestrator functions** and you define stateful entities with **entity functions**. Durable functions manage the state, checkpoints, and restarts for you, using data stored in the storage account to keep track of the orchestration progress.

When you have more complex workflows and business logic that needs to be broken into multiple functions with stateful coordination, previously, you'd have had to come up with a creative solution using multiple services yourself to try and achieve this. That's the primary use case for durable functions. Let's briefly look at the function types and the typical patterns that durable functions help with.

Types of durable function

To achieve this kind of orchestration, durable functions have four types of functions:

- **Client functions** (or **starter functions**): These can use all the function triggers and are used to initiate a new orchestration workflow. If you want to test an orchestration workflow, you can't manually trigger an orchestrator function; you trigger the client function, which sends a message using an orchestrator client binding to initiate the orchestration.

- **Orchestrator functions**: These define the steps within a workflow and can handle any errors that occur at any point in the workflow. Orchestrator functions don't actually perform any activities – they only orchestrate.

- **Activity functions**: These implement the steps within a workflow and can make use of all the input and output bindings available to functions.

- **Entity functions** (or **durable entities**): These define the operations for reading and updating small pieces of state and can be invoked from client functions or orchestrator functions, accessed via a unique entity ID.

Durable function patterns

There are typically six application patterns that can benefit most from durable functions:

- **Function chaining**: Where multiple functions need to be executed in a specific order with the output from one function being passed to the input of the next. An orchestrator function keeps track of the sequence progress.

- **Fan-out/fan-in**: When multiple functions need to be executed in parallel and progress needs to wait for all those functions to complete. Usually, there would be some aggregation done on the results returned from the functions.

- **Asynchronous HTTP APIs**: Useful when coordination is required between long-running operations and external clients. Once the long-running operation starts, the orchestrator function manages polling the status until the operation completes or times out.

- **Monitor**: When there's a recurring process within a workflow that needs to be polled until certain conditions are met, such as monitoring something for a change in state, for example. The orchestrator function will call an activity function that checks whether these conditions are being met.

- **Human interaction:** A lot of business workflows need to pause for some kind of approval. The orchestrator function uses what's called a durable timer to request approval, and then waits for an external event (receiving approval) before moving to the next function. Optionally, you might decide to have a timeout and run another function to take some remediation action or escalation if the external event didn't happen. We will talk about both scenarios later in the chapter.

- **Aggregator:** When data needs to be aggregated over a period of time into a single, addressable entity. This data might come from multiple sources, at varying volumes. The aggregator may have to carry out an action on data as it arrives, and external clients may need to query the said data. This makes use of durable entities.

To demonstrate a durable function, we're going to create one and this time, we're going to do our development in VS Code, so that you can see the development and testing experience locally, which is often the preferred way to develop functions.

Developing within VS Code

When developing locally, the first thing we will do is create a new local Azure Functions project, where we select the same kind of settings that we did in the portal. After this, we can develop and test our durable functions locally before deploying to Azure.

Creating a project

These are the steps we can carry out to create a local Azure Functions project within VS Code:

1. With all the technical requirements installed and VS Code open, create a new folder for the project.

2. Open the **Command Palette** with *F1*, *Ctrl + Shift + P*, or **View | Command Palette…**.

3. Start the storage emulator by entering `azurite: start` into the input box. This allows us to use local storage when developing locally without having to provision a storage account in Azure for local testing. You'll notice some new files and folders created.

4. Open the command palette again and this time, enter `azure functions: create new project`.

5. Browse to and select the folder you created for this, select **C#** for the language, **.NET 6** for the runtime, and **Durable Functions Orchestration** for the template, enter a name or accept the default, and accept the default namespace.

6. When prompted, select the **Use local emulator** option.

7. Once completed, open the `.cs` file and examine the code.

Within the generated code, we can see examples of a few of the function types previously discussed. The first is an orchestrator function (notice we're decorating the function with an OrchestrationTrigger decorator, which will be used in the population of the function.json file upon compilation):

```
[FunctionName("DurableFunctionsOrchestrationCSharp1")]
public static async Task<List<string>> RunOrchestrator(
    [OrchestrationTrigger] IDurableOrchestrationContext
context)
    {
        var outputs = new List<string>();

        // Replace "hello" with the name of your Durable
Activity Function.
        outputs.Add(await context.
CallActivityAsync<string>("DurableFunctionsOrchestration
CSharp1_Hello", "Tokyo"));
        outputs.Add(await context.
CallActivityAsync<string>("DurableFunctionsOrchestration
CSharp1_Hello", "Seattle"));
        outputs.Add(await context.
CallActivityAsync<string>("DurableFunctionsOrchestration
CSharp1_Hello", "London"));

// returns ["Hello Tokyo!", "Hello Seattle!", "Hello London!"]
        return outputs;
    }
```

This function uses the function chaining pattern previously discussed, where it's calling an activity function in sequence, passing in the name of a city, and returning a list of outputs from that activity function.

Next, we have the activity function (decorated with ActivityTrigger):

```
[FunctionName("DurableFunctionsOrchestrationCSharp1_
Hello")]
    public static string SayHello([ActivityTrigger] string
name, ILogger log)
    {
        log.LogInformation($"Saying hello to {name}.");
        return $"Hello {name}!";
    }
```

This activity function takes the name passed to it, logs a message, and returns a string value greeting the provided name.

Finally, we have the client – or starter – function, which triggers the orchestration function (decorated with `HttpTrigger`, although it could be any other trigger type):

```
        [FunctionName("DurableFunctionsOrchestrationCSharp1_
HttpStart")]
        public static async Task<HttpResponseMessage>
HttpStart(
            [HttpTrigger(AuthorizationLevel.Anonymous, "get",
"post")] HttpRequestMessage req,
            [DurableClient] IDurableOrchestrationClient
starter,
            ILogger log)
        {
            // Function input comes from the request content.
            string instanceId = await starter.
StartNewAsync("DurableFunctionsOrchestrationCSharp1", null);

            log.LogInformation($"Started orchestration with ID
= '{instanceId}'.");

            return starter.CreateCheckStatusResponse(req,
instanceId);
        }
```

This function has an HTTP trigger that accepts `GET` and `POST` requests, triggers the orchestration function, and uses the generated `instanceId` value in a log message, as well as for generating a message that can be used to check the status. We won't make any code changes this time.

In the file explorer, you'll see a file called `local.settings.json`. This file stores the application settings that are only used for local development. This is useful for us because we know the `AzureWebJobsStorage` value is used by our functions and we want to make sure, for development, we're using the local storage emulator, but in Azure, we want to use the storage account. The value of `AzureWebJobsStorage` is `UseDevelopmentStorage=true`, indicating that the storage emulator will be used locally.

Let's get ready to give this a test.

Developing and testing locally

Here are the steps we can follow to build and test our functions locally in VS Code:

1. From the activity bar of VS Code, click the Azure icon and expand the **FUNCTIONS** list.

2. Expand your subscription and you'll be able to see the function we created earlier within the portal. Feel free to look through and see what can be found there. You can also see the local project in the same area. Expand **Local Project** and **Functions**, then click **Run build task to update this list...** (you could also build however you would normally build your .NET projects):

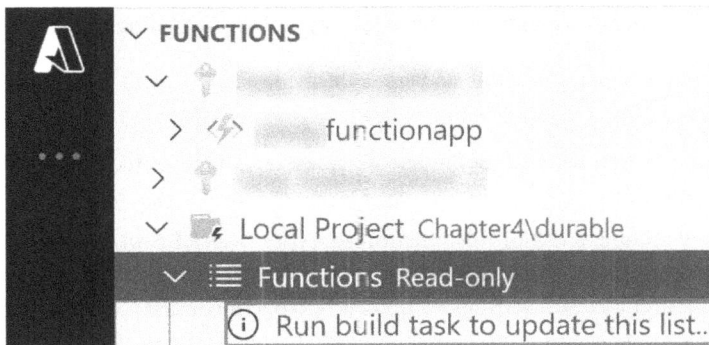

Figure 4.4 – The local and Azure-based functions listed

You can now see the three functions listed: we have our orchestrator function, activity function, and client (or starter) function.

3. Click on each of the functions and the `function.json` files for each will be displayed, where you can see the specific bindings, which should be somewhat familiar by now.

   Although we won't do it here, you could also right-click on the functions to add a binding, which would open a wizard to have you populate the relevant properties for the binding.

4. Run the program as you normally would, which is often using *F5*.

5. You will see our functions and their triggers in the terminal output. The client function has a webhook URL we can use to trigger. Visit that URL and you will see several pieces of information, including the `statusQueryGetUri` URI. The terminal output will also display output messages.

6. Copy the full URL value of `statusQueryGetUri`, which was generated by the client function using the `CreateCheckStatusResponse` call we saw in the code, then visit that URL.

   Here you can see the status as `Completed`, along with the output list from the orchestrator function and some other data.

7. Back in VS Code, right-click on the client function, select **Execute Function Now…**, and either accept the default JSON input or delete (it makes no difference in our case). You'll see the terminal output showing the durable functions running.

8. Stop the app running with *Ctrl + C* (or any other way you wish).

We've just created and tested a durable function locally without the functions being deployed in Azure – great job! Let's finish this up by deploying our function to Azure along with a new function app.

Deploying to Azure

There are several ways to deploy our app to a function app – we're just going to use one of them here:

1. Open the command palette as before and enter `Create new Function App in Azure…` `(Advanced)`.

    We're going to use the advanced method so we can select the resource group rather than allow it to create a new one.

2. Enter a globally unique name for this function app, choose **.NET 6** when prompted with **Select a runtime stack**, choose **Windows** when prompted with **Select an OS**, choose the appropriate resource group and location settings when prompted, choose the **Consumption** plan, select **Create a new storage account**, and enter a unique name for the storage account if the default isn't acceptable. Select **Skip for now** at the Application Insights resource creation step. Monitor the terminal output to see when it completes.

3. Open the command palette as before and enter `azure functions: deploy to function app`.

4. Select the newly created function app when prompted with **Select a resource**.

5. When prompted, select **Deploy**.

    We created the function app, but we could have also deployed the code to an existing function app, which is what we would do if we needed to update the code or deploy another function to the same function app.

    Upon completion, you should see the new function app with all our new functions created under your subscription in VS Code.

6. Execute the starter function within Azure by right-clicking on it and selecting **Execute Function Now…**, as we did previously.

7. Within the Azure portal, open the newly created storage account and go into the **Storage browser** blade.

8. Explore the tables you see, where you'll be able to see all the snapshots in history that the orchestrator function creates during the execution of the workflow, as well as the status for each instance.

You can also see various queues used for the orchestration. If you haven't worked out by now, the `AzureWebJobsStorage` application setting has indeed been pulled from the function app application settings and not our local setting. Detailed information on the performance and scale of Azure Functions, which details how the storage accounts are used, can be found in the *Further reading* section of this chapter.

You may have noticed some references to something called **task hubs**. Let's take a quick look at what that means in durable functions.

Task hubs

Task hubs are a logical container for storage resources used in durable functions orchestration such as the queues, tables, and containers we can see in our storage account. If one or more function apps share the same storage account, they should all be configured with their own task hub names. If not, they may compete against each other for messages, which could lead to them getting stuck in a specific state.

Task hubs can be defined in the `host.json` file, which could look as follows:

```
{
    "version": "2.0",
    "extensions": {
        "durableTask": {
            "hubName": "MyTaskHub"
        }
    }
}
```

Azure Functions automatically enforces the default deployment slots to have the task hub name match that of the site, which is why the task hub name we saw reflected the name of our function app. If using multiple deployment slots, you should configure task hub names for the non-production slots to avoid conflicts.

Durable functions provide a means to control timing, called **durable timers**. These should be used instead of the standard ways in which you would normally create timers in your chosen language.

Controlling timing

To create a durable timer, you would call the `CreateTimer()` method in .NET or the `createTimer()` method in JavaScript.

A very basic, crude, one-line example of creating a 1-minute timer in C#, which will pause the orchestration for 1 minute before continuing, is the following:

```
await context.CreateTimer(context.CurrentUtcDateTime.
Add(TimeSpan.FromMinutes(1)), CancellationToken.None);
```

If we wanted to create a timeout that canceled the task, we could create a new `CancellationTokenSource`, using a line similar to this:

```
var cts = new CancellationTokenSource()
```

Then, instead of `CancellationToken.None`, we could reference the `CancellationTokenSource` object with `cts.Token`, and after our timeout logic, we could cancel the durable timer with `cts.Cancel()`. If the function doesn't either complete or cancel, the orchestration status isn't set to *completed*.

One of the patterns we mentioned earlier was the human interaction pattern. Having the ability to wait and listen for external events is required for this to work, so let's take a look at this final topic.

Waiting for and sending events

To wait for an external event in C#, you would call the `WaitForExternalEvent<type>("<name>")` method in the orchestrator function, specifying the name of the event and the type of data it expects to receive. For example, to wait for an external event called `Approval`, which you would expect to return a Boolean value indicating whether or not something is approved, we could use the following:

```
bool approved = await context.
WaitForExternalEvent<bool>("Approval");
```

We could then check on the approval outcome using the `approved` variable.

Using the approval scenario again, if we had a client function that received the approval information, and that function should pass the information to the orchestration function listening for it, in C#, we could use the `RaiseEventAsync()` method as follows:

```
await client.RaiseEventAsync(instanceId, "Approval", true);
```

It's passing in the `instanceId` value, the name of the event (`Approval`, in this case), and the Boolean value.

If the orchestrator function wasn't listening for that event, the message would get added to an in-memory queue, so that it would be available should the orchestrator function start listening for that event later.

With that, we have come to the end of our journey into Azure Functions. Feel free to delete the resource group and all resources created during this chapter if you wish.

Summary

In this chapter, we explored what Azure Functions is, what hosting options are available, and some fundamentals around scaling, as well as the core concepts of triggers and bindings. From there, we developed and tested functions in the Azure portal using a data operation trigger, a timer trigger, and a webhook trigger. We then looked at how you can create stateful workflows using durable functions, where we looked at the different function types available and primary use cases, before developing our own durable functions locally within VS Code, making use of local development application settings and the storage emulator. Finally, we took a brief look at task hubs, controlling timing, and finished off with how to wait for and send events with durable functions.

In the next chapter, we will step away from focusing on compute solutions, and look at developing solutions that use Cosmos DB storage. We will be looking at the service, the available APIs for Cosmos DB, managing databases and containers, followed by inserting and querying documents. We will then move into the topics of change feed, partitioning and consistency levels, as well as optimizing database performance and costs.

Questions

1. What is the name of the file that holds the information on a function's triggers and bindings?

2. What information is contained in the `AzureWebJobsStorage` application setting?

3. Which durable function type does an orchestrator function call to implement the steps of a workflow?

4. Which file is used to define application settings that only apply to local development?

Further reading

- The languages supported by Azure Functions can be found here: `https://docs.microsoft.com/azure/azure-functions/supported-languages`.

- Documentation about common Azure Functions scenarios can be found here: `https://docs.microsoft.com/azure/azure-functions/functions-overview#scenarios`.

- The pricing details of Azure Functions can be found here: `https://azure.microsoft.com/pricing/details/functions`.

- Documentation on custom handlers can be found here: `https://docs.microsoft.com/azure/azure-functions/functions-custom-handlers`.

- The application settings reference can be found here: `https://docs.microsoft.com/azure/azure-functions/functions-app-settings`.

- A reference for the `host.json` file can be found here: `https://docs.microsoft.com/azure/azure-functions/functions-host-json`.

- Documentation on NCrontab can be found here: `https://github.com/atifaziz/NCrontab`.

- The Azure Functions developer guide can be found here: `https://docs.microsoft.com/azure/azure-functions/functions-reference`.

- Documentation on Durable Functions can be found here: `https://docs.microsoft.com/azure/azure-functions/durable/durable-functions-overview`.

- Performance and scale information on Azure Functions can be found here: `https://docs.microsoft.com/azure/azure-functions/durable/durable-functions-perf-and-scale`.

Part 2: Developing for Azure Storage

This part introduces Azure storage solutions for persisting unstructured and semi-structured data. You will learn how to provision, configure, and optimize Azure Cosmos DB and Azure Blob Storage. We will cover the main NoSQL storage solution, Cosmos DB, and introduce different APIs of the database. This part teaches you how to provision, optimize, and scale the Cosmos DB account and how to manipulate and query for documents from SDK. Furthermore, Azure Blob Storage will be introduced as the main storage for binaries and text files. This part will also explain how storage is used to persist data for modern web applications running in Azure. You will learn how to manage blobs and your metadata, optimize costs, and configure the high availability of Azure Blob Storage. Finally, you will also be able to choose appropriate storage solutions based on requirements.

This part covers 15-20% of the AZ-204 exam questions.

The following chapters will be covered under this section:

- *Chapter 5, Developing Solutions That Use Cosmos DB Storage*
- *Chapter 6, Developing Solutions That Use Azure Blob Storage*

5

Developing Solutions That Use Cosmos DB Storage

In this chapter, we are going to discuss the extremely powerful **NoSQL database** service running in Azure called **Azure Cosmos DB**. We are going to focus on various aspects of Cosmos DB, such as high availability, geo-distribution, transactional support, security, scale, and performance. Moreover, we'll learn about another affordable and popular NoSQL service called **Azure Table Storage**, whose API is now incorporated in Cosmos DB.

You will also become familiar with NoSQL technologies and be able to select one that is appropriate for your project. You will also get hands-on experience in provisioning, configuring, and querying Cosmos DB and Azure Table Storage.

We're going to cover the following main topics in this chapter:

- Understanding the benefits of NoSQL databases
- Exploring Azure NoSQL platforms
- Developing a solution for Azure Table Storage
- Developing a solution for Azure Cosmos DB

Before jumping into the Azure services, let us find out what NoSQL technology is and what benefits it provides within modern cloud development.

Technical requirements

The code files for this chapter can be downloaded from `https://github.com/PacktPublishing/Developing-Solutions-for-Microsoft-Azure-AZ-204-Exam-Guide/tree/main/Chapter05`.

Code in Action videos for this chapter: `https://bit.ly/3xEg2GC`.

Understanding the benefits of NoSQL databases

NoSQL technology is a unique type of database that does not use tables and relations. This type of database is commonly used to store unstructured or semi-structured data as key-value pairs, broad columns, graphs, or documents without relations, named non-relational databases. There is significant market demand for databases designed to store these simple data types and files (e.g., JSON files) with minimum overhead. The advantages of NoSQL databases are a simple design, horizontal scale, control over availability, and the avoidance of relational schema overhead and limitation.

Many NoSQL databases also have a restriction that relational databases do not have. The use of specific query languages in NoSQL storage raises the learning curve for the developers who have to maintain the data. In addition, the inability to do ad hoc joins between tables leads to data being stored in a single database. The lack of defined interfaces makes connecting and maintaining apps with database changes challenging. Relational databases cannot always be lifted and shifted easily in NoSQL storage. Most NoSQL stores do not support real **Atomicity, Consistency, Isolation, and Durability (ACID)** transactions.

If the database consists of several nodes, all updates rely on eventual consistency when the main instance is updated, and other nodes obtain restive updates eventually. As a result, data requests might not return updated data promptly or may read the incorrect data, conditions known as stale reads. Furthermore, data consistency is more difficult for distributed transactions running across numerous databases than with relational databases. Despite these challenges, the popularity of NoSQL databases is skyrocketing.

Let us imagine a new project needs to be developed for an e-commerce web application to search for parts used in car manufacturing. The original relational approach requires the development of an **Object Relational Mapper (ORM)** and the design of tables storage for various parts of the car. For example, wheels, doors, and mirrors should be stored in the appropriate tables. Then, developers must create complex joins to retrieve search results for parts used for manufacturing different models. Then, the project's stakeholders decide to change gear and start selling flowers. Developers must redesign the ORM and data structure to meet the company's requirements. It may take a month to build and a month to redesign the structure for relational storage, but for non-relational storage, developers do not have to redesign the table structure. They can store all the cars and flowers in the same database with a different format serialized in JSON. Development and modification will be lightning fast with non-relational approaches. When the changes to requirements are unlikely to affect the data structure, the project can be migrated to the relational platform.

So, we have just covered the pros and cons of NoSQL solutions. You see the main pain points of NoSQL technology (lack of consistency, transactions support, and forced schema). You can also see how NoSQL technology can help you with persisting JSON data and save the time required to implement sophisticated ORMs. Now, you can evaluate the NoSQL platform provided in Azure and choose the appropriate service for your needs.

Exploring Azure NoSQL platforms

Azure Cosmos DB is a platform as a service technology hosted in the cloud, containing many of the advantages of a NoSQL database and removing many of the aforementioned disadvantages to simplify consumption and data management.

Probably the first and most unique ability of Cosmos DB is the support for different APIs. The API for MongoDB, the Cassandra API, Gremlin API, Table API, and Core (SQL) API are among the database APIs available in Azure Cosmos DB. Cosmos DB represents real-world data using these APIs by employing key-value, graph, column-family, and document data models. These APIs enable developers to interact with Cosmos DB as if it were any other database technology, without maintenance and scalability overhead, and chiefly, without code modification. Developers can leverage existing applications communicated with Gremlin, Cassandra, or MongoDB with changes only made to connection strings. Cosmos DB implements the latest version of the aforementioned APIs and provides a powerful platform hosted in Azure. That is an additional point for simplifying migration from on-premises or IaaS platforms to affordable PaaS ones.

Another benefit of Cosmos DB is that it's a fully managed service with high horizontal scalability and availability of up to 99.999% out of the box. Cosmos DB instances can be deployed in different regions and synchronized with updates. These instances can be provided with a single write and multi-read option, or with a multi-region writes option.

Furthermore, we should mention that Cosmos DB supports five levels of consistency, optimistic concurrency and conflict resolutions, partitioning, indexing, and transactions. Cosmos DB is easy to scale and regularly updated by Microsoft. We should also mention the provisioned and serverless modes available for hosting Cosmos DB in Azure. In addition, we should emphasize that Cosmos DB provides a free tier and makes it easy to get started with powerful instances of NoSQL databases for your solution.

Cosmos DB is the best but not the only available NoSQL storage in Azure. We should also mention **Azure Table Storage** as a simple and easy alternative for NoSQL storage, and ideal for storing structured non-relational data. We should take a close look at the Azure Table Storage service because the same concepts apply to the Azure Cosmos DB Table API. Azure Table Storage will be explained in the next topic, so let's take a look.

Developing a solution for Azure Table Storage

Azure Table Storage is a PaaS service that is ideal for storing non-relational data in the cloud by providing a simple key-attribute store. Because Azure Table Storage is a free schema service, it is simple to modify the data model as your application's requirements change. For many types of applications, access to Table storage data is rapid and cost-effective, and it is often less expensive than the standard SQL for equivalent amounts of data, or the Cosmos DB service.

Azure Table Storage is part of the Azure Storage platform and provides the most valuable features of Azure Storage, such as high availability and performance, encryption for data at rest and transit, and easy access through a RESTful interface by using SDKs available from many development languages. The cost of storing data is the cheapest in Azure, consisting of the capacity cost and transactional cost. In addition, Azure Table Storage has almost no limits on storage capacity. The only valuable limitation of Azure Table Storage is the maximum size of a single entity is 1 MB and the maximum number of properties of an entity is 255. Azure Table Storage is not available within Premium account types and requires the provisioning of *general-purpose* storage accounts.

There is a tool we recommend using to access Azure Table Storage. **Azure Storage Explorer** is a thick multi-platform desktop application and web-based application available in the Azure portal. Azure Storage Explorer is ideal for working with tables. It supports pagination, querying, and the import and export of entities to CSV and JSON formats.

In the following sections, you will learn how to provision Azure Table Storage with an Azure storage account and will be able to explore the account's services with Azure Storage Explorer. Let's take a look at the structure of Azure Table Storage and how to provision the service using the Azure CLI.

The structure of an Azure Table Storage account

PaaS Azure Table Storage is provisioned as part of the Azure storage account from the Azure portal, Azure PowerShell, the Azure CLI, or ARM templates. The Storage account must be deployed with the DNS queue name in the data center of your choice. The account name and the name of the tables must start with a letter and must be 3 to 63 (alphanumeric) characters long. The Azure storage account must be provisioned with a **Standard** performance tier to enable the support of Azure Table Storage. The storage account will be covered in further detail in *Chapter 6, Developing Solutions That Use Azure Blob Storage*.

The structure of Azure Table Storage consists of the following components:

- **Account**: This provides an HTTPS-enabled endpoint of connection for RESTful requests.

- **Table:** This is a collection of entities usually logically grouped (e.g., customers, orders, or products).

- **Entity**: This is a collection of properties close to a data row but with a free schema of types and names for properties.

- **Property**: This is a meaningful combination of key-value pairs for storing NoSQL data. Three properties must always exist for each entity. The unique combination of `PartitionKey` and `RowKey` in the table is required to persist and retrieve each entity. The third mandatory property is the timestamp of the last modification. Each property of the entity has a data type (*string, int32, int64, decimal, guid, boolean*, and *binary*). It's indexed and can be selected based on its values and data type. It's important to understand that an entity with a property named `StockCount` can coexist in the same table with different data types, for instance, the value *100 (int32)* and *out of stock* values (*string*):

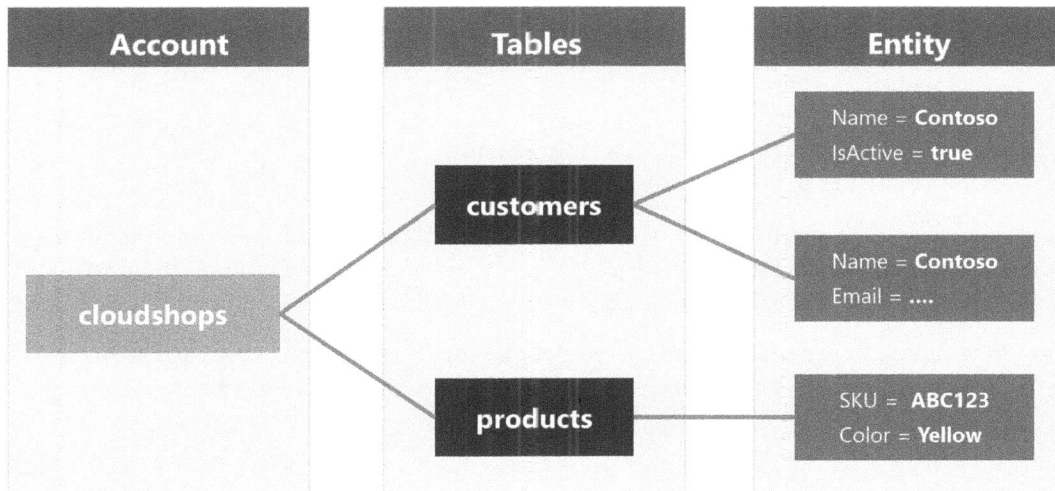

Figure 5.1 – An illustration of the Azure Table Storage account structure

Provisioning Azure Table Storage with the Azure CLI

One of the many ways to provision Azure Table Storage is using Azure CLI commands. In the following script, we will build a new storage account and create a table. The script also generates an **Shared Access Signature (SAS)** for access to the table through the RESTful interface. When you execute commands from the script, your new Azure Table Storage account will be provisioned. The commands can be completed from local Bash or Cloud Shell from the Azure portal:

```
https://github.com/PacktPublishing/Developing-Solutions-for-Microsoft-
Azure-AZ-204-Exam-Guide/blob/main/Chapter05/1-table-provision/table-
account.azcli
```

Querying Azure Table Storage with a RESTful interface

When Azure Table Storage is provisioned, the services can accept HTTPS queries to the provided RESTful interface. The queries will retrieve the entities from tables and must follow the rules of *OData* syntax. For example, you can get a list of the entities from customer tables by using the following requests. However, you need to provide the SAS from the previous demo and replace myaccount with the name of your account. Then, you need to execute the following link in the browser:

```
https://myaccount.table.core.windows.net/customers()
```

Another example only retrieves the customers who are active (using the isActive = true Boolean property). You can execute the following link in the browser by adding the SAS and replacing the account name with yours:

```
https://myaccount.table.core.windows.net/
customers()?$filter=IsActive%20eq%20true
```

The syntax rules are required to make code comparison operations with the following acronyms: lt, gt, le, ge, and eq. For example, instead of '>', '=<', and '=', you must use gt (great), lq (less or equal), and eq (equal) operations. The query string also needs to be properly encoded.

Azure Table Storage is extremely fast at querying entities by ID (PartitionKey and RowKey). For the best speed, both keys need to be provided in the query. The following example will retrieve the single entity:

```
https://myaccount.table.core.windows.net/
Customers(PartitionKey='ReSellers',RowKey='Contoso')
```

> **Important Note**
> The query rules require the name of the tables, the name of the properties, and the values to be case sensitive.

The following C# example will create a few additional entities and query them back in the same way we did from the RESTful interface. Finally, the items and tables will be deleted:

```
https://github.com/PacktPublishing/Developing-Solutions-for-Microsoft-
Azure-AZ-204-Exam-Guide/tree/main/Chapter05/2-table-sdk
```

The following table explains the classes used in the project:

Class	Description
TableServiceClient	Provides synchronous and asynchronous calls to the RESTful interface of table storage. The TableServiceClient class supports a full stack of operations with entities (get, query, delete, and upsert), and operations with tables (create and delete). The class instance must be properly initialized with a storage connection string before use.
TableEntity	Represents an entity from Azure Table Storage retrieved as a result of a query operation on TableServiceClient. It contains the required properties, RowKey and PartitionKey, for appropriate storage and requests entities from the table with a free schema attribute set. The Item[String] function can be used to retrieve or set attribute properties.

Table 5.1 – C# SDK classes used for connecting to Azure Table Storage from code

Summary of Azure Table Storage

The Azure Table Storage service offers cheap and powerful storage for NoSQL data in Azure, available for connecting, creating, modifying, and querying entities by using a REST interface and SDK. Because Azure Table Storage is schemaless, it is ideal for persisting a bottomless number of entities and using **LINQ** to save and restore objects directly from the code. Moreover, the Table API is supported by Cosmos DB, and will help you to upgrade your project to a scalable solution with minimum effort.

Developing a solution for Azure Cosmos DB

Cosmos DB is another powerful service that combines the advantages of NoSQL technology and the large scalable infrastructure hosted in Azure. The main Cosmos DB advantages include the following:

- It has one of the highest SLA availabilities for databases hosted in Azure.
- It is a strong PaaS managed by Microsoft.
- It has serverless and provisioned throughput with the support of autoscaling.
- It supports multiple consistency levels.
- It has a flexible pricing model, including a free tier.
- It supports well-known APIs.

Those advantages make the Cosmos DB service unique within all cloud NoSQL services and provide customers with the best migration experience between on-premises well-known databases and the Azure PaaS platform. Let's begin our journey through Cosmos DB by outlining which advantages are provided by each API, including the Table API we have already discussed.

Exploring Cosmos DB APIs

Let us look at the APIs available with Cosmos DB and discuss their advantages. It does not matter which API you select; you will receive a fully managed and scalable service with the advantages of the NoSQL database mentioned at the start of the chapter. The only concern is whether you already have experience with or have developed an application working with one of the well-known interfaces. In this case, Cosmos DB provides you with an easy lift-and-shift to the PaaS. If you start a new project and want to leverage the most powerful interface provided for Cosmos DB, we recommend you choose the Core (SQL) API.

The Table API

The data in this API is stored in a key-value format, and it provides clear and simple storage for your objects in code. We have just familiarized ourselves with Azure Table Storage, and the **Table API** in Azure supports the same features. You can reuse the same code to upgrade your application to Cosmos DB. If you are currently utilizing Azure Table Storage, you may experience latency, fixed throughput, impossible worldwide distribution, limited index management, and poor query performance. The Table API helps you avoid these constraints; therefore, it is recommended to migrate your project to Azure Cosmos DB. Be aware that the Table API only works with **Online Transaction Processing (OLTP)** scenarios.

The API for MongoDB

This API is compatible with the MongoDB Wire Protocol and uses the BSON format to store data in a document structure. It is an excellent choice if you want to leverage the larger **MongoDB** ecosystem, tools (MongoDB Shell, MongoDB Compass, or Robo 3T), and skills while still taking advantage of Azure Cosmos DB scaling, geo-replication, and high availability. However, Cosmos DB does not utilize any native MongoDB code; it is compatible with the 4.0, 3.6, and 3.2 MongoDB server versions. Your application that already worked with MongoDB can easily be switched to Cosmos DB by updating the connection string.

The Cassandra API

The **Cassandra API** guarantees backward compatibility with Apache Cassandra products. It provides a locally distributed and horizontally scaled database to store large volumes of data. The API uses a column-oriented design to store data. You can benefit from the elasticity and fully managed nature of the Cosmos DB service and still use native Apache Cassandra capabilities. For example, you can use the **Cassandra Query Language** through the CQL shell while connected to Cosmos DB. If you choose the Cassandra API, you do not need to manage the Java VM, OS, updates, clusters, or nodes. The Cassandra API only works with OLTP scenarios.

The Gremlin API

The **Gremlin API** lets you store data, and query edges and vertices. This API works best for scenarios that involve vigorous data, as in, data with complicated relationships. It combines the advantages of graph techniques with the managed highly scalable infrastructure of Cosmos DB. The Gremlin API supports wire protocol with the open source Gremlin – thus, you can create your application using the open source Gremlin SDKs. The Gremlin API ingests and queries data using the same **Graph Query Language** as Apache TinkerPop. Currently, Gremlin API only supports OLTP scenarios.

The Core (SQL) API

The **SQL API** maintains data in the document format, so originally the services of Cosmos DB were named DocumentDB. The SQL API provides a natively understandable query language based on T-SQL so that developers can leverage their relational skills to query NoSQL data. The SDK client library is frequently updated and accessible for most programming languages. The SQL API is the ideal option if your project is migrating from relational databases such as PostgreSQL or Oracle. The SQL API provides separation between analytical and operational workloads. Furthermore, internal objects in SQL API, such as stored procedures, triggers, and user-defined functions, are implemented in JavaScript, which enables developers to use well-known languages and a tested SDK library, instead of it using its own based on T-SQL.

Important Note

All further information and code samples will be provided for the Core (SQL) API, because it is a native Microsoft Azure API, and it will be the focus of the exam questions.

Provisioning

Provisioning Cosmos DB accounts can be done from the Azure portal, the Azure CLI, or PowerShell. When you create a new account, you must provide a unique DNS name, choose the main region, and then add additional regions for global distribution to achieve 99.999% of SLA. For capacity mode, you can choose between provisioned throughput and serverless platforms. Choosing provisioned throughput will charge you a fixed amount per month, even if you do not use the account, and the serverless plan will charge based on consumption, or **Request Units (RUs)**. Remember that you can apply for a free tier within the first provisioned plan of your subscription.

When you create an account, it is also important to choose between the aforementioned APIs. After provisioning, you cannot change the API for your account. The next step is to build a container with documents (with the SQL API), collections with documents (with the API for MongoDB), tables with rows or items (with the Cassandra or Table API), or graphs with nodes (with the Gremlin API). The structure of the Cosmos DB account is provided in the following figure:

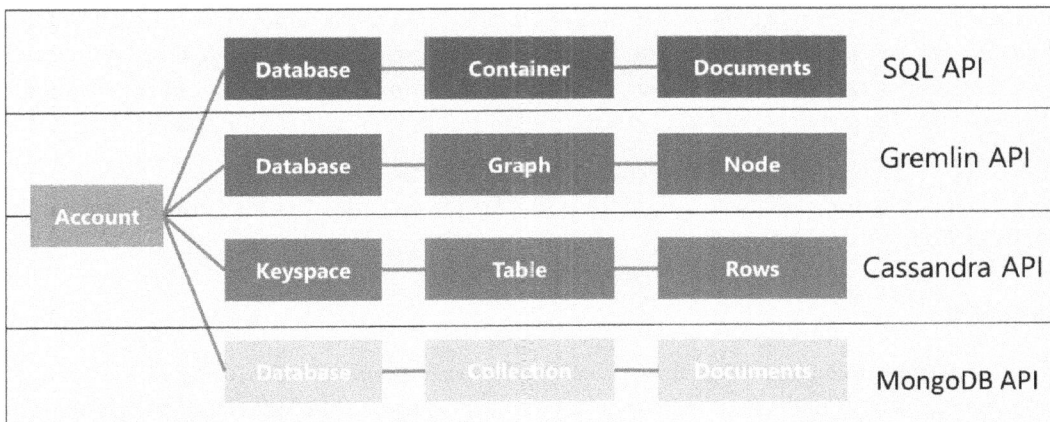

Figure 5.2 – The structure of the Cosmos DB account

Using the Azure CLI to provision Cosmos DB

Let us take a close look at the SQL API. The documents you will create in the container will be stored in JSON format, and can be indexed and searched by SQL queries using the properties you provide. In the following script, you will build a new account-supported SQL API and a container with provisioned throughput. The following script can be executed from bash locally or Cloud Shell from the Azure portal:

```
https://github.com/PacktPublishing/Developing-Solutions-for-Microsoft-
Azure-AZ-204-Exam-Guide/blob/main/Chapter05/3-cosmos-provision/
cosmos-account.azcli
```

When you complete the script, you can open the provisioned Cosmos DB from the portal and observe its settings. Let's take look at one of the best features of Cosmos DB – high availability.

High availability

Cosmos DB is a fully managed multi-region service that transparently controls the information of individual compute nodes. Users do not need to be concerned about patching or scheduled maintenance. Cosmos DB supports multi-region deployment and allows users to choose regions and test failover. Moreover, the common application architecture is based on multi-write access to the different regions where Cosmos DB is deployed. Those regions are synchronized by replicas depending on the selected consistency level. The different applications can update documents in one region and read or read-write with multi-region configuration.

Azure Cosmos DB may be set up to allow writes across different regions. This is beneficial for reducing write latency in geographically distributed applications. Using multiple write regions does not ensure write availability during a region outage in Azure Cosmos DB. A single write region with a service-managed failover is the ideal option for achieving high availability in the event of a region failure. The general availability of Cosmos DB with two or more Azure regions is an SLA level of 99.999%.

High-availability settings can be found on the portal for the exact database in the **Replicate data globally** section.

Indexing

Each JSON document stored in the database is converted into a tree representation, where each property is represented as a node in the tree. When you run the query, it uses the **Index Seek** algorithm. Index Seek is the most efficient way to run queries because it only reads necessary index pages and only loads the items in query results. An appropriate index strategy will reduce **Resource Units (RUs)** consumption and charges.

You can specify an indexing policy to include or exclude nodes from the indexing process. If a node is excluded, its parent nodes will be excluded as well. The node or property in the document is referenced by a path such as /Customer/Name/? or /Customer/*. The wildcard includes all nested nodes and ? includes only the exact value of the current node. The index of the root level, /*, can be overwritten with the exact settings of the include and exclude path. For example, you can include everything /* and exclude /Customer/?, or vice versa, you can exclude everything /*, and only include the property you want to index.

The default indexing policy indexes all properties. You can specify a custom index of the following types for the properties in a document:

- A **range index** suits a single field containing a list of *string* or *number* values. The index is useful in range queries with filtering, ordering, and joining requests. The range index is a default indexing policy, and it is already optimized for best performance. We recommend configuring range indexes for any single string or number properties.

- A **composite index** improves the efficiency when filtering or ordering operations are performed on multiple fields.

- A **spatial index** uses geospatial objects. Properly setting up indexes will improve your query performance and reduce RUs.

You can find indexing settings on the portal for the exact container in the **Indexing Policy** section of **Data Explorer**. The indexing policy is provided as JSON settings and has **includedPath**, **excludedPath**, and **compositeIndexes** sections.

There are a few recommendations for using *composite indexes*:

- The query performance will be optimal if queries hit a composite index in the same order of the fields it set up. For example, if you query for a customer with a specific name and family name, you can create a composite index for the Name and FamilyName fields.

- The composite index can also include ordering (ASC or DESC). For example, you query for a customer list and want to order your customers by family name, then by name. When you build a composite index, you need to provide fields in the same sequence that you want them to be ordered, with the same ordering direction (ASC or DESC) as in the query.

Time to live

Azure Cosmos DB's **Time to Live** (**TTL**) feature allows you to remove documents from a container automatically after a specified time. You can set TTL at the container level, applied to all documents by default. You can also set TTL at the document level to override inherited TTL at the container level. When you specify TTL for a container or an item, Azure Cosmos DB will automatically delete the objects after the time when they were edited. The TTL value is set in seconds and -1 makes it equal to infinity. The default value is *null* (not defined). You can modify the TTL value in **Container Settings** in Data Explorer.

Inserting and querying documents

You have provisioned a Cosmos DB account with a container and you can now use that account to insert documents and run queries. The Cosmos DB SQL API accounts allow you to query objects using SQL (one of the most well-known and widely used query languages) as a JSON query language. In the following examples, you will learn how to use these powerful query capabilities directly from C# code and the Azure portal.

Connecting to a Cosmos DB account from code

Let us look at the code snippets provided in the following GitHub repo. Remember to update the connection information with values provided in the **Keys** section for the account on the Azure portal. You need to update your URI endpoint and *primary key*. You will also have a chance to compare RU consumption for each of the queries:

```
https://github.com/PacktPublishing/Developing-Solutions-for-Microsoft-
Azure-AZ-204-Exam-Guide/tree/main/Chapter05/4-cosmos-sdk-generate
```

The following table will explain the classes used in the code snippet:

Method	Description
CosmosClient	Provides a logical representation of the Azure Cosmos DB account on the client side. This client allows you to configure and perform queries in the Azure Cosmos DB database service. The instance of the class must be configured with an endpoint and key before use. The class is responsible for providing operations with the Database class.
Container	Provides operations for reading, replacing, or deleting specific containers and documents in a container.
Database	Provides operations for reading or deleting an existing database and building a Container class instance.

Table 5.2 – The C# SDK classes used for manipulating a Cosmos DB account from code

Now, you can open Data Explorer and observe items created in Cosmos DB. You can also create documents manually or import them from files. Each document should contain a unique field ID and, after saving, have additional technical fields such as etag. A new document obviously should contain valid JSON data to be successfully created. In the next task, you will run a query and observe the RU's information under the **Query Stats** tab.

Here are a few query examples you can run:

```
--select the order by its number (1 result, 2.8 RUs)
SELECT * FROM c WHERE c.OrderNumber = "NL-21"
```

```
--select orders from a specific city (3 results, 3 RUs)
SELECT VALUE  {
   "Order City": o.OrderAddress.City,
   "Order Number" : o.OrderNumber }
FROM Orders o
WHERE o.OrderAddress.City IN ('Redmond', 'Seattle')


--products by ordered count
SELECT products.ProductItem.ProductName as Name, SUM(products.
Count) as Count
   FROM Orders o
   JOIN products IN o.OrderItems
   GROUP BY products.ProductItem.ProductName
```

Next, you can use the following code snippets to learn how to execute queries and process the results from code:

```
https://github.com/PacktPublishing/Developing-Solutions-for-Microsoft-
Azure-AZ-204-Exam-Guide/tree/main/Chapter05/5-cosmos-sdk-query
```

User-defined functions

The SQL API lets developers leverage **User-Defined Functions** (UDFs). UDFs should provide in arguments (many or non) and return a result (a single argument). Using UDFs, you can extend Azure Cosmos DB's queries by returning its results as fields or using function results in a WHERE filter. UDFs will help you to avoid wordy SQL queries because UDFs are created in JavaScript. JavaScript has many useful functions and libraries that can be used to express complex business logic. Here is an example of a simple function implementing a search by using a regular expression:

```
function Match(input, pattern)
{
    // Return TRUE if the input matches the pattern.
    return input.match(pattern) !== null;
};
```

Here is an example of a query where UDFs are used:

```
SELECT c.OrderNumber, c.OrderCustomer.Name,c.OrderCustomer.
IsActive
FROM c
```

```
WHERE udf.Match(c.OrderCustomer.Name, 'Level[1-5]') and
c.OrderCustomer.IsActive = true
```

However, there are some cases where you should avoid using UDFs, as follows:

- If Cosmos DB already has the functionality. The native Cosmos DB query functions will always work better than custom UDFs.

- If the query only has a UDF in the WHERE filter. UDFs do not utilize the index, so executing a UDF will require loading documents. To improve performance and avoid loading each document, combine a UDF and the additional filter options in the WHERE clause.

Stored procedures

A **stored procedure** in Cosmos DB is developed in JavaScript language and contains logic that can process a collection of documents as a single transaction. A stored procedure resource has a stable structure, expecting input and providing output. The stored procedure is saved as a document in the Cosmos DB container. It can be executed against documents in a specific partition. The partition value is what you usually provide when executing stored procedures.

Cosmos DB stored procedures can use the JavaScript libraries to conduct operations such as creating, reading, updating, deleting, and querying documents, as well as reading from and writing to the request body. It usually returns a JSON document and can accept a JSON document as a parameter. Many developers use stored procedures to complete bulk inserts or update a substantial number of documents within a single transaction. The following code example can be created as a storage procedure (with a name such as HelloWorldSp) and executed from the portal. The return should contain Hello, World!. You can test the following function from Data Explorer by creating a new stored procedure and executing it:

```
function () {
    var TheContext = getContext();
    var TheResponse = TheContext.getResponse();
    TheResponse.setBody("Hello, World!");
}
```

Triggers

Azure Cosmos DB supports two types of triggers: **pre-triggers** and **post-triggers**. Pre-triggers contain the JavaScript code executed before inserting or modifying an item, and post-triggers contain the code executed after inserting or modifying an item. Pay attention to trigger execution. They do not automatically execute before or after the operation as they are executed in relational databases. Triggers registered for a specific database operation (*all*, *create*, *delete*, or *replace*) should be explicitly called from the SDK.

The pre-trigger is most common and is used to validate an item that is being created in Cosmos DB. For example, a pre-trigger can validate a JSON structure. It can look for specific values or fields and throw exceptions if the field is not found. As a result, if the exception is generated, the document creation process is interrupted and the operation is rejected.

The following code snippet should build a simple pre-trigger for *create* or *replace* operations. The trigger will validate if the passed object (`Order`) has the `OrderCustomer` field:

```
function validateOrder() {
    var theContext = getContext();
    var theRequest = theContext.getRequest();
    // item going to be created
    var item = theRequest.getBody();
    // validate properties
        if (item["OrderCustomer"] != undefined &&
item["OrderCustomer"] != null) {
        // update the item that will be created
        theRequest.setBody(item);
    } else
    {
        //cancel operation
        throw new Error('OrderCustomer must be specified');
    }
}
```

Create the `validateOrder` trigger within the Azure portal because it's going to be used from the application code.

Leveraging a trigger validation from code

From the following C# code snippet, you will learn how to invoke triggers when creating documents in the Cosmos DB container. You must use the console application to submit documents for validation by leveraging the trigger. You need to update the Cosmos DB key and endpoint as you did for the previous demo. At the end of execution, you will receive an error message for a document that is not accepted by the trigger.

Pay attention to how the trigger was involved in the document creation process:

```
CreateItemAsync(doc, partitionkey), new ItemRequestOptions(){
PreTriggers= <list of triggers> });
```

The relevant code files can be found at: `https://github.com/PacktPublishing/ Developing-Solutions-for-Microsoft-Azure-AZ-204-Exam-Guide/tree/ main/Chapter05/6-cosmos-sdk-trigger`

The Cosmos DB REST API

The Azure Cosmos DB **REST API** allows you to build, query, and remove documents or database collections programmatically. To perform operations on Cosmos DB resources, you should generate a call through HTTPS to the particular resource using a supported method: `GET`, `POST`, `PUT`, or `DELETE`. For a successful call, the authorization header should be provided with a token generated from the Cosmos DB REST API and used for a single operation.

The following workload should be submitted as a `POST` request to the URL:

```
https://{account}.documents.azure.com/dbs/{db-id}/colls/{coll-
id}/docs
{
    "query": "SELECT * FROM Orders o WHERE o.id = @id",
    "parameters": [
    {   "name": "@id",   "value": "NL-21" }   ]
}
```

Optimistic concurrency

The Cosmos DB SQL API supports **Optimistic Concurrency Control (OCC)**. This control prevents clients from overriding the updates of others and losing valuable information as a result. Concurrent access occurs when several processes attempt to update the same document. One process will succeed to update and the other will fail.

The Cosmos DB SQL API supports OCC through an additional value, an _etag system property. The etag value is updated every time a document changes and clients need to verify the _etag value loaded from the database with the document and compare it with the current _etag value from the database. If the value is different, the operation of saving changes for this document can override previous changes. This type of check is maintained in the Cosmos DB SDK for replacement operations. Your code should configure a conditional check for _etag, as in the following example:

```
var ac = new AccessCondition { Condition = readDoc.ETag,
            Type = AccessConditionType.IfMatch };
await client.ReplaceDocumentAsync( readDoc,
    new RequestOptions { AccessCondition = ac });
```

Controlling the concurrency is required if more than one client is working on writing and deleting operations in a Cosmos DB container. If you have only one client, the OCC is not required.

Networking settings

The Cosmos DB firewall allows all connections to the internet by default. You can create custom rules to allow connection from a range of IP addresses, single IP addresses, and selected private networks. Cosmos DB network integration also supports access through private endpoints configured for specific Azure services. As additional options, Cosmos DB supports limiting access from the Azure portal and the data center used for provisioning. You can observe the settings in the **Networking** section on the Cosmos DB main blade.

Encryption settings

A Cosmos DB account is encrypted at rest by default with a Microsoft key and support customer keys for encryption referenced from **Azure Key Vault**. Meanwhile, developers can enable the **Always Encrypted** technology commonly used in Azure SQL for encrypting specific fields in the stored documents. In this case, applications need to implement client-side decryption because the data traveling from the database server is encrypted. The Always Encrypted technology supports *randomized* and *deterministic* encryption, and is recommended to enable for fields with credit card numbers, and other **Personally Identifiable Information (PII)**.

Backups and recovery

Backups in Cosmos DB support backing up the whole account with one of the two modes:

- **Continuous backup** mode allows you to restore data to any point in time from the past 30 days.
- **Periodic backup** mode (default) allows a backup to be taken and persisted based on a specific policy. The retention policy is limited by month, with backup intervals at a minimum of 1 hour. Note that restoring the backup needs to be done by sending a request to the support team.

Partitioning in Cosmos DB

The container you build with the SQL API acts as storage for JSON documents and can be replicated across multiple regions and horizontally partitioned. When you build a container, you should provide a key for partitioning. Usually, the partition key is one of the common field values that exists in most of your JSON documents. You need to provide this field name when you create a container in the *path format*.

Scaling a container involves dividing data and throughput across physical partitions to provide multi-request processing. Logical partitions are internally mapped to a single physical partition. Cosmos DB containers often have numerous logical partitions and just one physical partition.

Physical partitions, as opposed to logical partitions, are fully maintained by Cosmos DB. Let us say that a logical partition is a collection of documents that all share the same partition key. The scope of database transactions is likewise defined by a logical partition. You can use a transaction with snapshot isolation to update objects within a logical partition. New logical partitions are created transparently when new objects are added to the database.

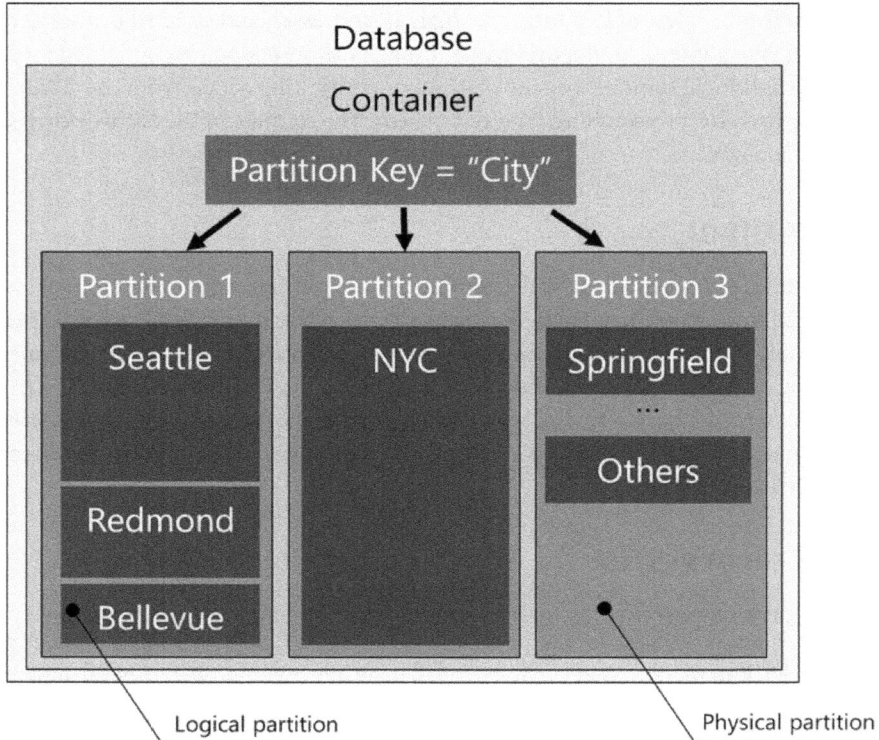

Figure 5.3 – A partitioning algorithm in Cosmos DB

Again, all documents in the container will be split into partitions to improve the performance of queries. This is acceptable if all documents in the container have a unique partition key. For example, you can use Item ID as the partition key. It is normal to have a large amount within the logical partition. The problem can occur if most of the documents will be stored in the same partition. This partition can reach its storage 20 GB limit and become a hot partition. You should avoid hot partitions when you plan your partition strategy.

The simple idea of partitions is that they provide parallel execution of your requests on the individual partition. The documents added to the container are automatically grouped into logical partitions based on the partition key. Each item has an item ID that must be unique inside a logical partition, in addition to a partition key. The combination of the ID and partition key specifies the logical partition for the document. The item's index is created by combining the partition key with the item ID. This index uniquely identifies the item. Selecting a partition key is a critical choice that will impact the performance of your application. Ideally, all documents should be divided between partitions almost equally to avoid hot partitions. Cosmos DB does not provide you with tools for managing the amount or size of partitions, but by choosing the partition key properly, you can avoid hot partitions and speed up queries.

The query retrieving documents from the same logical partition will provide better performance in comparison with cross-partition queries. When you model your partitioning strategy, try to predict most of the requests running by clients and choose the partition key accordingly. You should also avoid most of the requests hitting the same partition. When only one partition is loaded by queries, it becomes a throughput hot partition and can prevent your partition from properly scaling.

Leveraging a change feed for app integration

A **change feed** is an ordered log of changes in the container's documents. Transactions with any changes in Cosmos DB are tracked in the change feed. Then, the change feed can output the list of changed documents in the order they were modified. The change feed can be handled as a *first-in, first-out* queue and asynchronously processed by one or more consumers who connect the change feed.

All Azure Cosmos DB containers have the change feed enabled by default and it can be used to read changes from the database's regions. When the document is updated, the changes are tracked for all logical partition keys of all Azure Cosmos DB containers. This allows changes from large containers to be processed in parallel by multiple processors. For example, apps can request changes from feeds by providing an initial starting point using the `ChangeFeedOptions.StartTime` field.

Moreover, the change feed can be processed in the same way as the *post insert/update trigger* but also can be extended to external services. For example, document changes are placed in the feed and trigger an Azure function. That function, for example, can process updates in the third-party system through the web API or modify records in Azure SQL Database. Azure Logic Apps can also be triggered to generate templated emails depending on the document modification in the change feed.

In other scenarios, you can use a change feed to control deleted documents. You can capture delete operations by configuring the document's *soft-delete* flag. Then, set the TTL feature for your document and wait for deletion to capture deletes.

Consistency levels

Previously, it was explained that Cosmos DB globally distributed a database that supports deployment in several regions. For this type of service, consistency is an especially important topic. Services with frequently updated instances can suffer from data loss if they spread across multiple regions. The main challenge is to make all transactions sync *as soon as possible* to protect a region from failing and ensure that all regions contain up-to-date data. Meanwhile, the performance of the operation should not suffer because of the need to wait until all regions have accepted a transaction.

There are five consistency levels developers can choose and each level has different availability and performance trade-offs:

- **Strong consistency** offers a linearizability guarantee. It guarantees the sequence of operations and that a read operation will return the latest values. When a user performs a write action on the primary database, it is duplicated to the replica instances. Only when all replicas have committed and confirmed the write operation is it committed (and visible) on the main replica.

- **Bounded staleness consistency** guarantees the sequence of operation, but operations are replicated asynchronously with a staleness window. This consistency level allows specifying maximum lag in operations or time.

- **Session consistency** allows a single client to execute updates and reads in its session including monotonic writes, monotonic reads, write-follows-reads, and read-your-writes. This level ensures that all operations inside a user session are monotonic and guaranteed to be consistent across primary and replica instances. The application can extract the token from the response header and provide the token for the next request.

- **Consistent prefix consistency** ensures that out-of-order writes are never seen by readers. This level has a shaky consistency but ensures that updates appear in replicas in the right order (as prefixes to other updates) and without gaps.

- **Eventual consistency** has the loosest consistency and effectively commits any write operation against the primary instantly. Replica transactions are made asynchronously and will eventually (over time) match the primary. It provides the highest speed since the primary database does not need to wait for replicas to commit before completing transactions.

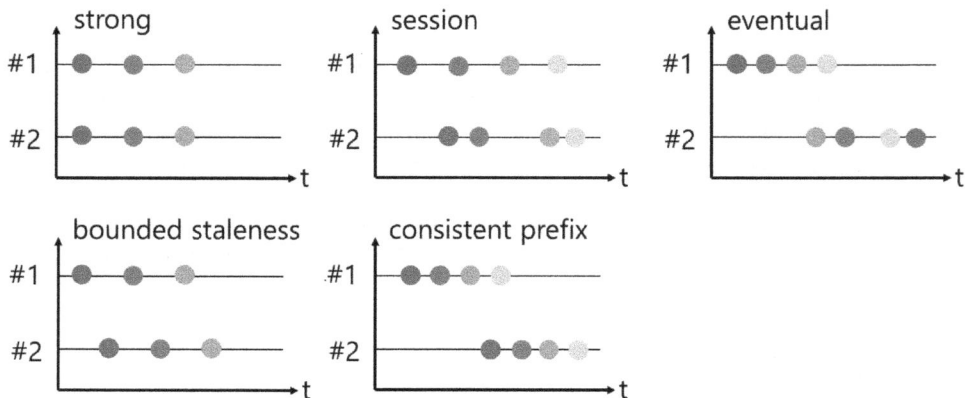

Figure 5.4 – Processing transactions for a globally distributed Cosmos DB account with two instances

The default consistency is set up at the container level and configured as *session consistency* to allow the clients to work in their sessions. This level can be changed manually or from code. The default consistency level inherits from the account to databases and to containers associated with that account. Be aware that the number of consistency levels might vary depending on the Cosmos DB API. The SQL API has five levels; another API might have only three. These levels are dictated by the original API's standards.

You can modify the default consistency level from the database account by selecting the **Default consistency** section.

Optimizing database performance and costs

There are a few options for optimizing performance and costs. Firstly, you need to provision optimal service. You can leverage the Consumption plan and Free tier. You also need to provision enough instances to meet the required availability. Each additional instance will multiply your total charge for the main instance. Remember the autoscale feature with Cosmos DB. Secondly, you need to perform request optimization and a recommendation will be provided shortly. Thirdly, you need to optimize transactional and backup storage to minimize costs. For many questions in the exams, you have to choose the optimal solution to meet the requirements and minimize cost.

Let us look at the first optimization aspect of selecting an appropriate throughput mode:

- **Dedicated provisioned throughput mode**: When each container has exclusive performance throughput. It works best if you spread your data between several containers and the application constantly queries all the containers with loads that are relatively similar.

- **Shared provisioned throughput mode**: When several containers in the same database share the provisioned throughput pool. This option can provide additional cost savings when your code exclusively works with only one of the containers, so that container will get more power. If you request documents from several containers at the same time, they must divide provisioned power between the containers. At the same time, you can create a container with provisioned or autoscale-exclusive throughput, which will not use the shared throughput pool.

When you provision a container's throughput, you can choose values from 400 to 1 million RUs, with a step of 100 RUs. All database operations will consume RUs, and the number is dependent on the operation type and the number of returned documents. You can monitor RUs for each of the requests you submit to the container. An RU represents the system resources (CPU, IOPS, and memory) that are used to perform the database operation. You can adjust the container throughput without interrupting the request working in the container. Remember, if you exceed the provisioned throughput with your requests, your request will fail and must be retried.

Cosmos DB accounts also support serverless throughput with unlimited RUs, charges based on consumption, and autoscale throughput, with help to adjust throughput based on demand and save costs. You can enable autoscaling on a single container and a database, and share it along all the containers in the database. In serverless mode, you do not have to provide any throughput when creating containers, but later, you get billed for the number of RUs that were consumed by your database operations.

Again, it is important to optimize queries to consume fewer RUs. You will pay less if you use serverless mode or don't hit the throughput limit when using provisioned mode. Just to be clear about consumed RUs, you can observe the query metadata and find out which request is optimal. For example, when only selecting the required fields, you will use fewer RUs than selecting all fields in a document. If you set up an appropriate filter for your request, you get fewer documents and use fewer RUs.

From a performance standpoint, it is faster to insert a bunch of documents than insert them one by one. It is also important to leverage the UDF and stored procedures to perform calculations on the database instead of the client application. Remember that the consistency level set up for your database can seriously affect the performance and consistency of the data. Strong consistency requires confirmation about completing all operations from all instances. Meanwhile, eventual consistency just submits and updates without waiting for a response, so your client application does not have to wait to submit another transaction. One more factor that can affect the performance of your database is *indexing*. Indexing will slow down updates – that is why when you are submitting a batch of documents, it is worth temporarily turning off indexes and putting them back after batch completion.

For storage and capacity optimization, be aware that the **reserved capacity** option is available for Cosmos DB, as for storage accounts or reserved VM instances. You can save up to 65% on pay-as-you-go prices with 1-year or 3-year reserved capacity options. The backup size and amount of persisted backups can also affect the capacity cost and need to be set up to the appropriate requirements.

Summary

In this chapter, you learned about Cosmos DB, which is the best NoSQL service available in Azure. Azure Cosmos DB provides a convenient way to store JSON documents with indexing and query capabilities through a RESTful interface.

Cosmos DB is a unique service available for provisioned and serverless throughput with autoscale settings. The horizontal and vertical scale will let your solution adjust performance to the needs of the application and save cost. From a cost-saving perspective, Azure Cosmos DB provides a Free tier, with one instance deployed per subscription with provisioned throughput. Meanwhile, throughput can significantly affect the total cost, and developers can monitor current use and optimize queries by decreasing throughput consumption, which is measured in RUs.

Cosmos DB supports several APIs to simplify *lift-and-shift* scenarios for customers moving from the IaaS to PaaS model. Cosmos DB can be provisioned with the Core (SQL), Cassandra, Gremlin API, and API for MongoDB. Meanwhile, the Azure Table API allows developers to migrate to Cosmos DB from the storage account and leverage a managed scalability model. The SQL API provides the best experience for developers using their SQL skills to query indexed documents. The SQL API also supports stored procedures, triggers, and functions developed on powerful JavaScript.

High availability is another benefit of Cosmos DB. An SLA level of up to 99.999% can be reached out of the box by the Cosmos DB service, provisioned in regions chosen by customers. It is also possible to build more than one instance of the database and allow multi-writes. Five different consistency levels will control updates on multi-instance databases and let you choose between the level of consistency and throughput.

This chapter has familiarized you with the NoSQL services provided by Azure, including Azure Table Storage and Azure Cosmos DB. You have learned about the main use case scenarios with Azure Table Storage and Cosmos DB. By now, you should know how to configure Azure NoSQL services, how to get connected from code, how to protect data, and how to avoid data loss. If you are going to take the AZ-204 exam, it's important to understand the principles of the NoSQL solution and its implementation in Azure.

In *Chapter 6, Developing Solutions That Use Azure Blob Storage*, we will continue to discuss data storage technology and look at the PaaS Azure Blob storage designed for persisting files. You will learn how to upload, download, search through metadata, and protect blobs in an Azure storage account.

Questions

1. Which APIs are supported by Cosmos DB?
2. What is the difference between a composite index and a range index?
3. What is the default Cosmos DB backup option?
4. Can you execute the Cosmos DB trigger from the Azure portal?
5. What language is used for storage procedures?

Further reading

- You can find recommendations about the optimal design of your Azure Table Storage, including partition and scale, here: https://docs.microsoft.com/en-us/azure/storage/tables/table-storage-design.

- If you want to get more information about the APIs supported by Cosmos DB, visit the following link: https://docs.microsoft.com/en-us/azure/cosmos-db/choose-api.

- You can read more about consistency levels at the following links:

  - https://docs.microsoft.com/en-us/azure/cosmos-db/consistency-levels

  - https://docs.microsoft.com/en-us/azure/cosmos-db/sql/how-to-manage-consistency

- You can learn details about change feeds for Cosmos DB here: `https://docs.microsoft.com/en-us/azure/cosmos-db/change-feed`.

- If you are interested in scaling, throughput units, and a serverless mode for Cosmos DB, visit the following link: `https://docs.microsoft.com/en-us/azure/cosmos-db/request-units`.

- Always Encrypted protection for Cosmos DB is introduced at the following link: `https://docs.microsoft.com/en-us/azure/cosmos-db/how-to-always-encrypted?tabs=dotnet`.

- Indexing policies are discussed at the following link: `https://docs.microsoft.com/en-us/azure/cosmos-db/index-policy#indexing-mode`.

- To get details about how partitioning works in Cosmos DB, follow this link: `https://docs.microsoft.com/en-us/azure/cosmos-db/partitioning-overview#physical-partitions`.

6

Developing Solutions That Use Azure Blob Storage

In this chapter, we are going to focus on a specific type of storage hosted in Azure to persist unstructured and semi-structured data called **Azure Blob Storage**. For a better understanding of the role of blob storage in a modern cloud application, you need to be aware of the general features of an **Azure storage account**, features such as tables, queues, files, and blobs.

Azure Blob Storage is the main part of an Azure storage account and is designed to persist and synchronize the state of processes in your solution. Internally in Azure, it is also extensively used. For example, Azure virtual machines persist files in Azure Blob Storage, content delivery networks can load static content from Azure Blob Storage, Azure App Services store log files in blobs, and Azure SQL Database keeps backups in Azure Blob Storage.

Later in the chapter, we will familiarize ourselves with the programmatic way to communicate with Azure Blob Storage to persist files with different formats such as JSON objects, PDFs, images, videos, and other binary files. You will learn how to create an account and upload or download files into it. You will also learn about high availability, performance, tiers, and price modes, and get hands-on experience in developing applications for Azure Blob Storage.

This chapter covers the following topics:

- Exploring Azure Blob Storage
- Manipulation with blobs and containers
- Managing metadata and security settings for storage accounts

Technical requirements

The code files for this chapter can be downloaded from `https://github.com/PacktPublishing/Developing-Solutions-for-Microsoft-Azure-AZ-204-Exam-Guide/tree/main/Chapter06`.

Code in Action videos for this chapter: `https://bit.ly/3dtxhU8`

Exploring Azure Blob Storage

Azure Blob Storage is the most important part of the Azure storage account and one of the oldest existing Azure services. Back in the day when the Azure classic services were released to customers, only a couple of services existed: VMs and storage to persist VM disks. Originally, Azure Storage was set up to persist large files, that were gigabytes in size, and provide random access to them. Now, most VM disks have already moved to managed disks but a storage account is still used to persist files – for example, *backups*, *logs*, and *performance metrics*. Modern Azure storage accounts are designed for persisting semi-structured data in tables and JSON files in blobs. Blobs are also good for persisting binary or unstructured data such as media, documents, or encrypted content. Azure storage accounts provide enormous resiliency, high availability, and strong security. Moreover, they are quite easy to connect and operate from code. You'll probably have a hard time finding a modern cloud solution that does not use Azure Blob Storage. So, why is this service so popular? Let's take a look.

Provisioning an Azure storage account

There are several ways that we can store things in Azure. We can create things called storage accounts and inside of a storage account, we can put files and **binary large objects** (or **blob**s). You can create different storage accounts for different purposes – you could put certain types of things in one storage account and other things in other storage accounts. You can use some level of organization to create a storage account, or rather, establish certain rules around how you create a storage account.

Azure storage accounts provide Web API access to files stored in data centers. When you provision blob storage, you need to choose the region where the files will be located. Let us imagine that your application is set up to broadcast recorded TV shows. Most of your customers are on the east coast of the US, so you can provision storage accounts in the East US data center and your users will have low-latency access to the files from the east coast of the US. What would you do if customers from the west coast or the central US would like to watch these shows? They must wait longer. Fortunately, we can provision geo-redundant storage accounts located in two regions and synchronize them. This helps to minimize latency.

The structure of Azure Blob Storage

Before we move on to the important aspects of availability and performance, let us look at the structure of Azure Blob Storage. When you start provisioning any storage in Azure, a storage account needs to be created first. The name must be DNS-unique and provided only in lowercase letters and numbers. Then, you need to create a container (or folder) for your files. Remember that Azure Blob Storage does not support container (folder) nesting and does not provide a hierarchical structure. Meanwhile, you are still able to use virtual folders in the path when you upload files to better organize the files in the container. The last step is to upload your files to the container to receive the URL with the filename to access the file if the container provides public access. The following schema represents the Azure storage account structure:

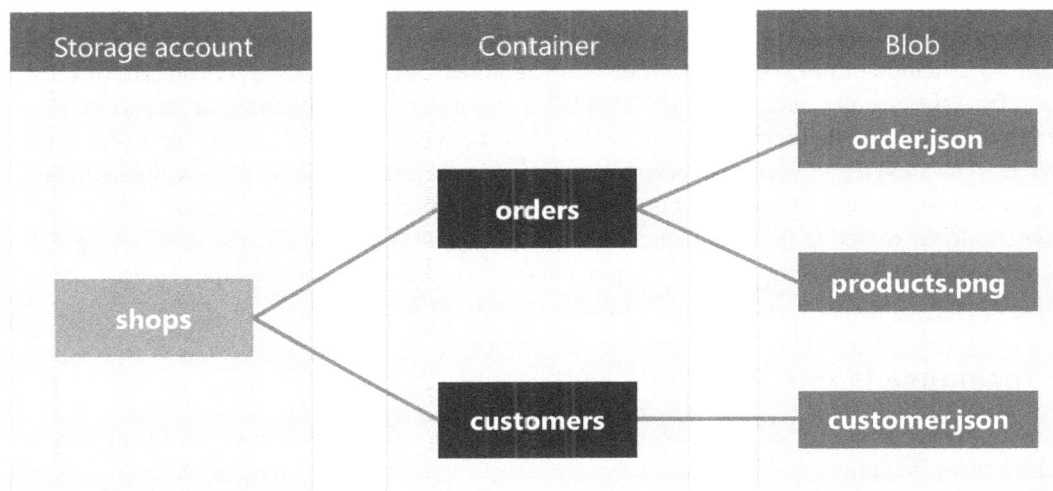

Figure 6.1 – The Azure storage account structure

From a security standpoint, the container you create to store uploaded blobs can be configured with a **private access level** (no anonymous access), so only users or apps with admin keys can get access to files. Alternatively, you can allow public access to blobs by configuring a container with a **blob access level** (with anonymous read access to the precise blob only) or with a **container access level** (with anonymous read access to all the blobs in the container). The public access models are useful if you are just storing image files referenced from your web portal. To access private files, you are required to obtain admin keys. Two admin access keys are generated per storage account and can be used for administrative operations including provisioning containers, uploading files, and cleaning up content. These keys should not be used by applications and applications should access the Azure storage account by using a **shared access signature** (**SAS**), as will be discussed in *Chapter 7, Implementing User Authentication and Authorization*. Another way of accessing the Azure storage account is through **role-based access control** (**RBAC**), as will be discussed in *Chapter 8, Implementing Secure Cloud Solutions*. For example, if you have read data access to a storage account, then you can read the blobs within that storage account.

High availability and durability

How safe is your data? Azure Blob storage provides 99.99999999% (11 nines) of durability achieved by three copies of your data being stored on different hardware and sometimes in different physical buildings. So, if one of the copies is lost because of a hardware failure, Azure always has a copy of your data and can restore it.

From an **availability** standpoint, Azure Storage provides several levels of redundancy in the primary region's **Locally-Redundant Storage (LRS)** and **Zone-Redundant Storage (ZRS)**. Zone redundancy always keeps a copy of your data in different buildings and each building will have a separate source of power and internet, so your data is well protected. Moreover, Azure can offer redundancy in a second region where another three copies of your data can be stored. For a second region, you can use only paired data centers – for example, East US-West US. You can choose **Geo-Redundant Storage (GRS)** and its twin, **Geo-Zone-Redundant Storage (GZRS)**. You can also choose **Read-Access Geo-Redundant Storage (RA-GRS)** if you need read access to the copy in the second region. This flexible schema will protect your application from data loss, should a data center experience an outage – access will automatically be routed to the second geo-redundant copy. It is useful in the case of accessing TV shows from the opposite coast of the US as previously discussed. Unfortunately, the geo-redundant options are more expensive than local redundancy from a cost standpoint.

Performance levels

Azure storage accounts provide two levels of performance: *Standard (v2)* and *Premium*. The premium level has many limitations and is expensive. For example, if you want to use the Azure Queue Storage or Table Storage service, you have to use the *Standard* level. The *Premium* level should be selected if storage performance is a key parameter. Premium storage provides an extra performance level. It can only be created with a single data center based on high-performance **solid-state drives (SSD)**.

Pricing models

When you provision storage accounts, the pricing model depends on redundancy parameters (for example, LRS, ZRS, and GRS) and performance tiers (*Premium* and *Standard*). It also depends on the capacity of data you are going to store and the number of transactions you use for data operations. In terms of data movement operations, leaving the data center also incurs an extra charge. In other words, you can upload files from on-premises for free but you must pay to download files. Moving files between data centers, including geo-redundant synchronizations, will also incur a charge because the data always lives in one of the data centers. Be aware of this when you choose your storage architecture. Please also refer to the **Azure Pricing Calculator** for further details.

Storage access tiers

You can also achieve some cost savings if you select the appropriate access tier for your files (**Hot**, **Cool**, or **Archive**). For example, log files are accessed often and can generate a lot of read-write transactions. For this type of file, it is better to select the *Hot* tier. The *Hot* tier has the highest cost for storage and the lowest cost for transactions. On other occasions, your image files can go days without being accessed. You can move them to the *Cool* tier (cold storage) to minimize the capacity cost but transactions will be more expensive. Remember to keep your files in the Cool storage tier for at least 30 days. Rarely accessed data should be stored in the *Archive* tier, which is the cheapest tier for capacity. Unfortunately, the transaction cost on the tier is quite high and you must keep files at least

180 days before deletion. Moreover, you might have to wait to download files from the *Archive* tier longer than usual because files are physically persisted on magnetic tape. You can find more details about cost optimization using access tiers at the end of this chapter.

Blob types

Choosing the *Standard* or *Premium* tier controls performance at the account level and some adjustments can also be applied on the blob level. Blob types, when used appropriately, can improve performance for specific scenarios.

The blob storage service offers three types of blobs: *block blobs*, *append blobs*, and *page blobs*. When you create a blob, you specify the blob type and it cannot be changed after creation. Each blob type is designed to handle specific types of objects in storage and provide the best access speed based on usage patterns:

- **Block blobs** let you upload blobs efficiently by composing blocks of data. Each block is identified individually and you can create or modify a block blob by updating a set of blocks by their IDs. A block blob can include up to 50,000 different-size blocks up to a maximum of 400 MB. Meanwhile, the maximum size of a block blob is limited to 4.75 TB. Block blobs are the default blob type and can be applied for storing images, documents, and configuration files. Moreover, only block blobs have the option to configure the blob access tier.

- **Page blobs** are designed for improving random access and are ideal for storing virtual hard disks. Each blob is a combination of 512-byte pages optimized for random read and write operations. When writing to a page blob, it can overwrite just one page and commit writes immediately, so it suits making frequent updates to virtual hard disks. The maximum size for a page blob is about 8 TB.

- **Append blobs** are optimized for append operations such as adding a new line in the logs. The type comprises blocks, and when it modifies an append blob, blocks are added to the end of the blob only through the *append block operation*. The maximum size of the append blob is about 195 GB. This type of blob is ideal for tracing and logging workloads.

Leveraging the Azure CLI to provision an Azure storage account

By now, you already know enough to build your Azure storage from the Azure portal or by using CLI commands. The code at the following URL will provision storage accounts and create a container with public access. We'll also retrieve admin keys for your storage account and upload image files to the container. Finally, you can retrieve the link to get public access to the file. Please copy your account name and the connection string provided in the output for the next demos. Alternatively, you can also complete all these tasks from the Azure portal:

```
https://github.com/PacktPublishing/Developing-Solutions-for-Microsoft-
Azure-AZ-204-Exam-Guide/blob/main/Chapter06/1-provision/demo.azcli
```

Data protection

When you have built your storage account, check out the additional features available from the portal:

- **Point-in-time restore** is used to restore one or more containers to an earlier state. If the point-in-time restore feature is enabled, then the versioning, change feed, and blob soft delete features must also be enabled to keep track of the changes.

- **Soft delete** for blobs and containers enables you to recover blobs that were previously marked for deletion, including blobs that were overwritten, for seven days by default.

- **Versioning** for blobs and feeds allows the use of versioning to automatically maintain previous versions of your blobs for recovery and restoration.

Static websites

You can enable your storage account to host HTML pages and static content. Web pages can include static images, styles, and client-side scripting – for example, JavaScript. When you enable this feature, the storage account will create a $web container where you can upload the static content and pages. Furthermore, you can provide the name of the default page (for example, index.html) and the name of the page for the file-not-found error. Server-side code such as **.NET** is not supported.

When you enable the setting, the URL for your static website will be available for requests for HTTP and HTTPS. If you create a geo-replicated account, you also receive the secondary endpoint.

In the following script, you will create another account in another data center for a static website in addition to the account you built before. Then, by executing the commands at the following URL, you can enable a static website and upload pages. Finally, you can test how the website works:

```
https://github.com/PacktPublishing/Developing-Solutions-for-Microsoft-
Azure-AZ-204-Exam-Guide/blob/main/Chapter06/2-static-web/demo.azcli
```

After completing all the commands from the script, you will notice that the home page of the site has a missing image. That will be fixed by the next script by syncing your first and second accounts. The script should be executed on local bash because it references the files in the folder. When you complete script execution, please copy and save the account name from the output for further reference.

You are already experienced with the main Azure Blob Storage services. You can provision a blob, upload files by using the Azure CLI, and establish a static website with your Azure storage account. You have also learned how to choose the optimal performance and access levels and select the appropriate availability level. You should now also be familiar with the security and data protection features. Now, you know a lot about Azure storage accounts, but it is not enough to leverage accounts from code. Let's look at how we can implement main operations with blobs and containers, which you have already learned about in theory.

Manipulation with blobs and containers

When we develop a solution to work with Azure Blob Storage, we mainly focus on uploading, downloading, and searching through blobs and their content. To complete these operations, you can execute the Azure CLI and PowerShell commands. You can also leverage direct REST calls. Those options are available but require tons of development time to code the operations you need. The better option is included in your project's SDKs available for C#, Python, Java, Node.js, and many other popular languages. The SDKs have already been tested and provide easy-to-adopt algorithms to implement main blob operations.

With SDKs, you can easily implement the container operations listed as follows:

- Creating and deleting a container
- Managing public access (at private, blob, and container access level)
- Managing container metadata (setting and reading attributes)
- Leasing a container (establishing and managing leases)
- Listing blobs (getting the list of the filenames in the container)
- Restoring a container (with the required soft delete settings enabled)

The SDKs can also help you to implement the following blob operations:

- Uploading and downloading blobs
- Deleting and undeleting blobs
- Replacing blobs
- Leasing blobs (establishing and managing leases)
- Copying or cloning blobs (including moving blobs between Azure data centers)
- Managing the metadata and tags of blobs
- Snapshotting blobs (creating a copy of a blob with the current state)
- Changing the blob tier
- Finding blobs by tags

When you leverage SDKs for implementing operations from code, there are several tools, services, and extensions to help you manage your storage account and monitor the changes you made from code:

- **Azure Storage Explorer**: A multi-OS Windows application that allows you to perform all the operations with an Azure storage account, including blobs and generating SAS. It is a free Microsoft tool available for download and installation. The equivalent of the explorer exists in the Azure portal and can be used through a web interface.

- **Azure Tools** or **Azure Storage Explorer** for **Visual Studio Code**: This allows you to access your storage account and observe containers and then upload and download files from it.

- **The AzCopy tool**: The console application allows you to leverage the full throughput of your internet connection by creating multiple threads for download and upload. This is an ideal tool for the manipulation of large files such as videos or hard disks.

- The **Import/Export service** and **Data Box**: This can be leveraged for the affordable physical movement of data between your on-premises storage and Azure data centers because you pay only for the shipping of the physical device.

Leveraging AzCopy for data transfer between storage accounts

In the following script, we will implement the operation of moving files between storage accounts with the AzCopy tool. You need to install the AzCopy tool locally and run the commands to transfer the logo file from the first account created previously to the second account where you built the static website. Please execute commands from the following script to be consistent with the next C# code example:

```
https://github.com/PacktPublishing/Developing-Solutions-for-Microsoft-Azure-AZ-204-Exam-Guide/blob/main/Chapter06/3-copy/demo.azcli
```

Implementing basic operations from C# code

Now, we can focus on the SDK packages available for .NET Core. The demo code at the following URL will create a container with an Azure storage account – then, it will upload and download files from the container. Please pay attention to the connection string for your storage account located at the top of the C# code file. Your connection string was retrieved from previous demo scripts. Alternatively, the connection string can be located in the **Access Keys** section of the Azure storage account on the Azure portal. Be aware that the connection string contains an admin key with full access to the account:

```
https://github.com/PacktPublishing/Developing-Solutions-for-Microsoft-Azure-AZ-204-Exam-Guide/tree/main/Chapter06/4-sdk-upload
```

The following table explains the classes used for accessing the Azure Blob Storage in the code example:

Class	Description
BlobServiceClient	Allows you to perform some operations with the blob storage including enumerating containers. The instance of the class needs to be configured with a connection string before doing operations with containers.
BlobContainerClient	Allows you to perform all operations with containers including creating, deleting, and enumerating blobs. The instance of the class needs to be configured from the exact `BlobServiceClient` instance by providing a container name.

BlobClient	Allows you to perform all operations with blobs including uploading, downloading, and deleting. The instance of the class needs to be configured from the exact `BlobContainerClient` instance by providing a blob name.

Table 6.1 – C# SDK classes for implementing operations with blobs

You just learned how to implement basic operations with blobs and containers from code and the Azure CLI. The next step is to maintain advanced settings to improve security and performance and reduce the cost of the solution. You will also learn how to leverage tags and metadata to quickly find the file you need to download.

Managing metadata and security settings for storage accounts

Let us return to the connection string you used from the previous code project. A connection string including an admin key should not be used for connection in the production environment. Configuring RBAC for resources also can help with accessing the Azure storage account. The safer option is generating SAS tokens and leveraging them to connect from code or scripts. Remember that an admin key provides high-level access and if revealed by hackers, may damage your data. The same can happen if you generate a SAS key with full permissions (you should follow the principle of least privilege).

To avoid a security breach of your storage account, you should not hardcode the keys in the code or store them in the configuration file. Microsoft recommends using Azure Key Vault to store connection information (such as the *connection string*, *SAS*, or *admin keys*). Moreover, the principle of least privilege should be applied to applications that manage storage accounts. The *SAS* technology will help granularly set up access to the Azure storage account and its content. The admin keys used for the management of the storage account can be rotated by manually switching your application from the primary to the secondary key and regenerating the primary key.

There is also an option to monitor key activities from selected storage accounts by configuring Azure Monitor and setting up alerts. Configuring security settings for Azure storage accounts is the responsibility of the customer. There are a few options that can help you to manage the security settings of your storage account, which we will discuss now.

Encryption

To implement encryption at rest, storage accounts are encrypted by default using **Azure Storage Service Encryption** (**SSE**). Encryption affects performance slightly but protects your data stored in the Azure Blob service. SSE is the only available and recommended option for encrypting storage accounts. However, you can decide which keys should be used for encryption: Microsoft keys or your own keys. When you configure encryption, you can choose keys managed by Microsoft, keys hosted by Azure Key Vault, or by third-party services. You also can manage the identity used by your storage account to access the key vault. Another tier of encryption can be supported at the file level. Files can be explicitly encrypted with available services such as **Azure Rights Management (Azure RMS)** or by leveraging SDKs.

For implementing encryption in transit, you have the option to use HTTP and HTTPS connections and only force an HTTPS connection with an Azure certificate. The HTTPS option is not applied when you use a custom domain name registered with your storage account.

Firewalls

Azure Blob Storage offers a layered security model to enable control and management of access to storage accounts from applications and Azure infrastructure and platform services. When firewall rules are configured, apps can request data over the specified set of networks or through the specified set of Azure resources. There is an option to limit access to your storage account from specified IP addresses and IP ranges.

On the Azure portal, you can configure storage accounts to allow access only from specific **VNets**. The allowed subnets or VNets can belong to the same subscription or different subscriptions. You can also enable a service endpoint to allow access from specific Azure services. Initially, when you deploy a storage account, the firewall rules are turned off. When you turn on the rules, it blocks all incoming requests for data by default unless the requests are sent by an allowed service or VNet. When you block requests, it includes access from other Azure services, the Azure portal, and telemetry services.

Metadata and tags

If you store a substantial number of files in a storage account, finding a specific blob is a non-trivial task. **Blob index tags** can simplify the process and provide the ability to manage *metadata* by using key-value pairs and indexed tags.

Metadata allows you to store company-specific data for your files such as department names and owner contacts. This data can be retrieved without downloading blobs programmatically, which reduces charges and improves the performance of search tasks. The metadata can be modified from the portal as well and is available for containers and blobs. Blobs do not inherit container metadata and can provide their metadata as a key-value structure. The blob context and its metadata can be indexed using **Azure Cognitive Services** and can be searched for using Web API requests.

Searching through blobs and their metadata requires using the indexing services explicitly provisioned in Azure. Meanwhile, searching through indexed tags of blobs is provided by the Azure Storage service. You can categorize and find objects within a single or multiple containers by making a search request and leveraging SDK objects to retrieve the corresponding blobs. If the object is modified or its index tag is modified, the object updates its index and remains searchable. The index will let your application find blobs that correspond to specific contexts – for example, orders by customer name or products related to a specific category.

Retrieving metadata by using C# code

From the code example at the following URL, you will learn how to store files in an Azure storage account with metadata and tags. You will also learn how to set up metadata and retrieve it from containers and blobs. Finally, the code demonstrates how to search through indexed tags and find the blob you need.

Note that you need to retrieve the connection string for your storage account and update it towards the top of the code. Your connection string can be retrieved from previous demos and is located in the **Keys** section of the account on the Azure portal. If you copy settings from the portal, you need to copy the **Connection string** value, not just **Key** value. Be aware that the string contains an admin key to allow full access to the account:

```
https://github.com/PacktPublishing/Developing-Solutions-for-Microsoft-
Azure-AZ-204-Exam-Guide/tree/main/Chapter06/5-sdk-meta
```

The following table explains the classes used for accessing metadata from Azure Blob Storage in the code example:

Class	Description
BlobClientOptions	Provides the client configuration options for connecting to Azure Blob Storage, including buffering, versioning, and retry attempts. This class will also help to retrieve geo-redundant secondary URLs.
BlobUploadOptions	Provides the configuration settings for blobs during the upload process. Includes settings for access tier metadata and transfer options to manage the upload process.

Table 6.2 – C# SDK classes for manipulating blob metadata

Life cycle management and optimizing costs

From the previous chapter, you will know that objects in blob storage, specifically in standard storage, have a different level of access to be both efficient in terms of space and efficient in terms of the cost of storing massive amounts of information. In the *Standard* storage account, we can store our data in the *Hot*, *Cool*, or *Archive* access tiers. A *Premium* storage account has only a *Hot* tier available.

As a rule, *hot data* is frequently accessed data and is stored for the notably short period of fewer than 30 days. For this type of file, we can efficiently use the *Hot* tier. For the *Cool* tier, we are going to write the data and not read it immediately. For example, backup files would be a suitable candidate for *Cool* storage. Meanwhile, rarely accessed data to be stored for over six months would be good a candidate for *Archive* storage. Effectively, based on the frequency with which you access your data, you can define whether the item should be stored in the *Hot*, *Cool*, or *Archive* tier. You can modify the blob tier from a storage account on the Azure portal or, better, set up a life cycle policy to migrate files from the *Hot* tier to the *Cool* or *Archive* tier, and finally be deleted. This is extremely useful for logs and backup retention.

You can create life cycle policy rules to apply to the objects within your storage account and automatically move your blobs from one layer or from one type of storage to another, and then blobs can be moved according to the rules. In a *Premium* account, you can only delete files by setting up a life cycle policy. When you configure life cycle policy deletion, remember the requirements from the storage account to store files on the *Archive* tier for at least 180 days and 30 days on the *Cool* tier to avoid cost penalties.

You can export rules and import rules using JSON. You can build a set of rules and then access those rules from the portal. You also can apply rules programmatically by using an SDK.

In the following schema, you can see how the life cycle policy can help to migrate files from different access tiers. By creating policy rules, you can migrate blobs between the *Hot*, *Cool*, and *Archive* access tiers, and then delete them. From the *Premium* performance tier, you can only delete files because the *Hot*, *Cool*, and *Archive* access tiers are not available in the *Premium* tier:

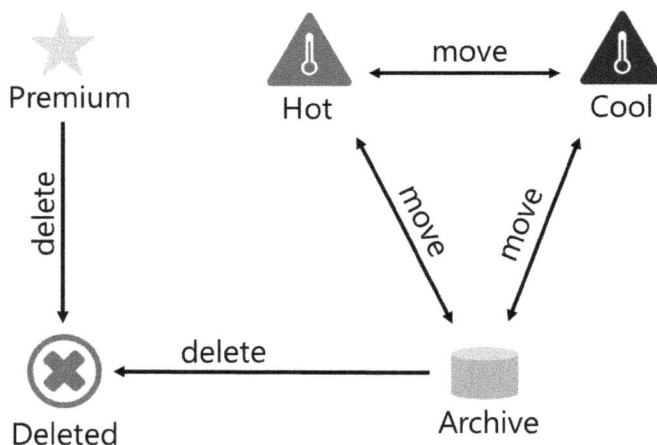

Figure 6.2 – File migration between tiers with the life cycle management policy

Cost savings

Let us look at pricing. The best tool for it is the **Azure Pricing Calculator**. Storage containers are commonly used resources in Azure subscriptions. Storage accounts are often deployed for logging (*VMs* and *Azure Functions*), persisting temporary data purposes (*Cloud Shell*), and site recovery transactions (*Azure Site Recovery*). After a few years of subscribing, the total charges for storage accounts can become significant, and controlling charges is important for any organization.

Charges for storage accounts can be split into three parts: *capacity*, *transactions*, and *data transfer*. Charges for the capacity of files, blobs, tables, queues, and other objects that you store in storage accounts can easily be calculated from Azure Monitor's storage account metrics and can be observed on historical charts. The capacity charges for *Standard* storage accounts depend on the tier, with the *Hot* tier having the highest charge. Meanwhile, the capacity charges for *Premium* storage accounts are even greater than for the *Hot* tier of *Standard* storage accounts. There are a few options for saving money on capacity – for example, appropriately changing tiers for files you store and deleting files you do not need anymore. A life cycle policy will help you move files between tiers and delete them after the retention period; another useful option to save costs is reserved capacity. Reserved capacity can help you to save up to 30% if you commit to a specific amount of storage data per month. Reserved capacity works similarly to **reserved instances**.

The second type of charge for storage accounts is *transaction* charges. These relate to the charges incurred when reading and writing blob files. They are usually billed in bulk in the hundreds and depend on the access tier. *Hot* tier transactions are the cheapest and *Archive* tier transactions are the most expensive for *Standard* storage. You don't have much control over transactions for storage accounts but deleting unused files will help you to decrease the number of them. You can also minimize transaction costs by reducing requests from code. For example, listing the blobs in a container will generate a transaction that can be replaced if you know the filename that you want to access.

The third type of charge for a storage account is for *data transfer* for files downloaded from the data center. You can upload files to the Azure Blob Storage service for free, but you must pay for any transfer from or between data centers in Azure. This cost depends on the size of the files and the region in which the requested data is downloaded. The transfer charge can be avoided by using the Import/Export service by shipping a storage disk directly to the customer from the Azure data center.

Summary

In this chapter, we explored the Azure Blob Storage service and learned about how to configure the service properly to achieve optimal performance and costs. You learned about the main features, including security, data protection, access, and the manipulation of blobs. Now that you are familiar with the provisioning process and blob manipulation operations, you can leverage Azure Blob Storage from code and persist your files in an Azure storage account to build a robust and reliable cloud solution.

Azure Storage is one of the oldest and most frequently used services for Azure deployments. It is provisioned as part of many solutions and is used for storing files of several types, including binary and semi-structured data. It supports a RESTful interface and can even host static websites or work as content storage for dynamic websites. A storage account can be provisioned with a *Standard* or *Premium* pricing tier with *Hot*, *Cool*, and *Archive* access tiers for files. A storage account results in charges for subscription owners based on capacity, transactions, and data transfer.

From a security standpoint, an Azure storage account allows public and private access to blobs and containers. It also allows you to filter network traffic based on firewall rules and can exclusively provide access to Azure virtual networks. Storage accounts support RBAC assignments and integration with

Azure Active Directory. Meanwhile, access to blobs by an application can be provided with admin keys or SAS. A storage account can be encrypted in a data center and can be limited to access only by HTTPS.

For development projects, access to storage accounts can be configured and managed with connection strings and SDKs that are available for Python, C#, Node.js, and Java. Storage accounts can persist data and metadata with files and allow you to search through indexed tags to quickly find the exact blobs you need. Usually, developers leverage storage accounts to store images, scripts, and static data, including JSON serialized objects. The SDK classes provide a wide variety of operations for storage accounts, containers, and blob manipulation by wrapping REST requests.

Overall, Azure Blob Storage provides affordable and reliable storage for files in the cloud with up to a 99.99% (4 nines) SLA. Geo-redundant storage can protect your application from data availability loss by providing read access to copies of files in paired data centers.

In *Chapter 7, Implement User Authentication and Authorization*, you will learn about implementing Azure security to better secure your solution in Azure and integrating with Azure Active Directory to leverage strong authentication and authorization protocols.

Questions

1.   How can you increase the availability of the Azure Blob Storage service?

2.   What features are available to protect data from deletion?

3.   Can you leverage an SDK to read blob metadata without downloading the blob?

4.   Can we migrate blobs between access tiers automatically?

5.   What type of data can be persisted in blobs?

Further reading

- You can learn more about the access tiers of blobs here:

  https://docs.microsoft.com/en-us/azure/storage/blobs/access-tiers-overview.

- You can find out more details about data protection algorithms, including soft delete and versioning, here:

  https://docs.microsoft.com/en-us/azure/storage/blobs/data-protection-overview.

- You can find more Azure CLI commands for implementing blob operations here:

  https://docs.microsoft.com/en-us/azure/storage/blobs/storage-samples-blobs-cli.

- You can learn further details about provisioning static websites with a storage account here:

  `https://docs.microsoft.com/en-us/azure/storage/blobs/storage-blob-static-website`.

- If you are interested in configuring metadata for blobs, indexing, and searching through values, you can find the details here:

  `https://docs.microsoft.com/en-us/azure/search/search-blob-storage-integration`.

- You can find more about how versioning is supported in a storage account here:

  `https://docs.microsoft.com/en-us/azure/storage/blobs/versioning-overview`.

- The following article explains the best practices for using SAS:

  `https://docs.microsoft.com/en-us/azure/storage/common/storage-sas-overview#best-practices-when-using-sas`.

Part 3: Implementing Azure Security

This part introduces the key security concepts relevant to developing solutions for Azure. We start with an introduction to the Microsoft identity platform, discussing service principals, permissions, consent types, and conditional access. We also cover the Microsoft Authentication Library, Microsoft Graph, and shared access signatures. We look at how to implement Azure Key Vault to securely and centrally manage secrets, including authorization and authentication with Key Vault, before moving on to the topic of managed identities, and finishing with an exploration of Azure App Configuration, including the management of feature flags within the App Configuration service.

This part covers 20-25% of the AZ-204 exam questions.

The following chapters will be covered under this section:

- *Chapter 7, Implementing User Authentication and Authorization*
- *Chapter 8, Implementing Secure Cloud Solutions*

7

Implementing User Authentication and Authorization

Identity management has evolved a long way from basic usernames and passwords, as have those who wish to compromise user accounts. Nowadays, there are so many considerations and complexities to authentication and authorization that creating your own solution tends not to be the best option.

In this chapter, we will explore the features and services that Microsoft offers to help developers handle user authentication and authorization without the need to create their own solutions. We'll start by exploring the **Microsoft identity platform** and covering the core features for controlling access to your resources. We'll then learn how to implement authentication using the **Microsoft Authentication Library** (**MSAL**), before moving on to **Microsoft Graph** and some of the ways it can help enhance your apps. We'll finish with a look at **shared access signatures** (**SAS**) for authorizing access to storage resources.

By the end of this chapter, you will understand which features and services are available to you from Microsoft for handling user authentication and authorization within your apps.

In this chapter, we'll cover the following main topics:

- Understanding the Microsoft identity platform
- Implementing authentication with the Microsoft Authentication Library
- Discovering Microsoft Graph
- Using shared access signatures

Technical requirements

To follow along with the exercises in this chapter, you will need the following:

- The latest .NET SDK: `https://dotnet.microsoft.com/download`
- Visual Studio Code: `https://code.visualstudio.com/Download`
- The code samples for this chapter can be found here: `https://github.com/PacktPublishing/Developing-Solutions-for-Microsoft-Azure-AZ-204-Exam-Guide/tree/main/Chapter07`

Code in Action videos for this chapter: `https://bit.ly/3RWeZcZ`

Understanding the Microsoft identity platform

Nowadays, there are open standards such as **OAuth 2.0** and **OpenID Connect** (**OIDC**) to help with handling user authentication and authorization, but even these have many complexities, especially when considering more than just a username and password – multi-factor authentication and conditional access, for example. The Microsoft identity platform provides several tools to help developers implement user authentication and authorization and does the heavy lifting for you.

We first made use of the Microsoft identity platform when we enabled authentication in *Chapter 3, Creating Azure App Service Web Apps*. At that point, we mentioned that we would discuss the details later, and here we are. As we saw in that chapter, the Microsoft identity platform helps to create applications that users can sign in to with their Microsoft work or school accounts, personal Microsoft accounts, as well as social or local accounts.

The Microsoft identity platform is built on top of the open standards previously mentioned: OIDC for authentication and OAuth 2.0 for authorization. OIDC is built on top of OAuth 2.0, so there are similarities between the two with regard to terminology and flow. Out of the box, the platform supports advanced security features such as multi-factor authentication, passwordless sign-in, single sign-on, and more, without the need for you to implement the functionality yourself. If your application is integrated with the Microsoft identity platform, you can natively take advantage of all the features on offer.

The platform contains multiple open source libraries (such as the **MSAL**) for various languages, and because it uses standards-compliant implementations of OAuth 2.0 and OIDC, it supports bringing in your own standards-compliant libraries as well. It also has a registration and configuration experience within the Azure portal, as well as the ability to programmatically configure your applications using the Microsoft Graph API and PowerShell.

Something we deferred discussing in depth until now when we enabled authentication on our web app was the **Azure Active Directory** (**AAD**) objects that are required for your applications to delegate identity and access management functions to AAD. Let's discuss those now.

Service principals

In order to delegate functions to AAD, your application needs to be registered with an AAD tenant, which creates an identity configuration for your application that allows integration with AAD. When we register an application, we control whether it's intended to be a single tenant app (only accessible within the AAD tenant in which you're creating the registration, also known as the **home tenant**) or a multi-tenant app (accessible from other AAD tenants as well).

You may remember from when we previously enabled authentication on the web app that we had an entry in **App registrations** and an entry in **Enterprise applications** within the Azure portal. We'll quickly go over each of these now:

- When you register an application with AAD, an **application object** is created within the home tenant, within the **App registrations** blade of AAD. This object contains metadata about your application, how tokens get issued in order to access the app, details of any resources the app might need access to, and which actions the app can perform. Each application will have only one app registration, even if it's been configured to be accessible from multiple tenants. This information is used as a template for creating one or more **service principals**.

- For your application to be able to access resources secured by AAD, a service principal needs to exist within the relevant AAD tenant to represent the application. Service principals are each tenant's representation of an application, located within the **Enterprise applications** blade of AAD. Key information from the app registration is used to create the service principal representing that application.

Each tenant that uses the application will have a service principal to represent that application, which can be used to define the access policy and permissions within that specific tenant. Only one app registration exists per application and that exists only within the home tenant of the application. So, the app registration is the global application object, and the service principal (enterprise application) is the per-tenant representation of that object, over which you have control of permissions and access policies, and so on. We'll see these in more detail throughout this chapter.

Before we delve into a practical exercise to look at application objects and service principals, we should also talk about the different permission and consent types, as these will form part of our upcoming exercise.

Permission and consent types

As previously mentioned, the Microsoft identity platform uses OAuth 2.0, which is a method through which an application can access web-hosted resources on a user's behalf. Web-hosted resources that integrate with the Microsoft identity platform have a resource identifier or application ID URI. For example, the Microsoft Graph resource has a URI of `https://graph.microsoft.com`. This is a first-party resource, but the same is also true for third-party resources integrated with the Microsoft identity platform.

Any web-hosted resources that integrate with the Microsoft identity platform can also define a set of permissions, allowing for third-party apps to request only the permissions they need to perform their functions. Users and admins can see what type of data the app can access, which we'll discuss shortly.

In OAuth 2.0, these types of permission sets are known as **scopes**. You will also see them commonly called **permissions**. When an application needs a certain permission, it specifies the permission in the scope query parameter, which is indicated by appending the permission value to the web-hosted resource's identifier or application ID URI. For example, an app that needs to sign you in with your AAD account and read your profile will need the `https://graph.microsoft.com/User.Read` permission (or scope). If you don't specify the resource (for example, simply using `User.Read`), the Microsoft identity platform assumes the resource is Microsoft Graph. Again, although this is a first-party example, the same is true for other web-hosted resources, such as your own web APIs, for example.

There are two types of permissions supported by the Microsoft identity platform that you should be aware of.

Permission types

These are the two permission types supported by the Microsoft identity platform:

- **Delegated permissions**: These are used when an application needs to act on behalf of the signed-in user when it makes calls to a target resource. Users or admins can consent to delegated permission requests. We saw an example of this with the **User.Read** delegated permission used when we enabled authentication on our web app previously.

- **Application permissions**: These are used when an application needs to make calls to a target resource without a signed-in user present, for example, if the application runs a background service. Only admins can consent to application permission requests.

Essentially, if the app is accessing something on behalf of the user, the user delegates permission to the app to act on their behalf. If the app acts on its own behalf without a signed-in user required, application permission is required to access resources. To grant permission to an application, consent is required. There are three types of consent.

Consent types

The three consent types available with the Microsoft identity platform are the following:

- **Incremental and dynamic user consent**: Using incremental – or dynamic – consent, you can request only minimal permissions upfront, then have the app request additional permissions as and when they're needed. When your app requests an access token, you can include the new scopes in the `scope` parameter. If consent hasn't already been granted for the requested permission(s), the user will be prompted to provide consent only applicable to those new permissions being requested.

One challenge is that this kind of consent only applies to delegated permissions, not application permissions. This means that if the permission(s) being requested require(s) admin consent and the user can't provide that consent, the permission won't be granted here.

- **Static user consent**: This specifies all the permissions your app needs within the app's configuration in the Azure portal. If consent hasn't already been granted for the permission(s), the user will be prompted to provide consent.

   One challenge with this is that when you're specifying all permissions upfront, your app needs to know every resource that it would ever need access to in advance. A common use case for this is so that admins can provide consent on behalf of an entire organization.

- **Admin consent**: When your app needs to request more privileged permissions, an admin will need to provide consent, rather than just a user. This allows admins to have control over authorizing apps to access highly privileged information. Admins can provide consent on behalf of the entire organization, so users won't get prompted when the scope is requested.

   For admins to be able to consent to permissions on behalf of an organization, these permissions need to be static permissions registered within the app registration portal.

   When you expose your own APIs, you can define scopes and whether only admins can consent to the scope or both admins and users can consent.

To demonstrate the different consent types, let's run through a very basic example:

1. Create a web app using your preferred method, which you shouldn't need step-by-step guidance on how to do by now. Create a new App Service plan if needed.

2. As we did before, go to the **Authentication** blade of the newly created web app and click **Add identity provider**.

3. Select **Microsoft** for **Identity provider**, leave everything as default, and click **Add**.

   We could have created an app registration beforehand and selected it here, but for the sake of this exercise, we'll just create a new one and have the default settings applied.

4. Within AAD, open the **App registrations** blade and open the newly created app registration, which will have the same name as your new app by default.

5. From within your app registration, go to the **API permissions** blade. Notice that the **Microsoft Graph** permission **User.Read** is there as before (which translates to `https://graph.microsoft.com/user.read`).

   This is an example of a delegated static permission. You can see that no admin consent is required, so each user will need to provide their consent for the first time unless an admin consents on behalf of the organization.

6. Using a private browser session, navigate to the URL of your new web app and before logging in, look at the URL (or use the dev tools and select the entry with `authorize?`), and note that the URL includes the `scope` parameter, `scope=openid+profile+email`, which consists of the standard OIDC permissions that the `user.read` permission uses. Don't accept yet.

You should see the following permissions being requested:

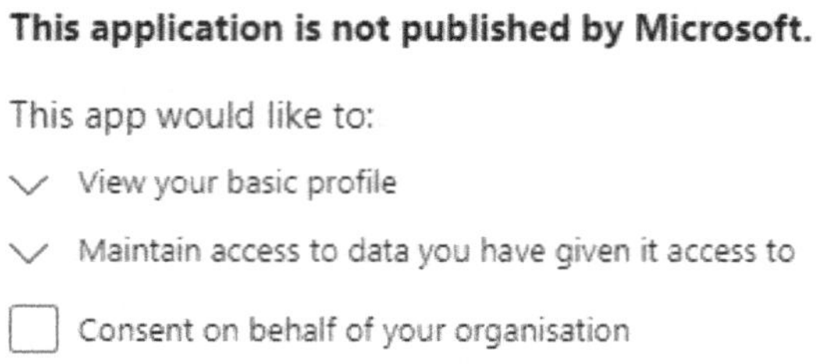

This application is not published by Microsoft.

This app would like to:

∨   View your basic profile

∨   Maintain access to data you have given it access to

☐   Consent on behalf of your organisation

Figure 7.1 – User.Read permissions requested

Because I'm an admin, I can check the checkbox to consent on behalf of the entire organization.

7. Change the URL to add `+calendars.read` at the end of the scope, like this: `scope=openid+profile+email+calendars.read`. This will tell your app to request consent dynamically to read the calendar of the user signing in.

When you commit that new URL, you should see the calendar permission being requested in addition to the previous permissions (still don't accept yet):

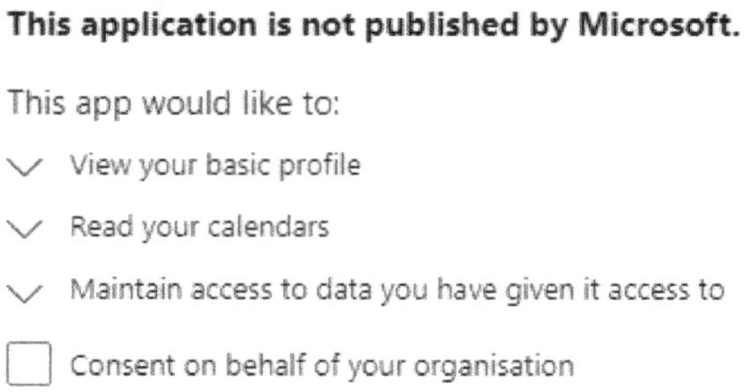

This application is not published by Microsoft.

This app would like to:

∨   View your basic profile

∨   Read your calendars

∨   Maintain access to data you have given it access to

☐   Consent on behalf of your organisation

Figure 7.2 – Additional Calendars.Read permissions requested

8. Click **Cancel** on the permissions and close the browser tab. We'll revisit this process again shortly.

We've just seen a very basic example of static consent with `user.read` and dynamic consent by adding `calendars.read` to the scope. We'll use dynamic consent more later when we start coding. Let's complete this section by showing admin consent. Now that we know our application needs to read the calendar of our users, as well as read their profile to be able to log them in, assuming we're happy with that, let's grant admin consent on behalf of the entire organization for both permissions:

1. Head back to the Azure portal and open the app registration again.

2. Open the **API permissions** blade and click **Add a permission**.

3. Add the Microsoft Graph delegated permission for **Calendars.Read**. You can use the search box after selecting **Microsoft Graph**.

4. We now have **User.Read** and **Calendars.Read** Microsoft Graph permissions in the app registration.

    As previously mentioned, the app registration is the global representation of the application, which is used as a template for the service principal in each tenant. Changes made to the app registration will propagate to each enterprise application/service principal. Let's go into our enterprise application and grant the admin consent for these static permissions.

5. From AAD, open the **Enterprise applications** blade and open the service principal for your application.

6. Open the **Permissions** blade and click **Grant admin consent for <tenant name>**.

7. Select your admin account and authenticate if needed, and you will see that both permissions have appeared for you to provide admin consent. Click **Accept**.

8. After a few moments, you can refresh the screen and both permissions will show as having admin consent granted.

9. Browse to the URL of your web app once more, making sure the `calendars.read` permission is added to the `scope` parameter in the URL as before. You shouldn't be prompted for any consent because it's already received admin consent.

Having certain permissions requiring admin consent provides some security, but you may also want to only provide access to the application if certain conditions are met from devices, such as multi-factor authentication, if the devices are enrolled within Microsoft Endpoint Manager/Intune, or depending on other conditions such as network location. This can be achieved using **conditional access**.

Conditional access

To demonstrate conditional access with the web app we have just created, let's create a conditional access policy that only allows access to the app if the device attempting to access it is of a certain operating system (just for demonstration purposes):

1. Within AAD, open the **Enterprise applications** blade and open the relevant service principal for the newly created app.

Remember, this is our tenant-specific representation of the application, so this is where we set up access and permissions for the application in our tenant.

2. Open the **Conditional Access** blade and select **New Policy**, then **Create new policy**.

3. Give this policy an appropriate title for what it will do. As a reminder, this will limit access to the app to only devices with an OS of your choice.

4. For the **Users or workload identities** section, select **All users** from the **Include** tab.

5. For the **Conditions** section, select **Device platforms**, and change **Configure** to **Yes**. From the **Include** tab, select **Any device**, and from the **Exclude** tab, select the OS from which you want to provide access to your app, then click **Done**.

6. From the **Grant** section, select **Block access**, which will block access to all OSs other than the one you excluded, and click **Select**.

7. Select **On** under **Enable policy**, followed by **Create**.

We have just created a conditional access policy blocking access to our app for all but the excluded OS. Feel free to look through the other options available, where you can grant access when certain conditions are met and require things such as multi-factor authentication.

A link to further information can be found in the *Further reading* section of this chapter.

8. Test the access to your app from a private browser session from both an OS that you excluded, which should be able to access the app, and another OS (if available) that you didn't exclude, which shouldn't have access. When attempting to access from a blocked OS, you should see something like the following:

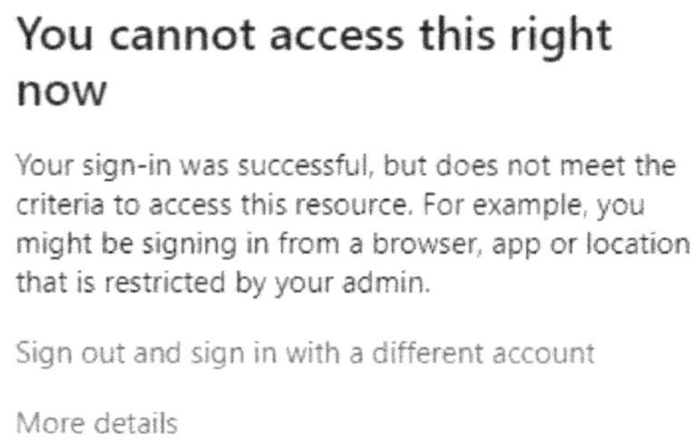

You cannot access this right now

Your sign-in was successful, but does not meet the criteria to access this resource. For example, you might be signing in from a browser, app or location that is restricted by your admin.

Sign out and sign in with a different account

More details

Figure 7.3 – Conditional access denying access to the application

We won't use this app or the App Service plan again, so feel free to delete those resources if you don't want to continue exploring and testing.

That was a very quick and simple example to both reinforce what we've been through regarding service principals and introduce you to conditional access policies. This is all we're doing with conditional access in this chapter, so feel free to remove the policy from the app to avoid preventing your own access.

For the most part, as we've just seen, conditional access doesn't require any code changes and there are no changes to the behavior of the app itself either. If the app requests a token indirectly or silently for a service, code changes will be required to handle challenges from conditional access.

Here are some scenarios that would require code changes for handling conditional access challenges:

- Apps that perform the **On-Behalf-Of (OBO)** flow
- Apps accessing multiple services or resources
- Single-page apps that use MSAL.js
- Web apps calling a resource

We've just seen that conditional access can be applied to web apps, but it can also be applied to web APIs that your app might access. Our app didn't require any code changes to handle conditional access challenges because it was not trying to access any resources or APIs. If our app was accessing an API that had a conditional access policy applied it would need to comply with that conditional access policy. Implementing challenge handling would be required in this scenario.

With the understanding of the Microsoft identity platform that we now have, let's look at how we can make use of the libraries available from MSAL, which make authentication and authorization easier within your application code.

Implementing authentication with the Microsoft Authentication Library

MSAL allows you to get tokens from the Microsoft identity platform for authentication and accessing secure web APIs. For example, MSAL can be used for getting secure access to Microsoft Graph and other Microsoft APIs, as well as any other web APIs, including your own. If you've heard of **Active Directory Authentication Library** (**ADAL**), which integrates with AAD, MSAL is the successor of ADAL and integrates with the Microsoft identity platform, instead of being limited to AAD authentication only.

There are MSAL libraries available to support several languages and frameworks using a consistent API, including Android, Angluar.js, iOS, macOS, Go, Java, JavaScript and TypeScript frameworks, Node.js, Python, React, and – as you might expect – the .NET ecosystem. MSAL can be used to acquire tokens for web apps, web APIs, single-page apps, mobile and native applications, daemons, and server-side apps.

As we mentioned earlier in this chapter, modern authentication can be extremely complex to implement yourself. MSAL handles a lot of the heavy lifting for you. For example, here are some of the things MSAL does for you:

- Uses OAuth and OIDC libraries directly, while you just use MSAL APIs
- Handles the protocol level details so that you don't have to

- Obtains tokens on behalf of users or an application as applicable
- Caches and refreshes tokens when required so that you don't have to handle token expiration yourself
- Provides support for any Microsoft identity
- Helps with troubleshooting your app by exposing actionable exceptions, logging, and telemetry

MSAL provides several different authentication flows, which can be used in various application scenarios.

Authentication flows

Here are some of the flows provided by MSAL:

Flow	Description
Authorization code	Obtains tokens and accesses web APIs on the user's behalf.
Client credentials	Accesses web APIs using the application's identity with no user interaction.
Device code	Signs users in to a device without a browser, from another device that has a browser, and accesses web APIs on their behalf.
Implicit grant	Used by browser-based applications to sign in and access web APIs on behalf of the user.
Integrated Windows authentication (IWA)	Acquires a token silently when accessed from an AAD-joined device without user interaction.
On-Behalf-Of (OBO)	Accesses a downstream web API from an upstream web API on a user's behalf, sending their identity and delegated permissions.
Username/password	Signs the user in by directly handling their password. This is NOT recommended.

Figure 7.4 – Some of the authentication flows provided by MSAL

A link to further information on the flows and application scenarios can be found in the *Further reading* section of this chapter.

Before we start creating applications that use MSAL, there are some key pieces of information to cover first with regards to client applications.

Client applications

The first thing to understand about client applications is that there are three categories, which have different libraries and objects available. These categories are as follows:

- **Single-page applications (SPAs)**: Web apps that acquire tokens by a JavaScript or TypeScript app running in a browser. These apps use MSAL.js. Support for these types of applications is more recent than the others and doesn't form part of the exam content at the time of writing.

- **Public client applications**: Apps that run on user devices, IoT devices, or browsers. Because these are easily accessible, they aren't trustworthy for keeping application secrets safe. Due to this, they can only request access to web APIs on behalf of the logged-in user (delegated permissions).

- **Confidential client applications**: Apps running on servers such as web apps, web APIs, or daemon apps. Because they're considered more difficult to access than public client apps, they are considered secure enough to be trusted with keeping application secrets safe. These clients can hold configuration time secrets and each instance of the client has its own configuration, which includes the client ID and client secret.

For your application to make use of MSAL, you need to initialize the app with MSAL. The recommendation when instantiating your app is to use the available application builders. For public client apps, we can use the PublicClientApplicationBuilder class, and for confidential client apps, we can use the ConfidentialClientApplicationBuilder class. Both provide the means to configure your app within code, a configuration file, or a combination.

It should be no surprise by now that if we want our application to integrate with the Microsoft identity platform so that we can sign users in, we need to register the application in our AAD tenant.

Let's take what we've learned so far in this chapter and create a new app that integrates with the Microsoft identity platform and uses MSAL to acquire tokens. We're going to create a top-level C# console app that uses MSAL.NET for this exercise, keeping things relatively simple:

1. Within AAD, create a new app registration that will represent our console app. Give it any name you'd like, leave it as a single tenant app, then, under **Redirect URI (optional)**, change the **Select a platform** dropdown to **Public client/native (mobile/desktop)**. Set the URI to http://localhost, then click **Register**.

    Because our app will be a console app running on our device, that makes it a public app, hence selecting this option.

2. Once created, go to the **API permissions** blade of the new app registration and note that the Microsoft Graph **User.Read** permission has been added by default. We could grant admin consent so that nobody gets prompted for consent but we won't.

3. From the **Overview** blade, make a note of the **Application (client) ID** and the **Directory (tenant) ID** values, as our app will need this information for the integration.

Notice that we're not creating any certificates or secrets because our app will be using the user's tokens and not those of the app/client itself. If we were creating a web app (which would be a confidential client app), we could use the credentials of the app registration instead of the user.

4. Create a new folder for this exercise if you wish, then create a new .NET console app with a name of your choice from a terminal session with the following:

```
dotnet new console -n "<app name>"
```

5. Navigate to the newly created project folder and add the MSAL .NET package by running the following command:

```
dotnet add package Microsoft.Identity.Client
```

6. Open the Program.cs file within VS Code and remove any prepopulated code so that we're starting afresh.

7. Add the MSAL.NET package to the project by adding the following statement:

```
using Microsoft.Identity.Client;
```

8. Add variables for the application/client ID and tenant ID, which are on the **Overview** blade of the newly created app registration:

```
const string _clientId = "<app/client ID>";
const string _tenantId = "<tenant ID>";
```

9. Use the PublicClientApplicationBuilder class to initialize the app with MSAL as a public client app:

```
var app = PublicClientApplicationBuilder
    .Create(_clientId)
    .WithAuthority(AzureCloudInstance.AzurePublic, _
tenantId)
    .WithRedirectUri("http://localhost")
    .Build();
```

Notice we're passing in the client ID of our app registration via the _clientId variable, as well as setting the authority to the public Azure cloud, passing in our tenant ID via the _tenantId variable. We're also setting the app to use the same redirect URI as the app registration. If the redirect URIs don't match, you will receive an error when trying to sign in.

10. Create an array of strings containing the scopes that we want to request. In our case, we're just going to request User.Read for now (we'll add more shortly):

```
string[] scopes = { "User.Read" };
```

11. We can now request the token interactively using the scopes variable:

```
AuthenticationResult result = await app.
AcquireTokenInteractive(scopes).ExecuteAsync();
```

12. Add a couple of lines that print out the ID token (authentication) and access token (authorization) to the console:

```
Console.WriteLine($"ID:\n{result.IdToken}");
Console.WriteLine($"Access:\n{result.AccessToken}");
```

Your code should now look like this:

```
using Microsoft.Identity.Client;
const string _clientId = "<app/client ID>";
const string _tenantId = "<tenant ID>";
var app = PublicClientApplicationBuilder
    .Create(_clientId)
    .WithAuthority(AzureCloudInstance.AzurePublic, _
tenantId)
    .WithRedirectUri("http://localhost")
    .Build();
string[] scopes = { "User.Read" };

AuthenticationResult result = await app.
AcquireTokenInteractive(scopes).ExecuteAsync();

Console.WriteLine($"ID:\n{result.IdToken}");
Console.WriteLine($"Access:\n{result.AccessToken}");
```

13. Confirm the application builds successfully with the following command:

dotnet build

14. Once confirmed, run the application to test it with the following command:

dotnet run

You should get the usual **Permissions requested** prompt, which you can accept. You should then have both tokens output to the console. If you wish, you can copy each token into `https://jwt.ms` as before and see what claims are contained within each token.

15. Add another scope to the `scopes` array, for example, `Calendars.Read`, so that the `scopes` line looks like this:

```
string[] scopes = { "User.Read", "Calendars.Read" };
```

16. Accept the permissions after running the app again with the following command:

```
dotnet run
```

You've just created an app that uses MSAL to request tokens and dynamic consent to request additional permissions through code. Congratulations!

Having to log in interactively every time is not exactly optimal, so you'd want to be able to acquire a token silently from the cache first and, only if that fails, try interactively. If this was a web app, the token cache would be handled for you. If you want to check out the mvc template arguments or the webapp template arguments, including `--auth`, you can find them here: `https://docs.microsoft.com/dotnet/core/tools/dotnet-new-sdk-templates#web-options`. As you will see from that page, you can pass in the app registration credentials, which get prepopulated in the app configuration.

With desktop apps such as the one we've just created, there's no built-in user token cache handling, because storing unencrypted (although encoded) tokens locally in a file would not be considered secure.

To see our example expanded to include creating a local user cache (for demonstration purposes only), as well as attempting to obtain the tokens from the cache silently, falling back to interactive if the app can't acquire a valid token from the cache, check out the example here: `https://github.com/PacktPublishing/Developing-Solutions-for-Microsoft-Azure-AZ-204-Exam-Guide/tree/main/Chapter07/02-auth-with-cache`.

The main point to note from the example code at the link is within the `ObtainTokenAsync()` method, where we first try to get the token from the cache with the `AcquireTokenSilent()` method, then if we get the `MsalUiRequiredException` exception, we try interactively as we did before. This is a common pattern with MSAL. We won't be using this example for any upcoming exercises, as it was just intended to demonstrate a common pattern for token acquisition without having to create a new web app.

With that, we've reached the end of the MSAL section of this chapter. You can see how the APIs exposed by MSAL make authentication so much easier than if we had to manage all the protocol-level details ourselves.

Now that we've got our app integrated with the Microsoft identity platform using MSAL, we can consider expanding our app to make use of the tokens we acquired and start interacting with data in Microsoft 365 using Microsoft Graph.

Discovering Microsoft Graph

At a very high level, Microsoft Graph is a REST API that can be used to interact with the data within Microsoft 365, available through REST APIs and client libraries.

You can use Microsoft Graph to access data on **Microsoft 365 core services** such as Calendar, Excel, Microsoft Search, OneDrive, Outlook/Exchange, Teams, and more. You also have **Enterprise Mobility + Security** services such as AAD, Advanced Threat Protection, and so on, **Windows** services, and **Dynamics 365 Business Central** services.

Microsoft Graph has three main components to help with the access and flow of data:

- The **Microsoft Graph API**: Accessible using a single endpoint (`https://graph.microsoft.com`) to interact with people-centric data and insights across the aforementioned services. You can access the endpoint using REST APIs or the available SDKs (which we will shortly).

- **Microsoft Graph connectors**: Used to bring data from external sources into Microsoft Graph applications and services to enhance experiences such as Microsoft Search, so that your chosen external data can be displayed alongside Microsoft 365 search results, for example. There are connectors for a lot of the most used data sources such as Salesforce, Jira, Confluence, and ServiceNow.

- **Microsoft Graph Data Connect**: Used to access data on Microsoft Graph at scale with granular control over data and consent for admins. While the Graph API can be used to access data in real time, Data Connect can access data on a recurring schedule and operates on a cache of the data in your Azure subscription rather than the data master. Because Data Connect uses a cache, data protection is extended to that cache.

   The Graph API can provide admin consent for the entire organization and specific resource types, whereas Data Connect can provide admin consent for select groups of users, resource types, and resource properties, and exclude users. Data Connect can also scope to many users or groups, whereas the Graph API can scope to a single user or the entire tenant.

Before we start querying, I'd like to introduce you to a useful tool for exploring Graph, so you can see the information you can get, which permissions are required, and what responses might look like. This tool is aptly named **Graph Explorer**.

Graph Explorer

We'll briefly look at Graph Explorer now before we make more use of it later, like so:

1. Navigate to `https://developer.microsoft.com/graph/graph-explorer` and sign in using the **Sign in to Graph Explorer** button if you're not already signed in. If you don't sign in, Graph Explorer will use sample data rather than real data, but you won't be able to do everything in this exercise, hence signing in would be ideal.

    Notice toward the top of the main part of the screen, where we have the method (defaults to **GET**), the API version (**v1.0** at the time of writing this), and the URL. The URL is made up of the API endpoint (`https://graph.microsoft.com`), the API version (which updates if you change the version dropdown), the resource you want to query (defaults to /me, so will query the context of the logged-in user), and it will also include any optional parameters.

2. Click **Run query** and see the response, which shows some basic profile data.

3. Click on the **Modify permissions (preview)** tab. Here, you can see consented permissions and consent to additional permissions, so that you can test the results when changes are made.

    Some of the queries you might test won't work until you modify the permissions by granting consent to Graph, which can be done here.

4. Click on the **Access token** tab and you'll be able to see the access token that was used in the query. You can also click on the { } button to open the access token in `https://jwt.ms`, as we did previously.

5. Click on the **Code snippets** tab above the response and you'll see some small snippets of code for different languages, which you can use to help build your apps that need to integrate with Graph. Notice that most of them have a reference to /me, which makes sense now that we know that means it's the context of the logged-in user. The C# code we're going to see shortly was generated with the help of Graph Explorer.

6. Add `?$select=givenName` to the end of the URL and click **Run query**. Adding this query parameter will only return the `givenName` property.

7. Changing the URL to `https://graph.microsoft.com/v1.0/users` and running the query will return a list of all users in the organization. Filter the results to only show your account by changing the URL to `https://graph.microsoft.com/v1.0/users?$filter=userPrincipalName eq '<your full login>'`, replacing `<your full login>` with the email address that you use to log in to Azure.

Feel free to explore a little more if you'd like. If we were to do the REST requests ourselves, we would need to acquire an access token, which we would add to an `Authorization` header with the value of `Bearer <access token>`. You'll see this header being referenced in the upcoming C# example as well. You can use the browser developer tools to see what happens behind the scenes when you run a query, and you'll see the content of the REST call that Graph performs.

A link to the reference for the Microsoft Graph API can be found in the *Further reading* section of this chapter. With a basic understanding of what makes up a Graph REST API query (method, version, resource, and optional parameters), let's look at querying using the SDKs.

Graph SDKs

The Graph SDKs consist of two components: a **core library** and a **service library**. The core library provides many features for working with Microsoft Graph, with support for retry handling, transparent authentication, payload compression, and more. The service library has models and request builders generated from Microsoft Graph metadata.

Let's expand the app we created earlier with interactive token acquisition to query Graph. You're welcome to use the example that uses the local user cache, but as it's not a good practice to have a local unencrypted cache, the upcoming exercise will be using the app without a local user token cache:

1. If not already cloned, clone the repository for this book locally by running this command from within a suitable directory:

    ```
    git clone https://github.com/PacktPublishing/Developing-
    Solutions-for-Microsoft-Azure-AZ-204-Exam-Guide
    ```

2. Open the Chapter07\03-graph directory in VS Code and open a terminal session from that directory.

3. Replace the placeholder text for the client ID and tenant ID with those relevant to your app registration.

4. Confirm that the project builds successfully, which will also install any required packages:

    ```
    dotnet build
    ```

5. Run the app to test it:

    ```
    dotnet run
    ```

    You should be prompted for authentication in your browser and once authenticated, you should be greeted with your given name. This queried Microsoft Graph to get your profile and then returned your given name from that profile data.

There are a few points to note in this code:

*   We're using System.Net.Http.Headers to construct the Authorization header and the Microsoft.Graph package, which is a service library and has a dependency on Microsoft.Graph.Core, which, as the name suggests, is a core library and a dependency for all of the Graph service libraries.

- An authentication provider is required for making Graph calls, so we're creating one using the `DelegateAuthenticationProvider` class. This sets the request `Authorization` header and you can see that it uses the same format mentioned earlier (`"Bearer <token>"`). It gets the token using a method that checks the local cache (if it exists, although this app isn't creating one) for a valid token and then interactively obtains the token if one can't be found in the cache.

- We're then creating a new Graph service client using the `GraphServiceClient` class, which, as you'll see, makes making calls to Graph relatively simple. This uses the authentication provider from the previous point.

- This line uses the SDK to perform a GET request to `https://graph.microsoft.com/me` and stores the result in a `user` variable:

  ```
  var user = await graphClient.Me.Request().GetAsync();
  ```

- Finally, we use the `user` variable to greet the logged-in user by their given name with the `GivenName` property.

If you'd like to see an example of this app being expanded to create a new calendar event, feel free to check out `https://github.com/PacktPublishing/Developing-Solutions-for-Microsoft-Azure-AZ-204-Exam-Guide/tree/main/Chapter07/04-graph-calendar-event`. As with the local cache example, this is purely for demonstration purposes and I didn't add any additional exception handling to it, as it's just intended to show that it is relatively easy to implement features such as these.

Now that we've covered how to implement authentication and authorization with MSAL and how to use the acquired tokens to query the Microsoft Graph, we should consider the situations in which you need to provide your app with secure access to resources within a storage account, without trusting your app with the storage account access key. This is where SAS come in.

Using shared access signatures

A SAS is a signed URI that provides defined access rights to specific resources within a storage account for a specified period. To use a SAS for accessing Azure Storage resources, you'll need to have two components:

- The URI of the resource being accessed, for example, `https://myaccount.blob.core.windows.net/container/file.txt`

- The SAS token that you would have created and configured

The SAS token itself is comprised of several elements and it's worth understanding the structure.

The SAS token structure

If we look at an example SAS token, we can inspect each element for our understanding: `sp=rd&st=2022-06-04T13:35:54Z&se=2022-06-04T21:35:54Z&spr=https&sv=2020-08-04&sr=b&sig=wX4run5CPuFbQkCezJxGwOEv%2BQ2ODjVEVxn5Yrzo8ug%3D`. Let's take each element and explore its meaning:

- `sp=rd`: sp stands for signed permission. In this case, we have `r` and `d`, which stand for read and delete.

- `st=2022-06-04T13:35:54Z`: st is the start time of the token's validity.

- `se=2022-06-04T21:35:54Z`: se is the end time of the token's validity.

- `spr=https`: spr stands for signed protocol. In this case, we're only allowing HTTPS requests to use the SAS token.

- `sv=2020-08-04`: sv stands for signed version. This is the version of the Azure Storage API to use.

- `sr=b`: sr stands for signed resource. In this case, we're granting access to a Blob resource, hence the b.

- `sig=wX4run5CPuFbQkCezJxGwOEv%2BQ2ODjVEVxn5Yrzo8ug%3D` is the cryptographic signature with which the token is signed.

Using our example, the full SAS URI would be `https://myaccount.blob.core.windows.net/container/file.txt?sp=rd&st=2022-06-04T13:35:54Z&se=2022-06-04T21:35:54Z&spr=https&sv=2020-08-04&sr=b&sig=wX4run5CPuFbQkCezJxGwOEv%2BQ2ODjVEVxn5Yrzo8ug%3D`. Providing a request is made using the specified protocol and within the validity period, the SAS could be used to read and delete (in our example) `file.txt` within the container called `container` (I'm treating you to my incredibly expansive imagination again) within the `myaccount` storage account. Using this SAS wouldn't require any AAD user credentials, as the SAS contains everything needed to provide access.

You might be wondering which key is used to sign the SAS token. This depends on the type of SAS you generate.

SAS types

There are three supported types of SAS available in Azure Storage:

- A **user delegation SAS**: Secured with AAD credentials and provides access to containers and blobs, so is only supported for the Blob service. Because a user delegation SAS is secured using specific AAD credentials, this is the recommended type of SAS to use where possible, as it's considered more secure to sign with AAD credentials than to sign with an account key. The URI of a user delegation SAS includes some additional parameters. For example, the user's

AAD object ID, `skoid`, or the AAD tenant ID, `sktid`. Other parameters are supported and can be found in the Microsoft documentation.

- A **service SAS**: Secured with the storage account key and provides access to a resource in one of the following services: Blob Storage, Table Storage, and Azure Files.

- An **account SAS**: Secured with the storage account key and provides access at the storage account level. This provides access to service-level operations such as getting and setting service properties, which you can't do with a service SAS. An account SAS can also provide access to more than one service within a storage account at the same time, unlike a service SAS, which is limited to a single service at a time.

Let's briefly demonstrate a SAS by creating the resources using the CLI, before jumping into the portal to look at the options available. You can generate a SAS using the CLI, but we'll use the portal because it's easier to demonstrate:

1. Create a resource group if you don't already have one that you want to use:

```
az group create -n "<name>" -l "<location>"
```

2. Create a storage account:

```
az storage account create -n "<name>" -g "<resource group
name>" -l "<location>" --sku "Standard_LRS"
```

3. List the account keys for the storage account:

```
az storage account keys list -n "<name>" -g "<resource
group name>"
```

These are the keys mentioned previously that are used to sign service and account SAS. As you can see from the output, they provide full permissions to your storage account, so you should keep these keys secure and rotate them regularly. The reason for having two keys is so that you can use one of the keys while you rotate the other to avoid access being lost.

4. Copy the value of one of the keys and use it in the following command to create a container:

```
az storage container create -n "<name>" --account-name
"<storage account name>" --account-key "<account key>"
```

5. Within the Azure portal, open the newly created storage account and the **Shared access signature** blade.

6. Select **Service** under the **Allowed resource types** setting and select either of the access keys for the **Signing key** setting, then select **Generate SAS and connection string**.

Notice that the URLs for the different services are populated, including the SAS token that is appended to the URLs. There was no option to use AAD credentials to secure the SAS because that's only available for the Blob service.

7. Open the **Containers** blade and open your new container.

8. Click on **Shared access tokens**.

    This time, we have a **Signing method** option available, one of which is the account key, which we've already used. The other option allows us to generate a user delegation key.

9. Select the **User delegation key** option under the **Signing method** setting and select **Generate SAS token and URL**. Check out the **Blob SAS token** value and notice the additional parameters included, which weren't there in the account SAS.

If you see a warning displayed about not having permissions, you could go into the **Access Control (IAM)** blade and assign yourself a role that does have permissions – **Storage Blob Data Contributor**, for example. This can take some time to apply. You may have to refresh the page after the assignment.

It may have crossed your mind that Azure doesn't appear to track these generated SAS tokens, so how would you edit or revoke one once generated? That's where stored access policies come in.

Stored access policies

Stored access policies provide another level of control over service-level SAS on the server side. Within a stored access policy, you specify permissions along with start and end times, which will be applied to any SAS that are assigned to the policy.

What this means is that you can create a SAS that uses a certain stored access policy, and it will inherit the permissions and dates from this policy. Another benefit of using stored access policies is that you can edit permissions and/or dates within the policy, and all SAS assigned to it will have those changes applied to them, so you can revoke all SAS assigned to a policy at once by changing the dates or deleting the policy.

Let's do a quick demonstration with the storage account and container we've just created:

1. Create a plain text (.txt) file and save a short message in there, then upload that file to the container created in the last exercise using the Azure portal.

2. From within the container in the Azure portal, open the **Access policy** blade and select **Add policy**.

3. Enter any identifier you'd like, select **Read** under the **Permissions** setting, set **Start time** to a time in the past, and set **Expiry time** to a time in the future, then click **OK**.

4. Once created, make sure you click **Save**.

5. From the **Overview** blade, right-click on your uploaded text file and select **Generate SAS** (clicking on the ellipsis or clicking on it and then selecting the **Generate SAS** tab also works).

6. From the **Stored access policy** dropdown, select the newly created policy. Notice that the permissions and times are no longer editable.

7. Click on **Generate SAS token and URL**. Notice that the SAS token now includes the policy name in the `si` parameter.

8. Copy the **Blob SAS URL** value to the clipboard, as we'll use that in the next step.

9. Open a new terminal session and run the following command:

```
curl "<SAS URL>"
```

The request should have been successful and displayed the content of your plain text file. You may need to add the `-UseBasicParsing` switch if this command doesn't work without it.

```
StatusCode         : 200
StatusDescription  : OK
Content            : Hello, World!
```

Figure 7.5 – A successful GET request using the Blob SAS URL to display content

10. Back in the Azure portal, delete the access policy, and click **Save**.

11. After up to 30 seconds, try the same `curl` command we just used, and you should receive an authentication error.

As you might imagine, associating SAS tokens with stored access policies provides flexibility and additional security, so is a recommended practice where possible.

Although we won't cover how to do it, generating SAS can also be done programmatically. This is common in situations where you have an app that requires users to read and write data to your storage account. In these scenarios, you might want to have a lightweight service authenticating the client and generating the SAS. Then, the client can use the SAS per the permissions and period defined by the SAS. A link to documentation on SAS can be found in the *Further reading* section of this chapter.

Summary

In this chapter, we have explored some of the key tools and features available to make building applications with authentication and authorization easier. We started with a detailed introduction to the Microsoft identity platform, which included explanations of app registration and service principals, followed by the different permission types and consent types, finishing with a demonstration of using conditional access to limit access to an application.

Building on this, we have looked at using the Microsoft Authentication Library to handle authentication and handle tokens in code. Once we had the tokens, we used them to query Microsoft Graph using the Graph SDK, after exploring Graph Explorer and the structure of Graph REST API requests. We finished off this chapter looking at how SAS can provide defined access to specific resources within a storage account, including using stored access policies for greater security and flexibility.

In the next chapter, we will stick with the theme of security and look at securing and accessing application secrets in Azure Key Vault. We'll look at implementing managed identities for resources in Azure and we'll finish by discussing how to store configuration in App Configuration.

Questions

1. Which one of the following can be used to bring external data into Microsoft Graph applications and services?

    A. Microsoft Graph Data Connect

    B. Microsoft Graph connectors

    C. Graph Explorer

2. Which types of permissions are required when an application needs to act on behalf of a signed-in user?

3. Which MSAL library supports single-page applications?

4. Which type of client application runs on user devices, IoT devices, and browsers?

5. Which type of SAS is recommended where possible and only available with the Blob service?

Further reading

*   The documentation on conditional access can be found here: https://docs.microsoft.com/azure/active-directory/conditional-access/overview

*   Further information about MSAL can be found here: https://docs.microsoft.com/azure/active-directory/develop/msal-overview

*   Further details on authentication flows and application scenarios can be found here: https://docs.microsoft.com/azure/active-directory/develop/authentication-flows-app-scenarios

*   The documentation on Microsoft Graph can be found here: https://docs.microsoft.com/graph/overview

*   The reference for the Microsoft Graph API can be found here: https://docs.microsoft.com/graph/api/overview

*   Further documentation on SAS can be found here: https://docs.microsoft.com/azure/storage/common/storage-sas-overview

8

Implementing Secure Cloud Solutions

Now that we've been through the authentication and authorization side of security, it's the time for us to talk about deploying apps securely in Azure. One of the benefits of hosting your applications in the cloud is the security capabilities that come with the platform.

In this chapter, we're going to start by talking about securing your application secrets with Azure Key Vault. This will also cover recommendations for providing access to your vaults and secrets. We're going to then look at how to authenticate your application with Azure resources using managed identities, exploring the different types of managed identities available within Azure.

We'll finish the chapter with a look at the Azure App Configuration service for centrally and securely storing your application configuration settings, including how to use the feature management capabilities of the service to centrally manage enabling and disabling features, among other things.

By the end of this chapter, you'll know how to secure and provide access to your application secrets, how to authenticate your application with other Azure resources, and how to centrally manage settings and feature flags for your applications, all of which will include exercises in code for demonstration purposes.

In this chapter, we'll cover the following main topics:

- Securing secrets with Azure Key Vault
- Implementing managed identities
- Exploring Azure App Configuration

Technical requirements

To follow along with the exercises in this chapter, you will need the following:

- The latest .NET SDK: `https://dotnet.microsoft.com/download`

- Visual Studio Code: `https://code.visualstudio.com/Download`

- The Azure App Service VS Code extension: `https://marketplace.visualstudio.com/items?itemName=ms-azuretools.vscode-azureappservice`

- The Azure Functions VS Code extension: `https://marketplace.visualstudio.com/items?itemName=ms-azuretools.vscode-azurefunctions`

- The Azure Account VS Code extension: `https://marketplace.visualstudio.com/items?itemName=ms-vscode.azure-account`

- The code samples for this chapter can be found here: `https://github.com/PacktPublishing/Developing-Solutions-for-Microsoft-Azure-AZ-204-Exam-Guide/tree/main/Chapter08`

Code in Action videos for this chapter: `https://bit.ly/3UAB3Mj`

Securing secrets with Azure Key Vault

I'm sure it won't come as a surprise to hear that storing credentials, connection strings, and other sensitive secrets in application code isn't a great idea. We hear about these secrets being leaked all the time, and there are many tools integrated into code repositories nowadays that warn you if potential secrets are detected within your source code.

Azure Key Vault provides a way to store your application secrets, create and control encryption keys, and manage both public and private certificates centrally and securely. With the **Standard** tier, your keys, secrets, and certificates are software-protected and safeguarded by Azure. With the **Premium** tier, you have the option to import or generate keys in **hardware security modules** (**HSMs**) that never leave the HSM boundary.

A key vault is a logical group of secrets, and as such, the recommendation is to use one vault per application per environment (dev/prod, for example). This helps prevent the sharing of secrets across different environments and applications and reduces the threat of secrets being exposed.

You can monitor a key vault's usage by enabling and configuring logging, with the ability to restrict access to and delete the logs as needed. You can send the logs to a Log Analytics workspace, archive them to a storage account, stream them to an event hub, or send them to a partner solution. Previously, you were able to send the logs to Azure Monitor logs, but at the time of writing, a preview feature of Azure Monitor called Key Vault insights can be used instead. A link to further details on this preview feature can be found in the *Further reading* section of this chapter. As far as the exam is concerned (again, at the time of writing), you can still send the logs to Azure Monitor logs.

Key Vault secrets are encrypted at rest transparently, meaning that the encryption happens without any user interaction required, and the decryption happens automatically when you request to read those secrets (providing you have the permissions to do so). They're also encrypted in transport using **Transport Layer Security** (TLS). The combination of **Perfect Forward Secrecy** (PFS) – which protects connections between client systems and Microsoft cloud services – and connections using RSA-based 2048-bit encryption makes intercepting and accessing this data in transit difficult.

Before a user or application can get access to any secrets or keys stored within a key vault, that caller needs to first be authenticated with AAD. Once they are authenticated, authorization determines what operations they are allowed to perform (if any). Let's first look at authorization because authentication will lead us nicely into the subsequent section.

Authorization

Key Vault supports two permission models (only one of which can be used for accessing secrets at any one time):

- **Role-based access control** (**RBAC**): You are probably already familiar with how RBAC works for Azure resources: you can assign roles that have certain permissions. RBAC controls access to the **management plane**, which is used for creating and managing key vaults and their attributes and access policies, and accessing the data stored within them.

- **Key Vault access policy**: Access policies control access to the **data plane** for managing secrets, keys, and certificates, but not the management of the key vault itself.

Before we move into authentication, let's create a new vault and explore the permission models. We'll do the initial setup using the Azure CLI before moving into the portal:

1. From a terminal session that's already authenticated with Azure, create a new resource group if needed:

    ```
    az group create -n "<name>" -l "<location>"
    ```

2. Create the key vault:

    ```
    az keyvault create -n "<unique vault name>" -g "<resource
    group name>" -l "<location>"
    ```

    This may take a few minutes. Notice that the vault name needs to be unique because it will create a globally unique URI in the format `https://<vault name>.vault.azure.net/`.

3. Create a new secret in the newly created vault with any name and value you want:

    ```
    az keyvault secret set --vault-name "<vault name>" --name
    "<secret name>" --value "<secret value>"
    ```

    Your secret is now encrypted in your new key vault.

4. Read the value of the secret, which will transparently decrypt the secret and make it readable:

```
az keyvault secret show --vault-name "<vault name>"
--name "<secret name>"
```

From the terminal output, you can see that there are multiple properties, including activation and expiration dates.

5. From within the Azure portal, open the newly created key vault and from within the **Secrets** blade, open your secret.

Notice that we have a version with a status. Every secret is versioned and can be disabled at any time if needed. When we ran the CLI command to view the secret, we could have specified the version. When a version isn't specified, the latest version is used.

6. Open the current version and notice the **Secret Identifier**, which contains the vault URI, the secret name, and the specific version of the secret. Also, notice the options for dates and to set its **Enabled** state to either **Yes** or **No**.

7. Click **Show Secret Value** and you'll see the decrypted value once more.

8. Come out of the secrets screens and open the **Access policies** blade.

Notice the options to allow access to different types of Azure resources as well as the **Permissions model** option previously discussed.

9. Leaving **Vault access policy** selected, explore the various drop-down options for **Key Permissions**, **Secret Permissions**, and **Certificate Permissions** against your user account.

10. Remove the **List** option for your account under **Secret Permissions** and click **Save**.

11. Open the **Secrets** blade and you should no longer be able to view any created secrets (you may need to refresh).

12. Revert the change to give yourself **List** permissions again and don't forget to click **Save**. Confirm that you are now able to see the list of secrets again in the **Secrets** blade (you may need to refresh).

13. Back in the **Access policies** blade, change the **Permissions model** to **Azure role-based access control** and click **Save**.

Changing the Permissions Model

When changing the Permissions Model, it's strongly recommended that you don't do this during production hours in a production environment. If users or services were previously able to access the secrets as part of the vault access policy, they may no longer have access unless they've been granted access via RBAC as well.

---

14. Head back to the **Secrets** blade, click **Refresh**, and you should no longer have permission to list secrets despite having access when we were using the access policy.

To give yourself access, you would need to assign yourself to an appropriate role within the **Access control (IAM)** blade, although we won't do that right now.

15. Switch **Permissions model** back to **Vault access policy** from the **Access policies** blade, and remember to click **Save**.

Don't delete the resources just created because we'll use them in the exercises that follow.

There is a lot more to Key Vault than we can cover in this chapter. For example, **soft-delete** is a feature that allows deleted secrets to be recovered if they were deleted in error. There is a lot of useful information and multiple resources in the **Azure Key Vault developer's guide**, a link to which can be found in the *Further reading* section of this chapter.

We have just completed a very basic demonstration of the authorization side of accessing a key vault. This was all done using your own user account, but as the exam is focused on development, we should talk about how your apps can get access. Let's talk about how to authenticate your apps with Key Vault.

Authentication

In addition to authenticating with a user account like we just did, you can authenticate with a service principal (either using a certificate or secret), which we discussed in the previous chapter. You can also authenticate with Key Vault using **managed identities**, which is the recommended approach.

With service principals, you are responsible for storing and rotating the secrets and certificates. We hear all the time about these credentials being leaked or stolen, sometimes being accidentally committed to source control, or things ceasing to work because someone forgot to rotate a secret and the previous one has now expired.

The answer to this problem is managed identities, which remove the need for you to manage these credentials yourself.

Implementing managed identities

With managed identities (previously called managed service identities), the secret and secret rotation is automatically handled by Azure. You don't even have access to the credentials. This is the recommended way to authenticate your application with Key Vault and can be used to authenticate with any resource that supports AAD authentication, even your own applications.

If you're building an application using popular Azure resources such as App Service which access anything that supports AAD authentication, using managed identities is generally the recommended best practice. You can provide all the permissions you need without having to manage any of the credentials yourself. A link to a list of services that can use managed identities can be found in the *Further reading* section of this chapter.

Internally, managed identities are a special type of service principal (not an app registration) that are only usable with Azure resources. If a managed identity is deleted, the corresponding service principal is also deleted automatically. It's important to understand the two types of managed identity, so let's look at each one individually.

User-assigned managed identity

A user-assigned managed identity is a standalone resource tied to an AAD identity that's trusted by the subscription in which it's created. Once you've created a user-assigned managed identity, you can assign it to one or more applications, which can also have one or more user-assigned managed identities for authentication (we'll demonstrate this shortly, don't worry). With this type of managed identity being standalone and assignable to multiple resources, its life cycle is managed separately to any of those resources.

Let's explore this by using Azure Functions to query our key vault using a user-assigned managed identity to authenticate:

1. Create a new user-assigned managed identity with a name of your choice:

    ```
    az identity create -n "<name>" -g "<resource group name>"
    ```

2. Within the Azure portal, open the resource group and open the newly created user-assigned managed identity. This may take a few moments, and you may need to refresh the screen.

3. Open the **Properties** blade and notice that you can see the **Tenant id**, the **Principal id** (which is the service principal's object ID), and the **Client id** (which is the service principal's application/client ID).

    If you wanted to confirm that a service principal is indeed behind this, feel free to check **Enterprise applications** within AAD, but make sure the **Application type** filter is changed to **Managed identities**.

4. Open the key vault created earlier and within the **Access policies** blade, click **Add Access Policy**.

5. From the **Secret permissions** list, select **Get** then click on **None selected** next to **Select principal**.

6. Search for and select your new user-assigned managed identity, then click **Add**.

7. With the managed identity now showing in the list, click **Save**.

That's our user-assigned managed identity created and permissions to get secrets from the vault assigned to it. We'll eventually assign the identity to a function app. Let's go ahead and create said function app:

1. Create a new folder for this exercise locally on your device and open it in VS Code.

2. Open the command palette using the menu or shortcut keys.

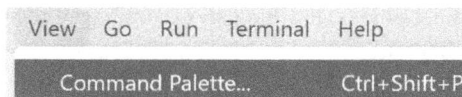

Figure 8.1 – VS Code view command palette menu

3. Start typing and then select the option for `Azure Functions: Create New Project....`

4. Browse to the relevant folder and select it, select **C#** for the language, choose the appropriate .NET version for the runtime, select **HTTP Trigger**, accept the default trigger name or create a new one, accept the default **Namespace**, select **Function** for the access rights selection, and wait for the project to be created.

5. Open a terminal from the current folder and add the `Azure.Identity` package along with the `KeyVault.Secrets` package with the following commands:

    ```
    dotnet add package Azure.Identity
    dotnet add package Azure.Security.KeyVault.Secrets
    ```

6. Once they have both been added, you can add them to your `.cs` file by adding the following lines near the other `using` statements:

    ```
    using Azure.Identity;
    using Azure.Security.KeyVault.Secrets;
    ```

    The `Azure.Identity` package is what we'll use to authenticate with Key Vault (it's not just for Key Vault) and the `Azure.Security.KeyVault.Secrets` package is what we'll use to get the secret we created earlier.

7. Replace the `Run()` method with the following code, putting in the client ID of the user-assigned managed identity, the URI of your key vault, and the name of the previously created secret that you want to get:

    ```
    public static async Task<IActionResult> Run(
        [HttpTrigger(AuthorizationLevel.Function, "get",
    Route = null)] HttpRequest req,
        ILogger log)
    {
        log.LogInformation("C# HTTP trigger function
    processed a request.");

        string userAssignedClientId = "Client ID of the user-
    assigned managed identity";
        var credential = new DefaultAzureCredential(new
    DefaultAzureCredentialOptions { ManagedIdentityClientId =
    userAssignedClientId });

        var client = new SecretClient(new Uri("Key Vault
    URI (in the format of https://<vault name>.vault.azure.
    net/)"), credential);
    ```

```
    KeyVaultSecret secret = await client.
GetSecretAsync("Name of secret you want to get");

    string responseMessage = $"Secret value: { secret.
Value }";

    return new OkObjectResult(responseMessage);
}
```

The key information to notice from this code is that we're using `DefaultAzureCredential`, which will try to get a token using the following credential types in the following order:

- `EnvironmentCredential` (credential stored in an environment variable)
- `ManagedIdentityCredential`
- `VisualStudioCodeCredential` (if you have the Azure Account extension installed and logged in)
- `AzureCliCredential`
- `AzurePowerShellCredential`

The list should be somewhat self-explanatory. `DefaultAzureCredential` is a popular choice for developers because when we're developing locally, it can use our VS Code credentials via the Azure Account extension, and when the code is running in Azure, it will use the managed identity provided in `DefaultAzureCredentialOptions`.

The code finishes off by using the `GetSecretAsync()` method to get the secret from the key vault using whichever credential was able to acquire a token from `DefaultAzureCredential`, before returning the secret value in plain text. Outputting the unencrypted value of a secret isn't something you'd usually want to do, but this is purely for demonstration purposes.

Let's test this locally to confirm it all works before deploying it to Azure:

1. Build and run the function with *F5*.
2. Open the GET URL shown in the terminal output from your web browser:

```
Functions:

    HttpTrigger1: [GET] http://localhost:7071/api/HttpTrigger1
```

Figure 8.2 – GET URL shown in the VS Code terminal output

It will take a few moments, but eventually the secret value should be displayed in your browser. This works fine locally using our credentials. Now we'll try in Azure.

3.   Stop the function running with *Ctrl + C* in the terminal window.

4.   Create a new function app using your preferred method, ensuring that you configure it to be .NET code with the correct version, your relevant region, and using the consumption plan.

5.   From VS Code, deploy your project to your newly created function app using your preferred method.

6.   Once that's complete, head to the new function within the Azure portal, get the function URL, and browse to it (or use **Test/Run** to create a **GET** request). You'll get an HTTP 500 error because none of the credentials DefaultAzureCredential wants to use are available.

7.   Go back to the function app (not just the function) in the Azure portal and open the **Identity** blade.

8.   Click on the **User assigned** tab and click **Add**.

9.   Search for and add the user-assigned managed identity created earlier.

10. Try the function URL or **Test/Run** again, and this time you should see the secret value being displayed.

To recap, we now have an identity with credentials we don't have to store, manage, or rotate. This identity can be assigned to one or more resources, such as a function app, and permissions can be provided for that identity that the relevant resources can use to authenticate with. We've also demonstrated how to access Key Vault secrets in code using DefaultAzureCredential to use whatever credentials are available in the current environment.

One thing that isn't especially obvious is that certain scenarios will default to attempting to use a system-assigned managed identity for authentication even if the resource doesn't have one and has a user-assigned managed identity assigned. I've been caught out by that in the past!

One example of this is if you try setting an App Service application setting (which we covered in *Chapter 3, Creating Azure App Service Web Apps*) value to reference a Key Vault secret, it will fail unless you either change the default behavior programmatically or configure a system-assigned managed identity. We'll come across this scenario shortly.

That brings us nicely onto the topic of system-assigned managed identities.

System-assigned managed identity

While a user-assigned managed identity is a standalone resource that can be assigned to multiple resources, with its own separate life cycle, a system-assigned managed identity is enabled within a resource and shares the life cycle of that resource.

Let's get straight into an example to demonstrate this. We're going to create a web app that reads an application setting, like we did in *Chapter 3*, *Creating Azure App Service Web Apps*, but the application setting value will be read from Key Vault:

1. Create a new App Service plan using the following Azure CLI command:

    ```
    az appservice plan create -n "< App Service plan name>"
    -g "<resource group name>" --sku "<SKU code. S1 for
    example>"
    ```

    This is assuming you're using the same resource group as before, or another existing one. By now, you should be able to create a new one if you need to.

2. Create an App Service web app that uses the newly created App Service plan:

    ```
    az webapp create -n "<web app name>" -g "<resource group
    name>" -p "<App Service plan name>"
    ```

3. Within the Azure portal, open the newly created App Service and open the **Configuration** blade.

4. Add a new application setting called KV_SECRET and give it the following value, providing your vault name and secret name: @Microsoft.KeyVault(VaultName=<vault name>;SecretName=<secret name>)

    We could have also used @Microsoft.KeyVault(SecretUri=https://<vault URI>/<secret name>/). The forward slash (/) at the end allows this to pick up newer versions of the secret, whereas if you don't add the slash, it doesn't.

5. Make sure you click **OK** and then **Save**.

    Notice that **Source** for this new setting displays **Key vault Reference**:

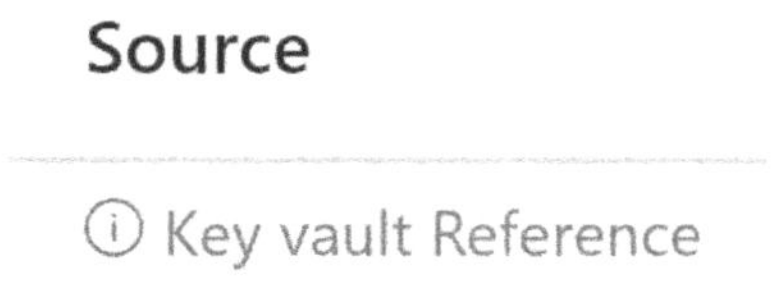

    ## Source

    ⓘ Key vault Reference

    Figure 8.3 – Application setting source showing as a Key Vault reference

6. Click **Refresh** followed by **Continue** and notice **Source** now displays an error icon:

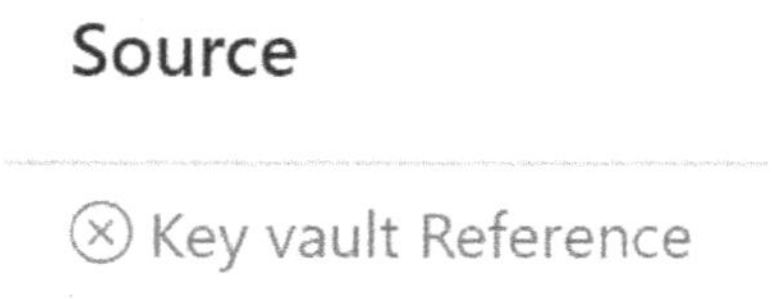

    ## Source

    ⊗ Key vault Reference

    Figure 8.4 – Key vault reference error on an application setting

7. Go to **Edit**, and you'll see the error is because no managed identity has been enabled on the App Service (although it still says **MSI** – **managed service identity** – which is the old name for managed identity):

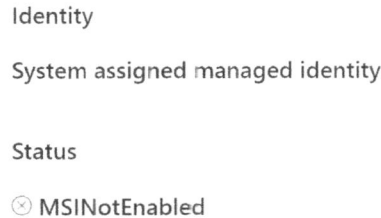

Identity

System assigned managed identity

Status

⊗ MSINotEnabled

Figure 8.5 – Key vault reference application setting error status

Notice that **Identity** is specifically saying **System assigned managed identity**. If we were to now assign our user-assigned managed identity to the App Service, this message would remain because the default behavior is for App Service to attempt authentication with a system-assigned managed identity. This can be changed, but we don't need to worry about that for this exercise.

8. Open the **Identity** blade and from the **System assigned** tab, toggle **Status** to **On**, and click **Save** followed by **Yes**.

We could have also used the following CLI command to enable the system-assigned managed identity if we didn't want to use the portal:

```
az webapp identity assign -n "<app name>" -g "<resource
group name>"
```

This has once again created a new service principal, but this time, it didn't create a standalone resource, unlike with a user-assigned managed identity. The life cycle of this system-assigned managed identity is intrinsically linked to that of the App Service.

9. Copy the **Object (principal) ID** value to the clipboard.

10. Add a new access policy to provide this new identity **Get** permissions to the secret in your key vault (make sure you set the **Secret Permissions** and not **Key** or **Certificate**) like we did before. You can either search for the App Service name or use the copied object ID. Make sure you click **Save** after adding it.

11. Go back to the **Configuration** blade and check the setting no longer shows an error. If you see an error that the key vault name isn't resolved, restart the App Service and refresh after a few moments.

12. Create a new folder for this exercise on your local machine and open a terminal session from it.

13. Create a new app using the .NET web app template:

```
dotnet new webapp
```

14. Open the folder with the newly created app files in VS Code.

15. Add a line of code similar to this in the `Pages\Index.cshtml` file:

```
<h3>Secret value: @(Environment.
GetEnvironmentVariable("KV_SECRET"))</h3>
```

If you run this locally, it will just display `Secret value:` with no value because that variable doesn't exist in this context.

16. Publish the app ready to deploy:

dotnet publish -c Release -o DeployToAppService

If you're already familiar with .NET, you'll know there are various ways to do this and create a `.zip` if you need to. Feel free to use your preferred method instead of the provided steps.

17. Assuming you're using the *Azure App Service* VS Code extension, right-click on the `DeployToAppService` folder and select **Deploy to Web App...**.

18. When prompted, select your App Service, and select **Deploy** when prompted.

19. Once it's deployed, browse to the App Service website and you should see the secret value displayed on the screen. If not, restart the App Service and try again.

To recap, we now have an identity linked to the app itself, which can be used to provide access to resources that support AAD authentication. If the application gets deleted, so does the identity.

We've been using Key Vault secrets during this chapter to explain concepts, and we have demonstrated how having a centrally managed secret store can be useful. What about configuration settings that aren't secrets? With cloud applications often being made up of many distributed components, wouldn't it be useful to have a central store of configuration settings that can be shared across these components? Enter Azure App Configuration.

Exploring Azure App Configuration

Azure App Configuration enables you to centrally manage your configuration settings, so you don't have to save all your settings in each individual component. In addition to configuration settings, you can also manage feature flags, which allow you to decouple your feature releases from code deployment, all managed centrally.

With App Configuration, you can create key-value pairs, and each setting can also be tagged with a **label**, so you can have the same key name multiple times but with different labels – perhaps a `Development` label and a `Production` label for the same key. This allows your code to reference a single key and have the value selected based on the environment (development or production, for example).

If you need security isolation between these environments, then you should create a new App Configuration store for each environment, rather than just using labels, because access control is at the per-store level.

As well as labels, you can organize your keys by adopting a hierarchical namespace approach to key names. For example, you could have all settings for an app in the MyApp namespace, and maybe add another level for service names, for example, MyApp:MyFirstService:MyAPIEndpoint and MyApp:MySecondService:MyAPIEndpoint. Ultimately, it's down to you how you want to manage this kind of thing. Keys are case sensitive as well, so bear that in mind.

All settings within App Configuration are encrypted at rest and in transit. This doesn't make App Configuration a replacement for Key Vault, however. Key Vault is still the best place to store secrets because of the hardware-level encryption, access policy model, and features such as certificate rotation, which is unique to Key Vault. You can create an App Configuration setting that pulls a value from a Key Vault secret, so your application can reference the App Configuration key and the value will come from Key Vault.

You can view and restore from historical revisions of each key, as well as compare two sets of configurations based on the times and labels you define. Unlike the app settings we've been changing so far, you don't always need to restart the service when you make changes to App Configuration keys. In fact, you can make your app handle dynamic configuration, so it will be updated with the latest key changes without needing a restart. The final exercise in this chapter will demonstrate this.

As with Key Vault, there's native integration with several popular frameworks for connecting to an App Configuration store, and we'll demonstrate this by using the **App Configuration provider for .NET Core** in an ASP.NET Core app shortly.

Also like Key Vault, you can use private endpoints to allow clients on a vNet to access data securely over a private link, and on-premises networks to connect to the VNet using VPN or ExpressRoutes with private peering, which allows you to configure the firewall to block all connections on the public endpoint.

Let's get started with creating a new App Configuration instance and have a look around. This exercise assumes we're using the same resource group as the previous exercises in this chapter, but feel free to create a new one or use a different one:

1. Create a new App Configuration resource using the CLI:

    ```
    az appconfig create -n "<unique name>" -g "<resource
    group name>" -l "<location>"
    ```

2. Create a new key-value pair (you don't need to use the same key and value as I have, as long as you use the same key for the steps that follow):

    ```
    az appconfig kv set -n "<App Config name>" --key
    "Chapter8:DemoApp:Greeting" --value "Hello, World!" --yes
    ```

    If we didn't add --yes, we'd have been prompted for confirmation before the key is created.

3. Create a new value for the same key, adding the `Development` label:

    ```
    az appconfig kv set -n "<App Config name>" --key
    "Chapter8:DemoApp:Greeting" --value "Hello from
    Development!" --label "Development" --yes
    ```

4. Create a new value with the same key, but with the `Production` label this time:

    ```
    az appconfig kv set -n "<App Config name>" --key
    "Chapter8:DemoApp:Greeting" --value "Hello from
    Production!" --label "Production" --yes
    ```

5. Within the Azure portal, find and open the **App Configuration** service (not your resource, just the service where the resources are listed).

    Notice there's a **Manage deleted stores** option. Soft delete is enabled by default on your App Configuration stores (just like in Key Vault), so if you delete one, you can recover it again if it's still within the retention period. Alternatively, you can purge the deleted stores unless purge protection is enabled. We didn't customize the retention period or enable purge protection, but you can.

6. Open your newly created App Configuration store and open the **Configuration explorer** blade, where you should see the key we just created. Click on the arrow next to it to expand and see the **Development** and **Production** entries for the same key, as well as the one without a label.

Key ↑↓	Value	Label
˅ Chapter8:DemoApp:Greeting	Hello, World!	(No label)
	Hello from Development!	Development
	Hello from Production!	Production

Figure 8.6 – New key-value pairs listed in App Configuration with both labels

If you haven't already noticed, you can click on the **Values** button with the eye icon at the top of the screen to display the values.

7. Right-click or click on the ellipsis (...) for one of the values and select **Edit**.

8. Change the value to something else and click **Apply**.

9. Right-click or click on the ellipsis (...) for the value you just changed and select **History**.

10. Expand the entries so you can see the changes in value, then click on the **Restore** button next to the original value. You'll see that the value has now reverted to the original.

11. Click on the **Create** button and select **Key Vault reference**. Notice that you can either browse through your Key Vault resources and secrets or input a secret identifier. We won't be using a Key Vault reference, so there's no need to create the reference, so you can click **Cancel**.

    Feel free to also check out the **Compare** blade. There you'll be able to compare the state of the current store with itself or another store at a specific date and time and filtered by label. Also notice there are many familiar blades, including the **Identity** blade we explored earlier in this chapter.

Now that we've seen how to create, edit, and restore a configuration setting, let's reference it within code.

App Configuration in code

Follow these steps to make use of App Configuration settings within an application's code:

1. From the **Access keys** blade, click on the **Read-only keys** tab and copy the **Connection string** value under **Primary key**. Keep this value safe because we'll need it shortly.

2. On your local machine, create a new folder for this exercise and open the new folder within a terminal session.

3. Create a new ASP.NET web app using the dotnet CLI:

    ```
    dotnet new webapp
    ```

4. Add the relevant AppConfiguration package:

    ```
    dotnet add package Microsoft.Azure.AppConfiguration.
    AspNetCore
    ```

5. Initialize a local secret store for storing the connection string:

    ```
    dotnet user-secrets init
    ```

6. Create a new local secret for the connection string, which we'll call AppConfig (make sure you use quotation marks around the connection string, because some terminal shells will truncate the string without them):

    ```
    dotnet user-secrets set ConnectionStrings:AppConfig
    "<connection string>"
    ```

7. Confirm that the connection string looks like it was saved correctly:

    ```
    dotnet user-secrets list
    ```

8. Within VS Code, open `Program.cs` and, after the line that calls the `CreateBuilder()` method, enter the following lines to set up the App Configuration connection:

```
var connectionString = builder.Configuration.
GetConnectionString("AppConfig");

builder.Host.ConfigureAppConfiguration(builder =>
{
    builder.AddAzureAppConfiguration(connectionString);
});
```

Because we didn't add any options to `AddAzureAppConfiguration()`, we'll be getting the value that didn't have a label assigned, because, by default, it will load configuration values with no labels/label values of `null`.

9. Open the `Pages\Index.cshtml` file and replace the code with the following:

```
@page
@using Microsoft.Extensions.Configuration
@inject IConfiguration Configuration
@model IndexModel
@{
    ViewData["Title"] = "Home page";
}


<h1>Message: @Configuration["Chapter8:DemoApp:Greeting"]</
h1>
```

We're using the .NET Core Configuration API to access the store, and we're using Razor syntax to display the message in the final line.

10. Confirm the project builds successfully:

    dotnet build

11. Run the program and then open the URL shown in the output in your chosen web browser:

    dotnet run

    You should be presented with the message we created in App Configuration.

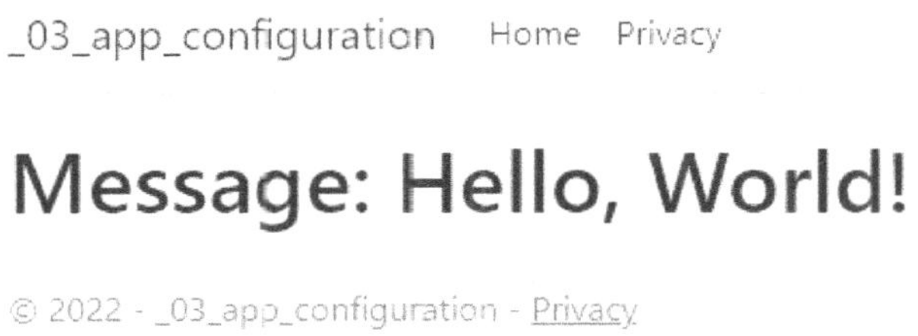

_03_app_configuration   Home   Privacy

Message: Hello, World!

© 2022 - _03_app_configuration - Privacy

Figure 8.7 – Website showing message from App Configuration

12. Stop the app with *Ctrl* + *C* in the terminal.

Great! That proves everything is working as expected. We could now edit that App Configuration value and run the app again, but we can be confident of the outcome. Let's instead make use of labels now. We're going to use `HostingEnvironment.EnvironmentName` to determine within which environment the app is running, which will correlate to our labels:

1. Back in the VS Code terminal session, run the following command to add the package required to filter App Configuration keys:

```
dotnet add package Microsoft.Extensions.Configuration.
AzureAppConfiguration
```

2. Open `Program.cs` and add the following line at the top of the file:

```
using Microsoft.Extensions.Configuration.
AzureAppConfiguration;
```

3. On the line immediately after the `var builder = WebApplication.CreateBuilder(args);` line, add the following line, which will allow us to access the user secrets (containing the connection string) in environments other than `Development`:

```
builder.Configuration.AddUserSecrets<Program>();
```

As you may already know, user secrets are only intended for development, so `AddUserSecrets<>()` is included in the default options for the `Development` environment but not others. We're changing that behavior for the purposes of this exercise.

4. Replace the `ConfigureAppConfiguration()` code block with the following, which returns any keys with a label that matches the current environment:

```
builder.Host.ConfigureAppConfiguration((hostingContext,
builder) =>
{
    builder.AddAzureAppConfiguration(options =>
```

```
        {
            options.Connect(connectionString)
                    .Select(KeyFilter.Any, hostingContext.
        HostingEnvironment.EnvironmentName);
        });
    });
```

5. Run the app again, as before, and browse to it. You should see the greeting you created with the `Development` label.

6. Stop the app running and this time, change the environment to `Production` and when you browse, you should notice the greeting you created with the `Production` label being displayed:

    ```
    dotnet run --environment Production
    ```

We've just seen how we can change the behavior of our app, without needing to make changes to our code, by using labels. We could have also made changes to the values in App Configuration. Consider the value this service can bring when you have multiple services using the same keys – change the value in one central location and all relevant services will be able to pick up the changes.

Another common requirement in modern development is to decouple feature releases from code deployment, so you can push code continuously into production without the risk of impacting production because the code is *hidden* behind a feature flag that is yet to be enabled.

Feature flags

The concept of a feature flag is very straightforward – it's a Boolean variable which has some code that executes based on the value of the flag. For example, you may have a new UI in development and although you're still deploying the code, the code that changes the UI sits behind a feature flag that defaults to `false`. You may have the option for users to opt into the new experience, so the flag gets changed to `true` and the new UI code runs.

You can also use a filter to evaluate the state of a feature flag. For example, user group memberships, device types, locations, and specific time windows can be evaluated and can ultimately determine the state of a feature flag. Feature flags can also act as a safety net – if something undesired happens as a result of enabling a feature, just toggle the feature back off.

App Configuration provides a centralized repository for your feature flags, so you can externalize feature flags and change their state quickly from Azure without having to modify or redeploy the application. Let's check out feature flags and how to use them in code. We'll also add the ability to automatically update when changes are made without needing to restart the app:

1. Within the Azure portal, open your App Configuration resource and open the **Feature manager** blade.

2. Click on **Create**. Leave the **Enable feature flag** box unchecked, enter demofeature for the **Feature flag name**, and add the Development label.

3. Check the **Use feature filter** box and explore the options available for filtering. When this is done, uncheck the box again as we won't be using a filter for this example. Then click **Apply**.

4. Repeat the process again, creating a new feature flag with the same demofeature name, but this time, add the Production label.

    Your list should now look like this:

Name	Label	Enabled
demofeature	Development	☐
demofeature	Production	☐

Figure 8.8 – Two feature flags with the same name and different labels

5. Open the project we were using for the last exercise in VS Code.

6. Add the FeatureManagement package to the project:

```
dotnet add package Microsoft.FeatureManagement.AspNetCore
```

7. Open Program.cs and add the following line to the top of the file:

```
using Microsoft.FeatureManagement;
```

8. Replace your builder.AddAzureAppConfiguration() block with the following:

```
builder.AddAzureAppConfiguration(options =>
{
    options.Connect(connectionString)
           .UseFeatureFlags(option =>
           {
           option.Select("demofeature",
hostingContext.HostingEnvironment.EnvironmentName);
           })
           .ConfigureRefresh(refreshOptions =>
           {
               refreshOptions.
Register("demofeature");
           })
```

```
                      .Select(KeyFilter.Any, hostingContext.
        HostingEnvironment.EnvironmentName);
          });
```

Here, we're allowing the use of feature flags and returning only those features with the name of `demofeature` and with labels that match our hosting environment, just like we did with the keys in the previous exercise. We're also using `ConfigureRefresh` to monitor `demofeature` for changes. Once changes occur, the app will update after the refresh interval, which is 30 seconds by default.

9. Add the following lines just before the `var app = builder.Build();` line:

    ```
    builder.Services.AddAzureAppConfiguration()
                    .AddFeatureManagement();
    ```

10. Just after the `var app = builder.Build();` line, add the following line so we can use the App Configuration middleware for the dynamic refresh we just configured:

    ```
    app.UseAzureAppConfiguration();
    ```

11. Open the `Pages\_ViewImports.cshtml` file and add the following line to add the feature management tag helper:

    ```
    @addTagHelper *, Microsoft.FeatureManagement.AspNetCore
    ```

12. Open `Pages\Index.cshtml` and add the following to the bottom of the file, which will display the text only if the relevant feature flag is enabled:

    ```
    <feature name="demofeature">
        <h1>Demo feature enabled!</h1>
    </feature>
    ```

13. Confirm the application builds and run it with the following two commands:

    ```
    dotnet build
    dotnet run
    ```

14. Browse to the local app page and you should see the same as in our previous exercise. Don't stop the app or close the browser tab.

15. Enable the feature flag with the **Development** label, wait around 30 seconds, then refresh the browser tab with the app page open. You should see that the demo feature text is now showing.

    Feel free to experiment further and add the `--environment Production` switch to the `dotnet run` command to see the difference if you wish.

Conceptually, we now have a way to deploy new code into production that will only be executed under certain circumstances, including the feature flag being enabled, without having to restart the app or make any additional code changes. Once a feature is rolled out to production, enabled, and fully tested, you probably want to clean up your code and remove the feature flag logic, so it becomes a normal part of the code.

That was a very basic example, but it has hopefully given you enough insight to grasp the concept and be able to answer any exam questions related to feature flags. Feel free to delete any resources created during this chapter if you want.

Summary

In this chapter, we explored some of the key services and features available for implementing secure solutions on Azure. We started off with a look into centralized secret management with Azure Key Vault, including how authorization and authentication work with it.

This led us onto the topic of managed identities, where we discussed user-assigned and system-assigned managed identities and used `Azure.Identity` to authenticate either with local credentials or – when the app is running in Azure – the managed identity via `DefaultAzureCredential`.

We finished off this chapter by exploring Azure App Configuration for centralized configuration management, discussing various ways to organize your settings with namespaces and labels, and how to reference them in code.

Finally, we ended the topic by discussing the feature management capabilities of App Configuration and some of the useful features, including making use of the feature in code and automatically refreshing without needing to restart the app.

In the next chapter, we're going to introduce the caching solutions available within Azure. We'll go into common caching patterns, Azure Cache for Redis, and how to use content delivery networks for web applications.

Questions

1. Which type of managed identity shares its life cycle with an Azure resource?

2. If you want to use App Configuration to read a secret value, what's the recommended approach to achieve this?

3. Which method of authenticating your app to Key Vault is recommended for most scenarios and doesn't require you to manage secret rotation?

4. Which Key Vault permission model is used for controlling access to the vault's management plane?

Further reading

- The Azure Key Vault Developer's Guide can be found here: `https://docs.microsoft.com/azure/key-vault/general/developers-guide`

- Key Vault insights (preview) documentation can be found here: `https://docs.microsoft.com/azure/azure-monitor/insights/key-vault-insights-overview`

- Managed identities documentation can be found here: `https://docs.microsoft.com/azure/active-directory/managed-identities-azure-resources/overview`

- A list of services that can use managed identities can be found here: `https://docs.microsoft.com/azure/active-directory/managed-identities-azure-resources/managed-identities-status`

- Azure App Configuration documentation can be found here: `https://docs.microsoft.com/azure/azure-app-configuration/overview`

- Documentation on using customer-managed keys to encrypt App Configuration data can be found here: `https://docs.microsoft.com/azure/azure-app-configuration/concept-customer-managed-keys`

- App Configuration feature management documentation can be found here: `https://docs.microsoft.com/azure/azure-app-configuration/concept-feature-management`

- To learn about using `ConfigurationBuilder` to configure ASP.NET apps to retrieve secrets from Azure Key Vault, check out the following learning path: `https://docs.microsoft.com/learn/modules/aspnet-configurationbuilder`

- To learn more about implementing feature flags in cloud-native ASP.NET Core microservices, check out the following learning path: `https://docs.microsoft.com/learn/modules/microservices-configuration-aspnet-core`

Part 4: Implementing Monitoring, Troubleshooting, and Optimization Solutions in Azure

This part will start by introducing guidelines for using cache technology to improve the performance of modern web applications. You will learn about use cases of Azure Cache for Redis and **Content Delivery Networks (CDNs)**. You will learn recommendations about data sizing, connections encryption, and cache expiration settings to build secure and optimized applications.

The rest of the part describes the main techniques of monitoring and troubleshooting applications running in Azure. You will discover Azure Monitor and Application Insights monitoring and telemetry services. The part introduces the main applications of instrumentation and monitoring frameworks hosted in Azure. You will learn how to use Application Insights and Azure Monitor to detect performance bottlenecks and handle errors. The chapter will also explain the alerting capabilities of the Azure platform.

This part covers 15-20% of the AZ-204 exam questions.

The following chapters will be covered under this section:

- *Chapter 9, Integrating Caching and Content Delivery within Solutions*
- *Chapter 10, Troubleshooting Solutions by Using Metrics and Log Data*

9

Integrating Caching and Content Delivery within Solutions

This chapter introduces guidelines for using cache technology to improve the performance of modern web applications. You will learn about best practices with **Azure Cache for Redis** (also referred to as Azure Cache) and **content delivery networks (CDNs)**. These **platform as a service (PaaS)** technologies help to improve loading speed for customer sites and reduce the load for backend and data storage. They also increase the availability of the static content cached on a CDN such as media, scripts, and configuration files with a hundred copies across the internet.

Another common scenario where caching technology can help is delivering updates. IoT devices and mobile devices can download and install updates synchronously without overloading the origin server. Popular packaging registries such as NuGet and registries of container images such as the Docker Hub benefit from a CDN by caching their binaries close to the clients who want to download them.

In this chapter, you will get recommendations on how to reap the maximum benefits from caching solutions, including managing data size, connection encryption, and cache expiration settings, to increase security availability and reduce costs.

In this chapter, we will cover the following main topics:

- Introducing caching patterns
- Exploring Azure Cache for Redis
- Exploring Azure Content Delivery Network

Technical requirements

In addition to the technical requirements outlined in previous chapters, you will require the following to follow along with the exercises:

- The **Azure Cache extension for Visual Studio Code** – downloadable from here: `https://marketplace.visualstudio.com/items?itemName=ms-azurecache.vscode-azurecache`.

- **Redis command-line tools for Windows** – downloadable from here: `https://github.com/microsoftarchive/redis/releases`.

- The code files for this chapter can be downloaded from: `https://github.com/PacktPublishing/Developing-Solutions-for-Microsoft-Azure-AZ-204-Exam-Guide/tree/main/Chapter09`.

Code in Action videos for this chapter: `https://bit.ly/3Bsut1l`

Introducing caching patterns

When we start introducing caching technology, we should look back and find out what cache technology is. The cache is a service that stores data, like in the database, but provides the fastest access and does not persist data longer than requested by time-to-live settings. The data stored in the cache is usually the result of previous calculations or commonly requested data retrieved with a higher speed than from the database. In other words, the cache is a temporary storage of precomputed data. What data can be cached for modern web services? Firstly, the output of pages. Millions of page views on modern websites that retrieve the same page that is rarely updated can cache the output to return the user the previously generated response and save website resources.

The idea of caching temporary output is not new. Caching solutions were generally used for application services such as websites way before Azure built its first data center. One of the first officially supported caching algorithms was output caching. It was introduced in ASP.NET and developers can use web server memory to temporarily cache output. It works perfectly for static or almost static legacy websites, but it is not suitable for modern websites now because changes happen so often and page content expires immediately after caching. Another recommended approach is caching content based on query parameters. It helps in some cases but significantly increases memory consumption and slows down websites. Overall, output caching is not the best approach for modern websites. Meanwhile, the caching of objects used for generating pages will improve performance like upgrading a database will.

For example, an e-commerce website page contains a list of products with their given prices and stock quantities. The product list is rarely updated and can be cached for days; meanwhile, the prices may change every hour and stock items may be updated every minute. So, caching output for minutes does not improve performance but can cause inconsistency with stock counts. Clients will complain if they see that a product available on the main page cannot be ordered because it is out of stock.

How do we solve these problems and speed up performance? Let's imagine a powerful technology established to temporarily cache the list of products for days, the price of products for hours, and the stock count for less than a minute. Let's imagine the app can access that service faster than going to the database. Otherwise, there is no reason to have the data cached. Let's imagine we can manually update this temporary storage when the data is changed in the source database (for example, an item is ordered and the stock count needs to decrease). **Azure Cache for Redis** should be considered for this kind of scenario.

The **Redis cache** is a powerful memory-based caching solution that can perfectly support our scenario and apply different treatments for each type of data. In other words, the Redis cache can perfectly support cache-aside patterns and can seriously improve your app performance. There is a trade-off between consistency and performance but you have all the power to manage and adjust data in the cache until it expires.

Let's look at how we can implement a *cache-aside pattern* in Azure. We will also recommend two scenarios for refreshing data in the cache and you can select which works for your application better.

First, if the data is stored in the cache, it needs to be pulled at high speed. It will work best if you have data cached on the same server. Unfortunately, the local cache of one server cannot be used for another, so this prevents scaling. Instead of using local memory, the cache can be deployed on the dedicated server with high-speed connections.

Second, the data needs to be updated when it expires. For that reason, we can use a custom **time to live** (TTL) for each type of data you use. When the data expires, it can be cleaned up from the cache so it can be replaced by updated data from the database. Here, we can make the data client load the data and store that data in the cache to speed up the next load. The alternative option is to have the cache server generate an event to trigger your application just before the data expires to load updated values from the database.

Both options have pros and cons. If you make the client server load the data from the database when it is expired from the cache, you will have a *cold* request first before the *hot* request will reuse the data from the cache. Alternatively, if you build a service to refresh the expired data from the cache, you will avoid the first *cold* request but must spend more memory loading the data that is not going to be reused. Because the price you pay for caching in Azure depends on your memory usage, the preload solution can be quite expensive.

Finally, you can combine the advantages of preloading data and minimize the size of stored data by providing custom settings for each data type that you cache. Moreover, you can manually monitor changes in the database and update the cache and the database in the same transaction.

Let's observe how the *cache-aside pattern* works for the e-commerce website we discussed previously. You will notice that the first request hits the database but the second request retrieved cached versions of products and decreased the database's load:

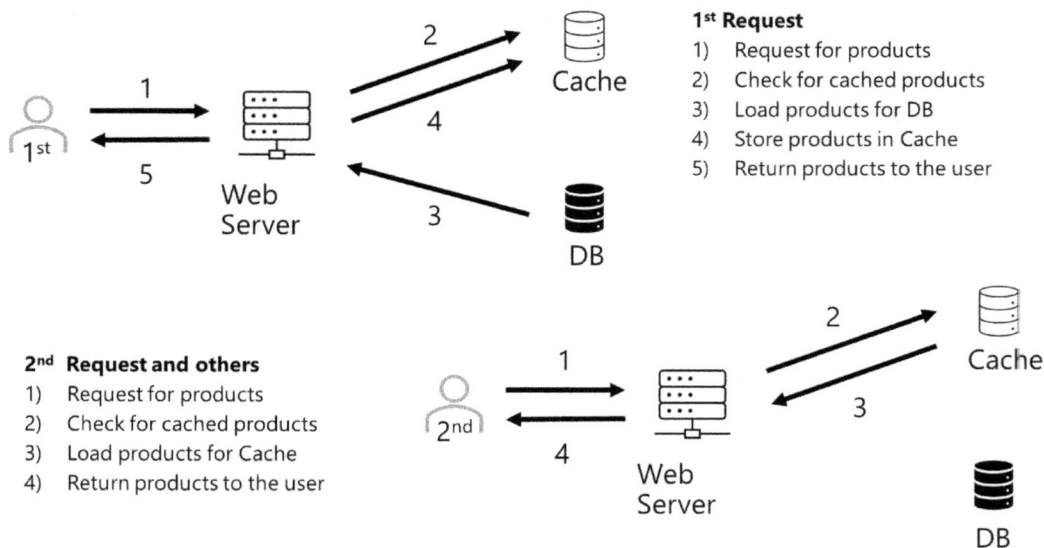

1st Request
1) Request for products
2) Check for cached products
3) Load products for DB
4) Store products in Cache
5) Return products to the user

2nd Request and others
1) Request for products
2) Check for cached products
3) Load products for Cache
4) Return products to the user

Figure 9.1 – Implementation of the cache-aside pattern with Azure Cache for Redis

You already know the benefits of caching and the main patterns used for building effective caching strategies and reducing consistency issues. Now is the best time to take a look at what caching services are available in Azure. We will start from Azure Cache for Redis and continue with Azure CDN.

Exploring Azure Cache for Redis

Azure Cache for Redis is the Microsoft implementation of well-known Redis software. **Redis** means **Remote Dictionary Server** and was initially implemented in 2009 as a memory management service implemented on C and hosted on a Unix-like platform. Redis provides open source NoSQL storage, allowing the persisting of complex data structures for key-value storage. Redis supports clustering technology, which prevents it from failing and losing data in memory.

Microsoft adopted Redis technology to successfully run in Azure as a PaaS with a single server tier and cluster as well. Moreover, Azure Cache for Redis provides Redis open source and a commercial product from Redis Labs (Redis Enterprise) as secure and dedicated instances with full Redis API compatibility. Azure Cache for Redis can be used for various scenarios, including a cache-aside pattern for content and data persistence, a message broker, and even a sessions service transparently integrated with the .NET platform. Azure Cache for Redis depends on the pricing tier, deployed as a standalone or cluster, along with other Azure databases such as Azure SQL or Cosmos DB. Because Redis technology is based on the TCP protocol, it requires a specific port to be opened for communication with services provisioned in Azure or on-premises.

When you provision Azure Cache for Redis, you need to select the appropriate pricing tier. There are several pricing tiers available to meet everyone's expectations:

- The **Basic tier** does not provide an SLA and should not be used for any production workloads. Meanwhile, it is ideal for development or testing. It does not support any clustering technology or geo-replication and this makes the service charges as low as possible.

- The **Standard tier** is suitable for production workloads and supports failover with primary/replica duplication. It still does not support cluster or geo-replication but provides an SLA of 99.9%. The Standard tier still does not persist the caching data during restarts, so your application should not rely on the persisting data in cache memory and should use the cache-aside pattern.

- The **Premium tier** provides the same features as the Standard tier and some advanced features such as clustering and data persistence that are important to many enterprises. It runs two nodes under the hood and can persist data during node restarts with an appropriate hangover to another synced node. Some useful features such as networking and importing are available only with the Premium tier.

- The **Enterprise tier** has all the functionality of the Premium tier, plus powerful enterprise-ready features such as Redis Search, Redis Bloom, and active geo-replication. Its availability has grown to an SLA of 99.999% and is suitable for business-critical applications.

- The **Enterprise Flash tier** has the same powerful reliability as the Enterprise tier but runs on fast non-volatile storage for massive cache implementations. In addition, it supports Redis Flash technology and provides a huge amount of memory, up to 1.5 TB.

Each pricing tier supports several sub-tiers with the ability to granularly manage required memory and connection. The number of client connections might also limit your application if using low-tier mode. Luckily, you can monitor connections from Azure Monitor and be notified when it reaches the limit to upgrade your instance to higher sub-tiers.

In the next paragraphs, you will learn more about Azure Cache by provisioning an instance in Azure and discovering its advanced settings, including pricing tiers, console commands, and security configuration. Let's learn how to provision the service from the Azure CLI.

Provisioning Azure Cache for Redis from the Azure CLI

Provisioning an Azure Cache for Redis instance can be completed from the Azure portal, the Azure CLI, and PowerShell. To complete provisioning, you need to choose the region where you want the service located, the unique DNS name, and the pricing tier. The region should be the same as you use for the hosting of your solution to avoid cross -data center charges for traffic. The pricing tier should be chosen based on the requirements for memory consumption. For example, for the Basic tier, you can choose sizes between 0.25 GB and 50 GB. If the consumption grows, you can upgrade your size and migrate to a higher tier.

By running the following CLI commands, you will learn how to provision your Azure Cache for Redis instance and retrieve the connection keys for the connection. The commands should be run in Azure Cloud Shell, bash, or the bash terminal, with the Azure CLI installed locally:

```
#create a resource group
az group create --location eastus2 --name AzureCache-RG
#to avoid name collisions generate a unique name for your
account
account=azurecache$RANDOM
#create Basic SKU instance
az redis create --location eastus2 --name $account --resource-
group AzureCache-RG --sku Basic --vm-size C0
#retrieve key and address
$key=$(az redis list-keys --name $account --resource-group
AzureCache-RG --query primaryKey -o tsv)
echo $key
echo $account.redis.cache.windows.net
```

The list of commands can be found at https://github.com/PacktPublishing/Developing-Solutions-for-Microsoft-Azure-AZ-204-Exam-Guide/blob/main/Chapter09/1-redis-provision/demo.azcli.

Upon successful execution of the previous commands, you should have provisioned an instance of the Azure Cache for Redis in your Azure subscription. In further tasks, you will learn how to configure the instance and access the Redis console.

Advanced configuration

From the Azure portal, you can find the instance you built and investigate the following advanced settings for security, diagnostics, and monitoring. You can also open the **Redis console** from the browser to run the commands to manage the instance.

Access key

To connect to the Redis instance in Azure from the SDK or console clients, you need to provide a connection key. There are two keys provided to meet compliance requirements for the periodic rotation of key values. You can choose the first key or copy the connection string with the key; then later, you can update the connection to leverage the second key and regenerate the first key without interrupting the application. Be aware that keys provide you full access to the key values and allow you to read, write, and manage the instance. You can find keys and connection strings from the **Access key** section of your Redis page on the Azure portal.

Firewall and virtual network integration

Azure Cache for Redis provides a variety of options for managing networking connections. You can rebind default port numbers. The 6379 and 6380 TCP ports are used for open and encrypted SSL connections. Remember that Azure Cache for Redis uses fast TCP communication instead of slow HTTPS requests.

The Azure Redis cache provides firewall rules customization. By default, no rules are defined, and connections are allowed from any IP address. You can replace the default rule with a rule for the exact IP or IP range. The private endpoint is available for leverage to connect specific types of services directly to the cache – Azure App Services, for example.

You can provide the firewall rules in the **Firewall** section of your instance on the Azure portal.

Diagnostic settings

There are several important metrics for Azure Cache for Redis that you need to monitor during production workload to avoid connection errors. A recommended best practice is setting up Azure alerts for these metrics to be notified when the workload exists in your instance. Here are two examples of important metrics:

- **Memory consumption**: A memory usage metric will allow you to monitor your current cache size and your maximum size depending on the tier level. During high memory pressure, your cache may start saving data on disk and significantly decrease performance.

- **Connected clients**: This is another important metric limited by the tier of your instance. New clients cannot be connected when the number of connections hits the maximum for your tier. High client connection numbers can also lead to a high server load when responding to repeated reconnection attempts.

For **Premium** and **Enterprise** pricing tiers, the Azure Cache for Redis instance can be configured with access from a virtual network. In this case, your cache instance can only be connected to virtual machines and applications within the virtual network of your choice.

The Redis console

There are several tools you can use to view and manage data stored in the cache:

- **redis-cli** – the original Redis client console, which you can install and run from localhost and use to communicate with the server in Azure. You need to provide connection information, including a hostname, port, and key. Remember that the console uses the default TCP ports 6379 and 6380 for the connection. Your client settings for SSL or no-SSL ports should match the settings on the server.

- The **Azure Cache extension for Visual Studio Code** – available for download and installation with your VS Code interface. When you sign in with your Azure account, the tool will retrieve a list of instances with a list of keys in it. You can create or delete existing keys from the UI.

- The **Azure Redis console** – a web-integrated tool that runs directly from the Azure portal and leverages connection through an automatically configured port on the server side. The tool only supports Redis commands and we will use this console in the next demos. You can find the console icon at the top of the **Overview** section of your Azure Cache for Redis page.

You have just learned about the different types of client applications that you can leverage to monitor and observe the content stored in the cache. In the next section, you will learn how to leverage the Azure Redis console to execute commands to operate with different data types.

Implementing basic operations with cached data

The Redis cache supports a variety of types to store any string or binary data in a key-value structure. It also supports the nested key-value structure. Each value associated with a key can be used as the key name of another key-value pair. The names of the keys should be self-explanatory, such as `user-name` or `product:price:usd`. A good naming approach will help you to manage the data in the cache explorer. For best performance, the value of the keys should be less than 100 KB and bigger values should be split into multiple keys.

The Redis cache supports the following types of data:

- **Strings** are the most common basic data values in Redis. With string data types, you can store JSON documents, binary representations of images, or cryptography keys. The maximum string value is 512 MB. The following operations can be used for creating and retrieving string values:

  - For retrieving or updating string values: `GET`, `SET`, and `GETSET`

  - For retrieving or updating binary values: `GETBIT` and `SETBIT`

  - For when an integer is stored in the string values and can be incremented or decremented: `INCR`, `DECR`, and `INCRBY`

  - For appending to strings: `APPEND`

  - For retrieving or updating part of a string: `GETRANGE` and `SETRANGE`

- **Lists** are lists of strings, sorted by insertion order. You can create a list by adding a new element to the empty key. You can remove elements and list existing elements. Accessing list elements is very fast near the start and end of the list but accessing the middle elements is slow. The following operations can be used for creating and retrieving lists:

  - For adding a new element to the top of the list: `LPUSH`

  - For adding a new element to the bottom of the list: `RPUSH`

  - For retrieving inserted items: `LRANGE`

- **Sets** are an unsorted collection of string elements. You can add, remove, and check for the existence of elements in a set. Sets can only add unique elements. This means that adding the same elements several times will override the same items, instead of adding a new item such as adding items in a list. The following operations can be used for creating and accessing items in sets:

  - For adding new values to a set: SADD

  - For retrieving the number of elements in a set: SCARD

  - For retrieving elements from a set: SMEMBER

- **Hashes** are collections that map string fields and string values. Hashes are used mainly to store objects. They can store a large number of elements compactly, so you can use hashes for storing your custom objects with a large number of fields. The following operations help to manage hashes:

  - For adding fields to a hash: HMSET

  - For listing all fields in a hash: HGETALL

Furthermore, Azure Cache for Redis supports the following technical commands that you can also run to get additional information about a cache instance:

- For retrieving the number of keys in a cache instance: DBSIZE

- For retrieving information about connected clients: CLIENT LIST

- For retrieving full information about instances, including size, IP address, tier, version, and such: INFO

In the following hands-on exercise, you will be able to run these commands to understand how they work. Then, you will be able to leverage SDKs to get connected to cache instances and store and retrieve data in string, list, set, and hash data types. There are several C# SDKs you can integrate into your project:

SDK name	Description
ServiceStack.Redis	The fork of the original C# client was written by Miguel De Icaza but significantly improved by adding new commands.
StackExchange.Redis	A well-known .NET client developed by Stack Exchange (Stack Overflow) for high-performance needs. We will use this package further for demo tasks.
BeetleX.Redis	A high-performance Redis client for .NET Core, the default supports JSON, the Protobuf data format, and asynchronous calls.
FreeRedis	This .NET client supports Redis 6.0+, clusters, sentinels, pipelines, and simple APIs.

Table 9.1 – Popular C# SDKs to manage Redis from code

In this section, you have learned what different types of data are available in Redis. Now, we'll move on to the next section to learn the commands to manipulate those data types from the Redis console.

Manipulating data in Azure Cache from the console

To get a better understanding of how caches manage different data types, the best option is to try to execute commands from the console and observe the results. To run these commands, you need to open the console in the Azure portal and execute the commands one by one. To get connected from `redis-cli`, you need to provide a name for your Azure cache instance and the access keys for the connection. To run the Redis console from the browser, you can open the Azure portal, find the instance you built from the previous demo, and select the **Overview** section. At the top of the page, under the name of your cache instance, you can find the console icon to run the console. Run the complete list of commands that can be found here:

```
https://github.com/PacktPublishing/Developing-Solutions-for-Microsoft-
Azure-AZ-204-Exam-Guide/blob/main/Chapter09/2-commands/commands.txt
```

To observe the results directly from the cache instance, you can install the **Azure Cache extension for Visual Studio Code**, open the **Azure** tab (next to the extension), and find the **Cache** section. If you've already run a command to set values, you will see **DB 0** and a list of the keys that you can open to observe the value.

Manipulating data in Azure Cache from C# code

Now you already know how to configure, test, and monitor your cache instance. You know how to leverage commands for observing the data in the cache. In the next task, you will build a C# console app to read and write data in different formats including lists, sets, and hashes. In the same way as you operated with the previous simple command from the preceding console, you can implement code to persist objects from a database with the cache-aside pattern. The following link contains a ready-to-go project to demonstrate your connecting and data manipulating operations:

```
https://github.com/PacktPublishing/Developing-Solutions-for-Microsoft-
Azure-AZ-204-Exam-Guide/tree/main/Chapter09/3-redis-sdk
```

The following table lists the classes used for accessing and manipulating data of Azure Cache for Redis in the previous code example:

Class	Description
RedisKey	Represents the key stored in the cache. It can implicitly convert string to and from and binary values.
RedisValue	Represents the value (string or binary data) of the key.

Class	Description
ConnectionMultiplexer	Has multi-purpose usage, mostly for accessing the Redis database and also retrieving server metrics such as status, subscribers, and slots. It also handles connection state change events. This thread-safe class instance should be configured just once.
IDatabase	The main database interface, implementing all operations with keys and values. It maps the Redis console commands to use ReadisKey and RedisValue. It has asynchronous and synchronous commands.

Table 9.2 – SDK classes for data manipulation in Azure Cache for Redis

In the previous code example, you explored commands to persist different types of data in the cache. In the next section's code examples, you will build a session service for the graceful scaling of a web application.

Leveraging Azure Cache for persisting web sessions

In the following code example, we implement a session state service for sharing state information between website instances. Usually, legacy applications do not provide appropriate session handling for session information. As a result, session values get lost when the user's request is routed to another server instance, or the number of instances is scaled in. Losing session values can lead to application crashes and harm your users. Azure Cache for Redis provides a solution with a centralized session store that makes your application pass session values to another instance through writing and reading the session data from cache.

Let's look at the following ASP.NET Core configuration with session handling implemented. Before you run the project, you need to update the `appsettings.config` configuration file and provide your Redis instance connection string in the `AzureRedis` parameter:

```
https://github.com/PacktPublishing/Developing-Solutions-for-Microsoft-
Azure-AZ-204-Exam-Guide/tree/main/Chapter09/4-redis-stateserver
```

In the project, you can observe how the session state is enabled in `StartupRedis.cs` by adding `builder.Services.AddSession` and `builder.Services.AddDistributedMemoryCache` to the initialization code. The **StackExchange** provider for Redis is also configured in the same file to persist the session.

When testing how the cache hosts the session during server restarts, you need to run the project. Then, you should enter the **session value** in the text field and save it by clicking on the **Set** button. The update automatically refreshes and pulls the value from the session to the page, and you can observe the values. The values are also saved in Azure Cache for Redis transparently.

Then, you can restart the web server, clean up the session in memory, and mimic swapping slots or scale in. When the server starts again, you can refresh the web page and retrieve the stored value. Now, the values are transparently loaded from Azure Cache for Redis back to the session and appear on the page. The following screen demonstrates the session loaded from the cache:

ASP.NET Core Session State Provider for Azure Cache for Redis

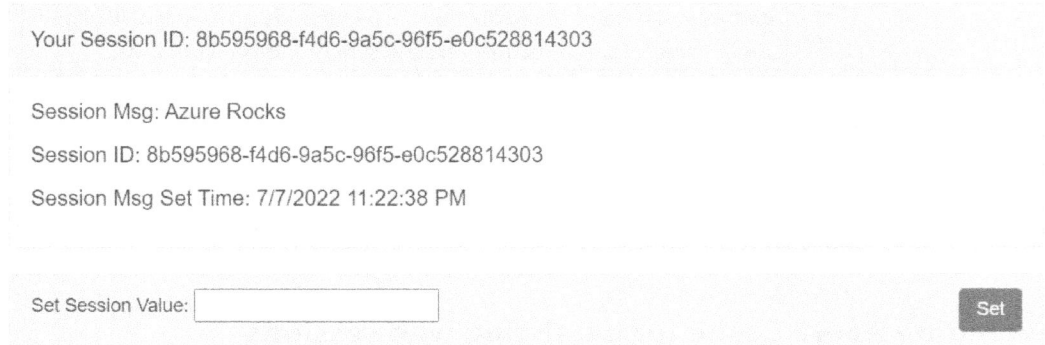

Your Session ID: 8b595968-f4d6-9a5c-96f5-e0c528814303

Session Msg: Azure Rocks

Session ID: 8b595968-f4d6-9a5c-96f5-e0c528814303

Session Msg Set Time: 7/7/2022 11:22:38 PM

Set Session Value: [   ]   Set

Figure 9.2 – The page loaded the Azure Rocks session value from the session stored on Azure Cache

In addition to session state, there are other cache scenarios when the cache is used as a message broker. For example, one application is used for updating data in the Redis cache and another application will read the updated data. Leveraging Azure Cache for Redis is not an optimal solution in terms of price, but ideal in terms of performance. Meanwhile, we recommend using **Azure Service Bus** or **Azure Queue** for implementing a message broker pattern. These messaging services will be explored in *Chapter 13, Developing Message-Based Solutions*.

How to cache your data effectively

When you design and develop an application, you need to be aware of the following guidelines about the appropriate use of Azure Cache:

- First, you need to choose data for caching. You should not cache every piece of information in your source database. This decision should be based on the data source and workload of your application. The greater the amount of data you have and the greater the number of people that need to access it, the greater the benefits of caching become, because caching minimizes the latency of handling large amounts of concurrent requests in the original data storage. Consider caching data that is regularly read but hardly updated. Again, you should not utilize the cache as the official repository for crucial information. Caches can be restarted or information lost under high memory pressure. That means you should not store the data you cannot lose in the cache. If your application is updating any data, you can update the cache and source or update the source and wait until the cache data expires and it will be replaced with a new copy.

- Second, you need to properly configure the expiration time. You can set Azure Cache for Redis to expire data and shorten the duration when the data persisted in the cache. It makes your application retrieve data from the dataset more often and the performance decrease again. According to the cache-aside pattern, when cached data expires, it is deleted from the cache, requiring the application to retrieve the data from the original data store. When configuring the cache, you may provide a default expiration policy, as well as a specific expiration for each object. You can trace the queries to your database and analyze how often it's updated based on choosing a shorter expiration for corresponding objects. Specify the expiration period for the cache and the objects in it wisely. If you make it too short, objects will expire too quickly, and you will not get any performance gain. If you make the period too long, you have a risk of getting inconsistent data.

- Third, implement availability and scalability. It is important to understand that the cache is not a critical service in your application. The application should be able to function if it is unavailable. The application should not become unresponsive or fail while waiting for the cache service to resume. Always use an asynchronous pattern and retry policy for retrieving data from the cache. Remember that the basic tier of Azure Cache for Redis does not provide any SLA and should not be used for production workloads. Moreover, the standard tier may not be the best choice because of the low SLA and inability to leverage cluster technology. Clustering can increase the availability of the cache. If a node fails, the second node of the cache will still be working and will provide the service. You should be aware that the scaling of your cache instance can take a significant amount of time (up to an hour) and some of the pricing tiers will not allow downgrading to a lower tier, but you can still scale available memory.

You have already learned about the advantages of using Azure Cache for dynamic content managed from the application server and replacing the database. The next section of the chapter will introduce the caching technology available for static content. Let's take a look at how caching static content can improve modern web applications.

Exploring Azure Content Delivery Network

You are already familiar with how to cache dynamic content with a cache-aside pattern. Now, let's take a look at static content caching technology. The cache-aside pattern is still in play but now it needs to cache static files such as images, videos, JavaScript files, and CSS files. For legacy websites, these files are usually stored on the server, and delivery to the customerdelivery to the customer takes time takes time. Caching those files close to the user can significantly speed up loading and let the web server focus on processing dynamic pages. Azure proposes a solution by caching static files globally as close to users as possible with its **CDN**.

A CDN is a distributed network of endpoints that can host and deliver web content to users quickly and efficiently. To reduce latency, CDNs cache content on edge servers in **point of presence** (**POP**) locations close to end users. POP works like an old-school proxy in corporate networks but is geographically spread across many locations. Azure CDN provides developers with a global option for rapidly delivering high-bandwidth content to customers. Azure CDN also helps minimize traffic from the origin server and suits scenarios involving delivering application updates. The following figure represents how static content can be cached on POP servers:

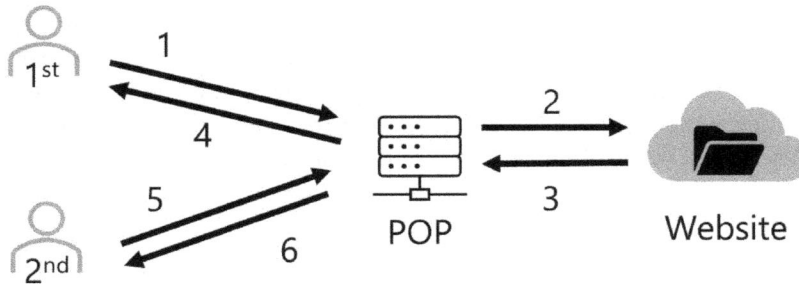

1ˢᵗ Request:

1) File requested
2) File does not exist on the POP and the request is sent to the server
3) File provided and cached on POP
4) File returned to the user

2ⁿᵈ Request and others:

5) File requested
6) Cached copy of file returned to the user

Figure 9.3 – Implementation of the cache-aside pattern with CDN

Azure CDN supports two caching modes: loading assets on demand (based on the user request) and prepopulating assets from the origin to minimize delays with the first request. If you prefer to use an on-demand model, the first user request will initialize loading the asset directly from the origin and store it on the POP server. The first request might be executing slower than the others because it has to wait until the POP loads the content from its origin. All other requests can load the copy of assets directly from the POP server. The consistency issue discussed here can be avoided by configuring an appropriate **TTL** for each type of file.

The prepopulating or preloading approach will help you avoid the slowness of the first request, but will generate a traffic spike on the server because the content has to be loaded by the command, not demand.

The Azure CDN will leverage partner networks (Akamai and Verizon) and does not store files in Azure data centers unless you provision Azure CDN with the standard tier from Microsoft or choose content caching with **Azure Front Door**.

Azure Front Door

Azure Front Door is the networking service that allows access to the Microsoft global networking edge. This service provides you with fast and secure access to a web application deployed as PaaS. Front Door is an advanced load traffic manager working on Layer 7 and supports HTTP/HTTPS protocols. It can analyze traffic and protect your web application from cyberattacks. It's a globally available service that can route customer traffic from the entry point to the nearest available application backend. Azure Front Door is based on routing settings, health monitoring checks, and failover configuration.

You might be curious as to why Azure Front Door is combined with CDN services. Originally, the classic Azure Front Door was responsible for providing scalable and secure entry points for the fast delivery of content. Now, this service is responsible for caching content, as well as for the fastest delivery of content. It means that Front Door now can offer CDN services. Previously, Microsoft offered CDN services from its data centers; now, these services have migrated into one, with a secure cloud CDN offering content caching and acceleration, intelligent threat protection, and global load balancing for your websites. We will further discuss configuration concepts with Front Door and CDN services and also discover another product provided in Azure CDN.

Dynamic site acceleration

Caching static content is a trivial task but caching dynamic content sometimes is not possible using the traditional approach. Another technology can be leveraged with Azure CDN to help cache dynamic content. **Dynamic site acceleration (DSA)** is an algorithm responsible for delivering dynamic content, involving the following techniques:

- **Route optimization: Border Gateway Protocol (BGP)** does not always provide optimization choices and faster routes can be taken through a point of presence. The route optimization algorithm can measure the latency from the network and use that information to choose the fastest and most reliable path to deliver dynamic content from the origin server to the end user.

- **TCP optimizations**: TCP is the standard for IP communication and is used for delivering information between browsers and websites. When initializing a connection, several back-and-forth requests are required to set up a TCP connection. The network connections also can slow down communication. Azure CDN handles this problem by optimizing TCP packet parameters and leveraging persistent connections.

- **Object prefetch (Akamai products only)**: Traditional pages loading in the browser started from content followed by the browser loading page's assets such as styles and images. Prefetch is a technique used to retrieve assets embedded in the HTML page while the page is rendered in the browser and before the browser requests those objects.

- **Adaptive image compression (Akamai products only)**: This feature automatically monitors network speed and applies standard JPEG compression methods to improve delivery time when the network is lagging.

You have learned about the main technologies that help Azure CDN and Azure Front Door to successfully manage traffic and to cache static and dynamic content. Now is a good time to learn how to provision your Azure CDN instance.

Provisioning Azure CDN

When you provision Azure CDN, you need to deploy the CDN profile and CDN endpoint. Several endpoints can be configured on the same CDN profile. For provisioning Azure CDN, you do not need to provide an exact location because the location is set to "Global Network." It means the servers will be located in all available geographical regions. All you need to do is to choose a unique name and select a product. Each product you choose has a different specification and price. You cannot change the product you have selected after deploying Azure CDN. The following products are available to select:

- **Standard from Microsoft (classic)**: Microsoft CDN products support many Azure services, especially Azure Blob storage, commonly used by customers to store static content. The Standard tier of Microsoft CDN is based in Azure data centers, implements DSA, and is presently combined with Azure Front Door. After configuration of the CDN endpoint, the cached objects will immediately be available. It supports general delivery optimization and the customization of caching rules. It provides extended monitoring and allows you to involve your SSL/TLS certificate. From a pricing standpoint, this product is the most affordable. At the same time, the CDN does not support tokens or preloading assets.

- **Azure Front Door**: This product combines a standard Microsoft CDN with Azure Front Door. This provides the advantages of fast delivery based on the Azure edge network and high availability and security based on a load balancer, combined with a web application firewall, and also provides out-of-the-box CDN caching algorithms.

- **Standard from Akamai**: Akamai CDN is a well-known and highly geo-distributed network, allowing the use of adaptive image compression and object prefetching. It requires a few minutes to make objects available after finishing the endpoint configuration. Akamai CDN supports sophisticated optimization algorithms. The CDN does not support cache/header settings and URL redirect/rewrite, tokens, or preloading assets. You are also unable to involve an SSL/TLS certificate.

- **Premium and standard from Verizon**: The Verizon CDN is the most configurable and geo-distributed CDN network available when you provision Azure CDN. The standard tier supports all general features, including the preloading of assets. Premium Verizon supports individual portals where customers can configure additional parameters, such as tokenization and detailed monitoring and reporting. The premium tier is expensive but recommended for business-critical applications.

After provisioning a CDN profile, you can configure one or more CDN endpoints. An endpoint's configuration requires a DNS unique name, origin host and port, origin type (Azure Blob, Azure Web Apps, and custom origins are supported), a path for caching, and a content optimization type.

After configuration of the CDN endpoint, you will receive the DNS address and be able to reroute user requests to the provided address.

The pricing model of Azure CDN depends on the product selected for provisioning. Features between content delivery networks will vary. The charges depend on use and consist of charges for traffic moving between zones, configured cashing rules, and enabling DSA. Traffic charges are the most significant and depend on the zone of request and the zone of origin location. Each zone charge depends on the chosen CDN and will vary.

Provisioning with the Azure CLI

In the script, you need to execute Azure CLI commands locally in bash or upload the files you need to Azure Cloud Shell. The script will use static files provided in the folders and upload them to the storage account. Then, you build a CDN instance and download files directly from the storage and from the CDN endpoint to compare the speed.

Please open the script to get familiar with the commands. First of all, the script will build a **resource group** and an Azure Blob storage account for hosting static files. The storage account is created in the South Korea data center, but you can choose another location far away from your current location (Australia, for example). You have a few files to cache: an image, video, and JavaScript file will be uploaded to the storage account. Second, in the same folder, you can find an HTML file and you need to run a command to replace the links in the file with links to your Blob storage. The file can be opened locally to observe the overall performance. The third step is provisioning a CDN profile and endpoint to cache files from Blob storage. You also test the speed of loading from the CDN. The script will create a Microsoft-tier CDN because it will be updated faster than other tiers. If you are interested in exact measures, you can use the **curl** tool. Refer to the following link for further details:

```
https://github.com/PacktPublishing/Developing-Solutions-for-Microsoft-
Azure-AZ-204-Exam-Guide/blob/main/Chapter09/5-cdn-provision/demo.azcli
```

Advanced CDN configuration

Now you know how to provision Azure CDN and create endpoints to cache static content. In the next section, you will learn how to use advanced CDN features, such as caching rules and global filters. You will also learn about preloading and purging content features. From the previous demo, you have provisioned the Azure CDN profile and endpoint and now you can observe the existing settings of your account.

Caching rules

Let's start with caching rules and management to control caching behavior. In general, publicly available content can be cached based on caching rules. Caching rules are managed by TTL values. The default TTL for each file can be obtained using the **Cache-Control** header value from the origin server and can be overwritten using internal Azure CDN rules.

CDNs can override cache settings through the Azure portal by configuring CDN caching rules. The origin-provided caching settings are disregarded if you add one or more caching rules and set their caching behavior to **Override** or **Bypass** the cache. For any other content without the **Cache-Control** header value, Azure CDN automatically applies a default TTL of 7 days, unless it's explicitly overridden by caching rules.

Azure CDN offers two ways to control how your files are cached: using caching rules and using query string caching. You can configure **global caching rules** for each endpoint in the profile to affect all requests to the endpoint. The global caching rule can override any source settings with **Cache-Control** headers. You also can configure **custom caching rules** to match specific paths and file extensions. Custom rules are processed in order and can override the global caching rule as well.

Purging cached content

Caching rules will help users to get the refreshed content when the TTL expires, but this approach does not include cases when the content is updated or modified at the source. The CDN might still have the old version, even if the file is updated at the source. To avoid this scenario, best practice recommends generating a new URL for a new version of your assets. Another popular approach is to purge a specific path or file type/name when the file is updated at the source.

Purging cached content will force all edge nodes to retrieve newly updated assets. You can purge all files on the nodes or purge files in the specific path, for example, /pictures/logo.png. You also can purge the files or folder by providing a wildcard, for example, /pictures/*.

Be aware that purge functionality will remove content from the edge nodes but the browser cache and proxy servers can still have content cached. The files will be eventually updated after the expiration of the TTL. Additional delays can also be caused by a purge operation taking approximately 2 minutes. That is why best practice recommends generating a new URL for the new version of the content.

Preloading

From the previous discussion of the CDN caching pattern, you will remember that first requests can take longer because the edge server has to request a file from the origin and save it locally for the next request. The second request for the file will be significantly faster if the file has not expired yet. To avoid this first-hit delay, CDN *gurus* initialize and preload the content. Preloading provides a better customer experience and will reduce spikes of network traffic on the origin server. Content preloading works best for large files, such as software updates or movies that need to be simultaneously released to a large audience. You can preload content by providing an exact path to the file or by using regular expressions.

> **Note**
> Be aware that the preloading feature is available only with Azure CDN Standard from Verizon and Azure CDN Premium from Verizon.

Geo-filter

When a user requests a website with CDN, the content is delivered by default for all available locations based on the CDN product deployed. Meanwhile, you can limit access to the content based on the country or region. The total charges for CDN depend on the zones, so blocking some countries can prevent the caching of content in specific regions and decrease charges.

You can configure geo-filtering for specific paths and recurring folders or configure rules for the root folder (for example, /, /pictures/, or /pictures/logo.png). Neither wildcard nor regular expressions are supported in the path. Only one rule can be applied to the same relative path. When you configure the rule, you can apply a list of the countries/regions and an **Allow** or **Block** action. The **Allow** action lets users from the specified countries/regions get access to assets requested from the recursive path. The **Block** action will deny access to the content requested from the recursive path. The **Allow** action is configured by default so all users from all regions can access the content.

> **Note**
>
> Be aware that the geo-filter feature is not available for Azure CDN Standard from Microsoft. Consider the fact that applying geo-filter will apply 10 minutes after saving the settings.

Configuring a website to leverage the CDN

This demo will continue the previous demo where you provisioned a CDN profile and endpoint. Now, files from the storage account should be cached by the CDN. Now it is time to prepare and upload your HTML page to test the CDN in action. Next, you need to replace the links to your CDN endpoint by running commands from the script. Run the command from the bash console to upload an HTML page to the static website on the storage account you built before. You can open a generated link to observe the caching performance. You can also compare it with the HTML file pointed to the storage account from the previous demo. The performance increase should be visible. Please note that files can be cached on the browser side and for ideal comparison, you should clear the cache from the *F12* Developer Tool.

The next task is providing custom TTL policies for content. You will set TTL on the JavaScript file on the origin level by using the **Cache-Control** header. If your cache still retrieves the old version, you will use the purge command and the test page will load the latest JavaScript script. You can download the script from the following URL:

```
https://github.com/PacktPublishing/Developing-Solutions-for-Microsoft-
Azure-AZ-204-Exam-Guide/blob/main/Chapter09/6-cdn-advanced/demo.azcli
```

Manipulating a CDN instance from code

You have already learned how to manage Front Door and CDN resources from the Azure portal and the Azure CLI. Now is a good time to get familiar with the SDKs you can leverage to manage resources. Let's introduce the best management SDK for .NET Core, named Fluent. The exact package to manage CDN resources, Microsoft.Azure.Management.Cdn.Fluent, can be added to the project. You also can register a service account and provide it access to your subscription/resource group with contributor rights. The app ID, secret, and tenant can be saved in the configuration file.

The following code snippet will help you configure the instance of the Azure class to get access to the resources in your default subscription:

```
using Microsoft.Azure.Management.ResourceManager.Fluent;
var credentials = SdkContext
        .AzureCredentialsFactory.FromFile("yourconfigfile");
var azure = Microsoft.Azure.Management.Fluent.Azure
        .Configure()
        .Authenticate(credentials)
        .WithDefaultSubscription();
```

The following example demonstrates how to create a CDN profile:

```
using Microsoft.Azure.Management.Cdn.Fluent;
ICdnProfile profileDefinition = azure.CdnProfiles.
Define("YourCdnProfileName")
        .WithRegion(Region.USEast)
        .WithExistingResourceGroup("YourResourceGroupName")
        .WithStandardVerizonSku();
```

This example will define the endpoint for the previous CDN profile:

```
cdnendpoint = profileDefinition.DefineNewEndpoint()
        .WithOrigin("your_origin")
        .WithHostHeader("your_origin")
        .WithQueryStringCachingBehavior(
            QueryStringCachingBehavior.IgnoreQueryString)
        .Attach();
```

As you can see from the previous code snippets, the manipulation of CDN resources is a trivial task and you have a powerful SDK to manage Azure resources. This is another example of infrastructure as code and it will be covered in *Chapter 13, Developing Message-Based Solutions*.

Summary

In this chapter, you have learned about caching with Azure Cache for Redis and Azure CDN. Both caching services can be successfully used for the cache-aside pattern to implement caching for static and dynamic content and configured with a custom expiration time to avoid inconsistency with the source of the data. Azure Cache for Redis is a PaaS available in Azure with a large scale of different price tiers. Azure Cache for Redis supports multiple data types such as strings, integers, lists, sets, and hashes to store strings, binaries, and object fields. Azure Cache for Redis should be used as temporary storage and the application should not rely on the cache data.

Azure CDN is designed for caching static data such as images, videos, and documents. The CDN can also help to speed up the loading of static content such as media, CSS, and JavaScript files. Azure CDN works as a proxy server for your customers and helps them to cache files very close to their location. The CDN network supports a variety of locations to store files, including Microsoft, Verizon, and Akamai data centers. Configuration settings will help you set up different caching policies for files in the path, specific extensions, and depending on the region/country of requests.

By provisioning and configuring Azure CDN and Azure Cache resources, you get experience required for the exam. Now, you can leverage caching technology in your web-based solution and recommend the appropriate size and configuration, depending on the requirements of exam questions.

In the next chapter, you will learn about monitoring technologies and tools that help you minimize downtime and proactively diagnose possible performance bottlenecks and avoid crashes. Let's move on to the next chapter.

Questions

1. What Azure Cache for Redis SKU does not provide an SLA?
2. What Redis command is used to set TTL?
3. What is the difference between a Basic and Premium SKU for Azure Cache for Redis?
4. What protocol and port are used for connection to Azure Cache for Redis?
5. What CDN products are available with a Premium SKU for Azure CDN?
6. What are the three ways of controlling TTL in Azure CDN?

Further reading

- From the following link, you can learn additional Redis commands: `https://redis.io/commands`
- You can find more details and learn about scenarios to use Azure Cache here: `https://docs.microsoft.com/en-us/azure/azure-cache-for-redis/cache-overview`

- Here, you can get code examples and descriptions about hosting session state services on Azure Cache for Redis: `https://docs.microsoft.com/en-us/azure/azure-cache-for-redis/cache-aspnet-session-state-provider`

- You can learn details about caching features for Azure Front Door here: `https://docs.microsoft.com/en-us/azure/frontdoor/front-door-caching`

- You can read how to generate a service account to use the Fluent SDK here: `https://docs.microsoft.com/en-us/dotnet/azure/sdk/authentication`

- Learn more about the configuration of Azure Cache and the required network settings to get connected: `https://docs.microsoft.com/en-us/azure/azure-cache-for-redis/cache-configure#access-ports`

- A list of the available commands for managing Azure Cache for Redis can be found in the following documentation: `https://docs.microsoft.com/en-us/cli/azure/redis?view=azure-cli-latest`

- The process of purging CDN endpoints is discussed at the following link: `https://docs.microsoft.com/en-us/azure/cdn/cdn-purge-endpoint`

- Caching best practices can be learned about at the following link: `https://docs.microsoft.com/en-us/azure/azure-cache-for-redis/cache-best-practices-memory-management`

10
Troubleshooting Solutions by Using Metrics and Log Data

This chapter introduces the main services of instrumentation, monitoring, and troubleshooting solutions hosted in Azure. You will learn how to use Application Insights and Azure Monitor to detect performance bottlenecks and handle errors. This chapter will also explain the alerting capabilities of the Azure platform. You will also learn how to instrument your code to get maximum insights from your application. You will learn about advanced techniques for monitoring performance metrics and diagnostics issues on PaaS and IaaS platforms.

In this chapter, you will deploy web apps to Azure App Service and learn how to monitor performance metrics and investigate logs with Application Insights and Azure Monitor. You will also learn how to track communication and monitor dependency performance. You will then learn how to investigate logs and metrics by using **Kusto Query Language** (KQL).

In this chapter, we will cover the following main topics:

- Monitoring and logging solutions in Azure
- Analyzing performance issues with Azure Monitor
- Exploring Application Insights
- Using KQL for Log Analytics queries
- Discovering Monitor workbooks

Technical requirements

The scripts provided in the chapter can be run in Azure Cloud Shell or be executed locally. The Azure CLI and Visual Studio Code are ideal tools to execute the code and commands provided in the following repository:

`https://github.com/PacktPublishing/Developing-Solutions-for-Microsoft-Azure-AZ-204-Exam-Guide/tree/main/Chapter10`

The code and scripts in the repository will provide you with examples of provisioning and developing applications for Azure Web Apps and using Application Insights to troubleshoot issues.

Code in Action videos for this chapter: `https://bit.ly/3R25zLH`

Monitoring and logging solutions in Azure

Azure Monitor is a well-known free monitoring tool that is commonly used to monitor infrastructure services but can also be successfully used for essential monitoring services and security activities. Azure Monitor is a highly extensible tool and can be used for analytics queries running on the **Log Analytics** platform. The Log Analytics platform includes multiple extensions for specific services, platforms, and databases. Moreover, Azure Monitor can persist data for free only for a limited time. Data persisting limits can be exceeded by leveraging the **Log Analytics service**. Furthermore, in this chapter, we will learn about **Application Insights** – a powerful monitoring framework available in Azure.

For services deployed in Azure, Azure Monitor functions as a monitoring hub and collects lots of performance data and logs in its internal database. The idea behind the monitoring hub is to allow the individual Azure product groups to decide what would be best to monitor and report. For example, Azure **virtual machines** (**VMs**) report their **CPU usage**, **networking**, and **disk activities**. Meanwhile, **Azure Web Apps** services report their **request rate**, **memory usage**, and **exception rate**. All services in Azure report their metrics to a single location in Azure. This consolidation has lots of benefits, including allowing running analytics queries across different services' metrics to find out the real cause of a problem.

Performance metrics are collected from most computer and database services automatically, but by default are persisted for only 30 days. These metrics are usually available as a chart that can be observed on the **Monitoring** page of the resource. The metrics can be queried by Log Analytics and exported in files. Collected performance metrics, including default and customized charts, can be added to a dashboard. You can share dashboards with users of your organization and monitor multiple services at the same time with live metrics. Performance data and logs can also be persisted in the storage account. For example, Azure VMs can automatically export the collected performance metrics to **Azure Table Storage**. Azure Web Apps can be configured to export HTTP request logs to **Azure Blob Storage**.

Azure Monitor collects logs for 90 days. It starts overwriting old logs after 90 days, and at any time, the most recent 90 days of information is captured. With the activity logs, you can find out who provisioned resources, who restarted VMs, and who modified the resource settings. This information also includes health monitoring of the global Azure platform, which is helpful when you perform troubleshooting. The logs of the VM, for example, the **application event logs** in Windows or **system logs** in Linux, can also be forwarded to an Azure Storage account. The logs can persist for years to meet compliance requirements. Then, the storage account can be pulled by the Log Analytics workspace to be indexed and queried with analytics requests.

Azure Monitor exposes a RESTful interface to connect to third-party services such as Datadog and Grafana. In the same way, it can be used by first-party Microsoft tools, for example, Power BI. The Azure CLI and PowerShell under the hood can call the services to export data in the files and parse them later with tools such as **Performance Analysis of Logs (PAL)**.

Azure Monitor is one of the many monitoring tools we can use in Azure to diagnose and troubleshoot applications. We mentioned several other services previously that will also help you monitor and troubleshoot applications running in Azure. Let's look at a quick overview of the main features of Azure monitoring services.

The Azure Log Analytics service requires an Azure Log Analytics workspace to be provisioned to install monitoring tools to monitor the state of VM updates, security baselines, the performance of the server, web requests and app crashes, database size, and load. You can also develop analytics queries with KQL with the collected data and metrics collected in the tables. A request's result can also be provided as a chart to the monitoring dashboard and can be used as a source of Azure alerts. You will see some KQL examples at the end of this chapter.

Application Insights is another well-known brilliant telemetry service commonly used for web applications that can be used for online monitoring and troubleshooting. Application Insights is a web API service running in Azure. Moreover, Application Insights can perform event tracking and performance tracing in real time. The tracking technology is implemented by the client-side application, reporting the loading and rendering time, and the server-side SDKs, reporting the performance of the server. As a result, Application Insights provides developers with a 360-degree view of the application's performance and user activities. Application Insights includes sophisticated services to track performance on the dependent services (such as storage account and database), produce custom events and metrics, and collect dumps for application crashes.

Azure Monitor workbooks are a combination of telemetry charts and graphs, widgets, and Markdown text areas with descriptions. You can build your workbooks to monitor all aspects of the application's performance collected from multiple data sources across Azure. You can print and export the workbook as a report.

In the next sections of the chapter, you will learn details about the services to help you choose the appropriate platform for monitoring and troubleshooting your application and configure performance metrics and log collection.

Analyzing performance issues with Azure Monitor

To better understand monitoring and troubleshooting tools in Azure, we need to deploy Azure Web Apps first, then configure its diagnostic settings and provision an Application Insights instance. After completing this task, from the Azure CLI, you will be able to collect and analyze the web application performance metrics.

Provisioning cloud solutions to explore monitoring features

The following script will help you deploy web app, a storage account, and Azure SQL Database: `https://github.com/PacktPublishing/Developing-Solutions-for-Microsoft-Azure-AZ-204-Exam-Guide/blob/main/Chapter10/2%20-%20ai%20config/demo.azcli`

The solution will be used in the next parts of the chapter to demonstrate monitoring and diagnostic features. To run the provisioning script, you should install the Azure CLI locally (`https://docs.microsoft.com/en-us/cli/azure/?view=azure-cli-latest`). Later, Visual Studio Code (`https://code.visualstudio.com/Download`) will be involved in observing and deploying the code to Azure App Services.

Once you finish provisioning services from the preceding demo script, you can find the web application in the portal and open its **Overview** page. At the top of the page, you can find the URL to observe the application's content. Follow that link to open the website in a separate browser window. You can refresh the website page several times to generate some activities and observe the requests with Azure Monitor in the **Monitoring** section of the App Service blade.

Exploring Azure App Service diagnostic settings

Let's observe the **Monitoring** section of the newly deployed App Service. You can configure monitoring features in the **Diagnostic settings** section.

In **Diagnostic settings**, we recommend you select all categories of logs and all categories of metrics. There are several options to persist the logs: with a storage account, a Log Analytics workspace, and Event Hubs. You can also configure the partner solutions: Elasticsearch, Kafka, and Datadog. Choose a storage account because it is the simplest way to set and observe the collected output. Note down the storage account's name to observe its content later.

Let's now look at the **App Service Logs** option in the **Monitoring** section. This feature will let you collect some valuable information for diagnostics: **Application logging**, **Web server logging**, **Detailed error messages**, and **Failed requests tracing**. Enable those settings and keep collection parameters by default. Those logs will provide you with additional information in the event of application crashes. You can pull client settings, request settings, and exception stack traces. You can also collect the tracing of the application if your web application is built with the diagnostics flag enabled. These logs are extremely helpful if you do not have access to the application code and must deploy a prebuilt solution. You will also notice that logs are available for download by using the internal FTP server running with the application. Do not forget to save the settings when you leave the page.

After you have enabled App Service logs collection, let's explore another monitoring feature, named **Log Stream**. You can find this feature in the **Monitoring** section of your application. When you open Log Stream and refresh the page of your web application, you will see the activities show up on the console. You can see the updates in real time. These settings will help you troubleshoot the exception in combination with logs you persisted in the storage account.

Let's open the storage account you set up in the **Diagnostics settings** section previously. In the storage account, you can navigate to **Containers** and find the containers whose names start with log or insights. In the containers, you can find collected files. Performance metrics will be collected in Azure Table Storage. Observing the results is no trivial task. You can download them by using a query for a specific time frame and build charts in Excel. If the files are too big to open in Excel, you can use BI analytics tools such as Power BI.

> **Important Note**
> There is a significant delay, of several minutes, before the logged data shows up in the files and tables.

Azure Monitor for Azure Web Apps

The next task is observing the **Monitoring** section of the Azure web app. If you return to the **Overview** page, you will discover five charts: HTTP 5xx, Data In, Data Out, Request, and Response Time. These charts are available to zoom in by clicking on the chart and selecting the time frame. For example, on the **Request** chart, you can find several requests from the previous page load. You can refresh the website page to display more requests.

You can observe several metrics by adding new metrics or filtering the metric values and combining them on the same chart to get the root cause of the issue. For example, you can combine **Response Time** and **Http Server Errors** to study the effect of the error handling on request processing. You can also combine **Response Time** and **Memory working set** to study whether the memory pressure affects the performance of your application.

The following chart is a good example of how monitoring helps with detecting performance issues in the production service. The symptom is a random small spike in **Average Response Time** (orange) followed by a significant spike in **CPU Time** (light blue). By adding these charts together and also adding **Data In** calls (dark blue) you can observe that the CPU spike matches the data load spike generated almost at the same time. Upon investigating the weird correlation further with logs, the data transfer activities were recognized to be large SQL queries executed during the first small spike, then a minute of awaiting the database response, and then high CPU usage due to the return of a large dataset requiring processing:

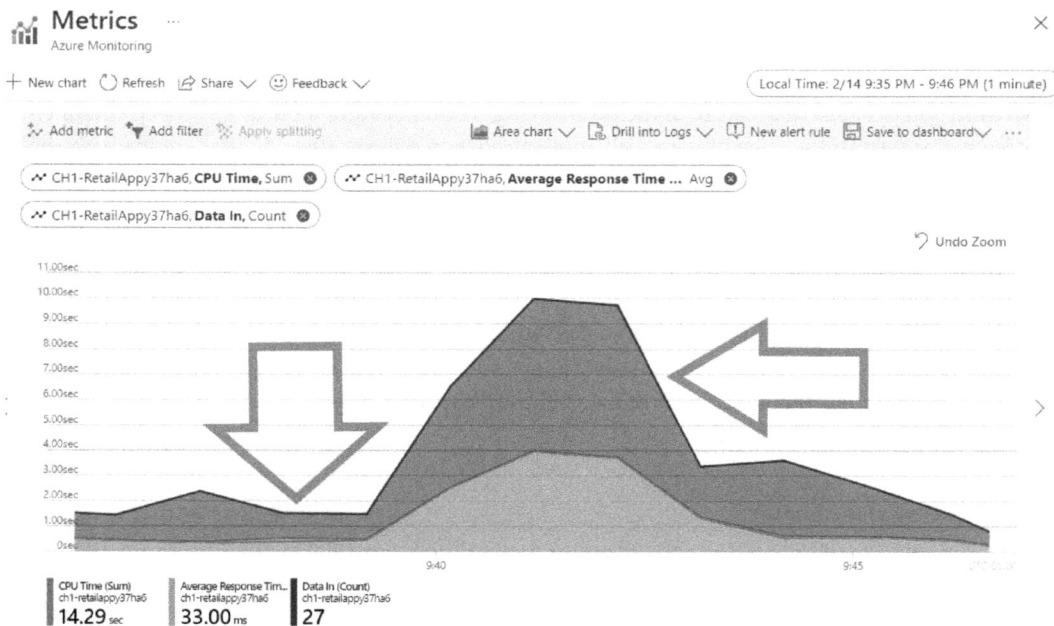

Figure 10.1 – Azure Monitor metrics demonstrating CPU spike issue

The errors and downtime of your solution could be related to issues in the Azure infrastructure In the next section, you will learn how an Azure outage can affect your solution.

Azure Service Health

Another useful metric of many IaaS and PaaS services is **Resource health**. This metric is also available for Azure Web Apps and can be found below the **Support + Troubleshooting** section. **Resource health** consists of an indicator with traffic light colors. Most of the time, it shows **Available** (green), which means that the service is available and functioning well. Sometimes, the indicator can indicate an **Unknown** state, but this is a rare situation. Sometimes, it shows an **Unavailable** (red) status, which means that the service has health issues and the Azure team is likely working on a solution. During that time, your service might experience delays or not respond at all. The time frame of issues should not exceed the SLA provided for the service.

When you design your solution in Azure, remember the whole solution's SLA can be lower than the SLA of its services. For example, the total SLA of an Azure Web Apps (Basic tier) and Azure SQL Database should be calculated with the following formula:

99.95% (Azure Web Apps) * 99.99% (Azure SQL Database) = 99.94%

The total SLA of the solution will be 99.94%. This means about 1 minute a day and 7 minutes a week of possible downtime when service health issues affect the application.

On the **Service Health** page, you can also observe the history of status changes and find information about affected services and downtime.

Configuring Azure alerts

The best way to be notified of a specific type of event or changes in metrics is by setting up an Azure alert. Alerts, for example, can be configured from the Azure portal in the **Monitoring** section on the Azure App Services page.

Configuring alerts includes three steps that need to be completed in sequence: **Scope**, **Condition**, and **Actions**. You need to determine the **Scope** first. The default scope is the website you want to be monitored. Depending on the resource type, the monitoring metrics and events can vary. Next, you need to select **Condition**. For example, for App Service, you can monitor the count of **Http Server Errors** or **Requests in Application Queue**. For logs, we can use the **Restart Web App** event to monitor whether the web application has been restarted by enterprise admins.

Next are determinate conditions. You can configure one or more conditions with thresholds determined by OR logic. For each condition, you need to select performance metrics or events. Then, you need to provide the **operation** for comparing the metric with a threshold (less than, equal to, or greater than), then the **aggregation type** (sum, count, or average), and **threshold values** with **units** of measurement. You can also configure very important metrics for **aggregation granularity** and **frequency of evaluation**.

The **aggregation granularity** is the interval over which data is measured by the aggregation type function. The default 5-minute interval is optimal. If you decrease the interval, your alerts will be affected by spikes in metrics more often. If you increase the interval, alerts can miss some significant changes and be late with notifications.

The **frequency of evaluation** allows you to configure the period when the conditions are not evaluated. This setting is valuable for an automated response. For example, say you set up a scaling script with an automation account and trigger that with an Azure alert webhook. In this case, after triggering the scaling changes, the alerts should pause until the scaling is complete and load has been properly shared between scaled instances.

The last step to configure Azure alerts is setting up **Actions**. By the way, there might be no action provided at all, so there will be no notification. **Actions** lets you set a preferred notification action. SMS, a call to a cell phone, and email are available options for individuals or groups of individuals. An action can also trigger Azure services, such as Azure Functions, Logic Apps, and Automation account scripts, as well as a general webhook available for third-party integration. Then, you need to provide the name of the alert, a description, and the severity to complete the process of setting up alerts.

> **Important Note**
>
> Monitoring **Requests in Application Queue** will be better than monitoring **CPU Time** to identify the website's loading performance. Be aware that CPU activities might be a result of the activation of background processes.

Azure Monitor is the greatest tool to monitor infrastructure performance and collect activity logs. It is quite easy to monitor the application and service health with Azure Monitor diagrams and build a dashboard with the charts provided by Azure Monitor. Meanwhile, Azure Monitor has a few important limitations, such as being unable to create custom metrics, search and parse custom logs, profile application code, and persist performance metrics for more than a month. Those gaps are covered by Application Insights, the powerful and customizable telemetry framework hosted in Azure. In the next part of the chapter, you will learn how to use Application Insights for your application.

Exploring Application Insights

Back in the day, it was always difficult to collect user activity and performance information about a classic web application hosted on-premises or with a hosting provider. Large enterprises developed their own frameworks, which were difficult to adapt and connect. Implementing new monitoring and reporting activities also required significant support effort. Now, the monitoring and telemetry challenge has been successfully solved by connecting to a lightweight service hosted in Azure. The service is easy to adapt and extend and is available for multiple platforms and languages. This service is named **Application Insights**, which accurately describes what the service provides to developers. Application Insights collects all possible insights about application performance and user activity.

Application Insights is a well-known telemetry framework that collects data from instrumented application code and tracks application activities, performance, custom metrics, and exceptions. Application Insights provides a 360-degree view of the performance of web applications by tracking the client code with JavaScript objects executed in the browser and tracing requests and their metrics from the server side with the SDK. If the code is unviable for instrumentation, Application Insights provides an installer for the server with limited capabilities for handling request metrics and collecting trace and fatal errors. Moreover, Application Insights can be used by not only web applications but also desktop and mobile applications, as well as by add-ons for Microsoft Office applications. Application Insights' SDK supports multiple languages, including C#, Python, Java, and Node.js, as well as working in browsers running JavaScript. The Application Insights SDK library is already integrated into the C# MVC scaffolding template.

Tracking telemetry is implemented as an async web request to the Application Insights endpoint located in Azure. The endpoint tracks the request without affecting the performance of the corresponding application. Later, the telemetry can be analyzed with Azure Log Analytics, monitored by Azure alerts, and viewed directly from Visual Studio and the Azure portal.

In the following subsections, you will learn how to provision and configure an Application Insights instance and how to connect a website to the telemetry service to monitor activity, troubleshoot crashes, and profile application performance.

Provisioning and configuration

The provisioning of Application Insights is usually completed as part of provisioning Azure App Service. It is also provisioned for Azure Functions and is automatically configured to collect telemetry. Application Insights should be provisioned in the same region as the website to minimize traffic charges and latency. The latest changes are required to use a workspace-based instance connected to an existing Log Analytics workspace. The workspace will be used for persisting telemetry data and running Kusto queries for deep analysis. The location of the workspace should be the same as the Application Insights instance.

Provisioning Application Insights with the Azure CLI

In the previous deployment script, you already provisioned a web application and a SQL database. In the following script, you will provision and configure the Application Insights instance and connect it to your web application:

```
https://github.com/PacktPublishing/Developing-Solutions-for-Microsoft-
Azure-AZ-204-Exam-Guide/blob/main/Chapter10/2%20-%20ai%20config/
demo.azcli
```

Notice that the connection string with the Instrumentation key value will be retrieved and Azure Web Apps configuration records will be created with the value.

Once you finish provisioning and linking Azure Web Apps to Application Insights, we need to check whether Applicant Insights is configured properly. You can open the Azure portal and then the web application, and you will find the **Application Insights** section in **Settings**. If the **Enable...** button exists, you should click on the button and configure the settings for the .NET Core application. The following settings should be enabled for .NET Core: **Profiler**, **Snapshot debugger**, and **SQL commands**. The settings should be switched **on**. In the next tasks, you will deploy a website to use the profiling and debugging options.

Discovering security settings

There are two aspects of security of Application Insights that need to be configured: the networking isolation and authentication for accessing reports.

Networking isolation can be implemented by enabling firewall rules to accept or not accept ingesting telemetry data and query requests from public networks. The firewall rules allow all or nothing from public traffic. For services running in Azure, such as the web app you deployed previously, you can enable Private Link to allow only Azure services such as Azure Web Apps or Azure Virtual Network. Private Link will use only the Microsoft backend network.

To configure the application to send telemetry, Application Insights provides a connection string with the instrumentation key. There is no other authentication required to send the insights to the service. Meanwhile, accessing collected telemetry requires authentication with your Microsoft or Azure AD account. Alternately, the application can obtain API keys to get access to the Application Insights reports from outside of the Azure portal.

Integration with DevOps

Integration with DevOps services is valuable when you analyze insights and detect exceptions. Application Insights supports integration with Azure DevOps and GitHub. You can build a work item (bug) template to submit collated insights to the DevOps service for further processing and fixing. For example, from the Application Insights UI, you can find the crash record and submit the work item with all the information about exceptions added automatically. The integration is implemented as a template you can build in the DevOps solution and referenced as a URL in the Application Insights settings. Then, you need to provide additional fields in key-value format with collected insights.

In the following task, you will learn how to deploy web application code to an Azure instance and observe the performance, activities, dependencies, exceptions, and many other important metrics in real time. But first, let's deploy the web application.

Instrumenting code to use Application Insights

We have developed the ASP.NET Core MVC website for you, which represents a small e-commerce application with order processing algorithms. From the website, you will be able to list, create, modify, and observe the details of ordered items. The web application uses Entity Framework connected to Azure SQL Database and Azure Blob Storage to demonstrate your ability to track dependency requests. When you deploy the application to Azure, you will be able to observe performance per page, user requests, dependencies, SQL queries, and so on. Execute the following script to build and publish your web application as a ZIP archive:

```
https://github.com/PacktPublishing/Developing-Solutions-for-Microsoft-
Azure-AZ-204-Exam-Guide/blob/main/Chapter10/3%20-%20asp%20core/
deploy.azcli
```

Before running the script, you need to pull the full project located in the same folder and update your web application's name in the script with the name generated in the previous script execution.

Once the application is deployed, you can visit the application to generate some activity on the website. You should click on the **Details** link for some of the products to generate requests to Azure SQL and Azure Blob Storage. You should create a new order by selecting a customer from the list and providing the product's name and description. You can also edit and delete random orders. To generate and track an error, visit the **Privacy** page. A few minutes later, Application Insights should have enough data to build a chart for observations. Let's move on to the next section to learn more about available charts, metrics, and logs.

Charting and dashboards

In the following subsections, you will learn about the metrics and logs collected by Application Insights. You will also learn about services such as **availability test** and **application map**. You will learn about monitoring exceptions, profiling, and collecting snapshots for troubleshooting crashes.

Live metrics

Let's start with the live metrics dashboard. Application Insights supports a live diagram dashboard located in the **Live metrics** section of the Application Insights instance. On this dashboard, you can monitor in real time the main performance parameters, including **Request Rate**, **Committed Memory**, **CPU Total**, and **Dependency Call Duration**. When you open **Live metrics**, open the website in another browser window and generate some requests to observe them on the dashboard:

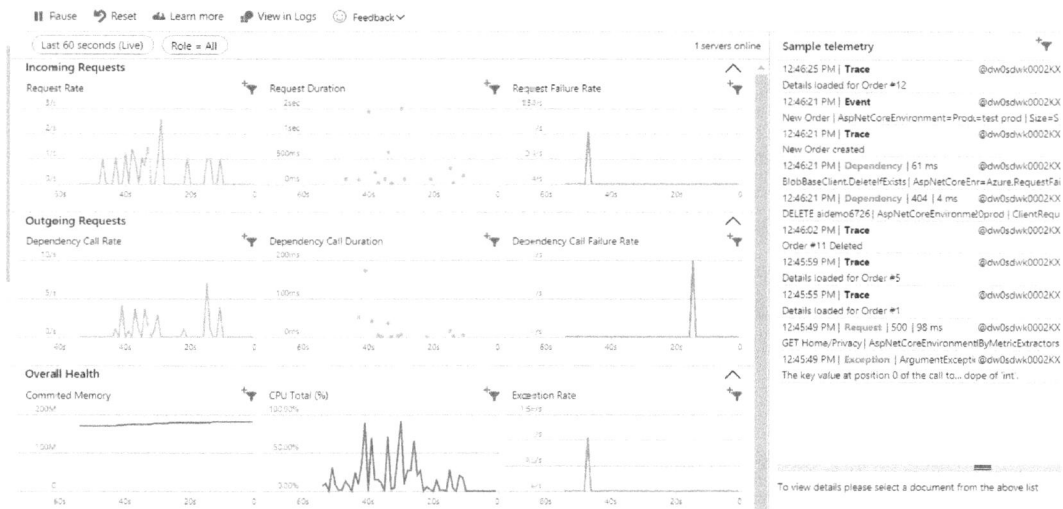

Figure 10.2 – Live metrics dashboard for the web application deployed previously

Additional charts can be found in the **Overview** section of the Application Insights instance. The charts include **Server Requests**, **Failed Requests**, and **Availability** metrics.

Performance

Detailed request performance metrics are located in the **Performance** section of Application Insights. You can observe the **Operations** tab to learn about operation time per page and the total count of requests per page. This chart helps you identify the pages with a performance bottleneck, drill down to individual requests, pick one, and observe transaction details with a histogram of calls, including dependency calls. In the following screenshot, you can observe the performance graph and by-page metrics:

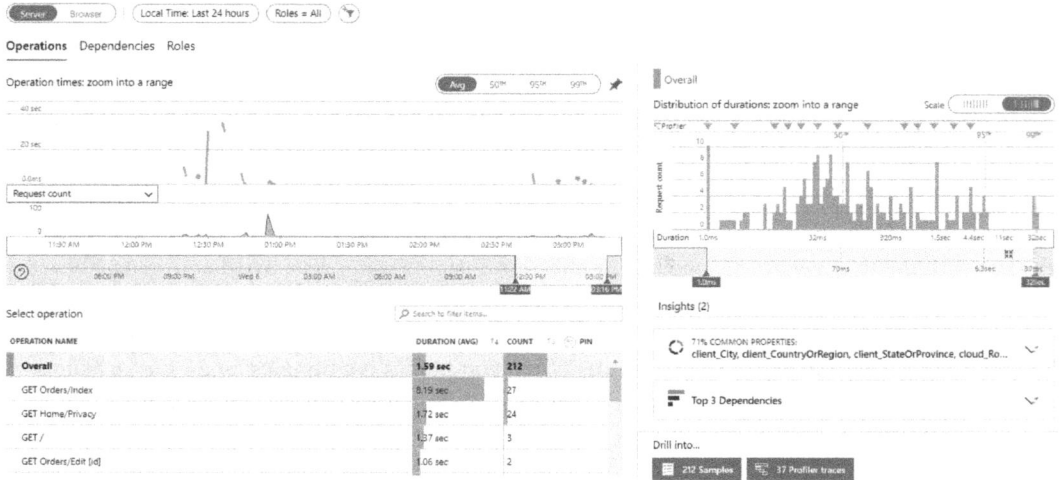

Figure 10.3 – Performance chart with page performance details

On the **Dependencies** tab in the **Performance** section, you can also monitor dependency calls, including the performance for each type of dependency, including Azure SQL and Azure Blob requests. Then, you can pick an individual request and analyze its performance over time.

Another tab, named **Roles**, will let you observe the services hosting your solutions. For website instances, it could be VMs and Azure App Service. The roles are configured in the code and can be assigned as architectural tiers (such as front and mid-tier or backend).

Profiler

The previous screenshot showed the performance details. You can dive deep into an exact request or observe collected profile information. You can also click on the blue **Profiler traces** button in the bottom right of the performance screen. The profile will demonstrate the performance trace collected from the application for each executed request. You can also observe the slowest requests to find out what your application is waiting for and where the bottlenecks are. For example, the following screenshot is taken from the application you deployed previously. You can observe the profile of the **Index** page performance. The process was retrieving the orders list from the database and waiting for 89% of the time to get the result in an asynchronous function:

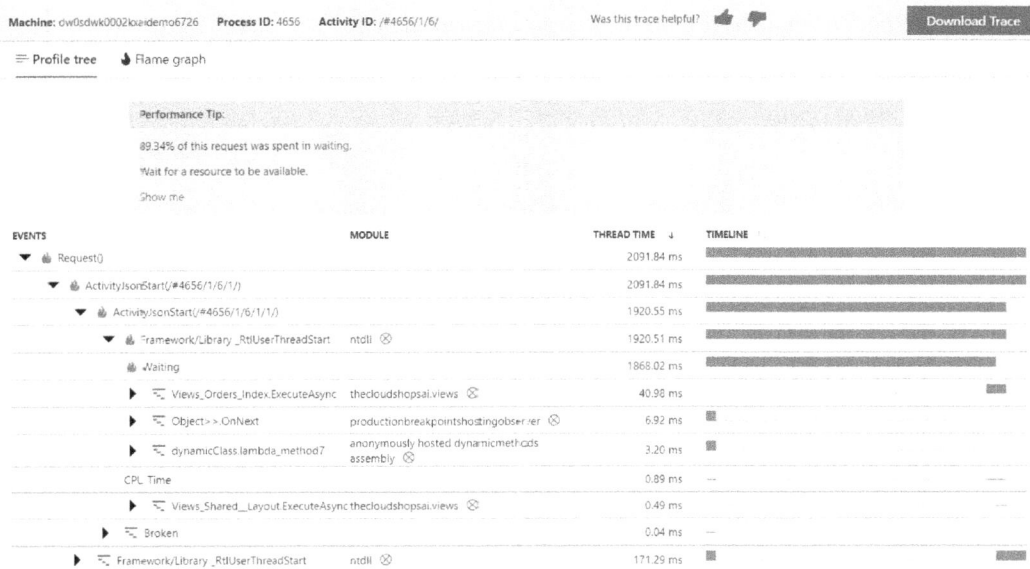

Figure 10.4 – Profile of the loading orders call

The issue seems to be on the database side, which is taking 1.8 seconds in total. The trick is to use views and indexes to improve the performance of the database.

Usage

Another important part of web application monitoring is user behavior. This information could be interesting for the marketing department, which wants to measure the interest of users in products and pages on the website. Application Insights automatically collects user information, except for IP addresses. The rest of the information, about the platform, browser, home country, and city, is available for each request. To learn more about your users, you can observe a session summary. For instance, you can pull the exact session to see the path of the users on the website and visited pages. You can find the **Users** and **Sessions** sections under **Usage** on the Application Insights page.

If you set up client-side event collection with the JavaScript SDK for Application Insights for your website, you can monitor users' events, such as navigation from the links and clicking on the page buttons. These client-side events are indexed and available for searching in the **Events** section of the **Usage** group. You can also build funnels with session parameters to filter out users with specific behaviors, for example, users who prefer to follow recommendations and read reviews on your website, or users who prefer to find an exact product by searching or browsing by category. The **Funnels** section can be found in the **Usage** group.

To better understand users' behavior on the website, you can create a flow chart based on the events collected from users' sessions:

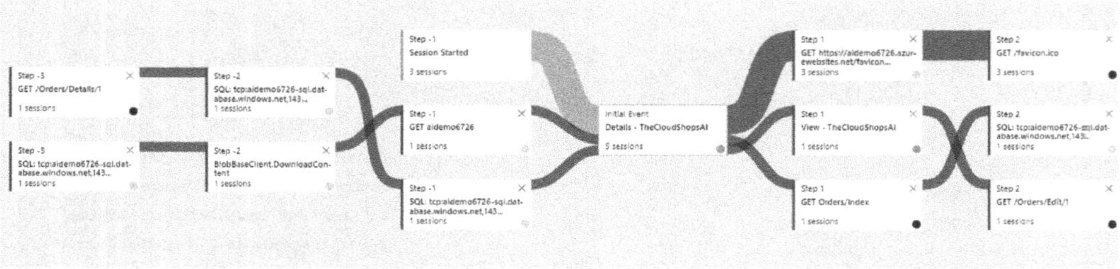

Figure 10.5 – User flow chart for Details page views

For example, most of the users (the thick blue lines) visit the website from the home page, then click on the ticket from the grid and follow to the page where the details about the ticket are located. Meanwhile, some of the users visit the page directly, probably from a search engine. This behavior can be tracked in the **User Flows** section of the **Usage** group. In the preceding screenshot, you can observe the graph built for the **Details** page and included dependency (Azure SQL and Azure Blob Storage) requests.

Exception troubleshooting

One of the brilliant functionalities of Application Insights is the tracking and diagnostics of crashes and exceptions. For properly instrumented code, non-fatal and fatal exception information could be collected, including a stack trace to the problematic function, request parameters from the browser, and even taking a snapshot with debugging information. You can find statistics of exceptions listed by web page, exception type, and timeline. The exception provides a function and activity flow chart to help you determine what other requests to the dependent services were sent. It can also find similar exceptions and help you find the correlation between exceptions and user activity.

If you would like to troubleshoot exceptions, you need to select exceptions from the available lists of exception types (such as HTTP exceptions and **NullReference** exceptions). Then, you need to pick the recommended or latest exception and observe its profiling output. In the following screenshot, you can observe the exception retrieved from the **Privacy** page. It is a System.NullReferenceException exception with a call stack retrieved from the code. You can also notice the SQL dependency call above the exception. From the **Call Stack** output, you can see that the exception happened in the HomeController class, in the Privacy method. The method corresponds to the **Privacy** page where the exception occurred.

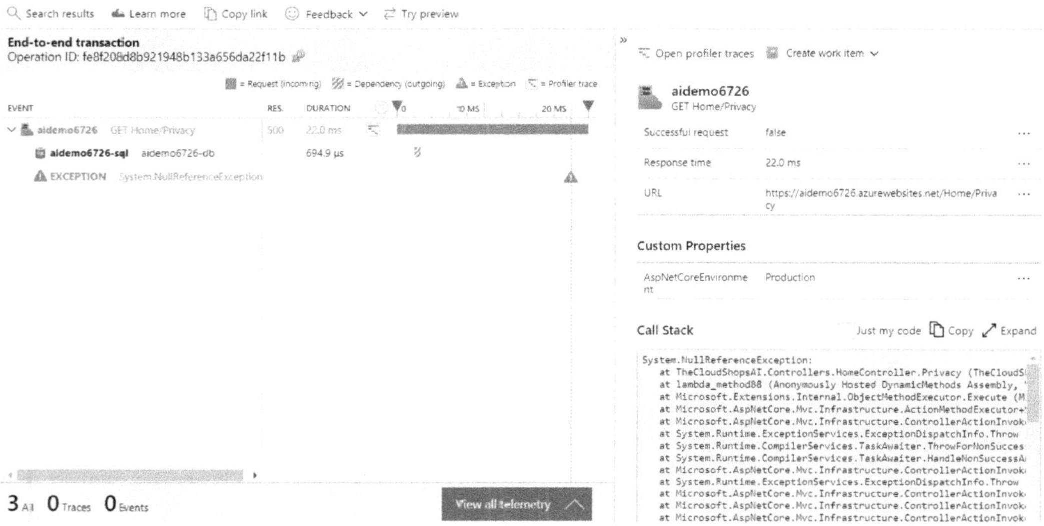

Figure 10.6 – Troubleshooting a NullReference exception collected by Application Insights

Finally, a properly configured Application Insights instance can persist **debug snapshots** collected on the server side when an exception happened and let you download the dump file. The dump file can be opened in Visual Studio and give you the same debugging experience you have when debugging your code locally. Currently, only .NET Core is supported for snapshot collection. Alternatively, you can open a snapshot on the Application Insights UI and observe the function calls and input parameter values. Collected exceptions are located in the **Failures** section of the Application Insights instance.

Availability test

Availability is an important metric and can be calculated based on the Azure SLA, as explained previously. Real solution availability depends on many factors, including exceptions and outages on the servers. Application Insights can set up HTTP pings from the selected data centers to ping your application with the provided URL and record the latency. This option can be configured manually and represent a chart with available (green) and failed (red) requests. You can configure the availability test for your application by choosing **Availability** from the **Investigate** section, adding the tests from the menu at the top, and selecting the URL for testing and the test locations. After a few hours, you can observe the results of your application's availability, which will look similar to the following:

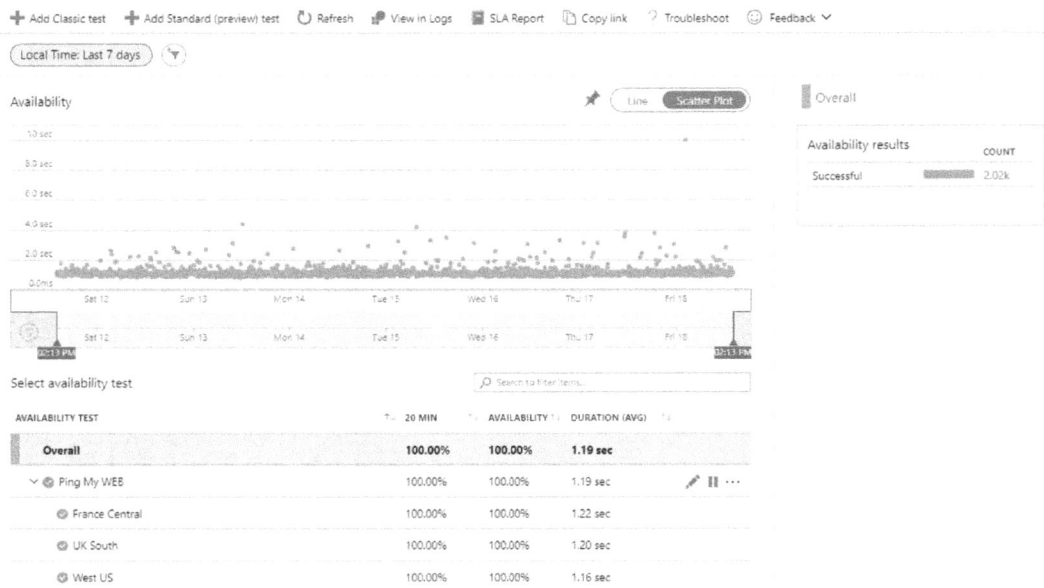

Figure 10.7 – Application Insights availability test results

Application map

The ability to track dependency calls is essential information for troubleshooting exceptions. The best chart of dependency calls made by the whole solution can be found under **Application map** in the **Investigate** section. Look at the following screenshot of the application map built as a result of monitoring the application as previously provisioned. The map consists of an instance of the web application (**aidemo6726**), Azure SQL (**aidemo6726-db-SQL**), Azure Blob (**aidemo6726**), the code profiling service (**profiler**), and calls to the Azure Storage containers (**blobbase**). The following chart shows the percentage of failed requests (16%). Most of those happened when the **Privacy** page was requested:

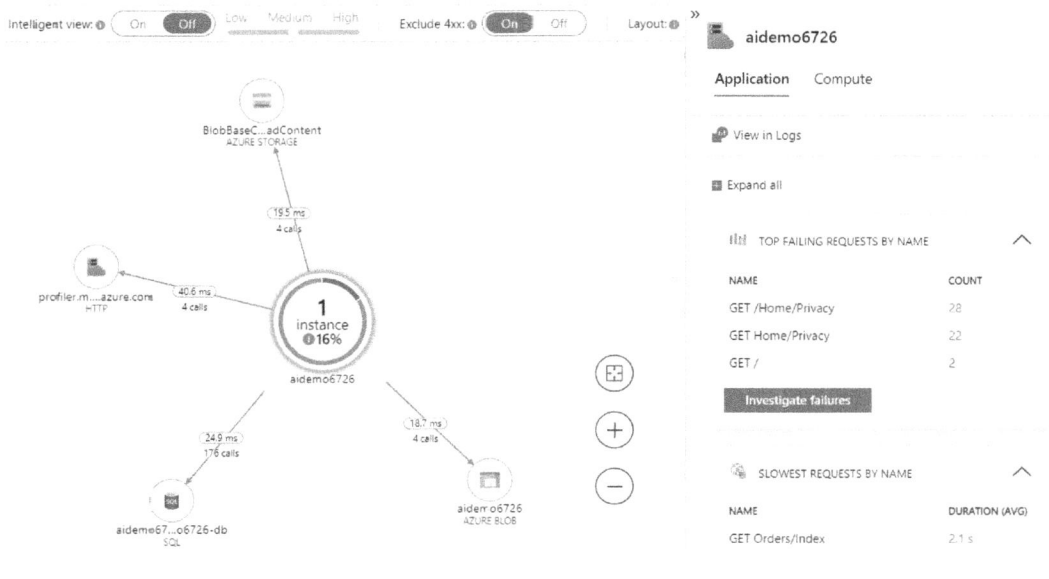

Figure 10.8 – Application map for the deployed application

The application map helps you understand the solution architecture and monitor the requests. It is interactive, and you can click on each of the circles to get details about operations, their performance, and exceptions. You can drill down into the metric to observe collected details. You can also troubleshoot the dependency problem. For instance, if the dependent database is not available for connections, you will see connection errors according to each dependent resource. In the next sections, we discuss how to configure the monitoring features from the code and how to get the most out of code instrumentations.

Instrumenting the code

In the following subsections, you will learn about code instrumentation features. Luckily, the minimum monitoring information can be collected without instrumentation code. This is good news for companies who do not have access to the code of the application they host. Meanwhile, the most valuable troubleshooting information you can get is the application code instrumented to track events with Application Insights. Let's discuss how to use client-side telemetry for JavaScript, server-side telemetry, track traces, exceptions, and custom events, and observe collated insights on the Azure portal.

JavaScript – client

The general approach to client-side monitoring is enabling a JavaScript library for Application Insights. The following code snippet can be added to the master page of your application. You can install it by executing the following command or referring to the original GitHub snippet (`https://github.`

com/Microsoft/ApplicationInsights-JS#snippet-setup-ignore-if-using-npm-setup):

```
npm i --save @microsoft/applicationinsights-web
```

Once you have added the required package to your web application page, you can track any client-side events, such as button clicks, text validation, AJAX calls, and also exceptions that happen in the user's browser. The following code snippet will track a custom trace and create a custom event:

```
import { ApplicationInsights } from
          '@microsoft/applicationinsights-web'
const appInsights = new ApplicationInsights(...config...);
appInsights.loadAppInsights();
appInsights.trackTrace('Some debug trace info')
appInsights.trackEvent('User clicked on [check-out]')
```

Because the Application Insights library can track client-side requests (AJAX), the tracking info is quite useful for diagnostics and monitoring single-page applications (such as React).

C# – server

The server-side instrumentation is available for multiple languages, including Python, Java, Node.js, and C#. Many other languages provide community-based support for Application Insights. By default, Application Insights tracks common performance counters and performance of the client requests on the server side, as well as standard dependencies such as SQL, queues, and Azure Blob. All unhandled exceptions are also tracked by default. Meanwhile, the code instrumentation approach will allow you to track handled exceptions and trace information, custom metrics and custom events, and custom dependencies to the related services. This information will give you a 360-degree view of your application and help you troubleshoot delays and crashes.

The following code snippets will demonstrate to you how to use SDK functions to instrument the code:

- **Debug trace**: Tracing custom information can be implemented by calling the following function. You can set the severity of the message and provide information that helps with debugging:

```
telemetry.TrackTrace($"Order #{id} Deleted",
                           SeverityLevel.Warning);
```

- **Custom events**: Custom events help developers track specific events generated in the business logic, such as creating a new order. The following example demonstrates how to create custom events and events with parameters:

```
telemetry.TrackEvent("New Order added");
telemetry.TrackEvent("New Order",
```

```
new Dictionary<string, string>() {
    { "Product" , order.ProductName },
    { "Size" , order.Size.ToString() },
    { "Client" , order.Client.Name },
});
```

- **Custom metrics**: The requirement of tracking custom events is quite common for modern web applications. For example, you can track the application metrics, such as the number of received records in a recordset, or business metrics such as adding products to the cart before checking out. The following code describes how a custom metric can summarize the number of orders with additional details:

```
telemetry.TrackMetric("Orders", 1);
telemetry.TrackMetric("Orders", 1,
        new Dictionary<string, string>() {
            { "Order #" , order.ID.ToString() }
        });
```

- **Error tracking**: The default functionality can track the unhandled errors (crashes) without instrumentation of the code. Meanwhile, you can get more details if you instrument the code. The code guidelines always recommend not swallowing exceptions. You can always track error information for further debugging instead of swallowing it. The following code example tracks the exception if the updating client does not exist and creates a new one:

```
try {
        _context.Clients.Update(theOrder.Client);
        _context.SaveChanges();
}
catch (Exception ex) {
        telemetry.TrackException(
        new Exception("The Client does not exists",ex));
        _context.Clients.Add(theOrder.Client);
        _context.SaveChanges();
}
```

- **Custom dependency**: Appropriate tracking of a dependency enables telemetry to granularly collect insights and provide details about what dependency operation was executed. The following code example will track dependency calls to the web API:

```
using (HttpClient httpClient = new HttpClient()){
    Stopwatch sp = Stopwatch.StartNew();
```

```
var result = httpClient.PostAsync(url, data).Result;
sp.Stop();
telemetry.TrackDependency("WebAPI",
    "Create Product", data,
    DateTime.Now.AddMilliseconds(-sp.
ElapsedMilliseconds),
    sp.Elapsed, result.IsSuccessStatusCode);
}
```

All operations mentioned before to track events and metrics, errors, and debug messages can be found by using **Transaction search** features on the Application Insights interface in the Azure portal. **Transaction search** is located in the **Investigate** section. The following example represents dependencies, custom events, and metrics collected from the application you deployed. It has a search field to help you find specific events or messages by keyword:

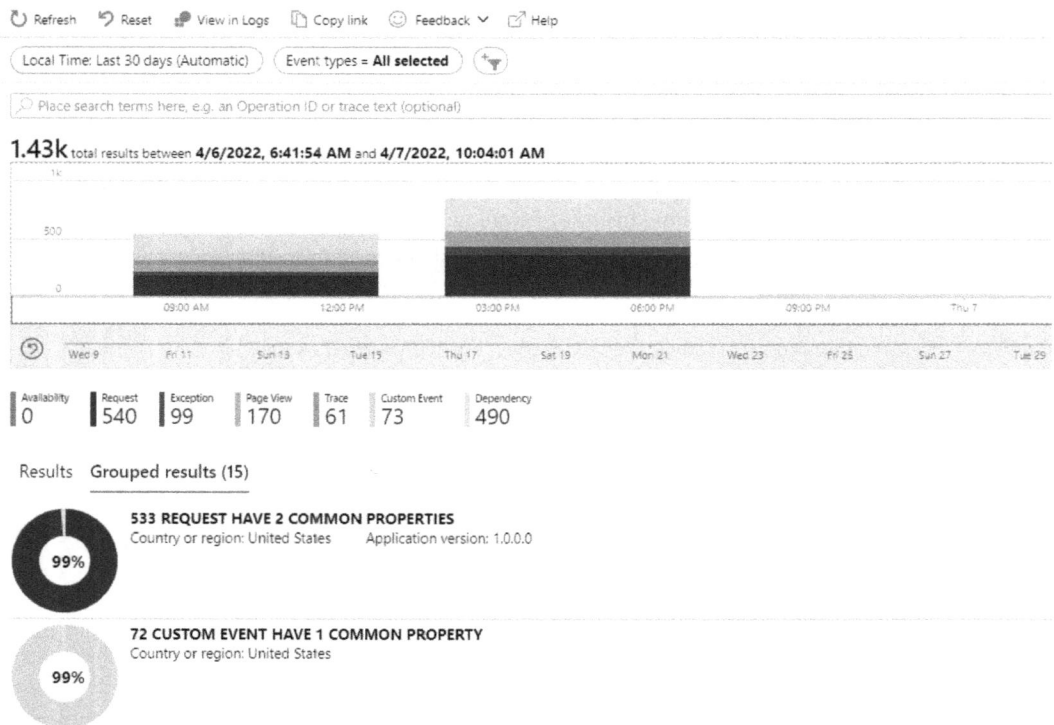

Figure 10.9 – Transaction search output

Transaction search helps you find the exact record and drill down to its parameters. Meanwhile, the search will not be able to represent results as a chart. The best approach, in this case, is to find a specific record of the metric you want to represent as a chart and copy parameters, then click on **View in Logs** and create a KQL query based on previously copied parameters. In the next section, you will learn how to use the Log Analytics workspace to build powerful queries to retrieve data from Application Insights. As a result, you can build custom charts for performance metrics, logs, and custom metrics and events and build interactive dashboards to monitor the health of the solution.

Using KQL for Log Analytics queries

Before we use KQL queries to build a custom chart, let's get familiar with the syntax and architecture. The data you can query with KQL is stored in the internal database provisioned as part of the **Log Analytics workspace**. In the previous sections of this chapter, you provisioned a Log Analytics workspace. Then, you provisioned the Application Insights instance and provided the workspace as a reference. As a result, all collected logs and metrics are stored in the workspace's database and are available for querying.

The Log Analytics services provide you with a rich UI to build and run queries. The UI supports navigation through the tables in the database and its fields. It also supports autofill to help you with KQL syntax. Let's learn the main syntax structure of the queries. To start querying collected data, you open the Log Analytics workspace instance or open **Logs** in the **Monitoring** section of the Application Insights instance. Close the **Pick Template** window and proceed to the queries.

On the left, you will see tables such as **pageViews**, **requests**, and **exceptions**. You can click on a table to observe its columns. By double-clicking on a table or field, you can paste the name into the query window. You just need the name of the table to run your first query. Let's say you double-click on **requests** and get the requests query. Click on the play button at the top. If you do not see any output, adjust the time range next to the play button. You should see the records from the requests table. Now, you can add a filter to find a query with an error. Let's provide the following query with where on the line after the name of the table and add the success column, as follows, to get only fail requests:

```
requests
| where success == false
```

For comparison, you can use the more than (>), less than (<), equal to (==), and not equal to (!=) operators to filter records. Also, the contains operator can help with finding string values. Let's modify the query and use contains to get only requests to the details page:

```
requests
| where success == true
| where url contains 'details'
```

One more modification we will add is to sort the output by `duration` values:

```
requests
| where success == true
| where url contains 'details'
| order by duration
```

In KQL, we can summarize the output equal to the `GROUP BY` behavior in T-SQL. Let's summarize request `count` to get the column named `hits` with 100 hits step of bucketization :

```
requests
| where success == true
| where url contains 'details'
| summarize hits=count() by bin(duration,100)
| order by duration
```

The query should provide you with something similar to the following table results. The values might depend on the performance and size of your web applications:

Figure 10.10 – Executing KQL queries on the requests table

In the next example, let's try a more sophisticated query:

- `let` will be used to create variables, including date and time variables, by providing your value in the `datetime` function with the format `YYYY-MM-DDTHH:MM:SS.SSSZ`

- Reuse the calculated `dataset` with a list of filtered records

- Summarize results by using the `sumif` function (summarization with conditions)

- Render results as a line chart with the graph of the `Overall` number of requests

The resulting KQL request is provided in the following snippet:

```
let start = datetime("2022-04-06T00:00:00.000Z");
let end = datetime("2022-04-07T23:59:00.000Z");
let timeGrain=1m;
let dataset=exceptions
    | where timestamp > start and timestamp < end
    | where type == "System.NullReferenceException"
;
dataset
| summarize failedCount=sumif(itemCount,severityLevel==3) by
bin(timestamp, timeGrain)
| extend request='Overall'
| render timechart
```

Replace the start and end values with the values from your time range when you did the test. After executing the requests, it provides output similar to the following:

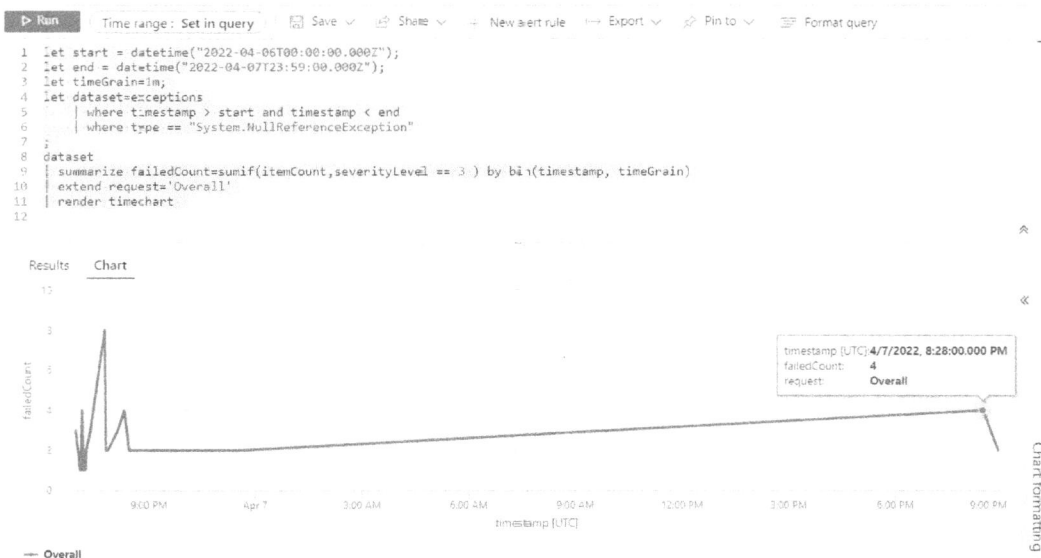

Figure 10.11 – KQL query execution interface showing the result as a chart

Of course, learning about KQL features is not enough to be proficient in the syntax. The documentation provided on the portal contains useful query examples that you can leverage to build charts on dashboards and workbooks. Furthermore, you can set up Azure alerts for the specific values received from queries and be notified when they hit the thresholds. In the following section, you will learn about a new monitoring interface named **Azure Monitor workbooks**.

Discovering Monitor workbooks

Workbooks are another great tool for reporting and monitoring in Azure. Let's compare Azure workbooks with other monitoring tools and services, such as Azure dashboards and Power BI:

- **Power BI** is one of the reporting tools that can be used for monitoring. Power BI reports consume the telemetry data pulled from Azure Monitor and Azure Log Analytics through web APIs. Power BI reports can be printed and published on the server and can also be shared as part of the Power BI dashboard with users in the Azure AD tenant and anonymous users.

- An **Azure dashboard** represents live activities and includes metrics and logs. The dashboard supports different types of tiles, including charts, images, videos, and Markdown. Usually, a dashboard is a single-page view of the most important metrics of the application that automatically updates. Dashboards support KQL charts, Application Insights, and Azure Monitor metrics. They aren't designed to be printed as a report or exported. A dashboard can only be shared with Azure AD tenant users.

- **Azure workbooks** can use sophisticated KQL queries, where you can combine different sources of data, support Markdown, and interact with charts, such as with filtering or ordering. Azure workbooks are based on reporting visuals for simplifying observation and printing reports. Notice that updates are not loaded automatically into a workbook. You need to refresh the workbook to observe the latest metric values. Meanwhile, some charts from the workbook do not exist on Azure dashboards and provide rich configuration settings to adjust the context and time interval. Moreover, Azure workbooks have a template you can use instead of starting from scratch.

Let's build a simple workbook to monitor exceptions logged by the Application Insights instance of the Azure Web App you deployed previously in the chapter. You need to select **Workbooks** in the **Monitoring** section of your Application Insights resource. **Workbooks** is located under **Logs** in the same section. Alternatively, you can search for the **Workbooks** section in the portal. Then, you need to create a new workbook by choosing empty **QuickStart** templates.

You can add a new section by clicking on the **Add** link and choosing the **Text** item. Then, switch to **Markdown text** and add the following snippet:

```
## Null Reference Exceptions
The time chart of exception occurrences in the application for
the **last day**
```

You can also add a diagram by selecting the **Add Query** item and providing the following KQL query. It is a modified version of the query you used previously. The start and end of the period should be hardcoded in the query and provided globally from drop-down filters at the top of the item:

```
let timeGrain=1m;
let dataset=exceptions
    | where type == "System.NullReferenceException"
;
dataset
| summarize failedCount=sumif(itemCount,severityLevel == 3 ) by
bin(timestamp, timeGrain)
| extend request='Overall'
| render timechart
```

After you finish creating them, your workbooks should look as follows:

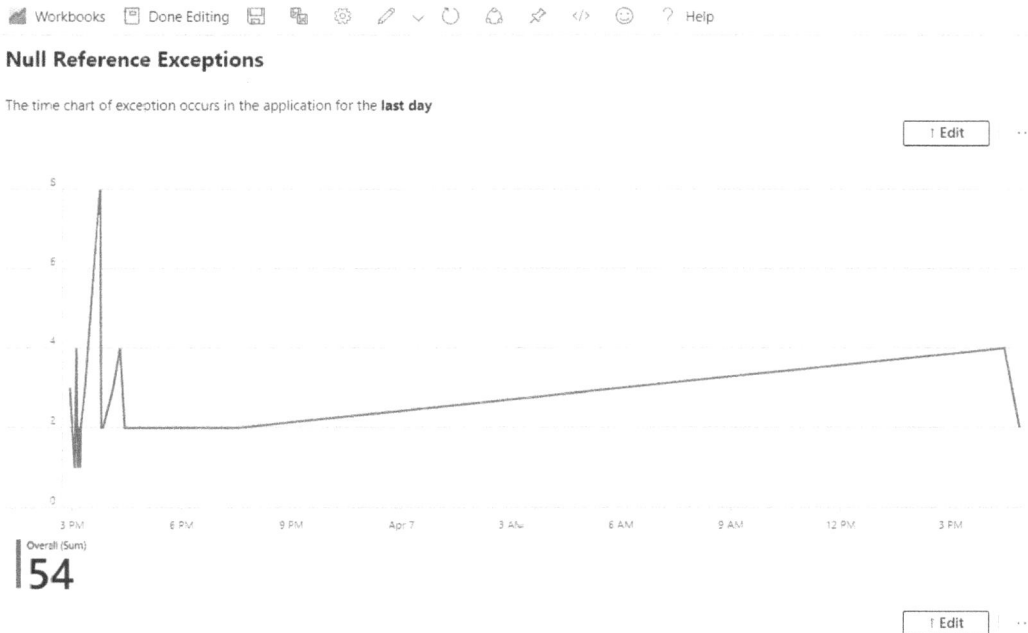

Figure 10.12 – Azure workbook created with Markdown and query items

You can keep going and investigate other quick-start templates available for Application Insights resources. For example, the **Performance Counters**, **Dependency failures**, **Exceptions**, and **Active Users** workbooks visualize the main metrics of the application and help with troubleshooting issues.

Summary

In this chapter, you have learned about a variety of monitoring tools available in Azure. You played around with Azure Monitor and were able to retrieve performance counters for your application, such as request rate, CPU usage, and failed requests. You learned about different options for persisting and analyzing logs by using Azure Blob Storage and Log Analytics workspaces. You also learned about Application Insights – the most powerful tool for monitoring and troubleshooting applications running on Azure platforms or on-premises. You got familiar with a variety of useful charts provided by Application Insights to monitor and detect bottlenecks in performance, investigate crashes, and collect dependency metrics of the solution's components. You also learned how to instrument the code to collect custom metrics and custom events, and handled exceptions. We introduced essential skills of root cause analysis by using custom KQL queries and custom charts. You learned about various ways of representing collected metrics and logs, including Azure workbooks and Azure dashboards. You were also made aware of the availability test and Azure alerts as the best way to be informed of an application outage. All of these skills and knowledge will be verified through exam questions and also help you successfully monitor and troubleshoot your enterprise application running on the Azure platform.

In the next chapter, we will continue our journey through Azure platform services and learn about the implementation, hosting, and protection of mid-tier web API services with API management resources.

Questions

1. What metrics are collected with Azure Monitor?

2. What is the difference between an activity log and an application log?

3. How do you collect dependency metrics for Application Insights?

4. How do you set up tests to determine when the application does not work or produces errors?

5. Does code instrumentation require collecting crash information?

Further reading

-   The following link introduces best practices for logging and monitoring with Azure Monitor:

    ```
    https://docs.microsoft.com/en-us/azure/azure-monitor/best-
    practices
    ```

-   You can discover a recommended technique for troubleshooting metrics of web applications with Azure Monitor at the following link:

    ```
    https://docs.microsoft.com/en-us/azure/azure-monitor/essentials/
    metrics-troubleshoot
    ```

- You can find recommendations about implementing Application Insights for ASP.NET Core websites at the following link:

  `https://docs.microsoft.com/en-us/azure/azure-monitor/app/asp-net-core`

- You can learn more about tracking custom events and metrics in code at the following link:

  `https://docs.microsoft.com/en-us/azure/azure-monitor/app/api-custom-events-metrics`

- The following link demonstrates how to debug crashes collected by Application Insights snapshot debugging:

  `https://docs.microsoft.com/en-us/azure/azure-monitor/app/snapshot-debugger`

- The following article explains how to collect logs from a VM that runs websites:

  `https://learn.microsoft.com/en-us/azure/azure-monitor/agents/data-sources-iis-logs`

- You can read more about setting up Application map at the following links:

  - `https://learn.microsoft.com/en-us/azure/azure-monitor/app/asp-net-dependencies#where-to-find-dependency-data`

  - `https://docs.microsoft.com/en-us/azure/azure-monitor/app/app-map?tabs=net#composite-application-map`

Part 5: Connecting to and Consuming Azure and Third-Party Services

This part begins with introducing the **API Management (APIM)** services and their advantages and limitations. You will be able to provision services and connect internal web APIs. You will learn how to build advanced policies to cash, throttle, and mock the backend response. Then, you will learn how APIM can help scale and protect modern web applications.

Then, event-driven solutions will be introduced. You will learn how to provision, get connected, and communicate with Event Grid, Event Hubs, and IoT Hub services in Azure. This part will help you understand the advantages and limitations of the event-based solutions to choose the best one according to your requirements.

You will discover the implementation of messaging solutions in Azure based on Service Bus queues and Storage queues. You will learn how to provision, get connected, and communicate with messaging services in Azure. You will also learn the advantages and limitations of the services and learn how to describe the scenarios where they should be used.

Before moving to the final part of the book containing the mock exam, we cover a few of the fundamentals of DevOps, providing some clarity around what it is and some DevOps practices implemented within successful teams. As well as providing some food for thought, this provides insight into some of the topics you may encounter should you want to start studying for the *AZ-400: Designing and Implementing Microsoft DevOps Solutions* exam after passing the AZ-204 (which we're sure you will!).

This part covers 15-20% of the AZ-204 exam.

The following chapters will be covered under this section:

- *Chapter 11, Implementing API Management*
- *Chapter 12, Developing Event-Based Solutions*
- *Chapter 13, Developing Message-Based Solutions*

11
Implementing API Management

In this chapter, we will learn about the concept of web API services and their implementation in Azure. We will learn how to provision our internal web API service and document its interface with Swagger. We will also see how to provision and manage the powerful Azure **API Management** (**APIM**) service to govern our enterprise web APIs. APIM has many advantages and some limitations, and soon you will know about them.

The demo scripts provided in this chapter will help you provision APIM and connect your backend APIs to the service. In this chapter, we will learn how to configure security, caching, and throttling settings for APIM, and we will find out how to granularly configure each operation in our APIs with policies. In the last part of the chapter, we will be introduced to the policies syntax and learn how to use advanced policies to cache and throttle the requests to our APIs. Furthermore, we will also learn how APIM can help scale and protect modern web applications.

Everything related to APIM services will be discussed in this chapter. The following main topics are on the agenda:

- Understanding the role of web API services
- Discovering APIM services
- Connecting existing web APIs to APIM
- Exploring APIM configuration options
- Using advanced policies

Before jumping into APIM, let us find out what web API technology is and what benefits it provides for modern cloud development.

Technical requirements

The scripts provided in the chapter can be run in Azure Cloud Shell as well as executed locally. The Azure CLI and Visual Studio Code are ideal tools to execute the code and commands provided in the following repository:

https://github.com/PacktPublishing/Developing-Solutions-for-Microsoft-Azure-AZ-204-Exam-Guide/tree/main/Chapter11

Code in Action videos for this chapter: https://bit.ly/3BuvzKf

Understanding the role of web API services

What is a web API in the modern web application world? A web API is a well-known and widely used technology to transfer data through communication channels on the internet. Web APIs are usually implemented on servers as a group of endpoints and used for connections from a variety of clients. Endpoints support the **Representational State Transfer** (**REST**) interface, allowing the manipulation of data objects by using HTTP verbs (GET, POST, PUT, and DELETE). The data formats engaged in communication are commonly represented in JSON or XML format. Furthermore, the **Open Data Protocol** (**OData**) can be used to filter and summarize data chunks exposed by RESTful interfaces. Also, OData provides a bunch of guidelines and best practices for operating with REST interfaces. Following the guidelines is a plus for any application working with web APIs.

Historically, there was a huge demand for transferring data between applications and databases. Applications, including web servers and individual clients working on desktop or mobile platforms, experienced lag when communicating and retrieving data. The root cause was that old databases did not support scaling to serve the significant number of client connections. Moreover, direct TCP communication was not allowed to go through firewalls. Finally, web services were able to help with data transfer tasks because web service is easy to scale, supports caching, and is accessible by the HTTP(S) protocol allowed by firewalls. The first web services that hosted web interfaces were based on **Simple Object Access Protocol** (**SOAP**) and supported XML chunks of data sent back and forth through HTTP(S) communications.

SOAP web services still exist and are supported by Azure technologies. Later, the REST protocol replaced SOAP communication because of the difficulties of implementing SOAP and the challenges with authentication. REST is a lightweight protocol optimized to transfer data most effectively through HTTP(S) requests. Nowadays, the REST protocol is supported by a wide variety of services in the cloud. In conjunction with OData, the REST protocol has become well known and is highly adopted in cloud-based solutions.

The web API service that supports REST protocol communication is named the **RESTful** service and allows other applications to access data. A good web API service must be documented, versioned, stateless, and scalable. All those aspects are already implemented in the ASP.NET Core MVC template and supported by various tools for tests, including Visual Studio Code extensions and third-party test applications. Most programming languages support HTTP clients and requests to get connected and effectively use the REST protocol to consume data from web API services. In Azure, the **Azure Resource Manager** (**ARM**) service is hosted on a web API and supports a variety of clients that use REST requests for communication. For instance, REST calls are wrapped in C# SDKs, the Azure CLI, and Azure PowerShell. The Azure portal also communicates with ARM with the REST protocol.

Let's take a look at how the ARM web API helps us to implement scale requirements. Recall that the ARM service is implemented as a web API and used for connection from the portal, automation services, SDKs, and other tools. The ARM web API is designed as a mid-tier service and can be scaled depending on the demand from the web UI (the Azure portal), automation tools (the Azure CLI or PowerShell), or SDKs (Fluent – `https://docs.microsoft.com/en-us/dotnet/api/microsoft.azure.management.fluent.azure?view=azure-dotnet`). Stateless services can be easily scaled and support the highest amount of connections that the backend can accept directly from the UI. The following diagram represents how the ARM web API is consumed by different types of clients:

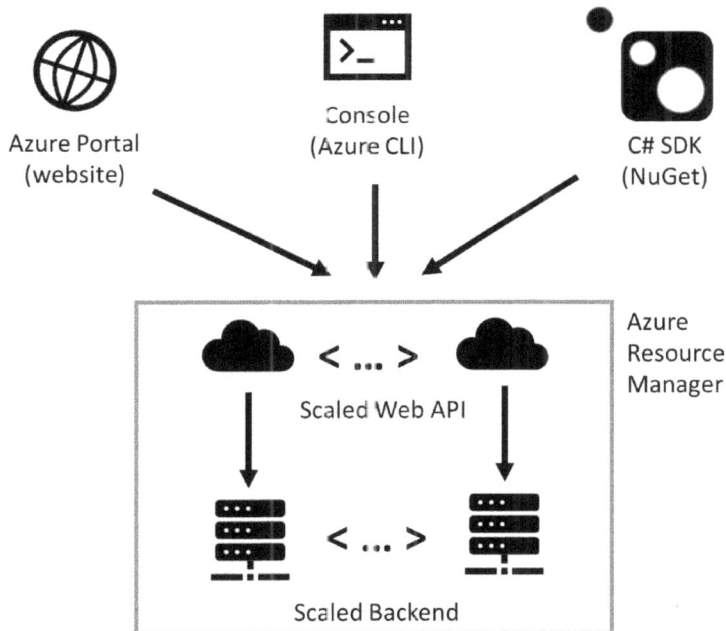

Figure 11.1 – ARM service architectural design

ARM is not the only example of a web API service used in Azure. Many other examples exist. Let's take a look at the Azure Cognitive Services implementation, which uses APIM. The following architecture helps with understanding how APIM helps protect Azure Cognitive Services. The client app sends a request to analyze an image and provide its subscription key for authentication. APIM accepts the request and orchestrates the calls to the backend and billing service. Then, APIM returns the result of image recognition from the ML model to the client app:

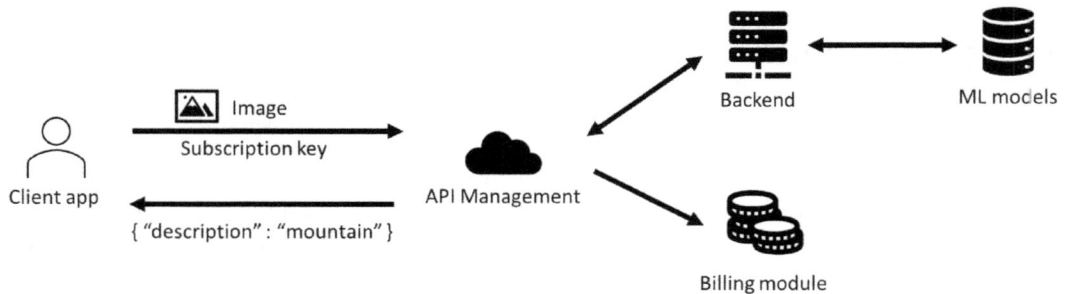

Figure 11.2 – Azure Cognitive Services architecture

You can visit the APIM console, which is represented as the APIM developer portal for Azure Cognitive Services, at `https://westus.dev.cognitive.microsoft.com/docs/services/`.

In the next parts of this chapter, we will discuss the advantages of APIM, which helps to protect and manage backend resources and expose a scalable web API out of the box.

Discovering APIM services

Previously, you learned how APIM is used internally in Azure to host Cognitive Services. Now, you'll move on to learning the details of the APIM service and the advantages of using it on modern websites.

The biggest advantage of the APIM service is its various ways of configuration, including security management, products and subscription management, and advanced policy configuration, which incorporates sophisticated algorithms of caching and throttling in the communication between clients and your web APIs. From an architecture view, the APIM service is designed as a façade service to protect the web APIs exposed by your organization. APIM implements orchestration of the request-response logic and allows communicating with multiple backends in a single client request. Moreover, the APIM service provides a rich interface for enterprise customers who want to provide data services for integrations (weather forecasts, stock prices, real-time flight timetables, etc.).

APIM has a powerful subscription and product management interface that allows it to control API use and provide billing information for customers. Another interesting service for integration provided by APIM is the developer portal. This portal includes up-to-date documentation about exposed endpoints, requested parameters, and versions of APIs. The dev portal also includes a testing tool to call APIs and trace the response.

Are there any limitations of APIM? There are almost no limitations except for a lack of protection from cybersecurity attacks. The service should be used in conjunction with **Web Applications Firewall** (**WAF**) services such as Azure Front Door. Another pain point for APIM customers is the pricing model. Currently, we have several tiers available to provision APIM:

- The **Developer** tier, with no SLA and a single scalable unit. It provides 10 MB of cache.

- The **Basic** tier, with a 99.95% SLA. It is scalable horizontally to 2 units and provides 50 MB of cache.

- The **Standard** tier, with a 99.95% SLA. It is scalable up to 4 units and provides 1 GB of cache.

- The **Premium** tier, which is deployed in several regions and provides 99.99% SLA with 10 instances to scale and 5 GB of cache.

All these tiers are charged monthly independent of usage. Previously, customers complained about the lack of consumption-based price tiers, so now, Azure has released a consumption-based APIM with a limited feature set but an affordable price. The Consumption price tier is based on usage and allows only one instance to be deployed per subscription.

In the next sections, you will learn how to provision APIM and how to connect existing APIs to the service, as well as how to configure products and subscriptions.

Provisioning a web API

Before we start learning about APIM, let's deploy a service exposed to web API operations to get the weather forecast. The following script will help you deploy an Azure web app to investigate the web API service and later connect it to your APIM. The following file should be executed in Bash to help you build and publish a website:

```
https://github.com/PacktPublishing/Developing-Solutions-for-Microsoft-
Azure-AZ-204-Exam-Guide/blob/main/Chapter11/01-provision-services/
demo.azcli
```

If the script has executed successfully, you should have an Azure web app provisioned and deployed with a demo weather service. The service might not respond to a direct call but should respond to you on the weather forecast endpoint. In the next section, you will learn how to generate documentation for your weather service and connect it to the new APIM instance.

Discovering OpenAPI documentation

Maintaining web API documentation is a recommended best practice. Back in the days when SOAP services were frequently encountered, documentation was provided as static documents in WSDL format. This static documentation had the main disadvantage that it was not up to date and often caused more confusion to developers than helped them to connect. Nowadays, enterprise organizations that want to consume your web API require up-to-date documentation of available endpoints and parameters. Good documentation also provides the request and response schemas expected by the web API and explains possible status codes returned by the servers. Status codes can flag specific cases, such as when incorrect parameters are provided (400), authentication is not completed (403), or the required item was not found in the database (404).

Documentation should be released depending on the interface version and must be up to date. Many frameworks can generate documentation based on the methods provided by the service (based on configuration attributes). One of the leaders of documentation and testing frameworks for web APIs is OpenAPI (aka Swagger). You can request the /swagger URL from your server to get the Swagger page that explains available methods, input parameters, and output schema.

On the Swagger page, you will see an operation named **WeatherForecast**, and if you click on it, you will see a button next to it named **Try it out**. By clicking on this button, the forecast will be generated and provided on a dark background output window.

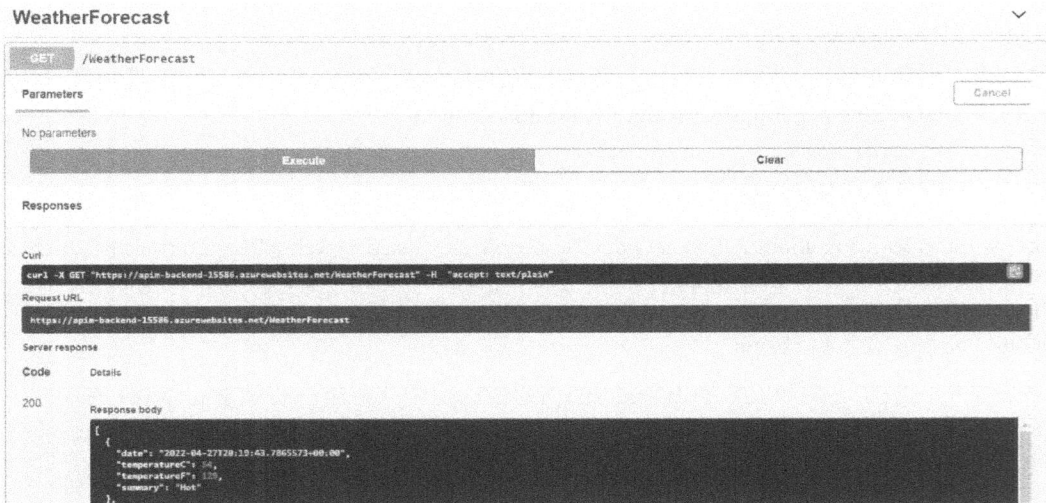

Figure 11.3 – Swagger interface with the weather forecast operation executed

Swagger is configured dynamically when the code is modified and provides descriptions with examples of input parameters and data schema. You do not need to waste time updating documentation manually because the documentation is generated on demand when requested from Swagger. The Swagger documentation is also generated for each available version of the API. Whenever you change the parameters or output schema or update endpoints, you should release a new version of the web API instead of changing the existing one. Meanwhile, the old versions should be accessible until the last customer migrates to the new version of your web API. Swagger also generates documentation based on the version. Let's request documentation URL /swagger/v1/swagger.json for the web API provisioned earlier. From the URL, you can notice that the web API version 1 will be requested. You can find the documentation URL on the Swagger page under **DemoCatalog**.

Click on the link and observe the JSON documentation of the API service. It should contain a description of the service and only one operation in the previously mentioned path. The operation named /WeatherForecast contains a response description.

Example output is provided here:

```
{
    "openapi": "3.0.1",
    "info": {
        ...
    },
    "paths": {
        "/WeatherForecast": {
            "get": {
                "responses": {
                    "200": {
                        ...
                    }
                }
            }
        }
    },
    "components": {
        "schemas": {
            ...
        }
    }
}
```

Copy the full URL address from the browser because you need this for the next script execution. In the next sections, you will use this OpenAPI documentation to import the service to APIM.

Provisioning APIM

To provision your APIM instance, you need to understand the workload patterns your clients will produce. For low-load patterns, the Consumption pricing tier works better than fixed tiers with the monthly load. Unfortunately, the Consumption tier does not support an internal cache, **virtual network (VNet)** integration, multi-region deployment, and self-hosted gateways for connection to the on-premises backend. Meanwhile, consumption-based tiers are optimal for proofs of concept and learning. You can start with consumption-based APIM and then upgrade it to a larger tier later when you need extra features or to scale performance.

> **Important Note**
> Provisioning the APIM instance might take about 40 minutes for all price tiers except the Consumption tier. Only one APIM instance per subscription is allowed with the Consumption tier.

When you provision an APIM instance from the Azure portal, you can specify the following settings to enable enterprise-grade features:

- A unique **name** for the resource, which can be used to register the FQDN and access web APIs. Later, you can register a custom domain for APIM.

- The **organization name** and the administrator's email address. These are required fields for setting up the developer portal.

- A preferred **location** should be chosen, preferably in the same data center where you have backend resources deployed. Additional traffic charges can be applied to your subscription for cross-data center communication.

- Choose the **pricing tier**, either **Consumption** or **Premium**, depending on the loading pattern.

- You can enable **Application Insights** to monitor request rates and collect crash information.

- **Scaling units** are available for pricing tiers starting from Basic and implementing horizontal scale by increasing or decreasing the number of units that host the APIM service.

- **Managed identities** can be used for communication with Azure resources such as Key Vault, which requires authentication and authorization with RBAC.

- **VNet integration** enables an internal firewall for managing external connections. Connection through the endpoint is also supported.

- **Protocol settings** allow you to enable different versions of TLS protocol support for client and backend connections.

APIM features such as connecting existing backend APIs, product and subscription management, an authentication platform, and integration with Git, will be configured later and explained in the next part of the chapter. For now, execute the following script in Bash to provision APIM for your subscription:

```
https://github.com/PacktPublishing/Developing-Solutions-for-Microsoft-
Azure-AZ-204-Exam-Guide/blob/main/Chapter11/02-provision-apim/demo.
azcli
```

The script generates the new APIM account and prints its name to the console. Please copy this name as you'll need it for the next execution. In the next part of the chapter, you will connect a previously deployed Azure App Services to the APIM you just provisioned.

Connecting existing web APIs to APIM

One of the major configuration tasks for APIM is managing connected backend services. There are several ways to connect your existing web API as a backend to APIM. One way requires manually providing each endpoint with parameters. It's a time-consuming process and only works for small APIs. There is another way to import documentation: from Swagger or from **Web Application Description Language** (WADL) and **Web Services Description Language** (WSDL) files. One more way of connecting is choosing an existing resource (e.g., Azure Functions, Logic Apps, or App Service) from an Azure subscription and APIM connects it automatically. In the next code snippets, you execute the Azure CLI script to connect existing services by providing OpenAPI documentation.

To execute the script, you need to update two values collected in previous script runs. First, you need to find the APIM instance name (the short name), and second, you need to provide the URL of the Swagger documentation from your weather API. This script will also connect several well-known services, and if it generates an error, it means the service is down and you can proceed with the next one:

```
https://github.com/PacktPublishing/Developing-Solutions-for-Microsoft-
Azure-AZ-204-Exam-Guide/blob/main/Chapter11/03-connect/demo.azcli
```

After executing this script, you will have four services connected to the provisioned APIM:

- `weather-api`: A simple one-operation service that returns the weather forecast. You previously discovered this service through the Swagger interface.
- `color-api`: A RESTful service implementing the GET, POST, PUT, and DELETE operations on a list of colors. It is also able to retrieve a random color from the list.
- `calc-api`: A calculator service supporting only GET requests and providing addition, division, multiplication, and subtraction operations for integers.
- `conference-api`: An IT sessions catalog with an option to search by topic and session name.

These APIs provide a good opportunity to get used to the APIM interface to call and troubleshoot operations. If you choose one of the APIs, you will see a list of the available operations for the API. For example, if you choose **color-api**, select **ApiRandomColor**, and then click on the **Test** tab at the top, you will see the **Send** button, which allows you to call the operation and observe the output. It will look like the following:

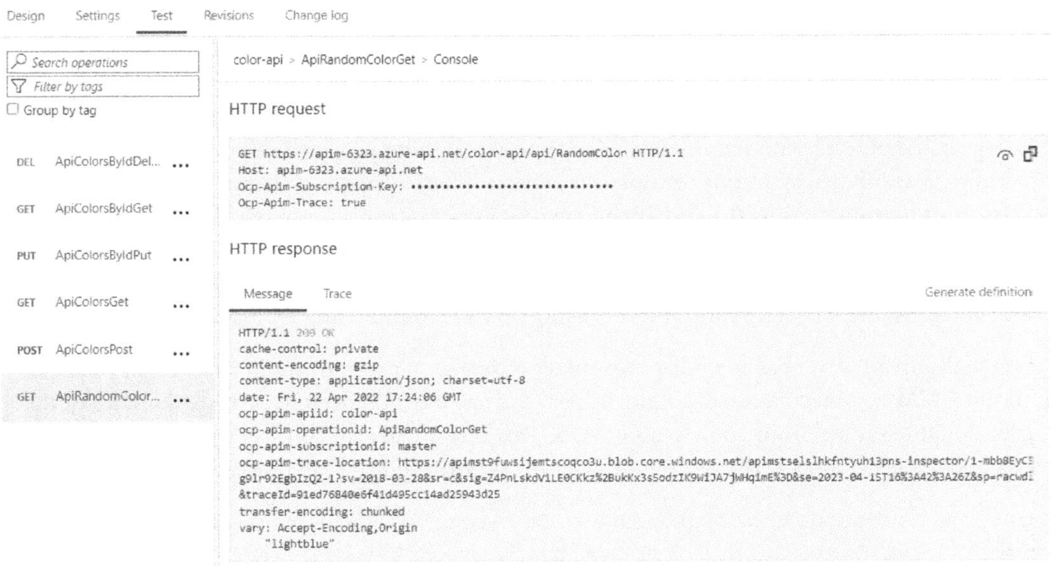

Figure 11.4 – Testing a connected API and observing the output

Products and subscriptions are other important configurations that are used to provide access to APIs. A few products were added during the previous script execution, and you can observe them on the APIM page in the Azure portal. In the next section, you will learn how to manage products, assign subscriptions, and distribute them between consumers. You will also learn about the configuration of APIM instances, which will help protect and improve the performance of your APIM and backend services.

Exploring APIM configuration options

Most of the configuration options are not available when you are provisioning APIM. When you finish deployment, advanced configuration options will be available for your APIM instance depending on the price tier you selected. Let's take a look at some of the configuration features. Some of the features you can observe from the portal, but other features might not be available for the Consumption tier you deployed from the script.

Products and subscriptions

Several terms need to be explained before moving on. An **API** is a set of endpoints or operations available for calling by clients to receive data. A **product** is a set of APIs groped logically. A **subscription** is a key provided for a customer who wants to call APIs included in the product. Usually, a product is linked to one or more subscriptions. Customers can obtain more than one subscription.

For enterprises that provide access through a web API to a variety of databases (e.g., forecasts, price change history, or analytics), it is important to control and track the access to the services and bill their customers accordingly. On other occasions, customers who want to adopt the enterprise service hosted on the web API can request trial access. Other customers might use a free access subscription to get limited functionality for proof of concept projects. All those needs are met in APIM's product and subscription management features. Companies that have deployed APIM can create several types of products:

- **A free product**, which can be accessed without a subscription. Those products should have the **Requires subscription** setting set to **Off**.

- **A billable product** is a product that requires a subscription to charge customers individually.

- **A trial product** is a product where subscriptions have limited access time during the trial period. APIM does not have handy settings to control the trial time, but in the access policies, you can verify the date when the subscription was created to control the length of the trial period.

A product is a logical group of APIs that are allowed to be used by client subscriptions. A new subscription can be generated at any time and assigned to the existing product. By adding a new API to the product, you are allowing access to all operations of the service. Alternatively, if you are building a free product, you can clone the registered API with a new name and delete the operation you do not want to share for free. You need to publish products to make them available for clients to call.

A subscription can identify the customer and link to the products that allowed access to the API. A subscription can be generated by the admin and shared with a customer or a customer can request it from the dev portal. A list of operations available as part of the product can also be obtained from the dev portal. A subscription is a number and letter combination that must be passed in an HTTP header named `Ocp-Apim-Subscription-Key`. A header should be provided for each request sent to the API's operations unless the product or API does not request a subscription.

In the previous script, you provision APIM and add three APIs to the APIM: Color API, the Calculator API, and the Conference API. Now, you can observe them from the Azure portal.

Authentication

Access to the development portal could be provided for unauthenticated users and users with an account created on the APIM instance manually. The user's email address and password are required to register the account. Alternatively, several identity providers can be used for the authentication process, including Azure Active Directory and Azure Active Directory B2C, a Microsoft account, Facebook, Twitter, and Google. You can also configure APIM to authorize developer accounts using the OAuth 2.0 and OpenID Connect protocols.

Authentication for API operation calls is implemented based on the subscription key related to the products. Meanwhile, additional authentication mechanisms can be implemented on advanced policy levels, such as verification of the request source (IP addresses) and certificate verification. More details about advanced policies will be provided in the *Using advanced policies* section of the chapter.

User accounts

From an APIM owner standpoint, the user account is a developer from an external organization who wants to adopt APIs. The APIM admin can create the user accounts manually, add them to the groups, and assign subscriptions to manage the visibility of the products for the user account. Several immutable system groups exist in APIM:

- **The Administrators group**, with full permissions to carry out operations on products and APIs. Azure subscription administrators are added to this group.

- **The Developers group**, with authenticated users who can test APIs based on the visibility of the products and request subscriptions. Developers can get access to documentation and monitor the usage of the services of their applications.

- **The Guests group**, for unauthenticated users who can observe APIs on the developer portal but cannot call them.

A custom group can also be created to manage a group of accounts manually. Admins can create a new account manually by providing a login and password or inviting users to create their accounts with self-service. The invite will be sent by email with a link to a registration page on the developer portal.

Networking

APIM can be connected to a VNet in Azure and on-premises. The API backend hosted on the network can be accessed by APIM securely and the backend should not be exposed for connection from the public internet. You can configure integration with an Azure VNet from the Azure portal to connect backends hosted on Azure VMs. If you are going to use Azure VMs, you must be aware of port requirements that allow APIM to monitor the state of the backend and use Load Balancer. You can also use private endpoints for connection to the Azure infrastructure. For connection to the resources, on-premises APIM needs to be integrated with a VNet that is connected to the on-premises network by site-to-site connectivity.

The dev portal

The dev portal is a website hosted on an APIM instance and is available for all pricing tiers except the Consumption tier. The dev portal allows clients who want to integrate with provided APIs to observe its documentation, test, and manage its subscriptions. The website pages are automatically generated and could be customized by the APIM owner. New products and APIs added will automatically appear on the portal when customers sign in.

Page customization includes editing layouts, menus, styles, widgets with text and media files, embedded HTML snippets, and inline frames. Custom logic on the pages is not supported out of the box but is available for customization from the portal code base on GitHub. Required updates could be requested as a pull request to merge with the managed portal logic or self-hosted on the client environment outside of APIM. This way of integration suits integration with a third-party system and provides a flexible way of customizing and implementing widgets with your logic.

Self-hosted gateways

Hybrid and multi-cloud companies need to run APIM instances in an isolated network. By deploying a self-hosted gateway, they can host a local APIM instance on-premises. The deployed gateway works as a proxy server and provides connectivity to registered Azure APIM resources for applications from the local environment. The self-hosted gateway is implemented as a Docker image. Then, it can be configured and managed from the Azure portal as a deployment with one or more nodes. Accounts are charged a fixed price per deployment, but their nodes run for free. If a company wants to provide access hosted on on-premises web API servers for an application running in Azure, it should consider using networking solutions such as a VPN or Azure Hybrid Connections.

External cache

The caching response is one of the most useful functionalities of APIM to protect backend APIs from hammering by client requests. Every client wants to get the most up-to-date data and will be able to call APIM often. The customer who owns the API could implement a throttling limit to prevent clients from calling the API often or implement caching logic to cache the frontend or backend output. The caching option is customer friendly and does not affect its functionality by throwing errors when the limit is exceeded.

APIM supports a built-in cache. The cache size depends on the price tier (10 MB for the Developer tier, 5 GB for the Premium tier). Often, the size of the built-in cache is not enough to support high-performance APIs. The workaround is using an external cache, for instance, **Azure Cache for Redis**.

If you connect an external cache instance to APIM, it will avoid cleaning up the cache memory during APIM updates, because the built-in cache is cleared when APIM restarts. You can also exceed the memory size of the cached output provided by the built-in cache. Moreover, you can use the external cache for the Consumption price tier, which does not support a built-in cache.

To adopt an external cache, the instance of the cache must be provisioned in Azure or on-premises. Then, the cache should be connected to the APIM instance by providing the connection string supported by `StackExchange.Redis`. When the cache instance is connected to APIM, the caching policies can be configured. In the next subsections, you will learn how to configure a caching policy and throttling limits.

Repository integration

APIM supports integration with a Git repository to persist configuration. This feature is especially valuable for companies that maintain advanced policies. The policy is that XML format configuration with inline code snippets must be versioned and persisted in source control. Moreover, the modification of the configuration, such as adding a new version of the API or modifying policies, can persist directly from the Git repo. Another advantage of configuring the Git repo for APIM is high availability. You can quickly restore the APIM configuration in the new instance in another region to replace a failed region.

Monitoring and troubleshooting

To monitor APIM calls, you can use Azure Monitor and Application Insights. Azure Monitor provides you with limited metrics to monitor and does not persist in the history of changes for more than a month. The main metrics recommended to be monitored are **Capacity** (displays the percentage of the resources in use and will let you know when your APIM requires an upgrade) and **Requests** (lets you know the current request rate for your APIM service). The metrics could be exported for persisting to the storage account and pulled to the Azure Log Analytics workspace to analyze.

The Application Insights service is explained in more detail in *Chapter 10, Troubleshooting Solutions by Using Metrics and Log Data*. It can offer the granular monitoring of individual requests and backend responses. The service can collect the exception output and monitor a variety of metrics, including dependencies on backend APIs.

The alerting service allows you to monitor the resource metric changes. For example, the execution time of the request, errors on the backend, restarts of the APIM instance, and so on. You can also be alerted to changes of custom requests configured in a Log Analytics workspace and events in activity logs, such as adding new subscriptions and publishing new products.

If you want to track the subscription, product, or API usage, the best option is to visit the **Analytics** page in the **Monitoring** section on the Azure portal. From the charts available on the page, you can monitor the frequency of the requests by subscription. You can also monitor operations, products, and subscription usage based on the time range and geography of the client. The information on the **Analytics** page could be used for the billing of clients.

Troubleshooting can be performed from the Azure portal by executing a request to the APIM operation. The **Test** functionality allows you to send a request to APIM and trace the flow on the **Trace** tab. The **Backend**, **Inbound**, **Outbound**, and **On error** tabs let you observe the output of each of the stages and traces of the inline code from the policy. The following screenshot shows you how to troubleshoot errors that might occur while calling the web API:

Figure 11.5 – Trace output for the operation of retrieving a random color from color-api

APIM policies are a powerful mechanism to granularly manage client activity. You already know about caching policies, throttling policies, and authentication policies, so you will now learn in detail how to use an advanced policy to protect your backend from overwhelming workloads.

Using advanced policies

The APIM policy is a powerful tool to manage many aspects of APIM communication. You can manage caching, header authentication, IP filtering, rewriting URLs, returning policies, converting output into a different format, and much more. A policy in APIM is provided as XML configuration applied for the operation it is specified for. You can also set up a global policy for APIs and refer to that policy in the exact policy for an operation, such as in the code when an inherited class can call the base class. This option allows you to minimize duplication of configuration and follow the **Don't Repeat Yourself** (**DRY**) approach.

The policy consists of four sections: `<inbound>`, `<backend>`, `<outbound>`, and `<on-error>`. Each of the sections can be extended with custom settings. The global policy for APIs can be referenced in the particular operation policy by including the `<base/>` tag in the policy. You can exclude the execution of the base policy by removing the `<base/>` tag from the section. The following example demonstrates a different way to apply or exclude base policy execution for an API operation:

```
<policies>
    <inbound>
        <!-- this part will be executed before the global policy applied -->
        <base />
        <!-- this part will be executed after the global policy applied -->
    </inbound>
    <backend>
        <!-- global policy execution excluded -->
    </backend>
    <outbound>
        <base />
    </outbound>
    <on-error>
        <base />
    </on-error>
</policies>
```

Figure 11.6 – Default operation policy with references to the base policy

The global policy can be edited when you select **All operations** on the list of all operations and then click on the </> icon next to the **Policy** text. If you open the policy editor, you will find many code snippets on the left and will be able to add the snippet to the policy and configure it. The validation of the policy will occur when you hit the **Save** button.

In the following section, we will provide some policies that you can copy and paste into the APIM instance you deployed previously to check what is returned to the client. All the following policy snippets should be provided inside of appropriate blocks, <inbound>, <backend>, <outbound>, and <on-error>. To minimize the length of the code, only the appropriate block will be provided in the examples.

Mocking API responses

You can mock any part of the API response, including the status code, HTTP headers, and response body. The response can be fully generated on APIM without access to the backend. This approach also decreases the load on the backend, simplifies authentication on the backend, and provides a meaningful status code for a variety of business logic events.

The following example allows you to generate a specific status code of 404 when a requested item is not found in the database. The status code table will let you choose the appropriate code:

```
<inbound>
    <base />
    <mock-response status-code="404" content-type="application/
json" />
</inbound>
```

Alternatively, you can customize the response parameters directly from the APIM policy by using the `<return-response>` instruction. For example, you can also provide a specific HTTP status code by using `<set-status>`. You can also generate or override the value of the HTTP header with `<set-header>`, provided by the backend to hide the value from the client. The same approach can be used to access the backend service with some generated values (for example, authentication headers). In the same way, you can hardcode specific HTTP output by using `<set-body>`:

```
<inbound>
    <return-response>
        <set-status code="200" reason="Product found" />
        <set-header name="source" exists-action="override">
            <value>warehouse database</value>
        </set-header>
        <set-body>{"name":"#1 Product", "price": 500}</set-body>
    </return-response>
</inbound>
```

The preceding example demonstrates the static output generated on APIM without calling a backend service.

Caching an API response

To avoid overload of backend services, a variety of different caching policies can be applied to operations in APIM. You can persist, retrieve, and remove the cached content directly from a policy.

In the first part, you need to define what content will be returned from the cache. The rules need be provided in the `<inbound>` section and controlled by the `<cache-lookup>` instruction. You can persist the content based on specific query parameters; for example, output products per category should depend on the category ID and should be cached separately by the value of the category ID. In the same way, you can control cached content based on the HTTP header with `<vary-by-header>`. You can also cache content by developer (client) with `<vary-by-developer>` or per developer group, `<vary-by-developer-groups>`. You can also configure the cache instance (internal or external) and downstream. In the second part, you need to provide the persistence rules with `<cache-store>`:

```
<policies>
    <inbound>
        <cache-lookup vary-by-developer="false" vary-by-
developer-groups="false" downstream-caching-type="public" must-
revalidate="true">
            <vary-by-query-parameter>category</vary-by-query-
```

```
parameter>
        </cache-lookup>
    </inbound>
    <outbound>
        <cache-store duration="60" />
    </outbound>
</policies>
```

> **Important note**
> When you test a caching policy on the Consumption pricing tier APIM, it is required to connect the external cache. Other pricing tiers will use the internal cache.

The preceding policy will perform caching based on the `category` query parameter and persist the output for 60 seconds.

Throttling requests

The workload provided by client applications increases when your API gets popular. Many enterprises face the need to upgrade the backend because the server cannot handle the increasing workloads. Thousands of mobile devices, web applications, and services can overheat your APIM if you do not throttle the requests. There are also many examples when the provider is limiting the number of requests by the subscriptions or products. For example, the Free tier in Azure Cognitive Services allows the processing of a few requests in a second and a limited number of requests per month.

The throttling functionality can be applied to an operation or the entire API with a global policy with the `<rate-limit>` instruction. You can provide the maximum number of calls with input parameters and a renewal period. With the `counter-key` parameter, you can throttle limits by any calculated values of the response, the IP address, for instance. To control calls for long periods, you can use the `<quota-by-key>` instruction with the same parameters as a rate limit instruction. The following example provides a rate limit of 1 call in 10 seconds with the limit set for the IP address of the caller:

```
<inbound>
    <rate-limit calls="1"
        renewal-period="10"
        counter-key="@(context.Request.IpAddress)" />
</inbound>
```

In the following examples, the quota is set up for a total of 1,000 calls and 100 kilobytes of bandwidth per month (2,629,800 seconds):

```
<inbound>
    <quota-by-key calls="1000"
            bandwidth="100"
            renewal-period="2629800"
            counter-key="@(context.Request.IpAddress)" />
</inbound>
```

The syntax used here that starts with the @ symbol is called a policy expression and it contains inline code. It will be explained in the next section.

Controlling flow

You already learned about examples of implementing policies that help control output and improve the performance of your APIs. Now, you will be introduced to flow controls and inline code examples that help you bring custom logic to APIM responses.

The following example describes the <choose> instruction, which needs to be set up with at least one <when> and one optional <otherwise> element:

```
<choose>
    <when condition="Boolean expression">
  <!— some policy statements applied if the expression is true
-->

    </when>
    <otherwise>
  <!— some policy statements applied if none of the above
expressions is true -->
    </otherwise>
</choose>
```

In the following example, <choose> is applied to the validation of client certificates. Pay attention to the inline code syntax, which follows **C# syntax** rules, and use full references to the **.NET Framework** objects:

```
<choose>
    <when condition="@(context.Request.Certificate == null
|| !context.Request.Certificate.Verify() || context.Request.
```

```
Certificate.Issuer != "issuer" || context.Request.Certificate.
SubjectName.Name != "expected-name")" >
        <return-response>
            <set-status code="403" reason="Invalid client
certificate" />
        </return-response>
    </when>
</choose>
```

As you can see from the previous example, the configuration policy in conjunction with C# syntax is a powerful tool for granular customization of the policies available on APIM. Many other policies could be found from the drop-down list of the snippets available on the policy editor page. Detailed documentation for each policy and its parameters is provided in the *Further reading* section.

Summary

APIM is an important platform for enterprise customers who expose web API services to public clients. APIM is provisioned in Azure to protect a variety of backend services deployed as IaaS or PaaS or even on-premises. APIM is also an orchestrator service that implements orchestration of the backend requests, can combine several in one, caches the output, and manages throttling. The support of modern authentication algorithms allows the service to securely protect the backend and manage networking integration.

APIM exposes the developer portal, which helps clients to integrate, test, and monitor the consumption of the service. The variety of the pricing tiers allows deploying affordable instances and using consumption-based serverless instances for low-load scenarios. The APIM service is the perfect choice for companies that make money from selling historical data, forecasts, machine learning services, and many other services that communicate through public networks. Subscription and product configuration will allow companies to track the usage and generate billing for clients who call APIM. For instance, Microsoft hosts AI services (Azure Cognitive Services) on the APIM platform to let the clients connect to the services, manage subscriptions, and perform troubleshooting.

In the next chapter, you will learn about event processing and an event-based solution that is also built on top of web APIs and designed for big data ingestion, flow management, and IoT device streaming.

Questions

1. What is the REST standard and what HTTP verbs are used in REST?

2. Does APIM support horizontal scaling?

3. What are three ways to connect existing web APIs from your Azure subscription to the APIM service?

4. Are there any disadvantages to using a consumption-based pricing tier for APIM?

5. What is the policy expression syntax based on?

Further reading

- Use the following link to check out the OpenAPI documentation: `https://oai.github.io/Documentation/`.

- You can learn more about managing and configuring the developer portal on APIM from the following link: `https://docs.microsoft.com/en-us/azure/api-management/api-management-howto-developer-portal`.

- Learn how to connect an external cache and provision Azure Cache for Redis in the following documentation: `https://docs.microsoft.com/en-us/azure/api-management/api-management-howto-cache-external`.

- A variety of examples of advanced policies can be found here: `https://docs.microsoft.com/en-us/azure/api-management/api-management-advanced-policies`.

- You can get extra hands-on experience with APIM from the following labs: `https://azure.github.io/apim-lab/apim-lab/1-apimCreation/`.

- You can read more about client authentication policies from the following link: `https://docs.microsoft.com/en-us/azure/api-management/api-management-authentication-policies`

- Disaster recovery options are discussed in the following article: `https://docs.microsoft.com/en-us/azure/api-management/api-management-howto-disaster-recovery-backup-restore?tabs=powershell#what-is-not-backed-up`

12

Developing Event-Based Solutions

In this chapter, we will be introduced to various event-based services available in Azure. We will become familiar with Azure Event Grid, Azure Event Hubs, Azure IoT Hub, and Azure Notification Hubs. We will also learn about the advantages and limitations of these services and find out which service is better to use in business scenarios. Furthermore, we will look at use case scenarios where we can leverage event-based services. Then, we will be able to compare event-driven solutions and detect their pros and cons.

By the end of this chapter, you will be able to configure event-processing services in Azure and you will know how to leverage them in your solution. By using the provided code snippets and scripts, you will be able to provision and connect to the services, generate events, and consume the events from the code.

In this chapter, we will cover the following topics:

- Understanding the role of event-driven solutions
- Discovering Azure Event Hubs
- Consuming event streams with Azure IoT Hub
- Exploring Azure Event Grid
- Comparing Azure event-based services

Technical requirements

The scripts provided in the chapter can be run in Azure Cloud Shell, but they can also be executed locally. The Azure CLI and Visual Studio Code are ideal tools to execute the code and commands provided in the following repository: `https://github.com/PacktPublishing/Developing-Solutions-for-Microsoft-Azure-AZ-204-Exam-Guide/tree/main/Chapter12`.

The code and scripts in this repository will provide you with examples of provisioning and development applications for Event Hubs, IoT Hub, and Azure Event Grid.

Code in Action videos for this chapter: `https://bit.ly/3xBkdmt`

Understanding the role of event-driven solutions

An event-driven solution plays a significant role in the modern world to help services running on different platforms and environments communicate. An event is a small chunk of data rapidly transferred by producers and processed by consumers. Events can form a stream of events where each event represents the current state of the remote system. For instance, IoT sensors can generate measurements in a real production environment. Then, Azure Stream Analytics services can implement the event-processing platform and leverage Azure Machine Learning services to monitor and predict trends in changes and recommend adjustments and maintenance.

Another common example of leveraging events is the reactive programming model. Imagine a website that requires scaling at the time of peak load. You could build a service that can consume the events received from the monitoring system. When the workload hits the threshold, it triggers your system to scale the website. This is scaling by reacting to incoming telemetry events. There are many other examples of leveraging event-based solutions, including streaming from IoT platforms, reactive programming, big data ingestions, and logging user activities. To better understand where you can leverage event-based solutions, let's look at the services available in Azure.

There is some terminology that needs to be clarified before you go down the rabbit hole:

- **Event**: A small piece of valuable data that contains information about what is happening. Usually, the event body is represented in JSON format.

- **Event source or publisher**: The services where the event takes place.

- **Event consumer, subscriber, or handler**: The services that receive the event for processing or react to the event.

- **Event schema**: The key-value pairs that must be provided in the event body by the event publisher.

There are several services in Azure that allow you to build event-based solutions. Some of these services will be described in detail in this chapter. Other services will be described briefly because they will be proposed as part of the solution to exam questions:

- **Azure Event Hubs** is commonly used in big data ingestion scenarios that involve event source systems and big data services such as Azure Synapse Analytics and Databricks. Event Hubs can also be used to collect diagnostic logs on a high-loaded networking environment where millions of requests and packages need to be tracked for processing later.

- **Azure IoT Hub** is an extension of Event Hubs and is designed as a two-way communication resource between IoT devices and Azure. IoT Hub provides services to consume and analyze the streaming of events from IoT sensors. It also helps to manage device settings, call methods of the device to update firmware, and restart the device. Meanwhile, Event Hubs also support event streaming, but they do not support device-to-cloud communication.

- **Azure Notification Hubs** is designed to support notification delivery to mobile applications. Notification Hubs became an orchestration and broadcast service responsible for delivering notifications to a large number of devices based on different messaging platforms such as Android, iOS, and Windows. The Azure-hosted Notification Hubs is registered as a publisher and mobile devices are registered as notification consumers.

- **Azure Event Grid** is a service that implements a reactive programming platform. It is also a bridge between many Azure PaaS services. Azure Event Grid is also commonly used for creating event processing flows to react to changes and activity in Azure subscriptions. For example, a file uploaded to Azure Blob storage can trigger an event that is processed by Azure Functions and submitted as a message to Azure Service Bus to be consumed by a third-party system.

From a developer standpoint, you need to learn how to leverage the event-based services available in Azure to achieve high performance, scale the processing system, and develop applications that leverage stream processing and reactive programming models. In the following section, you will learn how to leverage the most common Azure event-based services in your solution.

Discovering Azure Event Hubs

Azure Event Hubs is an event-based processing service hosted in Azure. Event Hubs is designed to implement the classic **publisher-subscriber** pattern, where multiple publishers generate millions of events that need to be processed and temporarily stored unless the consuming services can pull those events. Ingress connections are made by services (publishers) to produce the events and event streams. Egress connections are used by services (consumers) to receive the events for further processing. The events received from Event Hubs can be transformed, persisted, and analyzed with streaming solutions and big data storage.

For instance, Event Hubs can be connected to Azure Stream Analytics to analyze the content of an event, use a window function to detect any anomalies, and push them to the Power BI dashboard for real-time monitoring. Another common example of leveraging Event Hubs is ingesting data in big data solutions. For instance, Event Hubs can support the Apache Kafka interface and allow Kafka clients to get connected to Event Hubs. From a telemetry standpoint, Event Hubs is a real hub for a variety of monitoring streams where metrics data can be temporarily persisted and pulled by the analytics application. Event Hubs is commonly used as the target of log forwarding from Azure services such as VMs and networking resources. Logs can be forwarded from the source and ingested into external **Security Information and Event Management (SIEM)** tools.

The following diagram depicts the common scenario of processing a stream of incoming events (bank transactions) to detect fraudulent activity and update a live Power BI dashboard:

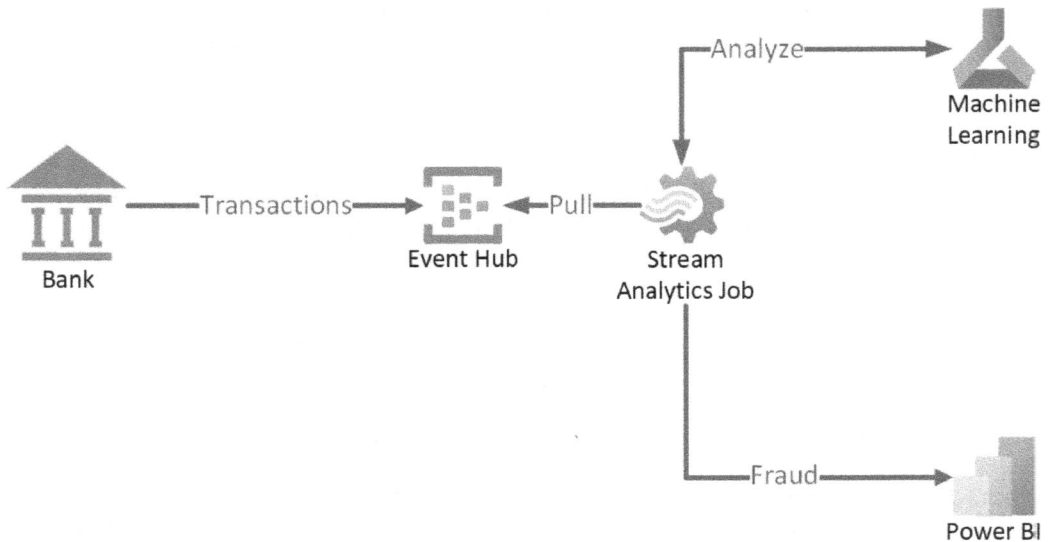

Figure 12.1 – Detecting fraud transactions with Event Hubs and ML algorithms

In the next subsection, you will learn about Event Hubs connectivity, configuration, scaling, and pricing to successfully leverage event-based services for your enterprise solutions.

Provisioning namespaces

An Event Hubs namespace is a virtual server that you need to deploy in Azure to provision Event Hubs. A namespace works as a logical container for hubs and provides isolation and management features for access control. When you provision a namespace, you receive the **Fully Qualified Domain Name** (**FQDN**) endpoint for connection. The network connectivity to the Event Hubs namespace can be managed from the firewall and is supposed to accept connections along with **MQ Telemetry Transport** (**MQTT**), **Advanced Message Queuing Protocol** (**AMQP**), AMQP over WebSockets, and HTTPS protocols. IoT devices commonly support those protocols and allow device-to-cloud connections to Event Hubs.

Pricing model

The Event Hubs namespace provides a different set of features, depending on the price tier:

- **Basic tier**: An affordable tier with minimum performance that doesn't allow dynamic partition scaling, capturing events, and VNet integration. The retention policy is limited to 1 day.

- **Standard tier**: This tier allows you to capture events in a storage account, integrate with VNets, and has increased retention for up to 7 days.

- **Premium tier**: An expensive tier that includes all sets of features and does not have any throughput limits. The retention policy is limited to 90 days.

- **Dedicated tier**: This tier has the same features as the Premium tier and is provisioned in an exclusive single-tenant environment.

Scaling

Event Hubs is a highly scalable solution designed for high-load data ingestion. The scaling process includes extending the number of throughput units and processing units.

The Basic and Standard price tiers are allowed to scale 40 **throughput units**, which are responsible for ingress and egress traffic. To increase throughput limits, admins can manually adjust the number of throughput units from the Azure portal. Each throughput unit will be charged individually per hour. An error will be generated when the load exceeds the available throughput.

Premium tier Event Hubs work in resource-isolated environments and allow horizontal scaling by increasing the **processing** units that represent units of the isolated environment. Because the Premium tier does not have any throughput limitations, ingress or egress requests can be made but will wait to be processed. The processing unit can handle the traffic that corresponds to about 10 throughput units in the Basic and Standard tiers. The Premium tier is allowed to scale up to 16 processing units.

Leveraging partitions

Partition numbers can also affect the performance of Event Hubs. The idea of partitions is the parallel processing of events individually on each of the partitions. The number of partitions is configured in the provisioning step, with a minimum of two, and cannot be changed later. The number of provisioned partitions should correspond to the number of throughput units with a 1:1 ratio.

In Event Hubs, the partition represents the logically separated queue, where the event is stored until it's pulled by the client. The queue supports the **First-In, First-Out** (**FIFO**) direction to retrieve events. When an event is received without a partition address being provided, it will be spread between available partitions. Later, events can be picked from each of the partitions individually.

Provisioning Azure Event Hubs

Provisioning Event Hubs consists of two steps. The first is namespace provisioning, which requires selecting pricing tiers, throughput units or processing units, and a location. After provisioning a namespace, Event Hubs can be provisioned with a certain number of partitions and with the number of days for event retentions. The rest of the feature set includes capturing events, network integration, and retrieving a **shared access signature** (**SAS**) key for connection, all of which can be configured from the Azure portal.

The following bash script will help you provision a namespace and an Event Hubs resource in your Azure subscription by leveraging the Azure CLI:

```
https://github.com/PacktPublishing/Developing-Solutions-for-Microsoft-
Azure-AZ-204-Exam-Guide/blob/main/Chapter12/01-eventhub-provision/
demo.azcli.
```

From this script, you can provision a storage account and configure event capturing. Later, when you run the publisher, you will be able to observe the captured events. The Avro file that contains captured events should look as follows:

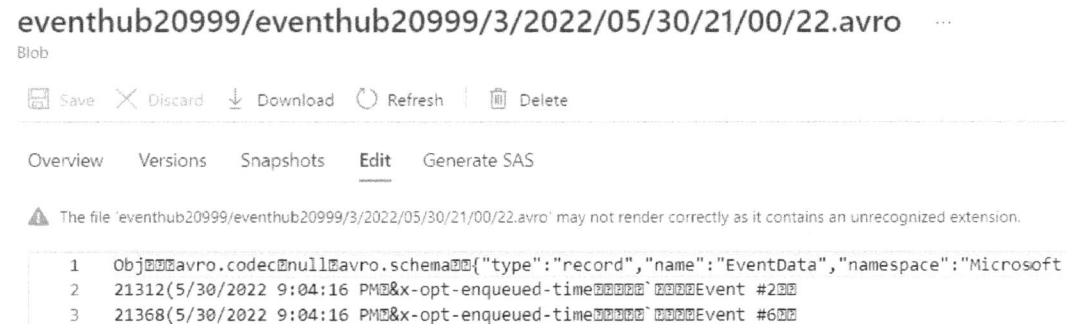

eventhub20999/eventhub20999/3/2022/05/30/21/00/22.avro ...
Blob

[◻ Save] [✕ Discard] [↓ Download] [◯ Refresh] | [🗑 Delete]

Overview   Versions   Snapshots   **Edit**   Generate SAS

⚠ The file 'eventhub20999/eventhub20999/3/2022/05/30/21/00/22.avro' may not render correctly as it contains an unrecognized extension.

```
1    Obj◻◻◻avro.codec◻null◻avro.schema◻◻{"type":"record","name":"EventData","namespace":"Microsoft
2    21312(5/30/2022 9:04:16 PM◻&x-opt-enqueued-time◻◻◻◻`◻◻◻◻Event #2◻◻
3    21368(5/30/2022 9:04:16 PM◻&x-opt-enqueued-time◻◻◻◻`◻◻◻◻Event #6◻◻
```

Figure 12.2 – Captured events from the Avro file opened from the Azure portal

Now, let's look at the event capturing feature.

Capturing events

Azure Event Hubs receives events from publishers and persists events based on the retention period before consumers pull them. All events received by Event Hubs can be copied to the buffer and then flashed to the blob. If an event is received or deleted because of the expiration time, its copy still exists in the blob and is available for analysis.

Event-capturing functionality is available for the Standard and Premium price tiers of Event Hubs. Be aware that capturing can produce extra charges for the Standard tier of Event Hubs, but those charges are included in the Premium tier. To minimize charges, you can specify the size quotas and time window of capturing. You can leverage Azure Blob storage and Azure Data Lake to capture events. Capturing functionality generates files in the provided container with time and date-based names per partition. The Apache Avro file format is used to capture and provide a compact binary structure to consume in Visual Studio Code and third-party tools.

In the previous script execution, you provisioned Event Hubs and also configured event capturing in a storage account. Later, when you build an application to send and receive events, you will also observe captured events in the storage account of the same resource group.

Consumer groups

Consumer groups are used to perform an independent read of events by the application. Consumer groups represent the view of events' state in the partition for events consumers. The service-published events can tag the event with a specific consumer group. A $Default consumer group is always created for each Event Hubs and other groups can be added up to the amount allowed by the pricing tier. The recommended best practice is to provide a single group for each downstream application that produces the event stream. Meanwhile, multiple readers of the same consumer group and the same partition can complicate event consumption and cause duplicates. The number of consumers should not exceed five consumers per group, per partition.

Connections with SAS tokens

The authentication and authorization of publishers and consumers are implemented based on SAS tokens generated with **listen**, **send**, and **manage** rights. The manage rights allow you to listen for and send events. Based on the principle of least privilege, publishers should only be allowed to send events, and consumers should only be allowed to listen to events. The default SAS token is generated with manage rights for all Event Hubs namespaces during provisioning. The SAS token works for all Event Hubs created with the namespace but should only be used for management purposes. After provisioning the Event Hubs, you can generate a SAS token based on the rights required for the service. That token should be used in the connection string for publishers and consumers. During the processing streams of events, the SAS tokens can also identify the producer.

Event consumption services

Many services are available in Azure to consume events from Event Hubs:

- **Azure Event Grid** can be connected to Event Hubs to publish and consume events and is usually used as a bridge to Azure Queue Storage, Azure Service Bus, Azure Functions, Azure Cosmos DB, and many others.

- **Azure Steam Analytics** is the most commonly used service in conjunction with Event Hubs to process events and ingest them into Azure Blob storage, Azure Queue Storage, Azure Service Bus, Azure Cosmos DB, Azure Synapse Analytics, and Power BI datasets. Compared to Event Grid, Azure Stream Analytics can leverage sophisticated filtering algorithms, including leveraging Azure Machine Learning services.

- Big data ingestion solutions also support Event Hubs as a source of streaming data. For instance, **Azure Synapse Data Explorer** can be connected to Event Hubs directly to pull and process events. Another example is the Azure Databricks solution, which operates with Event Hubs for Jupyter notebooks to submit and receive events.

Developing applications for Event Hubs

From the previous sections, you already know enough about Event Hubs to leverage your solutions. Now, you have a chance to observe how events can be submitted and consumed by C# applications.

From the following repository, you can build a publisher project and subscriber project to connect to the instance of Event Hubs provisioned earlier. To configure the project, you need to retrieve the connections string for Event Hubs with listening and sending rights. You also need the Azure Storage connection string, which enables your subscriber to persist checkpoints. Both strings were generated in the previous script run. You need to copy them from the output and update the `Program.cs` file.

To receive the events from Event Hubs, you need to start the consumer (the `subscriber` project). It will keep connected and show the body of events in the output when they are received. Then, you can run a `publisher` project (which produces 10 messages and outputs each message on the console). When you switch back to the subscriber console, you will see the received messages. These projects are located in the following repository: `https://github.com/PacktPublishing/Developing-Solutions-for-Microsoft-Azure-AZ-204-Exam-Guide/tree/main/Chapter12/02-eventhub-process`.

This example has demonstrated how a connection to Event Hubs is made with code. From the code, you can observe the following classes leveraged for communication:

Class	Description
`EventHubClient`	This class is responsible for generating events. It should be configured with connection strings to Event Hubs.
`EventProcessorHost`	This class performs event listening and should be configured with connection strings to Event Hubs and a storage account.
`SimpleEventProcessor`	This is a custom class that implements the `IEventProcessor` interface and functions to open and process received events and output their body.

Table 12.1 – C# SDK classes for event management with Event Hubs

Azure Event Hubs is quite a sophisticated service that we won't discuss in depth, though we have covered enough for you to be familiar with it according to the exam requirements. In the next section, you will learn how to consume events with Azure IoT Hub and Azure Stream Analytics.

Consuming event streams with Azure IoT Hub

Azure IoT Hub is another event-based service that we'll take a close look at. The Azure IoT Hub platform is very similar to Event Hubs. It has important differences though that are worth mentioning. First of all, Azure IoT Hub is designed for consuming streaming telemetry from IoT devices and also managing the devices that produce the streams. Azure IoT Hub can communicate with IoT devices if the devices need to be restarted or the firmware needs to be updated. Azure IoT Hub can also register devices to set up a secure communication channel and deregister devices if they are stolen. Azure IoT Hub should also support industry-standard communication protocols.

There are a variety of devices available on the market. Some IoT devices are powerful enough to get connected to the internet and provide telemetry from sensors. Other small, low-power IoT devices communicate with the hubs through the gateway. The devices can support TCP protocols, AMQP, and MQTT protocols, and their implementation through HTTPS. Because the amount of supported devices is quite high and telemetry streams can provide live updates with a high number of events, the performance of Azure IoT Hub is the most valuable metric.

Another bright side of Azure IoT Hub is its integration with other Azure services. Azure IoT Hub can be integrated with the powerful Stream Analytics service, which can use jobs to pull events from Event Hubs and IoT Hub and submit them to a SQL database, a storage account, Cosmos DB, or Power BI. Moreover, you can deploy Azure IoT Central, the service that's responsible for UI visualization of telemetry information and also managing device parameters and control connected to the device sensors.

Pricing model

Azure IoT Hub provides two pricing tiers with different features and different amounts of messages that can be consumed based on tier limitations. You can plan your deployment when you know the number of devices you are going to support and the number of messages they will send per month. IoT Hub will stop accepting messages if the number of messages per month allowed by the tier is exceeded. In that case, a scale-up will be required. The following price tiers are available:

- **Basic (B1-B3)**: This tier allows you to ingest 0.4 MB to 300 MB of messages and leverage all communication protocols (HTTP, AMQP, and MQTT). It also allows messages to be routed into Event Grid directly. Unfortunately, it does not support cloud-to-device messaging.

- **Standard (S1-S3)**: This tier allows you to ingest the same number of messages and has the same features as the Basic tier. The Standard tier also supports cloud-to-device messaging, device management through device enrolment, and device twins for configuration. The main difference between the Standard and Basic tiers is Azure IoT Edge support. The IoT Edge functionality allows you to orchestrate containers and their configuration on the device itself. For example, self-driving cars can leverage IoT Edge to spin containers with AI on the car and minimize the latency of communication.

- **Free (F1)**: This tier has the same features as the Standard pricing tier. Only one instance can be deployed per subscription.

Device registration

The device registration process can be performed manually from the Azure portal or by using the automation options. In the case of managing a large fleet of devices, the IoT Hub **Device Provisioning**

Service (DPS) should be used for device enrolment. Registering devices is a way to provide authentication and authorization for devices to send telemetry streams and receive controlling messages from the cloud. Two registration options are supported – one is with the use of SAS keys, while the other is a certificate. Both options can be revoked if a device is lost or stolen. In the provisioning script for Azure IoT Hub, you will register a device with a SAS key.

Azure IoT Edge

Azure IoT Edge is a service and software that enables you to bring logic and AI services to a device. The Azure IoT Edge package needs to be installed on the IoT device registered in Azure IoT Hub and configured with a connection string. IoT Edge is based on the IoT Edge agent and IoT Edge hubs Docker containers. The agent is responsible for updating restarts and updating configuration. The hubs is responsible for providing interfaces for communication. The IoT Edge runtime enables you to run custom code in separate containers and download and update container images to the new version when it's available.

Provisioning Azure IoT Hub

Provisioning IoT Hub does not require provisioning any namespaces as Event Hubs does. It only requires selecting a pricing tier and location with a unique name. All other settings, including enrolling devices, can be configured after provisioning. For device enrolment management, you also can leverage the IoT Hub DPS, but it's not required for managing a single device, which we will use in the following script.

Provisioning IoT Hub and enrolling a single device are automated with the Azure CLI in the following script. The commands from the script should be completed in Bash. The script's output should provide the connection string for the virtual device. The connection string should be persisted so that you can configure the upcoming code example: `https://github.com/PacktPublishing/ Developing-Solutions-for-Microsoft-Azure-AZ-204-Exam-Guide/blcb/ main/Chapter12/05-iot-hub/demo.azcli`.

After running the commands in the script, you can observe the deployed resources from the Azure portal. The following resources should be provisioned: Azure IoT Hub and virtual device, Azure storage account for monitoring output, and Azure Stream Analytics job to pull events from Azure IoT Hub. The device will report telemetry and the job will persist to the storage account, but only for messages with a humidity of more than 70%. The following schema will help you understand the flow of the event stream from an IoT device:

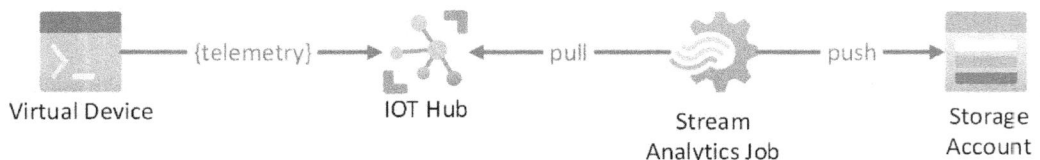

Figure 12.3 – Processing an event stream with IoT Hub and a Stream Analytics job

In the next section, we will learn how the IoT device can be configured to produce telemetry. The connection string from the script's output should be saved for the next step.

Developing applications for Azure IoT Hub

IoT devices are available on a variety of platforms and for many of them, Microsoft provides SDKs that can be leveraged for connection. The main functionality of the SDK is scoped for the following tasks:

- **Telemetry streaming**: A telemetry stream is usually provided with an event sent to Azure IoT Hub. The body of an event is formatted in JSON and contains values collected from sensors.

- **Receiving controlling messages**: A device can be registered for receiving cloud-to-device messages. The messages contain the body and key-value properties for transfer commands and states. The delivery of the messages is guaranteed.

- **Providing methods for invocation**: Invocation methods are another way of managing a device from the cloud. They are commonly used to restart a device and update the firmware. They can also be leveraged for remote control.

- **Handling configuration changes**: The device configuration (named device twins) describes the current device settings and contains the desired and reported properties for the device. The device itself should update its settings to the desired values and report the changes back to Azure IoT Hub. Those settings are persisted in the JSON file hosted on IoT Hub.

In the following example, you will learn how to connect your virtual device to Azure IoT Hub and provide telemetry streaming. Because a real device is difficult to set up and configure, we will use a virtual algorithm that works in a browser and mimics the communication between an IoT device and IoT Hub. The algorithm is represented by JavaScript code that can be modified. To complete the task, follow the following link and replace the value of `connectionString` in line 15 with the connection string from the previous script run: `https://azure-samples.github.io/raspberry-pi-web-simulator/`.

Once you have replaced the connection string, you can hit the **Run** button on the gray output console to start the telemetry stream. The JavaScript code will start producing messages with temperature and humidity values following this format:

```
Sending message: {"messageId":3,"deviceId":"Raspberry Pi Web
Client","temperature":29.837685611725128,"humidity":
62.19790641562577}
```

You can observe the messages from the console. The messages will be delivered to Azure IoT Hub, pulled by the Stream Analytics job, and stored in the container in Azure Blob storage with the name **state**. The filename will depend on the current date and time. The blob file should only contain messages that state `humidity` is higher than 70%. The file's content should look as follows:

2022/05/26/12/0_c658db67ee954dc495c513d8d22bf591_1.json   ⋯   ✕
Blob

🖫 Save   ✕ Discard   ⤓ Download   ⟳ Refresh | 🗑 Delete

Overview   Versions   Snapshots   **Edit**   Generate SAS

```
1    {"messageId":68,"deviceId":"Raspberry Pi Web Client","temperature":22.183423532311636,"humidity":74.9353367
2    {"messageId":69,"deviceId":"Raspberry Pi Web Client","temperature":31.732016284170115,"humidity":72.0054934
3    {"messageId":70,"deviceId":"Raspberry Pi Web Client","temperature":28.163384900294119,"humidity":77.7021022
4    {"messageId":71,"deviceId":"Raspberry Pi Web Client","temperature":27.964771374425421,"humidity":73.0935501
```

Figure 12.4 – The collected telemetry data from the virtual device in Azure Blob storage

The Raspberry Pi simulator is the only way to mimic event streaming between an IoT device and Azure IoT Hub. There are many others available, including the Azure code samples available on GitHub: `https://github.com/Azure-Samples/Iot-Telemetry-Simulator`.

This simulator is written in C# and enables you to learn about additional aspects of Azure IoT Hub device-to-cloud and cloud-to-device collaboration. In the next section, you will learn more about event-based technologies and how to receive and submit events to Azure Event Grid.

Exploring Azure Event Grid

Azure Event Grid implements a reactive programming model where a specific algorithm is triggered depending on the event processed on Event Grid. For instance, let's say that a blob stored on Azure Storage was modified (the file changed its access tier from Cool to Archive) and the appropriate event was triggered by Event Grid because it monitors modifications for a specific Azure storage account. The Azure function that monitors events from Event Grid received the event and processed the blob according to the business logic (sending an email to the administrator). Access tiers were introduced in *Chapter 6, Developing Solutions That Use Azure Blob Storage*.

This example of monitoring blobs uses a pure reactive programming model. The Azure function is not hammering the blob to pull the available changes. It waits to get triggered by Azure Event Grid and reacts depending on the logic. The solution schema is shown in the following diagram:

Storage   ―Tier Changed→   Event Grid   ―Trigger→   Function   ―Notify→   Admin
Account   App

Figure 12.5 – Monitoring changes in Azure Storage with Event Grid and an Azure function

Another scenario where Event Grid can be involved in event processing is a simple Pub/Sub-like Azure Event Hubs instance. The significant difference is that Event Grid can duplicate an event for all registered subscribers. This means that events can be delivered to each of the services that subscribed to those events. This logic, when one data change is duplicated for all registered subscribers, is known as a **topic**.

For example, let's say there is a request to monitor a resource group for modifications (tracking quotes per type of resource). The new VM was provisioned in the resource group and Event Grid triggers all subscribers for this type of event. Azure Logic App was triggered to update the third-party inventory system. An Azure Automation account was also triggered to run a PowerShell script to update the resource tag on the VM. Finally, a custom tracking portal was triggered to log the monitoring event. Three subscribers are registered for updates on the resource group and all of them will receive a copy of the event to notify them that the VM has been provisioned. The subscription approach will enable you to monitor events without removing them from Event Grid. This is unlike Event Hubs, which delivers the event only once and then removes it from the server.

The solution schema with three subscriptions (Logic App, Automation, and web portal) can be seen in the following diagram:

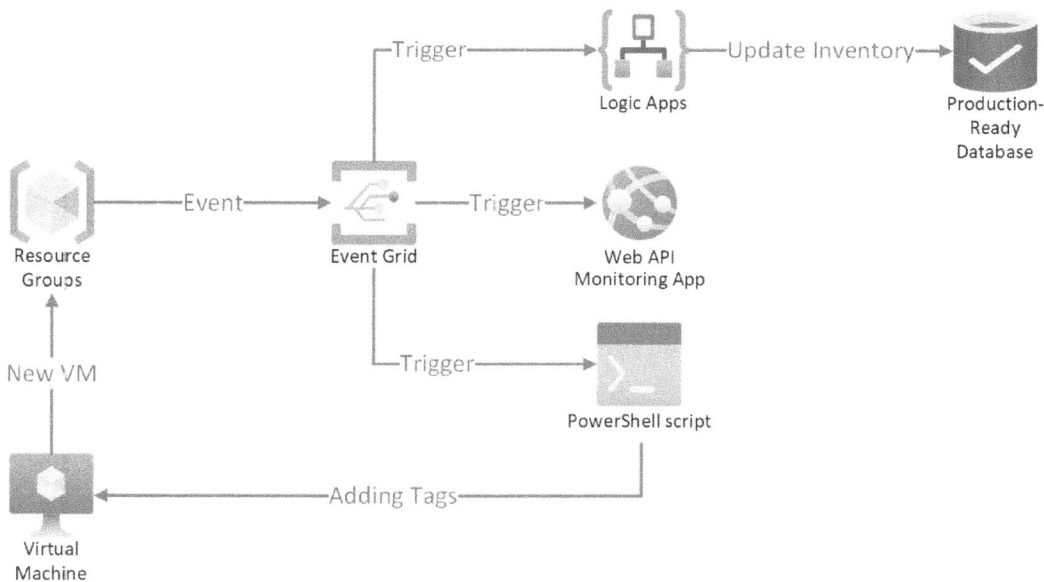

Figure 12.6 – Resource group change monitoring with Event Grid

Since you are already familiar with most of the event-based processing terminology, in the next few sections, only new terms will be explained.

Event sources and handlers

Based on the preceding examples, there is a need to clarify Event Grid terminology to explain configuration aspects:

- **Event source or publisher**: For Event Grid, this is one of the following services: Azure Blob storage, Azure Resource Manager, Event Hubs or IoT Hub, Azure Service Bus, Azure Media Services, Azure Maps, or another Azure PaaS service. Moreover, Event Grid can work as a message broker. Your application can submit custom events to the public endpoint and they can be delivered to subscribers.

- **Event handlers or subscribers**: For Event Grid, these can be registered in one or many of the following services: Azure Automation runbooks and Logic Apps, Azure Functions, Event Hubs, Service Bus, and Azure Queue Storage. Moreover, you can register a custom webhook to a third party to be triggered as an internal Azure service.

The relationship between the event source and the event handler is implemented by an **Event Grid topic**. The endpoint that's used by the event source to send events is named the **event topic**. On the other hand, the **event subscription** is a record that contains event handler registration, the kind of topic it subscribes to, and the type of event it wants to receive.

The following schema represents event processing by Event Grid topics:

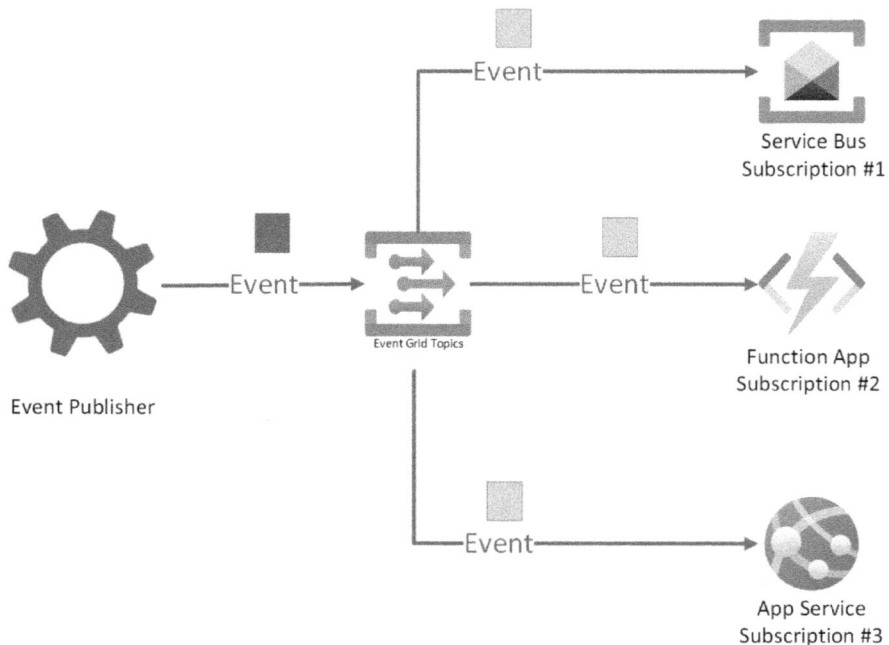

Figure 12.7 – Topic functionality – event processing from publisher to handlers

As you can see, event processing with topics in Event Grid is quite different from event processing in Event Hubs. The topic provides copies of events for each of the subscribers. The subscribers are represented by the different Azure services and process events according to the values defined by the schema.

Schema formats

The schema is a set of rules that define the event structure. Event Grid supports two schema formats: the default and the CloudEvent schema. The CloudEvent format is maintained for multi-cloud collaboration. According to the default event schema, the events processed by Event Grid are presented in JSON format and contain valuable information such as the type of event, subject, topic, ID, and version. The main payload of the event is stored in the data field and its format depends on the publisher. The following JSON structure represents the event received from Event Grid:

```
[
  {
    "topic": string,
    "subject": string,
    "id": string,
    "eventType": string,
    "eventTime": string,
    "data":{
      object-unique-to-each-publisher
    },
    "dataVersion": string,
    "metadataVersion": string
  }
]
```

The event, according to this schema, can contain the custom payload in the data field that depends on the event publisher. The field that existed in the default event schema can also be used for filtering. Your application that subscribed to the event should parse the JSON according to the schema and extract the data payload from the event. Each event can transfer a significant amount of data and can be used to deserialize an object and its state in the code. The maximum size of the event is 1 MB. You will see the real event payload in the next few sections as you provision your Event Grid instance.

Access management

The authentication and authorization process in Event Grid is handled by Azure Active Directory and access keys or SAS keys. These keys can be generated to access topics that submit events. Access keys provide full access to the topic and a SAS key should be used instead to provide specific rights for event management. Alternatively, Event Grid supports Azure AD identities, which can be used to provide role-based access to topics and subscriptions. In the provisioning script shown in the *Provisioning Azure Event Grid* section, you will see examples of retrieving the keys from the Azure CLI. Alternatively, you can pick access keys from the Azure portal.

Event Grid event domains

The event domain is a logical structure that helps manage a high number of event recipients and also provides security isolation for subscribers by managing authorization and authentication settings. An Event Grid domain is provisioned as a separate resource in the same way as the Event Grid topic. Domains can be formed by multiple topics that are used by subscribers to receive a copy of the event. Event Grid supports domain-scoped subscriptions when the subscriber receives events submitted to all the topics in the domain. From an access management standpoint, Azure RBAC is leveraged to manage subscriptions for each tenant in your application.

Delivery retries

Errors can occur while events are being delivered by Event Grid. Those errors can postpone or prevent delivery. The most common error occurs when the subscriber is not available and Event Grid keeps trying to deliver the event. You can customize the settings for how many times and how long Event Grid should keep retrying. You also can specify the *dead-letter* container on Azure Storage to persist the events that are not delivered after the retries end. When you design your solution with Event Grid, you need to be aware that the events could be delivered to the subscriber in the wrong sequence. This happens because retry attempts for event delivery can occur asynchronously. The retrying and dead-lettering of events are optional and are not configured by default. If the retry option is not configured, then Event Grid will drop events.

Filters

Another important concept that can affect delivery to handlers is filtering events. Filters allow you to subscribe only for a specific event (successful or unsuccessful resource deployment, update, and deletion). Filters are based on a specific file (key) delivered by the event. These field values are provided in the JSON payload of the event and can be analyzed by the event-delivering algorithm. You can build a filter based on the event type, subject, and values of the specific field. Moreover, you can leverage operators to combine the multiple filters with logical operators and string operators. Filtering is one of the powerful functionalities that can significantly reduce the number of events and number of handler runs, which positively affects the solution cost.

Pricing model

The Event Grid pricing model is designed for consumption use. The charges are based on the bulk of operations started after the first 100K of operations. These operations include ingress attempts, plus retrying attempts, to deliver the event. This means that the total charges represent multiplying the subscribed handler's counts by the number of processed events.

Provisioning Azure Event Grid

Provisioning an Event Grid service consists of two resources: the **Event Grid topic** and **event subscription**. If you start by provisioning the Event Grid topic, you can create an event subscription directly from the topic page. Alternatively, you can create an event subscription and choose what service will be used as an event publisher. The subscription for the service will be created automatically.

Manual topic creation is usually required for custom event processing scenarios. When Event Grid implements an event broker pattern, the event subscription for the custom topic is usually provisioned as a web-hosted service and uses webhook communication to push the event. Meanwhile, general web-hosted services can be replaced by Azure Functions, Azure App Service, Logic Apps, Event Hubs, and many others. Each topic can communicate with more than one subscribed service. When the custom topic is provisioned, you can pick the public endpoint and access key to submit the event. This scenario will be introduced later in this chapter.

When you created the event subscription from the Azure portal, you had to select the event source. You can choose several available services and objects, including the resource group or subscription. Resource groups and subscriptions will submit all activities to the subscribed consumers. In the following example, you'll build an event subscription for activities in a specific resource group and then trigger the event by updating the group's tag. The subscription does not leverage any filters, so all activities will lead to event generation

During script execution, you connect the Event Hubs instance that you previously deployed in your subscription. The name of this Event Hubs can be picked from the previous script output. You also need to run the consumer for the Event Hubs instance from the previous application. It should be appropriately connected to the Event Hubs instance by the connection string that was retrieved previously. No changes or code updates are required for Event Hubs and consumers. Here is the script to help you provision an event subscription and connect Event Hubs as a subscriber, and trigger events by updating the tag value. Be aware of the 1-minute delay in delivering the event to the Event Hubs consumer and keep it running while updating the tag. This is a PowerShell script, and you can execute it in PowerShell mode in Cloud Shell or locally if you install the Azure PowerShell module: `https://github.com/PacktPublishing/Developing-Solutions-for-Microsoft-Azure-AZ-204-Exam-Guide/blob/main/Chapter12/03-eventgrid-provision/demo.ps1`.

From the demo script, you will learn how to leverage event subscriptions. You'll become familiar with the event structure by observing it on your consumer application in the next section. The following schema will help you understand the event processing solution you have provisioned:

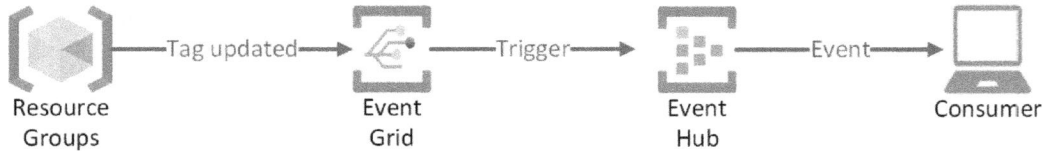

Figure 12.8 – Resource group change processing with Event Grid

The previously demonstrated solution does not involve any development skills, but the next example will leverage custom event handling in the reactive programming model. Let's take a look at how the event broker can be implemented with Event Grid.

Developing applications for custom event handling

The custom event handling process requires a web-hosted application that provides a webhook URL for event subscriptions. That URL will be used to deliver the events via an HTTP POST request. For event handling, you can leverage the well-known project, `Azure Event Grid Viewer` (https://github.com/Azure-Samples/azure-event-grid-viewer). This tool can be used to receive an event, persist it in memory, and demonstrate the event's payload. This tool is implemented as an ASP.NET Core MVC application and deserializes the event from the webhook request by using `EventGridEvent` from the `Azure.Messaging.EventGrid` package.

The following script will help you provision an event topic and deploy Event Grid Viewer to the App Service instance. Then, you can use the App Service URL to subscribe to the events. The script leverages Azure CLI commands and works better when run from Cloud Shell: https://github.com/PacktPublishing/Developing-Solutions-for-Microsoft-Azure-AZ-204-Exam-Guide/blob/main/Chapter12/04-eventgrid-process/demo.azcli.

Event submission to the custom topic is implemented by the console application. The application needs to be configured with the topic endpoint and access key provided in the output of the script run. Update the `Program.cs` file with appropriate values from the output. The code of the application is available at https://github.com/PacktPublishing/Developing-Solutions-for-Microsoft-Azure-AZ-204-Exam-Guide/tree/main/Chapter12/04-eventgrid-process/publisher.

This preceding example demonstrated how to submit custom events in an Event Grid topic endpoint. The following SDK classes were used in the project:

Class	Description
EventGridPublisherClient	This class is used to build a client to send the event and is configured with endpoint and access key information.
EventGridEvent	This event class represents events that deserialize in JSON with the required event schema.
AzureKeyCredential	Credential information that is used for client configuration with an access key.

Table 12.2 – C# SDK classes for event management with Event Grid

When you run the application, it generates a single event with the "This is the event data" text payload. You should be able to observe the event on the **Azure Event Grid Viewer** page. The following screenshot shows the viewer page with the event structure:

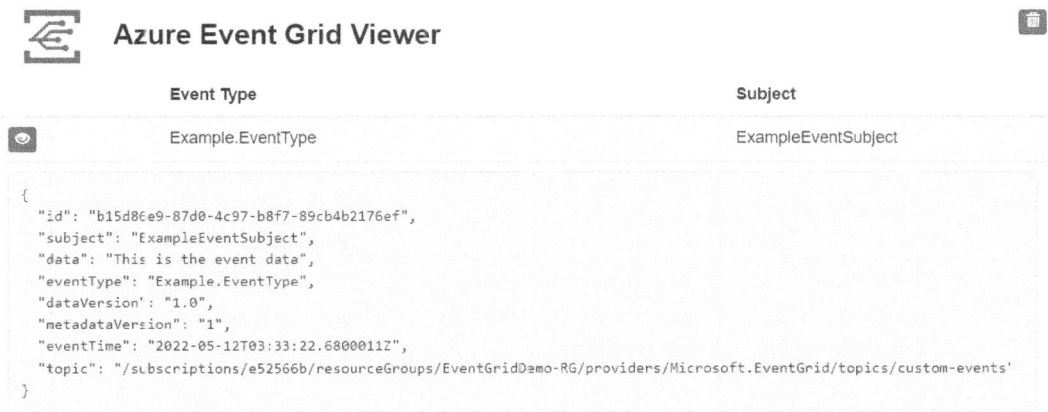

Azure Event Grid Viewer

Event Type	Subject
Example.EventType	ExampleEventSubject

```
{
  "id": "b15d86e9-87d0-4c97-b8f7-89cb4b2176ef",
  "subject": "ExampleEventSubject",
  "data": "This is the event data",
  "eventType": "Example.EventType",
  "dataVersion": "1.0",
  "metadataVersion": "1",
  "eventTime": "2022-05-12T03:33:22.6800011Z",
  "topic": "/subscriptions/e52566b/resourceGroups/EventGridDemo-RG/providers/Microsoft.EventGrid/topics/custom-events'
}
```

Figure 12.9 – Received custom event

In the previous examples, you learned how to provision Azure Event Grid and how to leverage custom Event Grid topics to submit an event. You also learned how to provision Event Grid topics to monitor resource group activities. You became familiar with the code of the application you built and consumed the event delivered through Event Hubs with an Event Grid subscription. Another application you built was submitting events to the custom Event Grid topic that was received by Event Grid Viewer.

In the next section, the available event-based services will be summarized in a table to help you understand their usage patterns.

Comparing Azure event-based services

This chapter has introduced you to several event processing services available in Azure. Some of the services can be used for the same task. For example, Azure Event Hubs and IoT Hub can process streams of data, and Event Grid and Event Hubs can be used as message brokers. However, some services may not be the optimal choice for specific tasks. For example, Event Grid has a delay in delivery events and is not designed for a high scale of events; you're better off choosing Event Hubs for high-scale workloads.

The following table will help you understand which of the services works best:

Service	Main Pattern	Pros	Cons
Event Hubs	Big data ingestion and streaming	High-scale. Event persistence. Capturing events. Low-cost.	An event can be received only once. Complex order support with multiple partitions. Server-managed cursor.
IoT Hub	Telemetry streaming	Two-way communication. Device registration and settings management. Free Standard tier.	No flexible pricing models. Sophisticated integration devices with Azure IoT Edge.
Notification Hubs	Event broadcasting	Multi-platform support. Free tier.	Lack of troubleshooting tools. A limited number of supported platforms.
Event Grid	Pub/Sub and reactive programming	Consumption-based pricing. Integration with other services. Topic support.	The events delivery sequence can be changed.

Table 12.3 – Comparing Azure event-based services

Knowing the pros and cons of the different event-based services will help you select the optimal service for your solution and recommend the appropriate choice for the exam.

Summary

Event-based technology plays a significant role in the data processing solutions hosted in Azure. The solutions based on event processing provide high-scale and high-availability services that are maintained in Azure with minimum administrative effort. Event-based services are commonly used for big data ingestion, telemetry stream processing, reactive programming, and mobile platform notifications.

Connectivity to the services and receiving events are implemented in custom applications based on SDKs and involve a variety of Azure services. Plug and play integration of Azure services is the biggest advantage of using event-based technology in Azure for asynchronous processing scenarios.

By completing this chapter, you can select the appropriate service based on your requirements and leverage it to process events in an enterprise solution for your company.

In the next chapter, you will learn about the differences between message and event processing and will be able to maximize outcomes from the message-based services in Azure, such as Azure Queue Storage and Azure Service Bus.

Questions

Answer the following questions to test your knowledge of this chapter:

1. What is a namespace?
2. How is Azure IoT Hub different from Event Hubs?
3. How long does an event persist in Event Hubs?
4. What service helps you connect Azure Functions and Event Hubs?
5. What type of authentication can be used to connect IoT devices to Azure IoT Hub?
6. What is a possible misconfiguration for an event handler that will not allow it to receive all events sent by Event Grid?

Further reading

To learn more about the topics that were covered in this chapter, take a look at the following resources:

- The following article will help you learn about Event Hubs features and terminology:

  `https://docs.microsoft.com/en-us/azure/event-hubs/event-hubs-features`

- The Event Hubs price tiers are discussed in the following document:

  `https://docs.microsoft.com/en-us/azure/event-hubs/compare-tiers`

- You can learn about Event Grid terminology in the following article:

  `https://docs.microsoft.com/en-us/azure/event-grid/concepts`

- The Event Grid event schema is explained in the following article:

  `https://docs.microsoft.com/en-us/azure/event-grid/event-schema`

- Learn how the capturing of events is implemented in Event Hubs:

  `https://docs.microsoft.com/en-us/azure/event-hubs/event-hubs-capture-overview#how-event-hubs-capture-works`

- The following article explains device-to-cloud communication for Azure IoT Hub:

  `https://docs.microsoft.com/en-us/azure/iot-hub/iot-hub-devguide-c2d-guidance`

- You can learn more about the combination of event-based and message-based solutions from the following article:

  `https://docs.microsoft.com/en-us/azure/event-grid/compare-messaging-services`

13
Developing Message-Based Solutions

From this chapter, you will learn how the messaging pattern can improve the reliability and availability of your solution in Azure. You will learn how to leverage the Azure Queue Storage and Azure Service Bus messaging services. You will be introduced to the publisher-subscriber concept and learn the difference between queues and topics. You will get to know how to provision, configure, and integrate messaging services with other Azure services, for instance, Azure App Service and Azure Functions. You also will be able to provision, connect, and manage the services from code. Furthermore, you will learn about the advantages and limitations of the respective services and be able to describe the scenarios where messaging services should be used instead of event-based services.

We'll finish off this chapter with an introduction to DevOps. We'll step away from the technical topics and discuss what DevOps actually means beyond being a frequently used buzzword, as well as some DevOps practices.

By the end of this chapter, you should understand better what role messaging solutions play in developing distributed systems running in Azure, and be familiar with services and SDKs that help you leverage the messaging services for your solution.

In this chapter, we will cover the following main areas:

- Understanding messaging patterns
- Exploring Azure Queue Storage
- Exploring Azure Service Bus
- Comparing Azure message-based services
- Discovering DevOps

Technical requirements

The code files for this chapter can be downloaded from `https://github.com/PacktPublishing/Developing-Solutions-for-Microsoft-Azure-AZ-204-Exam-Guide/tree/main/Chapter13`.

Code in Action videos for this chapter: `https://bit.ly/3BybjaF`.

Understanding messaging patterns

Messaging services are reliable services often used for communication across heterogeneous systems that might be disconnected from the networking. Messaging services were used for legacy Windows application synchronization, such as **Microsoft Message Queuing (MSMQ)**. Nowadays, the services are involved in the building of Azure infrastructure in data centers.

Messaging protocols provide required communication between services through the messaging broker that guarantees the delivery and ordering of messages. The broker is responsible for persisting messages while the services is temporarily unavailable. Other patterns of leveraging messaging services are messaging orchestration, load balancing, and reactive programming.

For instance, let's look at how provisioning resources on the Azure portal can be technically implemented by leveraging queues. When you provision resources from the Azure portal, the message with the task is sent to the queue to be picked up by the corresponding service. When the provision has started, you do not need to wait, and you can complete other activities on the portal. When the provision is complete, the corresponding service responds by dropping a message to the queue with the result of the provisioning process. The message is processed and the UI is updated. In the next section, we will examine these patterns closely.

The message broker and decoupling

The **broker pattern** has already been introduced in *Chapter 12, Developing Event-Based Solutions*. The broker pattern is implemented in the Azure Event Hubs and Event Grid services. In the pattern, we can define a **producer** (publisher) as a service that generates an **event** (message) with a **command** (task) to process. Then, the **consumer** (subscriber or handler) can pull the event (message) and process the command. The same pattern is implemented in the message-based technologies hosted in Azure.

For instance, Azure Queue Storage can be a broker for the communication of microservices running on the Kubernetes platform. The broker can help to decouple the producer and consumer of the messages. The messages are persisted by the producer in the queue and pulled by consumers to process. When the consumer finishes processing the message, the message is removed from the queue and the next message will be taken. One-way communication can be extended by the second queue where the consumer reports the result of processing to the producer. The following diagram represents two-way communication between the producer and consumer.

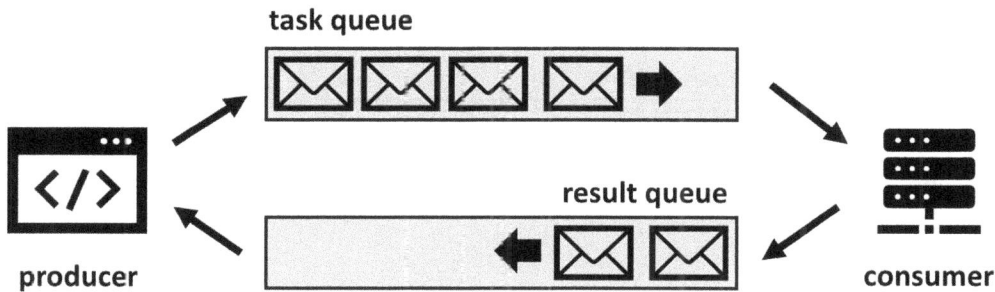

Figure 13.1 – Two-way communication with a message broker

The broker pattern schema here demonstrates one-to-one communication between the producer and consumer. Meanwhile, the producer can overload the consumer if the message requires significant time to process. This means that one-to-one communication between the producer and consumer should be converted to one-to-many, with many consumers picking messages one by one. This improvement introduces the load balancing pattern discussed in the next section.

Load balancing

Balancing the load is another useful function that helps the broker to scale the load. The number of messages depends on the publisher load. If the publisher implements a website that registers user requests at the peak of the load, it will produce a large number of messages. The consumer may spend the entirety of peak and off-peak hours processing the messages and this can delay processing. To solve these issues, the number of consumers can be increased manually or dynamically based on the number of messages in the queue.

By increasing the number of consumers picking up messages from the queue, we can speed up processing and constantly load all existing consumers. The publisher's load pattern can vary during peak and off-peak hours. Meanwhile, scaled consumers will be loaded constantly when they have work to do (that is, when they have messages in the queue). It helps to utilize all the consumers and scale them in when all the messages are processed. The following schema demonstrates how the balancing of the load works.

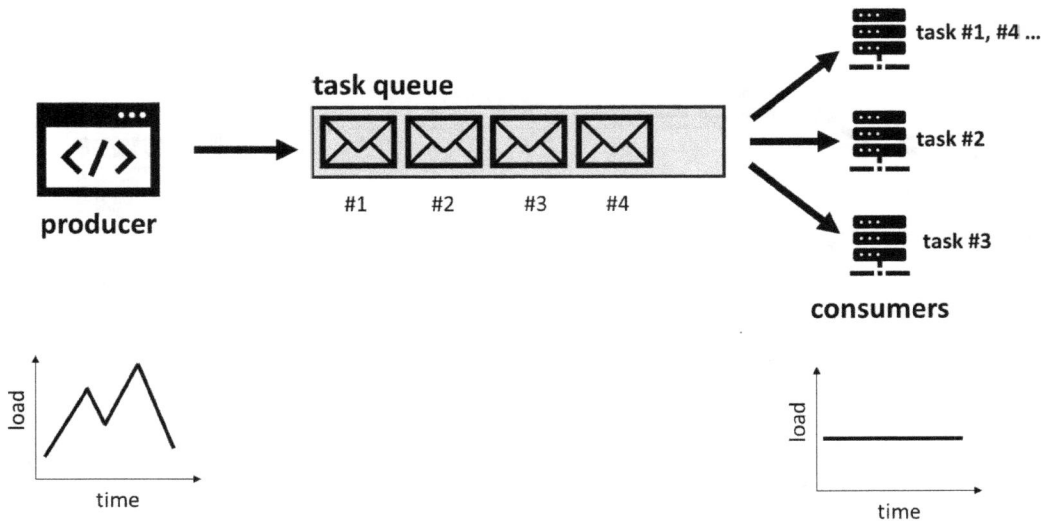

Figure 13.2 – Load balancing and scaling consumers

From the balancing example, you learned that the number of consumers can be adjusted dynamically. Scaling consumers helps to dynamically manage the number of consumers and reduce costs.

For instance, if the frontend is hosted on Azure App Service, and configured for dynamic scaling by CPU performance, the backend can be scaled by the length of the queue. Depending on the number of messages, we can get the scaled-out or scaled-in number of consumers and save costs, instead of paying for each of them 24/7. The following section will explain how this pattern is leveraged in Azure services.

Competing consumers

The **competing consumers pattern** is a combination of the message broker pattern and load balancing pattern. This pattern is designed to enable multiple producers and multiple consumers to coordinate with each other and increase the high availability and throughput of the whole solution. This pattern is commonly used in microservices architecture when each of the services is represented by multiple containers running on different environments or nodes. If one of the consumers fails, another consumer can replace it and process messages. The scaling of the consumers and producers can be implemented dynamically. Whenever the length of the queue grows, the number of consumers increases to meet the required throughput. Whenever the length of the queue goes down, the number of consumers decreases to save costs.

The competing consumers pattern can also help when services are hosted on a PaaS or IaaS platform or a combination of both. Moreover, the competing consumers pattern can be implemented on-premises and in hybrid environments. The following schema demonstrates how the single messaging service can help balance the load and provide high availability in the cloud environment.

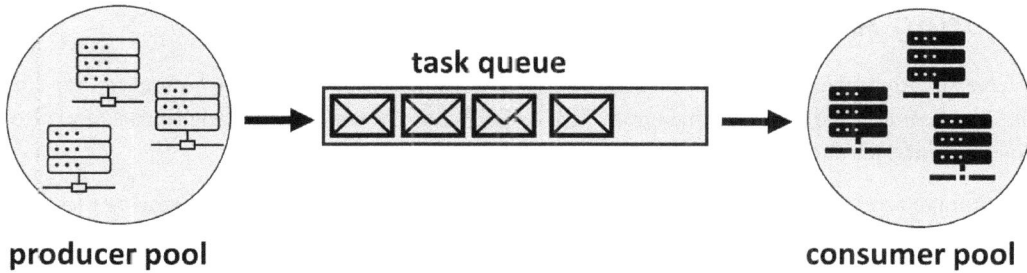

Figure 13.3 – Distributing the load between producers and consumers

When you implement the competing consumers pattern, you get the following benefits:

- Increases throughput with minimum effort that does not require code changes

- Improves the reliability of the solution because each of the services can be duplicated more than once

- Avoids complex configuration and message orchestration because the broker handles orchestration and supports out-of-the-box sequences

- Improves the scalability of the solution by increasing or decreasing the number of consumers and publishers depending on the load and queue length

- Saves costs by enabling dynamic scaling

- Monitors and manages messages manually by leveraging queue explorers

There are also some considerations you should make before you implement the pattern:

- Messages should contain self-sufficient data to avoid affecting external changes in the parameters or the task after they have been submitted.

- Message ordering is one of the functionalities provided out of the box, but you can change the order of processing by including the order ID in the task.

- Any exceptions during task processing can be handled by leveraging a "poison message" strategy. For instance, for three unsuccessful attempts made to process messages by different consumers, it should mark the messages as poison messages and move those messages to another queue (a **dead-letter queue**) for further processing.

- Retrying attempts should be used for pulling messages by consumers and pushing messages by publishers. The impact of potential connection loss can be eliminated by enabling retrying attempts.

In the next section, we are going to explore the services available in Azure to host queue services. It will provide the provision scripts and communication code, along with details about the configuration, security, and costs.

Exploring Azure Queue Storage

You have already learned a lot about Azure Storage from *Chapter 6, Developing Solutions That Use Azure Blob Storage*. The following paragraph will revise the topics you have already learned and also uncover new details about the queue service.

Azure Storage is one of the oldest services available in Azure, initially designed for storing files and blobs. Nowadays, Azure Storage supports additional services, such as Azure Table (a NoSQL database) and Azure Queue Storage (for simple messaging). Only the Standard storage tier supports these services and persists data in geographically separated regions. The service is based on Microsoft-managed infrastructure that is auto-scaled, on-demand, and recognized as serverless. All the hosted services on the Azure Storage platform support HTTPS RESTful interfaces for communication within Azure and on-premises solutions. Because of their high reliability, the services are commonly used within Azure solutions for logs and backup persistence. Another advantage of the service is the consumption-based pricing model. Charges are based on the capacity of the storage data and the number of transactions made.

Azure Queue Storage provides storage with queue mechanics that support a RESTful interface. The queue persists messages and the total capacity of these messages is close to petabytes. Meanwhile, the maximum size of the message is 64 KB. The queue serves as a simple queue that is commonly used as a list of tasks for consumers. To provision a new queue, you first need to provision a new **Azure Storage** account and select the availability option (local, zone, or region redundant), then create a new queue, and get a URL reference to use in REST requests.

From a security standpoint, storage accounts support encryption at rest and in transit using Microsoft-managed or customer-managed keys. Connections can be limited from public access by enabling a firewall and through connection to Azure VNets. Alternatively, SAS keys can be limited by a set of IP addresses. Managing services requires admin keys with full access. Meanwhile, permission for submitting and receiving messages can be limited for each of the publishers, also using SASs.

The cost of Azure Queue Storage depends on the chosen availability level, where local is the cheapest and geo-redundant is the most expensive. The cost is also based on the total capacity of storage consumed by the queue and the number of read-write operations. Extra costs can occur if the communication includes services outside of the selected queue region. Transfer charges will apply according to the respective transfer zones.

Simple queueing with Azure Queue Storage has many limitations, including forced **first-in-first-out (FIFO)**, the inability to fetch messages by ID, a limited lease/lock duration, and the limited size of the batch to process messages. Another significant limit is only having 64 KB as the maximum size of the message. There are other difficulties you might find when you try to pull messages from the queue. You can receive only an approximate number of the messages because the messages may be locked or hidden, and removed from the queue only when successfully processed by the subscriber. Also, due to the locking technique, the messages can change in order. So, the reviser might skip the message because it is locked and then return to it since the consumer fails to delete the message after the holding lock.

Provisioning Azure Queue Storage

Before you move on to take a look at the code examples, let's first find out how to provision Azure Queue Storage from the Azure CLI. The following script will build the locally-redundant storage, then enable the queue service by creating a new queue. This is a bash script and can be run from Cloud Shell or locally:

```
https://github.com/PacktPublishing/Developing-Solutions-for-Microsoft-
Azure-AZ-204-Exam-Guide/blob/main/Chapter13/01-provision-queue/demo.
azcli
```

In the script, we will pull the admin keys for the connection made from the code in the next demo. You can also observe the queue from the Azure portal to find out more about its settings and content. For the best way to monitor messages, you can download Azure Storage Explorer (`https://azure.microsoft.com/en-us/features/storage-explorer/`) or leverage the Visual Studio extension, named Azure Storage (`https://marketplace.visualstudio.com/items?itemName=ms-azuretools.vscode-azurestorage`).

Messaging from the code

The next code example will demonstrate to you a simple messaging broker that enables your publisher to submit the message and pull the message from the consumer. Pay attention to the following methods of receiving messages:

- **Receive and delete**: This is the general approach to working with the queue. The receiver pulls the message or a batch of messages and starts to process the message. Then, when finished, it must explicitly delete the message. During the processing time, the message is locked or hidden and is not available to be received.

- **Receive and update, then delete**: The same approach as the previous one occurs but the server can set a manual lock or hidden time per message to process messages that require extra time. The message must be explicitly deleted when the processing is finished successfully to avoid returning messages to the queue to be processed twice.

- **Peek**: This method is useful for observing messages within the queue and usually receives a batch of messages to minimize overhead communication. You can peek at the messages to monitor the content of messages without generating a dequeuing message from the queue.

For running the code, you need to update `Program.cs` with the connection string retrieved from the previous script run. To successfully run the example, you first need to run the publisher to submit several messages in Azure Queue Storage, then observe the messages by using one of the tools. You then run the consumer and choose the receiving method. You also can monitor the count of the messages when you select one method or another. All three of the aforementioned approaches are implemented in the consumer available in the repo here:

```
https://github.com/PacktPublishing/Developing-Solutions-for-Microsoft-
Azure-AZ-204-Exam-Guide/tree/main/Chapter13/02-connect-to-queue
```

The following classes were used for the submission and receipt of messages:

Class	Description
QueueClient	The class is initialized with a connection string and represents the queue to submit and receive the messages.
QueueProperties	The class instance receives meta information from the queue, including maximum batch size and an approximate number of messages.
QueueMessage	This is a received message class that contains the message body, message ID, and metadata. It stays hidden in the queue and needs to be explicitly deleted.
PeekedMessage	A peeked message class that stays in the queue.

Table 13.1 – C# SDK classes to operate with Azure Queue Storage

Azure Queue Storage is a simple messaging service that does not support enterprise features but it is extremely helpful for leveraging asynchronous communication between services. This service is the best choice if you need to minimize costs. However, the service does not provide duplicate removal or dead-letter queueing. The maximum size of 64 KB per message is also a significant limitation. In the next section, you will learn about the enterprise-grade service that helps you go beyond the limits of Azure Queue Storage.

Exploring Azure Service Bus

The orchestration of messages is a tough task that needs to be performed with high speed and consistency to suit the requirements of modern applications. Azure Service Bus is a service that runs on Azure PaaS to meet enterprise messaging requirements. In the following part of the chapter, you will become familiar with the features of Azure Service Bus and will be able to provision an instance for your solution. Then, you will learn how to leverage SDKs to get connected and submit and receive messages from topics and queues.

Before we cover the technical details of Azure Service Bus, let's take a look at what kind of scenarios the enterprise messaging service should be used for:

- **Message brokers:** Just as with Azure Queue Storage, Service Bus supports all simple messaging mechanisms to guarantee the delivery and sequence of messages with a FIFO approach. Because Service Bus supports up to 1 MB of size, the message can be extended with a variety of metadata fields and transfer any type of data, including binary code.

- **The transactional process**: One of the most useful functions of enterprise messaging is that it supports transactions. A transaction can include receiving and submitting multiple messages in multiple queues and keeping them hidden from other receivers until the transaction is committed.

- **Dynamic load balancing**: The orchestration algorithm allows several consumers to receive messages from the queue and is dynamically scaled depending on the queue message length. It implements the *competing consumers* pattern that we introduced and explained earlier.

- **Message broadcast**: The topics can support one or many relationships between publishers and consumers. Topics can be helpful when the messaging service is required to engage in processing more than one service by processing a copy of the same message. Topics will be covered in detail in the *Developing for Service Bus topics* section.

- **Relay communication**: As mentioned previously, cloud services and hybrid applications can be safely connected without direct connection through the broker. For instance, the relay service can be set up in Azure to connect Azure Web Apps and on-premises SQL. Relays will be discussed in detail in the *Exploring relays* section.

As you can see, Azure Service Bus is quite a complicated service, and this is reflected in its price. Let's get familiar with the pricing model before we recommend Azure Service Bus above other messaging services.

Pricing tiers

The feature set that you can use for your Azure Service Bus depends on the pricing tier. The following tiers are the available options:

- **Basic**: Only queue services available, no advanced services. The message size is limited to 256 KB. Incurs consumption-based charges per 1 MB of operations.

- **Standard**: Topics and queues are available with all advanced services except for redundancy and scale. The message size is limited to 256 KB. Consumption-based charges per 1 MB of operations.

- **Premium**: All advanced services, including geo-redundancy and horizontal scale by message units. The message size is limited to 1 MB (up to 100 MB in the preview feature of large messaging). Charges are made hourly per message unit.

Scaling

The horizontal scaling functionality is available on the Service Bus namespace level only within the **Premium** pricing tier. Up to 16 message units can be provisioned and scaled manually. Adding an extra message unit increases the total throughput of the namespace.

Another way to scale throughput is using engaged partitions. Depending on the partition key provided by the sender, messages will be hosted on the specific broker and storage will belong to it.

An increasing number of brokers and storage will let Service Bus increase the total throughput by processing messages in parallel.

Connectivity

The publisher and subscriber should provide specific SAS keys (or policies) to be accepted by the server. Usually, the keys are implemented as part of the connection string provided with the code. There are namespace-level policies and topic-/queue-level policies that are limited by the exact topic/queue. The policy allows **Listen**, **Send**, and **Manage** activities accordingly and should be followed to the minimum privilege recommendations. Moreover, Azure Service Bus supports **role-based access control (RBAC)** assignment, which gives access control to users and service accounts to allow them to manage activity.

Advanced features

Before we get into provisioning your Azure Service Bus, let's learn about the enterprise messaging features that are not available within the simple messaging service that Azure Queue Storage offers. Your feature requirements will help you choose between simple and enterprise messaging services:

- **Message sessions**: The session is the logical identifier of communication between the sender and the service hosting topics or queues. A session is supported by providing the session ID property to the sender who submits the message in the queue or topic. There are two possible patterns of seasoned connection: FIFO and request-response. The FIFO pattern guarantees the delivery of messages in the received order and provides the relation between messages. FIFO sessions suit a messaging broker scenario. However, the request-response pattern does not support sequences and is usually implemented using two single queues for request and response. The request should be matched to the response. The request-response sessions suit a relay scenario.

- **Message deferral**: This allows the receiver to engage in deferred retrieval of messages from the queue or topic. The receiver postpones message processing for later and keeps messages in the queue.

- **Dead-letter queues (DLQs)**: These support special treatment for undelivered and poisoned messages by storing them in a separate logical queue for further processing. The special treatment is usually implemented by manual processing of the message by the operator.

- **Deduplication**: This feature automatically deletes duplicates of the messages submitted by the publisher as a result of any connectivity issue. The duplicates are determined by their unique message IDs.

- **Transaction support**: This allows the consumer to complete several operations within the scope of the transaction. Messages can be retrieved, processed, and submitted in another queue or topic within the same transaction. If the transaction is canceled, all changes in the transaction scope will be reverted. If the transaction is completed, the changes will be visible to other consumers.

- **Auto-forward**: This feature enables Service Bus to automatically forward the messages from the original queue to another queue or topic and removes the message from the originally received queue. The auto-forwarding can be configured only for the same namespace server.

- **Idle auto-delete**: The feature automatically deletes the queue after a period of inactivity. The minimum interval can be set to 5 minutes.

Many of the features listed here are turned off by default. You can enable them later when you create a new queue or topic in the Azure portal. In the next section, you will learn how to provision Service Bus.

Provisioning Azure Service Bus

Provisioning Service Bus consists of two steps. First, you need to provision a namespace. Second, you need to provide the exact topic or queue. When you provision a namespace, you will register the globally unique address that should be used for the connection. You also need to choose the price tier, with the option to upgrade it to a higher level later. The Premium tier supports message units to scale throughput.

The topic or queue can be provisioned when the namespace is ready. Then, you need to choose the quote for the total amount of messages (5 GB is the maximum), a maximum delivery count, the maximum duration of time to live, and the lock duration of messages that are being processed. A set of advanced features can be selected based on the price tier.

The following script will help you to leverage the Azure CLI to provision the Standard tier namespace with one queue and one topic. Access policies will be provisioned as well. These resources will be used later for the connection from the code and you need to copy the provided connection strings from the output. The script should be executed in Bash:

```
https://github.com/PacktPublishing/Developing-Solutions-for-Microsoft-
Azure-AZ-204-Exam-Guide/blob/main/Chapter13/03-provision-sb/demo.azcli
```

When provisioning is complete, you can find the resource on the portal and observe its settings. The single queue should be provisioned and available for configuration. In the next part, you will learn how to work with queues.

Developing for Service Bus queues

At the start of the chapter, we introduced the message broker pattern. This pattern is used for simple messaging scenarios to send, receive, and peek at messages. In the following sections, you will see snippets of how to use transactions, sessions, and DLQs. The code will use the queue we provisioned earlier (simple queues and advanced queues with session and DLQ support).

Submitting and receiving

These projects will demonstrate how to implement simple operations with messages, as the previous code examples demonstrated with Azure Queue Storage. First, you need to run a **publisher** project to generate several messages submitted in the queue. Then, you need to run a **consumer** project to receive the message. When you start the project, you will observe the count of messages. The following options are available for testing:

- Receive messages with the `PeakLock` option, which requires explicit completion of the recipient removing messages from the queue. The removal of the message will be performed after finishing the processing stage.

- Receive and delete messages with automatic deletion.

- List all messages from queues.

To run both projects, the code needs to be updated with a connection string at the top of `Program.cs`. The connection info was received from the previous provisioning script output:

```
https://github.com/PacktPublishing/Developing-Solutions-for-Microsoft-
Azure-AZ-204-Exam-Guide/tree/main/Chapter13/04-queue-dev/simple-
messaging
```

Sessions

The following projects will leverage sessions that allow publishers and consumers to pull the messages that belong to specific sessions. The publisher and receiver should share the same session name to pump the messages through the Service Bus queue. The queue with advanced services will be leveraged to demonstrate session usage. First, you need to run a publisher project to submit several messages for two sessions in the queue. Then, you need to run a consumer project to receive the message by using the sessions. When you start the project, you will observe the message count. The following options are available for testing:

- Receiving a message from the next session – the sessions will be selected one by one. The code is also allowed to hardcode the exact session name.

- Listing all available messages for all sessions.

The code of `Program.cs` should be updated for both projects, with the connection string received from the previous provisioning script output:

```
https://github.com/PacktPublishing/Developing-Solutions-for-Microsoft-
Azure-AZ-204-Exam-Guide/tree/main/Chapter13/04-queue-dev/session-demo
```

Transactions and DLQs

The last code example will demonstrate how transactions and DLQs work with Service Bus. You need to run a publisher project first to generate several messages submitted in both queues. Each pair of messages will be sent in a transaction. Then, you need to run a consumer project to receive the messages. When you start the project, you will observe the message count in both queues, including the DLQ. The following options are available for testing:

- Operate messages within a transaction. The code will receive a message from the advanced queue and submit a message in the simple queue in a transaction. If the submission fails, the message will return to the advanced queue.

- Leveraging DLQ for poison messages. The code will try to process the message from the advanced queue and then fail with an exception. This message mimics a poison message and will be submitted to the DLQ.

- Receiving the messages from the DLQ. The code will pull messages from the DLQ to mimic special processing.

- Listing all messages from the queues. The code will peak all messages in batch but keep them in the queue for processing.

The following schema will help you understand the transaction flow and leveraging DLQ in the sample project.

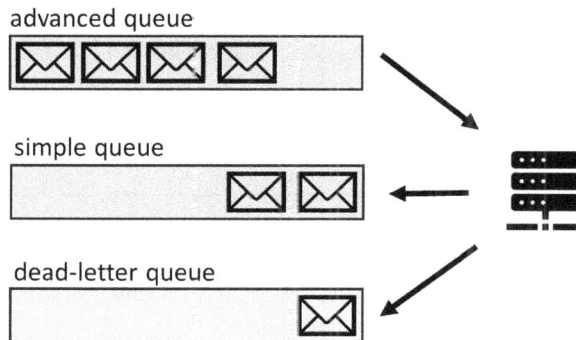

Figure 13.4 – A schema of transactional support and a DLQ

To run all projects from the following repo you need to update the code at the top of `Program.cs` with the connection string for the Azure Service Bus received from the previous provisioning script output:

```
https://github.com/PacktPublishing/Developing-Solutions-for-Microsoft-
Azure-AZ-204-Exam-Guide/tree/main/Chapter13/04-queue-dev/dlq-demo
```

Developing for Service Bus topics

In this example, you need to run two consumers that subscribe to the topic on Service Bus. The first consumer (**hotel-booking**) is responsible for hotel booking and the second consumer (**flight-booking**) is responsible for flight booking. Then, you need to start the publisher that will submit messages about all kinds of bookings on the topic. In the output of the consumers, you will see how they process the messages and what bookings are made. All three projects need to be run at the same time. The following schema will help you to understand the process.

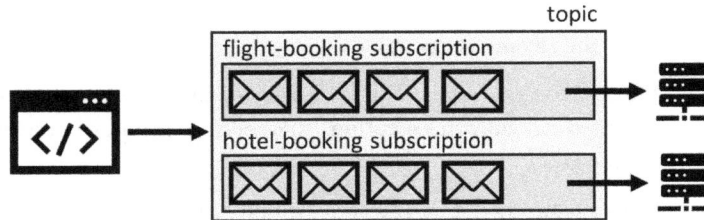

Figure 13.5 – An illustration of a sample of working with topics

Before you run projects, the code needs to be updated with a connection string at the top of `Program.cs`. The connection info was received from the previous provisioning script output:

`https://github.com/PacktPublishing/Developing-Solutions-for-Microsoft-Azure-AZ-204-Exam-Guide/tree/main/Chapter13/05-topic-dev`

You should notice that we now use `ServiceBusProcessor` instead of `ServiceBusReceiver`, which was configured to work with the queue previously. Both of these objects can be leveraged for connection to queues and topics. The following table should help you to learn more about objects that are used in the code:

Class	Description
ServiceBusClient	This class will help you to create a connected client configured with a SAS token. It also can be configured with options to support transactions.
ServiceBusAdministrationClient	This class exposes admin functionality, including the runtime properties with statistical information about a queue, for example, the number of messages in it.
ServiceBusReceiver	The receiver is created from the client class with configuration to a specific queue or topic. It also can be constructed with session support.
ServiceBusSender	The same as the receiver but used for sending messages and it does not require transaction configuration. The transaction label should be provided for each message.

ServiceBusProcessor	A processor class is allowed for subscription with delegates to two events: receiving new messages and errors. This class can be used to implement a reactive programming model.
TransactionScope	The transaction allows the submission and receipt of messages from different queues in the same transaction. The transaction can be manually committed or rolled back in the event of an error.

Table 13.2 – Azure Service Bus SDK objects

In the next section of the chapter, the Azure Relay service will be introduced. The Relay service will implement continuous messages to pump from producer to consumer in order to connect different types of environments, including hybrid and multi-cloud.

Exploring relays

A relay is an Azure PaaS resource that helps you to expose the services running in private networks to the services running in public clouds, or in another private network. For example, Azure Relay can help you to connect the services in your hybrid solution (a website in the cloud connecting to an on-premises database, for example). The main advantage of Azure Relay is that it does not require any VPN connections to be set up or any firewall to be configured. All traffic can be encrypted via HTTPS or TCP sockets and transferred that way.

Azure Relay supports one-way communication with a request/response approach. Two-way (bi-directional) communication is also supported by Relay. It completely separates both services but allows the exchange of information between services. It does not buffer any packages; it simply forwards them from the sender to the recipient. The drawback of this model is that it requires all parties of communication to be online.

Currently, Azure Relay supports two main technologies:

- **Hybrid Connections**, based on WebSocket and allowing communication with heterogeneous environments. This technology comes from Microsoft BizTalk services.

- The **WCF Relay service**, based on legacy relay for the **Windows Communication Foundation** (**WCF**) protocol, which allows remote procedure calls.

Provisioning Relay is similar to provisioning Azure Service Bus. The namespace needs to be deployed first, then one or many Hybrid Connections or WCF Relays can be deployed next. The following code example will help you to provision Azure Relay and Hybrid Connections endpoints:

```
https://github.com/PacktPublishing/Developing-Solutions-for-Microsoft-
Azure-AZ-204-Exam-Guide/blob/main/Chapter13/06-relay/demo.azcli
```

When you have completed provisioning Azure Relay, you can observe the instance from the Azure portal. The connection string provided in the output of the script should be used for the following projects. You can configure the server and client model to leverage one-way communication to transfer the messages from one application to another. You need to run both projects and hit the key on the client console application to see the message delivered on the server console:

```
https://github.com/PacktPublishing/Developing-Solutions-for-Microsoft-
Azure-AZ-204-Exam-Guide/tree/main/Chapter13/07-relay-dev
```

You also can shut down the server and see an error appear from submitting a message from the client console. This error confirms that both the client and server must be online to pump the messages.

Comparing Azure message-based services

In *Chapter 12, Developing Event-Based Solutions*, you learned about the Event Hubs and Event Grid services. Now, we can contrast and compare them with the message-based solutions hosted in Azure. First, let's talk about the similarities. The event-based and message-based solutions both leverage calls to public access endpoints. Both technologies can work as message brokers and transfer states for the synchronization of physically separate processes. Both services are enterprise-grade, hosted on Azure PaaS, and provide high availability and SLAs.

The difference between message-based services lies in the nature of the transferred data. With messages, a significant part of the data is self-defined and guarantees delivery and sequencing. However, events are small pieces of information and can be produced as a stream, with possible losses or changes made to sequences. Another difference is that event-based technologies are designed for the ingestion and processing of a large amount of data. Meanwhile, message-based technologies are focused on delivery and persistence. Surprisingly, one of Azure's event-based technology services is quite close to message-based technology. Event Grid implements topics in a similar way to Service Bus and transfers a significant amount of data with its event-like messages.

In the following table, we are comparing different message-based and event-based services hosted in Azure. Learning the pros and cons of the services will help you to select one of the services over another:

Service	Main Pattern	Pros	Cons
Event Hubs	Big data ingesting, streaming	High scale, event-persisting, capturing events, low-cost.	An event can be received only once. Complex order support with multiple partitions. Server-managed cursor.
Event Grid	Pub/sub, Reactive programming	Consumption-based price. Integration with other services. Topic support.	The events delivery sequence can be changed.

Queue Storage	Simple messaging	Unlimited queue size. Pay-as-you-go. Serverless architecture with geo-redundancy.	FIFO only. The small size of the messages. No advanced messaging. The delivery sequence can be changed.
Service Bus	Enterprise messaging	Scalable service. Variety of advanced messaging services. Access management.	Cost. 5 GB total message limit.
Azure Relay	Peer-to-peer communication	The communication is performed through a public network and does not require expensive VPN connectivity.	No message buffering. Both parties of communication must be online.

Table 13.3 – Comparison of Azure event-based services

As you will notice from the table, the differences and similarities between message- and event-based services are significant.

This brings us to the end of the technical topics required for the AZ-204 exam.

Before we wrap up the content and tackle a mock exam, it's worth addressing an important topic that is often misunderstood: DevOps.

Discovering DevOps

Too often, the word DevOps is passed around as a buzzword without an understanding of its meaning. Another unfortunate assumption is that you can simply tell a team of developers to *do DevOps*. Or, perhaps you can pay for a relevant training course or product, state that your company is now a DevOps company, and this will make it the case. This is all wrong.

Let's start with defining DevOps before we go any further into the topic.

What is DevOps?

If you were to ask a group of 10 people to tell you what DevOps is, you'd most likely get 10 different answers (maybe more). Some of the definitions may include implementing infrastructure as code, feature flags, automation, smaller deployments, or Agile planning, among other things.

None of these is wrong per se because DevOps can involve all these practices and more, but DevOps itself is a fundamentally simple idea.

One of my favorite definitions of DevOps is that given by Microsoft's Donovan Brown, which is *DevOps is the union of people, process, and products to enable continuous delivery of value to your end users.*

Let's address each part of this definition in the following subsections.

People

The term **DevOps** is a compound of **development** and **operations**. Traditionally, development teams would develop software in a silo and eventually give the software to the operations team to deploy. Often, operations teams would then need to carry out a lot of manual testing, configuration, phased rollouts, and potential workarounds for any bugs found in production that weren't discovered during development, among other follow-up tasks, which was a significant bottleneck.

Bringing development, operations, quality assurance, and other teams together as a multidisciplinary team with a shared definition of value and shared responsibility for the delivery pipeline has helped break down the silos. Imagine all of these disciplines coming together throughout the application life cycle. They all contribute to planning activities, concerns from operations can be voiced and addressed during development, and this ensures that testing happens in an environment that matches the state of the production environment, so that issues can be identified and addressed early. Any feedback or telemetry from production gets fed back to the development folks seamlessly on a regular basis.

DevOps isn't just about having these cross-functional teams within a single team. Nor is it just about having a team that can own a feature from end-to-end across different development areas (UI, database, and so on). DevOps defines a mindset, culture, and philosophy of working collaboratively that spans the entire software development life cycle throughout the planning, building, deploying, and operating phases.

One final point to make on the people side is that the DevOps culture needs to have executive support to be successful. Having your development and operations teams living by DevOps practices while the rest of the business is working in a way that doesn't support the DevOps culture is a recipe for failure.

Having the right teams and culture is a great start but it's also important that these people are following and supported by processes that enable innovation and the continuous delivery of value.

Process

We don't have enough space in this book to cover everything to do with DevOps, nor everything to do with DevOps processes. The key point here is that DevOps teams need to have and follow processes that support and enable the continuous delivery of value.

Legacy change advisory board processes and lengthy development milestones, which lack opportunities to gain frequent feedback by frequently deploying smaller iterations, are examples of processes that may act as bottlenecks to keeping your product relevant through continuous innovation.

While the people and process elements are key to succeeding with DevOps, there are also products that can help us align processes and better enable continuous planning, integration, deployment, and feedback.

Products

Various products exist that support the implementation of Agile and DevOps practices, such as Azure DevOps, GitHub, Jenkins, and many others.

Taking Azure DevOps as an example, which is one of the most complete single solutions on the market, the product might be used in a typical sprint (if you're working in sprints as part of **Scrum**, a topic for which you can find a link with more information in the *Further reading* section of this chapter) for the following:

- Product backlog refinement, prioritization, and estimation
- Sprint planning, forecasting, velocity, burndown, and capacity management
- Work item assignment and tracking
- Source code repositories for storing source code, configuration, and infrastructure as code files
- **Continuous integration** and **continuous deployment** (**CI/CD**) pipelines to automate building, testing, and deploying into various environments in stages, with granular orchestration

This list is by no means exhaustive but highlights that there are products out there that lend themselves perfectly to a DevOps environment. It's extremely important to understand that simply using a tool such as Azure DevOps doesn't mean you're working in a DevOps way.

Another important part of the definition is the word *value*.

Value

DevOps isn't just about automating a pipeline so we can rapidly deploy software; it's about delivering value. It's also important that teams have a clear understanding of what their definition of value is.

If people have different ideas of what value means, that could create a conflict of interests within the team. If you all have the same goal in mind, you have a better chance of success. Sometimes teams will have a value statement for each period, aligning all members to the definition of value for that period, if appropriate.

It's also important to notice that the term *end users* was carefully chosen.

End users

If you're only delivering value within your development or pre-production environments and the value isn't reaching your end users, something's not right.

In this context, end users don't need to be customers of your company, but perhaps whatever value you're delivering is delivered to internal users. Perhaps you're creating something that gets consumed by another team.

Often, the goal is to take the end-to-end process for delivering value – from planning to building, to deploying, to operating and monitoring – and shorten the cycle with smaller, more frequent deployments, each having a smaller risk surface area. This allows for frequent validated learning and feedback that can feed into the next planning session, and the cycle repeats continuously.

DevOps is such a huge topic that if we don't stop going into the theory now, we might never stop! We'll finish off this topic with an insight into some of the DevOps practices that we've seen success with over the years, some of which are mentioned in the *AZ-400: Designing and Implementing Microsoft DevOps Solutions* exam, should you wish to start exploring that after passing the AZ-204 exam.

DevOps practices

To keep this brief while still being insightful, I'll list some typical stages of the application life cycle in order and detail some of the practices I've seen implemented that have helped companies with successful DevOps implementations. Everything listed can be achieved using many different tools, so a specific tool won't be mentioned here:

- **Pre-planning**: During the execution of an iteration/sprint, which is a time-boxed period within which teams work to complete certain agreed tasks, a backlog of work items gets prioritized, and the items are refined further to ensure each work item contains enough detail and is ideally scoped well enough to be completed within a single period. Some teams will also estimate the level of effort, which helps with velocity and forecasting (if you do this, don't estimate backlog items in hours. Use story points, effort, or something similar).

- **Planning**: With a well-defined and prioritized backlog, teams can come out of a planning session with an agreed granular set of work items to be completed during the upcoming period. Often, these work items will appear in a sprint/iteration backlog with some visual tracking of progress, such as a **Kanban board**, for example.

  If the tool you use for collaboration has the capacity, you might choose to integrate the backlog or board into it, so that you have fewer tools to switch between.

- **Building**: Teams may have policies in place that require a certain branching strategy with branch protection policies. Developers might create a branch within their code repository that's explicitly linked to the work item they're addressing. When they're ready to commit their code, they might pull the most recent version of code from the main branch first, to ensure they have the latest code, and then confirm that whatever they're working on builds and passes all tests correctly.

  Perhaps a CI pipeline will run on each commit to the feature branch, checking out the branch, running any automated prerequisite tasks, confirming that everything builds successfully, and running automated tests (which might have previously been slow and laborious manual tests). This can help identify issues early and rapidly before they become impactful.

A pull request may be required before any code can get pushed to the main branch. When the developer creates a pull request to merge their code changes to the main branch, a policy can run that automatically triggers a CI pipeline.

The CI pipeline could pre-merge their code changes with the main branch code, perform the same or similar CI automation as on the feature branch, and generate some ready-to-deploy artifacts. These artifacts could then be used by a CD pipeline to automate deployment to a development environment, which is automatically created using infrastructure as code to ensure that the development environment is consistent with that of production. This allows approvers of the pull request to test the changes, as well as seeing the code changes.

- **Deploying**: Once enough approvals have been obtained in the pull request from the relevant code owners, the pull request can be completed, and the code is merged with the main branch. Automation can clean up the feature branch if that's an approach you want to take because it may no longer be required.

  Upon merging with the main branch, a CI/CD pipeline runs all the same automation as before, perhaps with some additional automated testing, and the artifacts are published for inspection and use later. Everything can be deployed to a UAT environment using infrastructure as code and those published artifacts.

  Once the automated UAT deployment has been confirmed as successful, approval can be obtained, triggering a deployment to production. Depending on the environment, this might make use of deployment slots, feature flags, or other deployment strategies. The artifacts that were deployed to the UAT environment need to be the same artifacts deployed into production; rebuilding artifacts can introduce additional risk.

  Again, many collaboration tools can integrate with these processes, so you can use a single tool to see the progress of pipeline runs, and grant or reject approvals for pull requests and deployments, without the need to open another tool. With the right tooling, policies, and automation, teams can innovate rapidly without sacrificing quality or stability.

- **Operating**: By now, you will already be aware of some of the monitoring tools available to gain valuable insights into systems in Azure. With additional integrations, I've seen teams have useful alerts that trigger an interactive message in their collaboration tool of choice, prompting immediate attention when required, as well as potential automated work item creation for tracking, and ideally automated remediation where possible.

- **Retrospectives**: At the end of each period, it's important to not only share what value has been delivered during that period but also to reflect on various aspects of that cycle, so learning points can be considered during the next cycle, encouraging continuous improvement. Again, collaboration tools have integrations that make this process easier.

Implementing Agile and DevOps practices into the software development life cycle as a continuous cyclical process has been proven to increase deployment frequency, reduce lead times for changes, decrease the mean time to recover, and reduce change failure rates significantly. You can explore these topics further, among others, should you wish to work toward the AZ-400 exam. For the purposes of the AZ-204 exam, however, we have concluded the topics we wanted to discuss.

Summary

Message-based services hosted in Azure implement asynchronous messaging and competing consumers patterns, which help to communicate between services in cloud-to-cloud and cloud-to-on-premises approaches. Messages always guarantee that the delivery and sequence of delivery are not changed. The message processing supports batches and transactions but is not ideal for high-performance loads. Meanwhile, the message queue publishers and subscribers can be horizontally scaled to process the messages at a higher speed.

For instance, Azure Queue Storage was introduced in this chapter. It enables you to save costs if your application does not need to leverage enterprise features. Furthermore, Service Bus offers a reliable, scalable, and adjustable service that provides you with enterprise-grade capabilities for a reasonable price. You learned the details about each of the services and learned how to communicate with both services via code. Now, in the exam, you can recommend the best service to meet the requirements of a given case study and leverage the best service for your company.

The final topic of this chapter was DevOps. Without delving too deep into the depths of the topic, we touched upon a few of the fundamental principles of DevOps and some DevOps practices.

You have successfully completed all the theory topics. In the next chapter, you can test your knowledge with mock exam questions, uncover knowledge gaps, and get closer to the real exam experience.

Questions

1. Can we back up a message queue?
2. Does Azure Queue Storage support transactions?
3. When the messages from Azure Queue Storage are successfully processed, why do they need to be explicitly deleted?
4. What is the maximum total size limit for the Azure Service Bus queue?
5. Which Azure Service Bus tier supports geo-redundancy?
6. What are DLQs used for?

Further reading

- To learn more about the competing consumers pattern, follow this link: `https://docs.microsoft.com/en-us/azure/architecture/patterns/competing-consumers`

- Asynchronous messaging is explained further at the following link: `https://docs.microsoft.com/en-us/azure/architecture/guide/technology-choices/messaging`

- A comparison of Event Hubs, Event Grid, Service Bus, and their features can be found at the following link: `https://docs.microsoft.com/en-us/azure/event-grid/compare-messaging-services`

- Compare Service Bus and Azure Queue Storage performance at the following link: `https://docs.microsoft.com/en-us/azure/service-bus-messaging/service-bus-azure-and-service-bus-queues-compared-contrasted`

- Advanced features of Azure Services Bus are introduced in the following document: `https://docs.microsoft.com/en-us/azure/service-bus-messaging/advanced-features-overview`

- Learn about retry implementation in SDKs at the following link: `https://docs.microsoft.com/en-us/azure/architecture/best-practices/retry-service-specific#service-bus`

- A useful article on DevOps culture can be found here: `https://www.martinfowler.com/bliki/DevOpsCulture.html`

- The Scrum guides documentation can be found here: `https://scrumguides.org/index.html`

Part 6:
Exam Preparation

As our journey comes to an end, we'll take this opportunity to test what we've covered during this book with some mock exam questions to help build familiarity with the types of questions you might be faced with in the exam, as well as testing your knowledge of the topics covered in this book.

The following chapter will be covered under this section:

- *Chapter 14, Mock Exam Questions*

Mock Exam Questions

At this point, we trust you have gained the knowledge and confidence to sit and pass the AZ-204 exam – we wish you the best of luck! Congratulations on making it to the end. We encourage you to take some time to review the *Further reading* sections of each chapter and do your own exploration. A single book can only cover so much – exercise your intellectual curiosity to expand your knowledge and understanding.

In this chapter, you'll go through a mock exam that will give you exposure to some of the types of questions you might encounter in the exam. You can find the answers to these questions in the *Mock Exam Answers* section at the end of this book. The exam itself has between 40 and 60 questions, and you'll have 100 or 120 minutes to answer them, depending on whether or not there are labs.

The questions in this mock exam are intended to give you an idea of the types of questions you might face in the exam. We can only cover certain types of questions in this book, but the exam can include other types of questions, such as drag and drop, simulations, and reordering lists.

A useful tool that Microsoft has made available for you to practice interacting with the different question types in a sandbox environment is the exam sandbox: `https://aka.ms/examdemo`. You don't need a login to access it. The questions are samples and not reflective of the exam questions, but they give a good idea of what question types you might be presented with during the exam.

We wish you the very best of luck! Please remember to revisit chapters where needed and do your own exploration and testing to cement your understanding.

Implementing IaaS solutions

1. You're developing a solution that requires multiple Azure VMs to communicate with each other with the lowest possible latency between them.

   Which one of the following features will meet this low-latency requirement?

   A. Availability zones

   B. Availability sets

      C.   Proximity placement groups

      D.   VM scale sets

2.   Your company uses ARM templates to define resources and their configurations that should be present in your resource group. After adding some additional resources to the resource group for testing, someone else deploys the same ARM template to the same resource group via the CLI, and you discover that the new resources you created have now been deleted while all other resources remain unimpacted.

Which one of the following commands could have had this impact?

A. `az deployment group create -g "RG-AZ-204" -n "Deployment_45" -f ./template.json -p deletenew="true"`

B. `az deployment group create -g "RG-AZ-204" -n "Deployment_45" -f ./template.json --mode Complete`

C. `az deployment group create -g "RG-AZ-204" -n "Deployment_45" -f ./template.json --mode Incremental`

D. `az deployment group create -g "RG-AZ-204" -n "Deployment_45" -f ./template.json --force-no-wait`

3.   You have a Dockerfile that you'd like to test locally before pushing it to a registry.

Which of the following commands should you use to build the container image on your local machine (assuming all of the prerequisites are in place)?

A. `docker run -it --im docker:file`

B. `az acr build --image dockerfile/myimage:latest --file Dockerfile .`

C. `docker build -t myimage:latest .`

D. `az acr run --file Dockerfile .`

4.   You've deployed an ASP.NET Core application to a single container in Azure Container Instances and need to collect the logs from the application and send them to long-term storage. A second container should be used to collect the logs from the application. You need to select a service that has the lowest cost and the fewest changes required to deploy the application.

Which one of the following services should you use to implement the solution?

A.   An Azure Container Instances container group

B.   A Kubernetes Pod

C.   Azure Container Registry

D.   A Log Analytics workspace

5. The following ARM template successfully deploys a storage account with the correct configuration, and you would now like to store it centrally for others to use. In its current state, colleagues would need to change the name of the resource within the template each time to create a new storage account.

    What changes should you make to the template so that colleagues can specify a name for the storage account without having to hardcode the value in the template each time?

```
{
    "$schema": "https://schema.management.azure.com/
schemas/2019-04-01/deploymentTemplate.json#",
    "contentVersion": "1.0.0.0",
    "resources": [
        {
            "type": "Microsoft.Storage/storageAccounts",
            "apiVersion": "2021-09-01",
            "name": "mysta",
            "location": "West Europe",
            "kind": "StorageV2",
            "sku": {
                "name": "Standard_LRS"
            },
            "properties": {
                "accessTier": "Hot"
            }
        }
    ]
}
```

A. Create a new version of the template with different values for the name each time a new name is required and store it in a source control repository.

B. No changes to the template are required. You can specify the name in the command line when deploying it.

C. Create a parameters section in the template and add the name so that it can be specified at deployment time.

D. Create a variables section in the template and add the name so that it can be specified at deployment time.

Creating Azure App Service web apps

1. You're developing a web app with the intention of deploying it to App Service and have been told that the messages generated by your application code need to be logged for review at a later date.

    Which two of the following would be required to meet this application logging requirement?

    A. A Linux App Service plan

    B. A Windows App Service plan

    C. Blob application logging

    D. Filesystem application logging

2. You're developing an API application that runs in an App Service named myapi, which has the https://myapi.az204.com custom domain configured. This API is consumed by a JavaScript single-page app called myapp with the https://az204.com custom domain configured.

    The part of the app trying to consume myapi isn't working, giving an error that includes the phrase The Same Origin Policy disallows reading the remote resource at https://myapi.companyname.com.

    Which one of the following is likely to be required to resolve this?

    A. Change the custom domain of the app to https://myapp.az204.com.

    B. Run the az webapp up command from myapp.

    C. Run the az webapp cors command from myapi.

    D. Move myapi to the same resource group as myapp.

    E. Run the az webapp cors command from myapp.

3. An App Service web app you're developing needs to make outbound calls to a TCP endpoint over a specific port, which is hosted on an on-premises Windows Server 2019 Datacenter server. Outbound traffic to Azure over port 443 is allowed from the on-premises server. Which Azure service can be used to provide this access?

    A. Private endpoint

    B. Hybrid Connection

    C. Private Link

    D. VNet integration

4. An App Service web app has been configured with the scale-out autoscale rules shown in the following screenshot. One is monitoring a storage queue, and another is monitoring the CPU percentage of the App Service plan:

Scale out			
When	ASP-AZ204-bacb	(Average) CpuPercentage > 70	Increase count by 5
Or	busy-queue	ApproximateMessageCount > 5	Increase count by 7

Figure 14.1 – Two scale-out autoscale rules in App Service

In a scenario where both rules are triggered at the same time, assuming the current instance count is *1* and the maximum is set to *15*, which one of the following scale actions would be performed?

A. The instance count increases to *7*.

B. The instance count increases to *5*.

C. The instance count increases to *12*.

D. The instance count doesn't change as the two rules conflict.

Implementing Azure Functions

1. You notice that a function hosted on a Consumption plan is always slow to run first thing in the morning. After the first run, the function runs again as expected.

   What is the most likely reason for this behavior?

   A. A long-running function that started overnight needs to finish before processing the early morning request.

   B. The **Always on** setting is turned off overnight and enabled at a scheduled time automatically.

   C. The function instances scaled to 0 due to being idle, and it takes some time for a cold startup.

2. You've inherited responsibility for a function that someone else created. This function uses a timer trigger, and you need to identify the schedule on which this function triggers.

   The trigger has been configured with the following NCrontab syntax: `0 0 */2 * * mon-fri`.

   What is the schedule on which this timer has been triggered?

   A. Every 2 days between Monday and Friday (Monday, Wednesday, and Friday)

   B. Every Monday–Friday for a month every 2 months

   C. Every 2 hours from Monday–Friday

3. Where do you configure triggers and bindings for a function written in Python?

   A. Update the `function.json` file.

   B. Decorate methods and parameters with the required attributes in code.

   C. Update the app configuration within the Azure portal.

Developing solutions that use Cosmos DB storage

1. Your company uses Cosmos DB with a SQL API to store JSON documents. The documents are often updated and sometimes deleted. You want to use the Cosmos DB change feed to track changes.

   Which statement from the following list about the Cosmos DB change feed is incorrect?

   A. The change feed is enabled in Cosmos DB by default.

   B. All modified documents are tracked in the change feed.

   C. The change feed is implemented in a first-in-first-out order.

   D. You can use SQL to query records in the change feed.

2. Which of the following factors determines the number of physical partitions in Azure Cosmos DB with Core (SQL) API provisioned with exact throughput?

   A. The storage and consistency level

   B. The storage and throughput

   C. The throughput and consistency level

   D. The number of documents and throughput

3. You develop a C# application to process credit card payments. You choose Cosmos DB with Core (SQL) API as a database to persist the payment info. The document schema is provided here:

```
{
  Id: ""
  customer: ""
  cardNumber: ""
  amount: ""
}
```

After reviewing your application design, the security engineer requests that you enable encryption for card payment information. The encryption technology must implement the following requirements:

• Encryption must be applied to all documents in the container.

- Encryption must protect sensitive payment information.

- Encryption keys must be controlled by the organization.

- The data must encrypted in transit.

What encryption technology can you implement to meet the requirements?

A. Enable **Transparent Data Encryption**

B. Enable encryption at rest with service-managed keys.

C. Enable encryption at rest with customer-managed keys.

D. Use **Always Encrypted** technology and configure the encryption policy with a /* path.

E. Use **Always Encrypted** technology and configure the encryption policy with a /cardNumber path.

4. You provision Cosmos DB with the Core (SQL) API in the two Azure regions. You keep the **Session** consistency level as the default consistency level for collection. Meanwhile, one of the applications that work with Cosmos DB must ensure that data is not being lost, and updates apply for both regional instances in real time.

What action should you take to meet the requirements?

A. Implement transactions and update documents in both regions individually.

B. Change the default consistency level for the collection to **Strong**.

C. Change the default consistency level for the collection to **Consistent Prefix**.

D. In the application's code, provide a **Strong** consistency level with RequestOptions when calling updates.

5. Your application is tracking payment transactions with a single instance of Cosmos DB with the Core (SQL) API. The hundreds of transactions arrive at the end of the business day and need to be ingested into Cosmos DB with Core (SQL) API as a single transaction per document. The business process required the data to be ingested with maximum speed.

What action should you complete to meet the requirements?

A. Change the default consistency level to **Eventual**.

B. Change the default consistency level to **Strong**.

C. Change the indexing mode to **Consistent**.

D. Change the indexing mode to **None**.

E. Implement a pre-trigger for creating operations.

Developing solutions that use Azure Blob Storage

1. Your company is going to host a single-page web application in Azure. You are required to provide a service with the following corresponding features:

   - Availability in at least two regions.

   - Support versioning for HTML and JS code.

   - Register the website with the yourcompany.com custom domain.

   - Use out-of-the-box features where possible.

   - Minimum cost.

   Which of the following services will you recommend?

   A. App Service on the Free tier

   B. App Service on the Basic tier

   C. An Azure Storage account

   D. An Azure VM

   E. Azure Container Instances

2. Your application generates log files that should be stored in the Azure Blob Storage. What is the best access and pricing tier that you recommend? The solution must minimize cost:.

   A. The Hot tier for Premium storage

   B. The Cold tier for Premium storage

   C. The Archive tier for Standard storage

   D. The Hot tier for Standard storage

3. You develop an application for IoT devices that persist files on Azure Blob Storage. You created a connection string using a single SAS key that allows read and write operations with the blobs. After the testing phase, one of the IoT devices was stolen, and the security engineer requested you revoke write access to the storage account from the stolen device.

   What will you do to revoke the access?

   A. Regenerate the access keys for the storage account.

   B. Revoke the SAS from the list of generated signatures on the Azure portal.

   C. Generate another SAS token with read-only permission.

   D. Update the SAS expiration time from the Azure portal.

4. Your application is connected to the Azure Blob Storage and periodically crashes with an exception. You discover the following code that produces the exception:

```
BlobContainerClient containerClient =
    client.GetBlobContainerClient(containerName);
Dictionary<string, string> metaData
        = new Dictionary<string, string>()
            {
                { "Department", "Marketing" }
            };
await containerClient.SetMetadataAsync(metaData);
```

What might be the reason for the exception?

A. The container does not exist.

B. The container's metadata format is not set properly.

C. The organization has not registered the marketing department in Azure AD.

D. Metadata can only be assigned to the blob, not to the containers.

Implementing user authentication and authorization

1. An ASP.NET Core application that you've successfully deployed to an App Service needs to authenticate users with their **Azure Active Directory** (**AAD**) accounts. When you enable authentication for your application within the Azure portal, which one of the following types of resources is required to integrate your app with AAD?

A. An application gateway

B. An application proxy

C. An app registration

2. You're developing an internal .NET Core application that will run on users' devices and require them to authenticate with their AAD accounts. You are using the Microsoft.Identity. Client NuGet package in your project:

```
var app = [missing word]
    .Create(_clientId)
    .WithAuthority(AzureCloudInstance.AzurePublic, _
tenantId)
    .WithRedirectUri("http://localhost")
    .Build();
```

Which one of the following is the missing word from the application code in the preceding code sample?

A. `PublicClientApplicationBuilder`

B. `PrivateClientApplicationBuilder`

C. `ConfidentialClientApplicationBuilder`

D. `ClientApplication`

3. An ASP.NET Core application you're developing on App Service connects to a container in an Azure Storage account using a SAS token, which is stored in an application setting of the App Service.

Your security team has advised that SAS tokens need to be managed in a way that allows you to modify the permissions and validity of those tokens.

Which three of the following can be performed to meet this requirement?

A. Run the `az storage container generate-sas` command.

B. Run the `az storage container lease change` command.

C. Run the `az storage container policy create` command.

D. Run the `az webapp config appsettings set` command.

E. Run the `az webapp config access-restriction add` command.

F. Run the `az appconfig create` command.

Implementing secure cloud solutions

1. An App Service web app you're developing needs to access a secret from one of your key vaults using an identity that shares the same life cycle as the web app.

Which two of the following commands should be used to enable this (in addition to any code changes that might be required)?

A. `az webapp identity assign`

B. `az keyvault set-policy`

C. `az identity create`

D. `az policy assignment create`

2. You're developing a solution that implements several Azure functions and an App Service web app.

You need to centrally manage the application features and configuration settings for all the functions and the web app. You're already using Azure Key Vault for the central management of application secrets.

Which one of the following services is most appropriate to use in this scenario?

A. Azure Key Vault

B. Application groups

C. API connections

D. App Configuration

3. Developers within your company have been doing local development and testing with application configuration key-value pairs in a local JSON file.

You need to import the key-value pairs into an App Configuration resource.

Which one of the following commands can be used to achieve this?

A. `az webapp config backup restore`

B. `az appconfig kv import`

C. `az keyvault backup start`

D. `az kv import config`

Integrating caching and content delivery within solutions

1. You are deploying a web application that uses Azure Cache for Redis to an Azure VM. You need to configure firewall rules to let the VM communicate with instances of the cache. What protocol should be enabled to allow communication?

A. TCP

B. UPD

C. HTTP

D. MQTT

2. You build an instance of Azure Cache for Redis and connect your web application to the instance. After starting the web application, you want to observe the values stored in the cache without exporting the full cache content.

What tool can you not use to view data stored in Azure Cache for Redis?

A. Visual Studio Code

B. `redis-cli.exe`

C. The Redis console from the Azure portal

D. Cloud Shell

E. The Azure CLI

3.   Your application uses Azure Cognitive Services to analyze communication with clients. The requests and responses use RESTful services and are formatted in JSON. Your manager notices that many requests from clients are identical and responses for them can be reused.

     You have been asked to recommend an Azure service to do the following:

     - Minimize the number of requests from your application to Azure Cognitive Services.

     - Configure how long the response can be reused.

     - Use out-of-the-box solutions where possible.

     - Minimize costs and provide the best performance.

     What service can you recommend?

     A.   Azure CDN

     B.   Azure Front Door

     C.   Azure Cache for Redis

     D.   API Management

     E.   An Azure Storage account

4.   Your company is developing an antivirus solution. Your application is used by millions of clients spread across the world. Whenever a new virus is detected, you update the binaries of your application. The updates are delivered as files of about 50 MB in size that need to be installed on the client machine. The update must be delivered ASAP. You have been asked to recommend an Azure PaaS service to distribute the updates.

     Which of the following services will help you implement the distribution of updates and minimize the cost?

     A.   An Azure Storage account

     B.   Azure App Service

     C.   Azure Data Lake

     D.   Azure CDN

     E.   Azure DevOps

     F.   Azure Container Registry

5.   Your company is hosting a website on Azure App Service. Additionally, your company is using a CDN to store JavaScript and media files. Recently, users have complained about JS errors occurring on the main page. After troubleshooting the error, you find the bug and fix it in the JS file. However, users are still complaining about the errors. After additional troubleshooting, you discover that users are still using the old version of the JS file with the bug.

What should you do to make sure that issue is fixed for the users?

A. Restart the VM of users who are still complaining about errors.

B. Ask the user to install the Edge Insider browser.

C. Restart your web app.

D. Purge the Azure CDN endpoint.

E. Delete the CDN and create a new CDN profile.

Instrumenting solutions to support monitoring and logging

1. Your console application is using Azure SQL Database. Your application is one of many other applications that query databases during the day. You suspect that the performance of the SQL database has been degraded. You want to collect information on query performance and compare it with the previous day.

    What actions should you take with a minimum administration overhead?

    A. From the Azure SQL instance, choose **Enable Query Performance Insight** to investigate the query performance.

    B. From Application Insights, choose **Application Map** and investigate the performance of SQL Server.

    C. From Application Insights, choose **Performance**, and then select **Profiler** to profile the request to SQL Server.

    D. From the Log Analytics workspace, connect your Azure SQL instance and choose **Query Performance Insights**.

    E. From Azure Monitor, choose the **CPU percentage** metric to monitor CPU utilization per request.

2. Your ASP.NET Core MVC application contains the following code in the `controller` class:

    ```
    // GET: Get Clients list
    public async Task<IActionResult> Index()
    {
        TelemetryClient telemetry = new TelemetryClient();
        Stopwatch stopwatch = new Stopwatch();
        stopwatch.Start();
        var clients = _context.Clients.ToList();
        stopwatch.Stop();
    ```

```
    telemetry.TrackMetric("TimeToTrack",
stopwatch.ElapsedMilliseconds);
    return View(clients);
}
```

What will the result of the execution of this code be?

A. Application Insights creates a performance record for the **Index** page view.

B. Application Insights traces a custom event when the **Index** page is requested.

C. Application Insights traces a custom event when the client list is loaded for the **Index** page.

D. Application Insights tracks the custom metric to log the time of loading the **Index** page.

E. Application Insights tracks the custom metric to log the time of loading the clients' list for the **Index** page.

3. You need to collect and query IIS logs from an Azure VM (IaaS) that runs your website. What are the activities you need to perform on the Azure portal and VM?

A. From the VM page on the Azure portal, configure log exporting in the storage account.

B. From the VM page on the Azure portal, configure log exporting to Event Hubs.

C. From the VM page on the Azure portal, export the activity log in CVS format.

D. Deploy the Azure Log Analytics workspace. From the workspace's page, connect the VM and enable IIS log collection.

E. From the VM page on the Azure portal, open the log interface and write a KQL query to find the log activities.

4. You are observing frequent crashes on your production ASP.NET Core web application hosted on the Azure App Service platform. When you try to run the application locally, you cannot reproduce the issue. Which of the following Azure techniques gives you the best troubleshooting experience? Choose the most effective and least invasive approach:

A. Add the tracing commands to the crashing function. Update the web app and reproduce the issue. Analyze the application logs with tracing commands.

B. Enable remote debugging, connect to the production web application, and set a breakpoint on the function that crashes. Reproduce the issue and investigate the variables and parameters.

C. Configure and collect the **Detailed error messages** and **Failed requests tracing** logs from App Service.

D. Configure Application Insights to collect a debugging snapshot and analyze it on the Application Insights page.

E. Configure Application Insights to collect a profiling trace for the crashed function.

Implementing API Management

1. You find the following code snippet of an APIM policy:

```
<policies>
    <inbound>
        <rate-limit-by-key  calls="7"
                renewal-period="60"
                increment-condition="@(context.Response.
StatusCode == 200)"
                counter-key="@(context.Request.IpAddress)"
                remaining-calls-variable-
name="remainingCallsPerIP"/>
    </inbound>
</policies>
```

What is the result of applying the preceding statement?

A. Any calls from any customer with any IP address will be accepted at a rate of seven calls per hour.

B. Any seven successful calls per minute will be accepted from customers with the same IP address.

C. Any seven calls per minute will be accepted from customers with the same IP address.

D. Any seven calls per hour will be accepted from customers with the same IP address.

E. If APIM returns an error, the call will be counted toward the rate limit of seven calls per minute.

2. Your company exposes a weather forecast web API on an API Management instance. Your APIM instance should call a backend web API that supports authentication. What type of backend authentication is not supported by APIM?

A. Managed identities

B. Basic authentication

C. Client Authentification Certificate

D. Windows Authentication

3. Your company creates an API Management instance and releases products to allow access to an the analytics web API. Which of the following listed features is not supported by API Management?

A. Import endpoint definition.

B. Allow developers to test your analytics API.

C. Provide public access to the web API endpoints.

D. Back up the usage data.

E. Generate a response for a request without querying the underlying web API.

F. Track policy changes in source control.

Developing event-based solutions

1. You need to diagnose the content of incoming events to detect malfunctioning applications. Thousands of incoming events from hundreds of applications are collected by Azure Event Hubs. Event Hubs is provisioned with the Basic price tier. What solution can you recommend to minimize cost and administrative efforts?

    A. Provision Event Grid, which is triggered whenever the event is received by Event Hubs and triggers an Azure function that logs the event in Cosmos DB.

    B. Scale Event Hubs to the Standard tier to increase the partition count, and reconfigure each of the connected applications to send the event for an individual partition.

    C. Scale Event Hubs to the Standard tier and enable the capturing of events in a Data Lake account.

    D. Enable Azure Monitor to track the received events by Event Hubs.

    E. Enable Azure Application Insights to track the received events by Event Hubs.

    F. Connect Event Hubs to a Log Analytics workspace, and use KQL to query the content of events.

2. Your IoT device constantly generates a stream of telemetry values collected by Azure IoT Hub (Basic SKU). You notice that the temperature value provided by the device is rising, and the device should be able to turn on the cooling system to avoid overheating. The device logic should be dynamically adjusted to the changes in temperature threshold. The threshold that is configured should be controlled on the server.

    You need to recommend a solution that minimizes the reaction time and minimizes the total cost of the solution. Which of the following would you choose?

    A. Collect historical data on the temperature, and train an ML model in Azure ML Studio. When the temperature value is received, the ML model can recommend turning on the cooling system.

    B. You configure an Azure Stream Analytics job to monitor reported temperature values. When the value exceeds the threshold, the temperature value is logged in a file located in an Azure Blob Storage. Azure Functions running on an IoT Edge device triggers when the file is updated and starts the cooling system.

C. Azure IoT Hub can use cloud-to-device communication and send a command to the device to start cooling when the temperature exceeds a certain threshold.

D. Azure IoT Hub can use twin settings to provide the temperature threshold, and the device will start cooling when the collected temperature exceeds the threshold. Upgrading Azure IoT Hub to the Standard SKU is required.

E. You can use Azure IoT Edge with a custom Docker container that measures the temperature and starts cooling when the temperature exceeds the threshold hardcoded in the container. Updating the threshold can be performed by rebuilding the container image.

3. You provisioned a new Event Hubs namespace named `namespeace1` and a new Event Hubs instance named `eventhub1` in your Azure subscription. Which of the following commands will help you generate the connection string for applications that are going to send events to Azure Event Hubs? The principle of least privilege should be used to select the required command:

A. `az eventhubs eventhub show --name eventhub1`

B. `az eventhubs eventhub authorization-rule keys create --eventhub-name eventhub1`

C. `az eventhubs eventhub authorization-rule create --eventhub-name eventhub1 --rights Send`

D. `az eventhubs eventhub authorization-rule create --eventhub-name eventhub1 --rights Manage`

E. `az eventhubs georecovery-alias authorization-rule keys list --namespace-name namespace1`

Developing message-based solutions

1. You're developing a message consumer for Azure Queue Storage. The consumer runs on the App Service WebJobs platform in Azure. You need to implement autoscaling rules to scale out the consumer instances horizontally when the total amount of messages in the queue increases by 100 messages.

What is the name of the metric you should use in the configuration of criteria for scaling?

A. Approximate message count

B. Count of active messages in the queue

C. Completed messages

D. Incoming messages

2. You develop a consumer application to process money transfer transactions from a bank. Each transaction is delivered in a single message. All generated transactions need to be processed in sequence. Losing any transactions is unacceptable. The solution should provide maximum tolerance for possible connections lost by the application.

    What service do you recommend for implementing transaction processing?

    A. Event Grid with a custom topic

    B. Event Hubs with an increased retention period

    C. Azure Queue Storage with the Geo-Redundant option

    D. Azure Service Bus queue with increased maximum deliveries

3. You are developing an application based on the Reactive programming model. The application should monitor Azure Service Bus and trigger custom logic when the message has been received. The application should always run as a service and react to the message in real time without restarts.

    Which of the following C# SDK classes should you use to implement requirements?

    A. `ServiceBusSender`

    B. `ServiceBusReceiver`

    C. `ServiceBusProcessor`

    D. `ServiceBusClient`

Mock Exam Answers

Implementing IaaS solutions

1. C is the correct answer.

   Although having VMs within an **availability zone** will bring VMs closer together than if they were in different availability zones or regions, **proximity placement groups** ensure that they are physically located close to each other for when you have low latency requirements.

   Feel free to revisit *Chapter 2, Implementing IaaS Solutions*, to review the availability options for VMs, including the useful links in the *Further reading* section of that chapter.

2. B is the correct answer.

   The default deployment mode is `incremental`, which will only make changes to the resources defined in the template if they need to be changed but won't delete any resources. The `complete` deployment mode will delete any resources within the deployment scope (the resource group, in this case) that are present within that scope but not defined within the template.

   This topic was covered in *Chapter 2, Implementing IaaS Solutions*.

3. C is the correct answer.

   Commands with `az acr` refer to Azure Container Registry and are not executed on the local machine. The `docker run` command requires a container to have already been built, which happens via the `docker build` command.

   This topic was covered in *Chapter 2, Implementing IaaS Solutions*.

4. A is the correct answer.

   ACI **container groups** allow you to host multiple containers on the same host machine, sharing the same life cycle, resources, network, and storage volumes. As the ACI infrastructure already exists, this option is more suitable than a Kubernetes Pod, which would require new infrastructure and therefore an additional cost.

   Azure Container Registry is used for storing but not running container images, and a Log Analytics workspace won't help with obtaining the logging information or writing it to long-term storage.

   Container groups were discussed in *Chapter 2, Implementing IaaS Solutions*.

5. C is the correct answer.

To have a name specified at deployment time without hardcoding the value in the template, you should create a `parameters` section in the template with a parameter for the name. You should also change the `name` value of the resource to get the value from that parameter. During deployment, the `staName` parameter (in this example) can be specified to create a new resource with that name, providing the name is available, as in this example:

```
az deployment group create -f .\sta.json -g AZ-204 -p
staName="mysta2"
```

The following is an example of how the template could look:

```
{
    "$schema": "https://schema.management.azure.com/
schemas/2019-04-01/deploymentTemplate.json#",
    "contentVersion": "1.0.0.0",
    "parameters": {
        "staName": {
            "type": "string"
        }
    },
    "resources": [
        {
            "type": "Microsoft.Storage/storageAccounts",
            "apiVersion": "2021-09-01",
            "name": "[parameters('staName')]",
            "location": "West Europe",
            "kind": "StorageV2",
            "sku": {
                "name": "Standard_LRS"
            },
            "properties": {
                "accessTier": "Hot"
            }
        }
    ]
}
```

This topic was covered in *Chapter 2, Implementing IaaS Solutions*. We could have also set the parameter to only be part of the name and used the `uniqueString()` template function to generate a more unique name.

Creating Azure App Service web apps

1. B and C are correct.

    Filesystem storage is intended for short-term logging and disables itself after 12 hours, so it won't be useful in this scenario, leaving Blob storage as the storage solution of choice. Windows apps offer application logging to both Blob and filesystem storage, whereas Linux only offers application logging to filesystem storage, making a Windows App Service plan a requirement to meet the needs of this scenario.

    This topic was covered in *Chapter 3*, *Creating Azure App Service Web Apps*, although filesystem storage only being designed for short-term logging wasn't specifically mentioned. This is an example where your own exploration would be useful because we can't cover every possible question in a single book.

2. C is the correct answer.

    The error indicates that **cross-origin resource sharing (CORS)** is blocking requests from `https://az204.com`. The command should be run from `myapi` rather than `myapp` because CORS is configured on the destination to specify where requests are accepted from.

    The CLI command could look as follows:

    ```
    az webapp cors add -g "AZ-204" -n "myapi" --allowed-
    origins "https://az204.com"
    ```

    This topic was covered in *Chapter 3*, *Creating Azure App Service Web Apps*.

3. B is the correct answer.

    Hybrid Connections can be used to provide Azure App Service web apps with access to resources in any network, including on-premises networks. This requires a relay agent within the network, which will relay the request from the web app to the on-premises TCP endpoint. The endpoint will then communicate with the web app over port 443 in an outbound connection from that TCP endpoint.

    Private endpoints relate to inbound connections to the web app, not outbound, and they use private links. As the on-premises network isn't a VNet, simply enabling VNet integration also won't help here.

    This topic was covered in *Chapter 3*, *Creating Azure App Service Web Apps*.

4. A is the correct answer.

    When multiple scale-out rules are triggered, autoscale evaluates the new capacity of each rule triggered and takes the scale action that will result in the greatest capacity of those triggered rules. In this scenario, that would be 7. Autoscale doesn't combine the instance counts of multiple rules – it only selects the single action that provides the greatest capacity.

    This topic was covered in *Chapter 3*, *Creating Azure App Service Web Apps*.

Implementing Azure Functions

1.   C is the correct answer.

     On the Consumption plan, functions that have been idle for a period will be scaled down to zero instances. After this happens, the first request may experience some latency because a cold startup is required to scale back up from zero.

     This topic was covered in *Chapter 4, Implementing Azure Functions*.

2.   C is the correct answer.

     This topic was covered in *Chapter 4, Implementing Azure Functions*, with a link to information on NCrontab syntax in the *Further reading* section of the chapter.

3.   A is the correct answer.

     With C# script, JavaScript, PowerShell, Python, and TypeScript functions, the `function.json` file needs to be updated to configure triggers and bindings.

     In C# and Java, you decorate methods and parameters in code.

     This topic was covered in *Chapter 4, Implementing Azure Functions*.

Developing solutions that use Cosmos DB storage

1.   D is the correct answer.

     The Cosmos DB change feed cannot be queried because it is a FIFO queue. Each modification is registered as a message in the queue and can be pulled by consumers.

     The change feed is discussed in *Chapter 5, Developing Solutions That Use Cosmos DB Storage*, in the *Leveraging a change feed for app integration* section.

2.   B is the correct answer.

     There are physical and logical partitions that exist for Cosmos DB. Its structure is controlled internally by Cosmos DB. The number of physical partitions depends on the throughput and storage capacity of the documents stored in the partition.

     Partitions are discussed in *Chapter 5, Developing Solutions That Use Cosmos DB Storage*, in the *Partitioning in Cosmos DB* section.

3.   E is the correct answer.

     The client-side encryption (Always Encrypt) meets the requirements because it protects data at rest and in transit and is decrypted only on the client side by using customer-managed keys from Azure Key Vault. When you apply encryption settings, you need to provide the path of a card number field. Full documents cannot be encrypted.

     The encryption topic is discussed in *Chapter 5, Developing Solutions That Use Cosmos DB Storage*, in the *Encryption settings* section.

4. B is the correct answer.

    If the update needs to be applied for both of the regional instances at the same time to minimize possible data loss, it means a strong consistency level for operation. The operation consistency must be the same or more relaxed than the default consistency. So, increasing the default level to strong is only one solution.

    Consistency levels are discussed in *Chapter 5, Developing Solutions That Use Cosmos DB Storage*, in the *Consistency levels* section.

5. D is the correct answer.

    The solution using of a single DB and consistency for a single DB makes no sense. Meanwhile, the indexing process affects the performance of inserting. One of the possible solutions is to set the index mode to none from the code before submitting the bulk. Then, return to the normal state.

    Disabling indexes is discussed in *Chapter 5, Developing Solutions That Use Cosmos DB Storage*, in the *Optimizing database performance and costs* section.

Developing solutions that use Azure Blob storage

1. C is the correct answer.

    The static website hosted on the Azure storage account provides the following:

    *   Availability in two regions if the GRS option is chosen.

    *   Versioning for all files in the blob including pages of the website.

    *   The option to register custom domains.

    *   Minimal cost in comparison with VMs and App Services.

        Websites hosted on a storage account are discussed in *Chapter 6, Developing Solutions That Use Azure Blob Storage*, in the *Static websites* section.

2. D is the correct answer.

    The premium storage account does not have access tiers. The Archive tier will be expensive because of writing transactions to append the log files. The Hot tier will be a more economically sound choice.

    The storage account access tiers are discussed in *Chapter 6, Developing Solutions That Use Azure Blob Storage*, in the *Life cycle management and optimizing cost* section.

3. A is the correct answer.

    The SAS is generated by using one of the admin keys. Regenerating the admin keys will break all SAS generated with the previous keys. This is an acceptable solution because the application is still in the testing phase and other devices are available for refreshing its SASs. Only SASs generated with a stored access policy can be safely revoked.

The SASs for storage accounts is discussed in *Chapter 6, Developing Solutions That Use Azure Blob Storage*, in the *Managing metadata and security settings for storage accounts* section.

4. A is the correct answer.

The code is taken from one of the demo projects for setting metadata. The code works without errors if the container exists. Before completing any operation with the container, the code should ensure that container exists and call the `CreateIfNotExists` function.

The code example is provided in *Chapter 6, Developing Solutions That Use Azure Blob Storage*, in the *Retrieving metadata by using C# code* section.

Implementing user authentication and authorization

1. C is the correct answer.

For applications to integrate with **Azure Active Directory** (**AAD**), an **app registration** must be created with at least the `User.Read` delegated permission assigned.

This topic was covered in *Chapter 7, Implementing User Authentication and Authorization*.

2. A is the correct answer.

Because this is an app that runs on user devices, it is therefore not trusted with application secrets and is only able to request access to resources on behalf of a logged-in user – this is a public client and not a confidential client.

This topic was covered in *Chapter 7, Implementing User Authentication and Authorization*.

3. A, C, and D are correct.

Use the `az storage container policy create` command to create a new stored access policy. Then, run the `az storage container generate-sas` command to generate a new SAS token that uses the new policy. Finally, run the `az webapp config appsettings set` command to update the relevant application setting of the App Service with the new SAS token.

This topic was covered in *Chapter 7, Implementing User Authentication and Authorization*, although not each of these CLI commands was explicitly covered. There will be examples in the exam you won't have seen before where you must use your judgment based on what you do know.

Implementing secure cloud solutions

1. A and B are correct.

The `az webapp identity assign` command will assign a **system-assigned managed identity** to the web app in question, which will share the same life cycle as the web app. The `az identity create` command will create a **user-assigned managed identity**, which is a standalone resource and won't share the same life cycle as the web app and therefore doesn't meet the requirements.

The az keyvault set-policy command will set an access policy on the relevant Key Vault, so you can provide the system-assigned managed identity with the permissions required to access the data plane of the vault. The az policy assignment create command relates to Azure Policy, not a Key Vault access policy, so it won't help in this scenario.

This topic was covered in *Chapter 8, Implementing Secure Cloud Solutions*.

2. D is the correct answer.

An **App Configuration** resource allows you to centrally manage both the application configuration settings and feature flags. App Configuration isn't a replacement for Key Vault for storing secrets, but you can also create a new App Configuration key that pulls the value from Key Vault (although it's not a requirement in this scenario).

This topic was covered in *Chapter 8, Implementing Secure Cloud Solutions*.

3. B is the correct answer.

You can import key-value pairs into App Configuration using the az appconfig kv import command. You can also export them from App Configuration into a JSON file using the az appconfig kv export command.

The az appconfig kv command was covered in *Chapter 8, Implementing Secure Cloud Solutions*, although the import command wasn't specifically mentioned.

Integrating caching and content delivery within solutions

1. A is the correct answer.

The TCP protocol is used for communication between the cache instance and the client.

The details about communication are provided in *Chapter 9, Integrating Caching and Content Delivery within Solutions*, in the *Firewall and virtual network integration* section.

2. E is the correct answer.

From the list of tools, only Azure CLI can not be used for observing values, but it can be used for managing the cache instance and importing and exporting data.

The details about communication are provided in *Chapter 9, Integrating Caching and Content Delivery within Solutions*, in the *Provisioning Azure Cache for Redis from the Azure CLI* section.

3. C is the correct answer.

Azure Cache for Redis suits server-side caching for reusing content better than other services from the list. It also provides flexibility with setting custom TTL for the response. Moreover, Azure Cache for Redis will provide better performance than a storage account because of TCP communication.

The cache-aside pattern and TTL were discussed in *Chapter 9, Integrating Caching and Content Delivery within Solutions*, in the *Introducing caching patterns* section.

4. D is the correct answer.

    The update file is static content and should be cached for clients with the appropriate service. Server-side caching (Azure Cache for Redis) does not help the client. The update of 50 MB does not suit general web hosting (App Service) well because the interruption to the connectivity will lead to downloads restarting. If the download speed is a requirement, the file should be located as close as possible to the clients. CDN servers (point-of-presence) will be the best choice. Downloading from an Azure storage account from another region will be slow and expensive. Outgoing traffic from the data center adds an extra charge to the subscription.

    Details about caching static content can be found in *Chapter 9, Integrating Caching and Content Delivery within Solutions*, in the *Exploring Azure Content Delivery Network* section.

5. D is the correct answer.

    The CDN endpoint still cached the old version of the JS file. You need to wait until the cached copy expires or purge the content.

    The same scenario with different messages (a web page where you press a button) is demonstrated in *Chapter 9, Integrating Caching and Content Delivery within Solutions*, in the *Configuring a website to leverage the CDN* section.

Instrumenting solutions to support monitoring and logging

1. B is the correct answer.

    Application Insights dependency tracking can collect SQL queries and their performance. You can get access to the collected information from the **Application Map** and **Performance** sections of the **Application Insights** page. Azure SQL Insights can only track query performance for all application requests. Profiler only helps for functions running from code.

    SQL dependency is explained in *Chapter 10, Troubleshooting Solutions by Using Metrics and Log Data*, in the *Application Map* section.

2. E is the correct answer.

    The code snippet represents working code from the controller that handles the client list loading from the DB (Entity Framework). The code tracks custom metrics with the elapsed time of the dependency collected by the Stopwatch class.

    The custom event was introduced in *Chapter 10, Troubleshooting Solutions by Using Metrics and Log Data*, in the *C# – server* section.

3. D is the correct answer.

    To collect logs from Azure VM, you need to connect the VM to the Log Analytics workspace by installing the agent. From the data collection settings, you need to configure the IIS log collection.

    The Log Analytics workspace and its structure were introduced in *Chapter 10, Troubleshooting Solutions by Using Metrics and Log Data*, in the *Using KQL for Log Analytics queries* section.

4. D is the correct answer.

    Debugging snapshots will help you to investigate the crash in a less invasive way. You can observe the snapshot from the **Application Insights** page or download and open it in Visual Studio. Live debugging and setting breakpoints can help with investigating the issue but freezes the application when the breakpoint is reached which interrupts request processing.

    Debugging snapshots was explained in *Chapter 10, Troubleshooting Solutions by Using Metrics and Log Data*, in the *Exception troubleshooting* section.

Implementing API Management

1. B is the correct answer.

    What is provided in the snippet policy will limit the requests and consist of the following parameters:

    ```
    <rate-limit-by-key calls="number" renewal-
    period="seconds" increment-condition="condition" counter-
    key="key value" remaining-calls-variable-name="policy
    expression variable name"/>
    ```

    APIM policy was explained in *Chapter 11, Implementing API Management*, in the *Using advanced policies* section.

2. D is the correct answer.

    APIM supports backend authentication with Basic and client certification and authentication with Managed Identity. The following policies can be configured for authentication with Basic:

    ```
    <authentication-basic username="username"
    password="password" />
    ```

    The following code snippet can be configured for authentication with client certificates:

    ```
    <authentication-certificate thumbprint="thumbprint"
    certificate-id="resource name"/>
    ```

    Windows authentication is not supported by APIM.

    The authentication basics were discovered in *Chapter 11, Implementing API Management*, in the *Exploring APIM configuration options* section.

3. D is the correct answer.

    The backup of usage data is not supported by APIM.

    The endpoint definitions that APIM supports importing were introduced in *Chapter 11, Implementing API Management*, in the *Connecting existing web APIs to APIM* section.

    APIM supports a portal for developers and lets them test published APIs. The portal was explained in *Chapter 11, Implementing API Management,* in the *Dev portal* section.

    APIM can expose publicly accessible APIs. Authentication settings were introduced in *Chapter 11, Implementing API Management*, in the *Exploring APIM configuration options* section.

    APIM can generate and mock responses without requesting backend services. The techniques were discussed in *Chapter 11, Implementing API Management*, in the *Mocking API responses* section.

    APIM supports integration with source control to track changes in the policies and settings. Integration was introduced in *Chapter 11, Implementing API Management*, in the *Repository integration* section.

Developing event-based solutions

1. C is the correct answer.

    To minimize cost and admin efforts, you should leverage out-of-box functionality such as event capturing. Event capturing is only available with the Standard and Premium tiers. The additional service Azure Data Lake should be deployed for storing captured events. The charges for Azure Data Lake are less than the consumption charges from Event Grid per each of the events and storing their content in Cosmos DB. Data Lake is a consumption-based service deployed as an extension for an Azure storage account. Capturing event content is impossible with Azure Monitor, Application Insights, or an Azure Log Analytics workspace.

    The capturing feature was introduced in *Chapter 12, Developing Event-Based Solutions*, in the *Capturing events* section.

2. D is the correct answer.

    There is no out-of-the-box functionality that meets the requirements. The IoT Hub should be upgraded to the Standard SKU to support dynamic settings management (or twin settings). The response time will be decreased if the IoT device starts cooling as soon as the temperature hits the threshold.

    The IoT edge will suit the requirements but will also require you to upgrade the IoT Hub and operate with Docker containers that increase the maintenance effort. The same is true for rebuilding containers.

B is a workable option but requires you to build expensive extra services.

The twin settings were mentioned in *Chapter 12, Developing Event-Based Solutions*, in the *Developing applications for Azure IoT Hub* section.

3. C is the correct answer.

   `az eventhubs event hub authorization-rule create` should be used with `Send` permission at most to follow the principle of least privilege.

   The connection string for Event Hubs is discussed in *Chapter 12, Developing Event-Based Solutions*, in the *Provisioning Azure Event Hubs* section.

Developing message-based solutions

1. A is the correct answer.

   The correct name of the metric for Storage Queue is **approximate message count** because the exact message count is not available.

   The approximate message count metric was discussed in *Chapter 13, Developing Message-Based Solutions*, in the *Exploring Azure Storage Queue* section.

2. D is the correct answer.

   Azure Service Bus Queue guaranteed the sequence of messages. The SDK automatically implements a retry pattern when the application experiences transient connection errors.

   Retrying attempts were mentioned in *Chapter 13, Developing Message-Based Solutions*, in the *Competing consumers* section.

3. C is the correct answer.

   `ServiceBusProcessor` provides callback architecture that allows the processing of received messages in real time by registering on `ProcessMessagesAsync` events.

   The `ServiceBusProcessor` class was demonstrated in *Chapter 13, Developing Message-Based Solutions*, in the *Developing for Service Bus topics* section.

Assessments

Chapter 1

1. Vertical scaling provides more power to a single resource, whereas horizontal scaling increases the number of instances of a resource.

2. The resource provider for virtual machines is `Microsoft.Compute`.

3. This is false. With SaaS, you only manage data and access as the consumer.

4. Virtual machines are an example of the infrastructure as a service model.

5. Azure resources can only be a member of a single resource group at any given time.

Chapter 2

1. This command will remove the Docker image named `my-image` and tagged `latest` from the local container registry.

2. Currently, multi-container container groups are only supported on Linux.

3. Adding the `apiProfile` element to an ARM template allows you to define the API version that all resources of a certain type should use.

4. No. Containers share the host's kernel and Linux containers will only work on a Windows machine if the Windows Subsystem for Linux is enabled. Linux can't emulate the Windows kernel.

5. One. A single container is still part of its own container group even if there are no other containers in the group.

Chapter 3

1. No. An App Service plan is the scale unit of the App Service apps. If the plan is configured to run five VM instances, then all apps in the plan run on all five instances. If the plan is configured for autoscaling, then all apps in the plan are scaled out together based on the autoscale settings.

2. The provider redirects the client to a URL in the following format: `https://<appservice>.azurewebsites.net./auth/<provider>/callback`.

3. True. Application logging is supported for both Windows and Linux App Service apps.

4. True. Enabling the private endpoint feature disables all public access by default, only allowing inbound traffic from a specified VNet.

5. Hybrid Connections can be configured to allow outbound calls from your app to resources within your on-premises network, providing the prerequisites are in place.

Chapter 4

1. The file with information on the triggers and bindings for a function is `function.json`.

2. `AzureWebJobsStorage` contains the storage account connection string for the function app.

3. Orchestrator functions call activity functions to perform the steps of a workflow.

4. Local application settings for functions are stored within the `local.settings.json` file.

Chapter 5

1. SQL (Core), MongoDB, Cassandra, Azure Table, and Gremlin (Graph)

2. Range index is designed for improving operations in a single field. Meanwhile, composite index improves operations in multiple fields.

3. The default backup option is periodic backup.

4. No, the Azure portal does not allow the execution of triggers. You must call triggers explicitly from the app code.

5. JavaScript is the language used for stored procedures.

Chapter 6

1. The choice of availability zone and the geo-redundancy option can increase the availability of Blob storage.

2. Soft delete can help protect data from accidental deletion.

3. Yes. The `GetPropertiesAsync` SDK function helps to get the property and metadata without downloading blob content.

4. Yes. Blob life cycle management migrates blobs between tiers.

5. Binary (unstructured) and semi-structured data can be persisted in Azure Blob storage.

Chapter 7

1. Microsoft Graph connectors can be used to bring external data into Microsoft Graph applications and services.

2. Delegated permissions are required for an application to act on behalf of a signed-in user.

3. The MSAL.js library supports single-page applications.

4. Public client applications are applications that run on user devices, IoT devices, and browsers. As such, they can't be trusted with storing application credentials.

5. It's recommended to use a user-delegated SAS with Blob storage where possible.

Chapter 8

1. A system-assigned managed identity shares its life cycle with that of its assigned Azure resource.

2. Adding a Key Vault reference key within App Configuration and referencing that key from your application provides all the functionality of App Configuration while maintaining the security and integrity of your application secrets.

3. Using managed identities is the recommended method to authenticate your app with Key Vault in most scenarios.

4. The role-based access control permission model is used to manage access to the management plane of a key vault.

Chapter 9

1. The Basic Azure Cache for Redis SKU does not provide an SLA.

2. The EXPIRE Redis command is used to set the TTL.

3. A Premium SKU cache runs on a cluster and a Basic SKU cache is a single instance without an SLA.

4. TCP protocol and ports 6379 and 6380 are used for connecting to Azure Cache for Redis.

5. Verizon CDN products are available with a Premium SKU for Azure CDN.

6. Using the Cache-Control header from the source or using Global and Custom caching rules you can control the TTL in Azure CDN.

Chapter 10

1. Performance metrics and logs are collected with Azure Monitor.

2. An activity log's tracking operation is completed from the portal with a resource. An application log tracks the activity of an application (e.g. diagnostic traces).

3. The App Insights SDK ships by default with a dependency collection model. Additional settings, such as the collection SQL command, can be specified from the code and portal.

4. Availability tests from App Insights can be configured with URLs to test and Azure data centers to send the monitoring requests from.

5. To collect crash information, the instrumentation of code is not required. However, the code must be instrumented to catch handled exceptions.

Chapter 11

1. REST is a representational state transfer protocol that allows the manipulation of data objects by using HTTP verbs (GET, POST, PUT, and DELETE).

2. Yes. Scale units are available for pricing tiers starting from Basic for implementing horizontal scaling of APIM resources.

3. You can connect existing web APIs in your Azure subscription to the APIM service either manually or by importing OpenAPI, WDAL, or WSDL definitions. It is also possible to connect the App service provisioned with the same subscription.

4. The consumption tier does not support an internal cache, VNet integration, multi-region deployment, or self-hosted gateways for connection to the on-premises backend.

5. The policy expression syntax is based on the C# language.

Chapter 12

1. A namespace is a virtual server deployed in Azure that provides connection endpoints to accept the connections from publishers and consumers.

2. An IoT Hub is based on Event Hubs functionality but has many differences, including scale and price tiers. The main difference is supporting two-way communication between devices and the cloud, which allows an IoT Hub to manage IoT devices.

3. Event Hubs on the Basic pricing tier can persist an event for only 1 day and Premium up to 90 days.

4. Event Grid can help you connect Azure Functions to Event Hubs.

5. SAS keys and X.509 certificates can be used to connect IoT devices to an IoT Hub.

6. Misconfiguring filtering for an event handler can prevent it from receiving all the events sent by Event Grid.

Chapter 13

1. The backup functionality is not provided out of the box but can be implemented with a custom service that triggers when new messages arrive from Event Grid and peeks messages without removing the message from the queue.

2. Transactions at the service level are not supported for Azure Queue.

3. When the message is received by the consumer, it needs to process the message and delete it, or the message will be restored in the queue after a timeout in case the consumer crashes while processing the message.

4. 5 GB is the maximum total size limit for an Azure Service Bus Queue.

5. The Premium Azure Service Bus tier supports geo-redundancy.

6. A DLQ is a logical queue that is used for keeping undelivered or poison messages. The message can be explicitly sent to the DLQ from the application code for special treatment.

Index

Symbols

A

‹packt›

Packt.com

Subscribe to our online digital library for full access to over 7,000 books and videos, as well as industry leading tools to help you plan your personal development and advance your career. For more information, please visit our website.

Why subscribe?

- Spend less time learning and more time coding with practical eBooks and Videos from over 4,000 industry professionals

- Improve your learning with Skill Plans built especially for you

- Get a free eBook or video every month

- Fully searchable for easy access to vital information

- Copy and paste, print, and bookmark content

Did you know that Packt offers eBook versions of every book published, with PDF and ePub files available? You can upgrade to the eBook version at packt.com and as a print book customer, you are entitled to a discount on the eBook copy. Get in touch with us at customercare@packtpub.com for more details.

At www.packt.com, you can also read a collection of free technical articles, sign up for a range of free newsletters, and receive exclusive discounts and offers on Packt books and eBooks.

Other Books You May Enjoy

If you enjoyed this book, you may be interested in these other books by Packt:

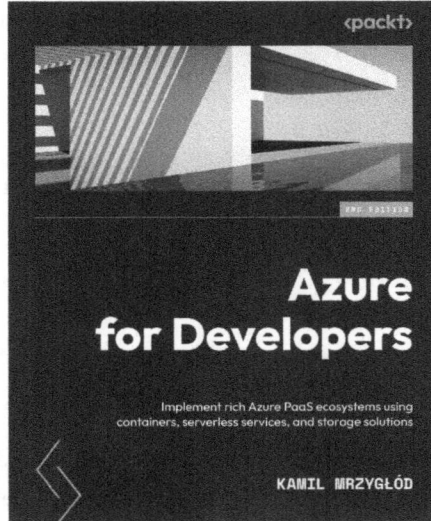

Azure for Developers - Second Edition

Kamil Mrzygłód

ISBN: 978-1-803-24009-1

- Identify the Azure services that can help you get the results you need
- Implement PaaS components – Azure App Service, Azure SQL, Traffic Manager, CDN, Notification Hubs, and Azure Cognitive Search
- Work with serverless components
- Integrate applications with storage
- Put together messaging components (Event Hubs, Service Bus, and Azure Queue Storage)
- Use Application Insights to create complete monitoring solutions
- Secure solutions using Azure RBAC and manage identities
- Develop fast and scalable cloud applications

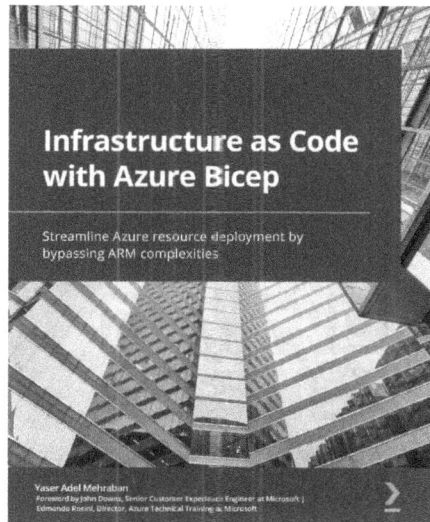

Infrastructure as Code with Azure Bicep

Yaser Adel Mehraban

ISBN: 978-1-801-81374-7

- Get started with Azure Bicep and install the necessary tools
- Understand the details of how to define resources with Bicep
- Use modules to create templates for different teams in your company
- Optimize templates using expressions, conditions, and loops
- Make customizable templates using parameters, variables, and functions
- Deploy templates locally or from Azure DevOps or GitHub
- Stay on top of your IaC with best practices and industry standards

Packt is searching for authors like you

If you're interested in becoming an author for Packt, please visit `authors.packtpub.com` and apply today. We have worked with thousands of developers and tech professionals, just like you, to help them share their insight with the global tech community. You can make a general application, apply for a specific hot topic that we are recruiting an author for, or submit your own idea.

Share your thoughts

Now you've finished *Developing Solutions for Microsoft Azure AZ-204 Exam Guide*, we'd love to hear your thoughts! Scan the QR code below to go straight to the Amazon review page for this book and share your feedback or leave a review on the site that you purchased it from.

`https://packt.link/r/1803237066`

Your review is important to us and the tech community and will help us make sure we're delivering excellent quality content.

Lightning Source UK Ltd.
Milton Keynes UK
UKHW031844011122
411475UK00007B/85

9 781803 237060